Appreciation for skills and the interpretation of the elements of design expression, inspires understanding and the desire to acquire these essentials of good craftsmanship. Let us seek opportunities to share and to exchange skills with others, especially craftsmen of other races and countries.

—LESTER GRISWOLD

The New Handicraft

PROCESSES & PROJECTS

TENTH EDITION

By LESTER and KATHLEEN GRISWOLD

VAN NOSTRAND REINHOLD COMPANY
New York Cincinnati Toronto London Melbourne

Previous Editions of *Handicraft*
First through Fifth Editions—1925-1931
Sixth Edition—1931
Seventh Edition—1937
Eighth Edition—1942
Ninth Edition—1951
Tenth Edition—1969
  Reprinted—1972

Van Nostrand Reinhold Company Regional Offices:
New York   Cincinnati   Chicago   Millbrae   Dallas

Van Nostrand Reinhold Company International Offices:
London   Toronto   Melbourne

Copyright © 1969 by Ruth Griswold Kremenak

Library of Congress Catalog Card Number: 68-59213
ISBN 0-442-22863-5 *(cloth)*—0-442-22862-7 *(paper)*

Published by Van Nostrand Reinhold Company
A Division of Litton Educational Publishing, Inc.
450 West 33rd Street, New York, N. Y. 10001

16   15   14   13   12   11   10   9   8   7   6   5   4   3

PREFACE

This *New Handicraft, Processes and Projects*, is the 10th Edition. It includes new project material and techniques recently developed for *Handicraft* in ceramics, metal, plaiting methods, plastics and wood. Selected subjects from the 9th Edition, basketry, bookbinding, lapidary and others which are of continued interest have been revised and described in more exact detail.

Basic skill principles and techniques have been retained for their inherent values and in recognition of the cultural common denominator they form between the people of today and those of other ages and races. For this reason some of the material on the crafts of the American Indian, which appeared in previous editions, has been retained.

The authors have embodied in *The New Handicraft* the results of many years of experience and observation. At this time they wish to express appreciation to the craftsmen, whose interest was inspired by previous editions of *Handicraft* and who have continued to acquire and share their skills. Their suggestions for the *New Handicraft Processes and Projects* have been of inestimable assistance.

In preparing this 10th Edition of *Handicraft*, it is our purpose to stimulate interest in crafts, help develop skills and provide the means of sharing with others the joy of creative achievement.

LESTER and KATHLEEN GRISWOLD
Green Mountain Falls, Colorado
September 20, 1968.

ACKNOWLEDGMENTS

We regret that space does not permit the recognition of everyone who assisted or made photographs available for this Edition of Handicraft. We are especially indebted to the following persons or organizations:

In Colorado Springs, Colorado:

RUTH APPLETHUN, *Home Demonstration Agent*
MARY FRANCIS BUNNING, *Craftsman*
CLARA GLOSS, *Ceramic Hobbyist*
CHRIS CHRISTIANSON, *Lapidarist*
BOB CHADBOURNE, *Metallurgist*
W. E. GLANDER, *Metal Craftsman*
LAWRENCE HELLER, *Ceramic Craftsman*
EVA CLARK KELLER, *Designer-Artist and Craftsman*
MRS. LILLIAN HEMMIE, *Rock Creek Lapidary*
WM. MASON, *Weaver*
KNUTSON-BOWERS, *Photographers*
FRED WILLS, *Master Potter*
VAN BRIGGLE ART POTTERY
JEAN and BOB WARREN, *Ceramic Models*
MRS. C. H. WOODARD, *Chimayo Blanket Collection Photographs*
HEIDI BRANDT (MRS. THOMAS BRANDT), *Artist-Designer and Craftsman*
DON ROLLER (deceased), *Silver Designer and Craftsman*
MRS. RUTH CRAWFORD (deceased), *Heirloom Woven Coverlet*

Other than Colorado Springs:

BEREA COLLEGE, Berea, Kentucky, *Weaving, Woodwork*
JIM BRESLIN (deceased), La Junta, Colorado, *Leather Carving*
EVIE CARMONA, Bay City, Michigan, *Ceramic Designer-Craftsman*
DESERT HOUSE CRAFTS, Tucson, Arizona
FRANCIS HANSON, Denver, Colo., *Art Instructor*
CLAUDE HANSON, Denver, Colo., *Craftsman-Designer*
SHIRLEY LYON, Lewiston, Idaho, *Photographer*
NEW MEXICO DEPT. OF DEVELOPMENT (formerly Bureau of Indian Affairs), Santa Fe, N.M., *Photographs of Pueblo Potters and Pottery*
MRS. LUCILLE MORRIS, Boulder, Colo., *Photographs of Maria Martinez Pottery*
PENLAND SCHOOL OF HANDICRAFTS, *Photographs of Pewter Work*
PROCTORS LAPIDARY, Loveland, Colorado, *Examples of Alabaster Projects*
ORTEGA BROTHERS, Chimayo, N.M., *Professional Weavers, Loom and Blanket Photos*
MR. and MRS. H. MERRIL TAYLOR, Farmington, N.M., *Wood Carvers*
ARTHUR E. VICTOR, Spokane, Washington, *Lapidary Publications*
MAXINE WEBER, Lewiston, Idaho, *Director of Ceramics Workshop*
MARJORIE B. LEAVENS, Carmel, California, *Examples of Chinese Cloisenne Enamel*

We wish to express our obligation and deep appreciation for the interest and service of Howard Tanner, Waupun, Wisconsin, who read the manuscript and made invaluable suggestions for its clarification and improvement.

Our work of research and composition was encouraged and sustained by friends and our daughters, Kay Phillips and Ruth Kremenak, who cooperated throughout the preparation of the material.

CONTENTS

Preface and Introduction.

1. **Design in Handicraft:** Elements of Ornamental and Structural Design: Principles of Arrangement; Project Designs; Examples of Pre-historic Mexican Designs   1

2. **Basketry:** Historical: Elements and Terms in Basketry; Indian Types and Techniques; Projects of Willow, Reed, Pine-needle, Raffia, Splint   7

3. **Bookbinding:** Historical; Terms and Techniques in Bookbinding; Re-binding a book, Process of Restoration; Binding of Note-books, Scrap-books and Albums: Leather, Fabric and Paper Covers   40

4. **Ceramics:** Historical; Classification of Clay; Preparation and Testing of Clay; Hand-built, Slip-cast and Wheel-thrown Processes and Projects; Decoration; Glazing; Firing; Kiln Construction; **Mosaics:** Materials, Techniques and Projects; **Indian Pottery:** Traditional Methods and Designs; Examples   47

5. **Decoration of Fabrics, Paper and Wood:** Processes of Design Painting; Block Printing; Silk Screen and Batik Methods   110

6. **Lapidary:** Classification of Stones; Cutting and Polishing of Specimens and Cabochons; Tumbled Stones for Free-form Mounting; Sphere and Bead Cutting; Alabaster Carving and Finishing; Alabaster Projects; Bases for Cedar Projects; Stone Flaking; Soft Stone Carving   128

7. **Leather Craftwork:** Classification of Leather; Selection and Cutting; Decoration and Assembly of Projects; Tool-making for Stamped and Carved Leather Decoration; List of Equipment. Lacing Steps and Principles   151

8. **Metal Craftwork:** Historical; Classification and Choice of Metals for Projects; Equipment and Processes in Metal work; Hammered, Raised, Pierced, Chased, Etched, Soldered. Projects of Aluminum, Copper, Pewter, Brass; Metal Foil; Making of Metal Stamping and Chasing Tools. **Enameling** on Copper; Historical Methods of **Cloisonne** and **Champleve** Enameling; **Silver work** and **Filagree**   218

9. **Plaiting Processes and Projects:** Cord, Thong and Yarn Methods of Plaiting, Tying of Ornamental Knots; Plaited Leather Thong Projects, Methods of Cutting   305

10. Plastics: Classification, Development and Uses; Processes for Cutting, Shaping, Carving, Cementing and Casting; Printing from Etched Plastic Plates 332

11. Weaving: Processes and Patterns for Weaving; Construction and Operation of the Two-Harness and Four-Harness Looms; Wool and Yarn-making Processes, Historical and Modern; Navajo Indian Traditions, Looms and Weaving Methods; Development of Navajo Indian and Spanish/Chimayo Looms and Weaving Patterns 352

12. Woodwork: Kinds of Wood for Craftwork; Equipment and Processes for Chip Carving, Outline, Relief and Figure Carving; Design Carving and Construction of Projects; Design Details and Carving of Pine Wood Chests; Spanish Colonial Furniture and Carving Designs 399

Index 459

INTRODUCTION

Regardless of the perfection of modern machine made products, greater value is still placed on articles made by hand. The personality of the maker, expressed by the imagination, skill and effort with which he worked, seems to become an intrinsic part of almost anything hand wrought giving it an unique value. The recognition and appreciation of this value is a part of our cultural heritage persisting with the progress of civilization.

Crafts, such as basketry, pottery, weaving, developed before the dawn of history, were first an essential part of elemental human existence, later providing a means of expression for the creative artistic impulses of many races. There often existed a similarity in such concepts and methods between races, despite great variance otherwise.

We of the United States have a rich heritage in the elements of many cultures brought to this country by the people of other lands and in those of the first American, the Indian, whose creative arts were developed centuries before the coming of Columbus. It is the privilege and duty of the craftsman to study, appreciate and further perfect these elements that they may be woven into the American culture as a fabric that embodies the best of civilization in its products of beauty and utility. A comparable perfection of human relationships may enable each individual to realize his greatest potential of character, intelligence and skill.

The individual whose occupation entails mental and emotional strain, or the continual outgoing of his own resources will find that concentration on a piece of craftwork will help to rebuild mental and spiritual resources. While the mind is absorbed in the activity, the emotions become stabilized and inner strength is restored. As a therapy for the convalescent from mental or physical disability, handicraft has been found a valuable help toward the rebuilding of health and confidence.

Craft programs are now recognized as essential for camps and other recreational fields as well as in education. The development of a balanced personality is advanced by a well planned craft program, thru the acquisition of skills, the satisfaction of creative self-expression and the developments of habits of application and accuracy. The teacher or leader who understands these principles and can inspire appreciation for them as well as impart the knowledge of techniques will enrich the learning experience of individuals, whether youth or adults, and give them a resource for life-long enjoyment.

CHAPTER 1

Design in Handicraft

An interpretation of art as applied to crafts refers to design as expressed in the ornamentation of a material having dimensions of form and proportion, as well as qualities of color and texture. The craftsman must first visualize the design, and within the limitations and possibilities of the material embody in an article of craft work the honest expression of his idea, developed in accordance with the decorative purpose or specific function of the finished work.

This requires imaginative understanding of the material and the principles of design, as well as a mastery of the required skills and procedures.

The concept of good handicraft design depends on an understanding of its suitability for the decoration of a specific article in a chosen material and the skills required for its application. Knowledge and recognition of these elements will not only enable the craftsman to design an article of beauty or utility, but it will enhance his appreciation of the fine arts and increase his sensitivity to design in all aspects of daily life.

Elements of design

The elements of design include: line, shape, form, or mass, space, color, and texture. They are defined as follows:

A *line* is the framework of a design, indicating the boundaries of shape and the division of space.

Shape is the unit within the framework. It may be regular, or irregular, symmetrical or asymmetrical, similar or with variation in size or contour, conforming to the framework.

A *space* or interval between lines or shapes becomes a related form or shape. It may serve to emphasize the main design motif.

Color, or the light reflecting quality, varies according to the hue or color designation, the value or degree of shade, whether dark or light, also the brightness or intensity.

Texture refers to the inherent surface quality of the material, such as the hardness or grain of wood, the plasticity of clay, the firmness of leather, the ductility of metal, and the varying degrees of these qualities in each material.

Examples of projects in wood, leather, clay, and metal are shown in Fig. 2.

1

Principles of Arrangement

The principles of arrangement of design units in handicraft must be correlated with the elements of design. They are defined as follows:

Rhythm, obtained by the repetition of the same decorative unit in regular order, singly or in combination. It may also refer to a related movement of line or form. Repetition is nature's rhythm, and any simple motif repeated, as in borders, corners, and all-over designs, expresses this principle.

Radiation is seen in leaves, flower petals, seed pods, and all growths emanating from a central position.

Balance, an equilibrium of design elements, depends on the division of space and the position of the design motif in relation to a central or axis line. As in nature, it may be symmetrical, equal-sided like the wings of a bird, or asymmetrical like certain trees, which have the appearance of balance although the sides are unlike.

Emphasis is achieved by means of a dominant theme, also contrast in size, shade of color, or arrangement. Emphasis is likewise attained by the opposing of forms dissimilar in character in such a way that they contribute to the effect of each other.

Proportion, or the relation of the parts of a design, is needed to achieve a harmonious pattern, based on the use of the preceding principles. The designs in Fig. 1 show these and other principles of arrangement. The sketches in A. show the development of a design from Nature; B. both Radiation and Symmetrical Balance; C. shows Repetition and Rhythm and D. Asymmetrical Balance.

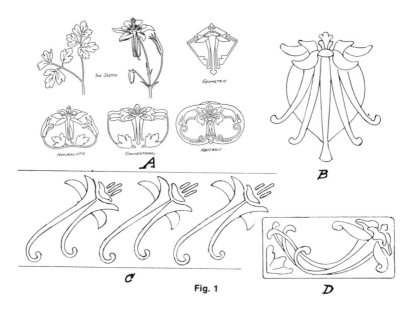

Fig. 1

Examples of Ornamental Design

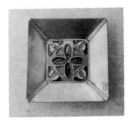  

Copper Tray with Tile Inset.   Black Walnut Carved Stamp Box Cover, One-Piece Box of Maple with Margin Carved and Stained.

Tooled Steerhide Bookend with Wide Lacing to Match.

White Ceramic Planter, Front Green Glazed with Decoration of White Engobe.

Design for Metal Etching Aluminum or Pewter.

Fig. 2

The true craftsman, like the artist, realizes that the elements of design and the principles of arrangement are interrelated and are likely to be merged as his design develops, Fig. 2.

Observation of design in nature and the recognition of the pleasing or satisfying aspects of design in man-made objects of quality, whether in museums, art galleries, or department stores, will help the individual develop sensitivity to good design and inspire him to express his own ideas in an original form.

Art has been defined as "design made manifest in material, interpretive as in painting, functional or decorative as in crafts." A fundamental law of design is that it must conform to the requirements of purpose.

Design motifs of ancient Mexico (sellos de antiguo Mexico)

At the suggestion of an art instructor, design motifs in Fig. 3 and 4 are included. They were taken from impressions of baked clay tablets or clay stamps (sellos) found in excavations of prehistoric Mexico and recorded by Señor Jorge Enciso. His research and the publication in 1947 of his sketches and data for hundreds of the stamps was made possible through the generosity of Senor Jose B. Iturbe.

Long before the Spanish conquest these stamps were used to decorate pottery and clothing, also to record symbolic rites and customs. Many geometric forms, mystical or religious figures and designs, and more realistic representations of flower, animal, and human life were found.

Some pottery designs, now used by the Indians of the Southwest United States, are similar to those of ancient Mexico, as well as the Mayan and Incan cultures of Central America. Indian pottery designs from the Denver Art Museum are shown in Fig. 91, page 109.

The elements or principles of design, evident in the stamps of ancient Mexico, might be considered instinctive, as they occur in the imaginative concepts of the prehistoric Mexican artist, who incised or modeled them on clay stamps, and made them permanent by baking (or firing). It seems that the elements of design, interpreted differently in every age, retain similarities which endure beyond time and have a special significance in relation to representative modern art.

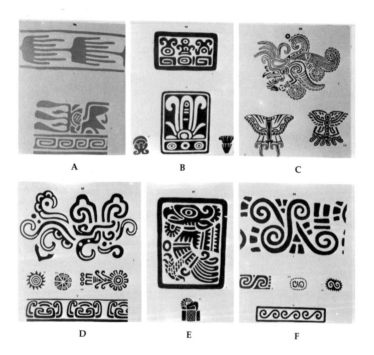

Enciso explanation of design motifs.

Upper Row:
A. Floral, cylindrical stamps
B. Earth in bloom, flat stamps
C. Mythical butterfly, flat stamps

Lower Row:
D. Floral motif, plain and cylindrical stamps
E. Representation of an eagle, flat stamp
F. Variation of blue worm motif, plain and cylindrical stamps

Upper Row:
A. and **C.** Variations of "stepped fret" and cylindrical cord patterns

B. Aquatic flower

Middle Row:
D. and **H.** Braided designs combined with shell and flowers

Center Row:
I. Book cover, jaguar design
E. Cylindrical
F. and **G.** Plain stamps, blue worm motifs

Lower Row:
J., K., L., M. Cylindrical and plain stamps, "stepped fret" designs, blue worm variation at top
N. Concentric circles and spirals, flat and cylindrical stamps

Fig. 4

Ornamental and structural design

The choice and development of an ornamental design for surface decoration must be governed by the nature of the material and the method of application. Every material, as mentioned, has the limitations and possibilities of its inherent qualities. These must be understood and considered in the selection of a suitable design and the medium of application.

The shape of the area to be decorated may conform to the shape of the article. The purpose for which the article is intended may suggest a design motif. In fitting the design motif to its space, it is desirable to test it on an area similar to that on which it is to be applied, leaving space for border lines or edge finishes. A study of the illustrated designs, Fig. 2, and the project examples will reveal some of the principles of design and arrangement.

Principles of Proportion in Structural Design

In the choice of a structural design, with or without surface ornamentation, the craftsman should follow the principles of form and proportion. The creative builder and artist of past ages discovered that there should be a balanced relationship in the proportions of width, height, and thickness. They determined that those qualities of space that satisfy the sense of balance may be developed within areas enclosed by rectangles. The principle of the so-called "Golden Oblong," as used by the Greek temple builders, is the ratio of the width to the height in any structural design. The geometric ratio of this "ideal rectangle" is 1 to 1.618 and so the proportions of 1 to 3, 3 to 5, 5 to 7, and similar ratios conform approximately to the "Golden Oblong."

The first step in planning a structural design is the construction of the area rectangle. It should have the best proportions for the article to be made according to its intended use, with space ratios agreeing as nearly as possible with the principles of the ideal rectangle. Any appendage, such as a handle, spout, or knob must be in proportion and in harmony with the theme of the design. The pewter tea set, Fig. 5A, conforms to this structural design principle.

A

B

Spun Pewter Tea Set from Penland School of Handicrafts, Penland, North Carolina.

Brown Lamp Base with incised design. Turquoise pedestal and background. Elements of the design around top of base and on lamp shade.

Fig. 5

CHAPTER 2

Basketry

Yucca Blossoms and Leaves in Spring

The Yucca plant, native to the southwestern United States, is the indispensable source of the strong fibrous leaves which the Pueblo and Hopi Indians have used for centuries for basket construction. This will be described in the section on Indian Coiled Basketry.

The botanical name is "Liliaceous Genus Yucca" and a typically Spanish name is "Candle of the Lord" from the beautiful spike of white blossoms which appears in spring and lasts until late summer.

Basketry

Many centuries ago, people learned to weave together various kinds of natural plant fibers for use in their shelters as mats, coverings, items of clothing, cradles for infants, and containers of many kinds. Fragments of woven fiber

7

found in excavations in widely separated parts of the world, now displayed in museums, indicate the knowledge was universal.

The techniques of the skilled primitive basket makers may be adapted in many forms and materials. Experimentation with native plant fibers is a challenge to the ingenuity of the modern basket maker. *Practical Basket Making* by George Wharton James describes many interesting examples of prize-winning baskets in which native materials and age-old techniques were employed.

As a camp or playground handicraft, basketry is always popular as well as inexpensive. To seek and prepare natural fibers for the adaptation of primitive techniques in basket construction is an excellent activity, and it helps to develop appreciation and understanding of early basket makers.

Preparation of Native Materials for Weaving

Willow tips or shoots are best cut in the spring when the appearing green leaves indicate the sap is rising, or in the early fall before the leaves drop; otherwise they may be too stiff to handle.

Cattail or *rushes,* many varieties of scirpus, the botanical name, should be gathered before they mature and dried slowly.

Yucca, a western plant, can be cut at any time. It retains the green color for some time when cut in the spring. The larger sections can be used for spokes, and the thin tips for weavers or for wrapping coils made of grasses or twigs.

"Rabbit bush" (rhu trilobata, a variety of sumac), widely used by the Indians of the Southwest, is more flexible in summer. The bark can be removed after soaking, and the sapwood cut into strips for wrapping coils made of the small twigs.

Grasses of many kinds, dried slowly in the shade, are widely used for coils and for wrapping by Indian basket makers.

Wild Honeysuckle vine, a material widely used in the highlands of our southern states, grows in 15 to 20 foot lengths and according to the basket makers is "cut in winter, when the sap is down, wound in rolls and boiled four hours, after which it is soaked overnight in water, rinsed and hung in the sunshine to dry."

A *variety of bamboo* which grows in the southern highlands is split into ¼ to ⅜ inch splints by the Cherokee Indians and mountain basket makers of this area. It is hard, tough, and durable, but difficult to weave and must be kept quite damp. The outer surface retains its smooth finish indefinitely, like the Asian bamboo.

Splints are made of ash or hickory; also other white woods such as oak, birch, and linden. Narrow splints are made from willow.

Splints made for spokes are ½ inch or more and cut thick enough to be rigid when dry. Weaving splints are thinner and more flexible, cut in widths from ⅛ to ½ inch. It is possible to make splints, Indian method, by beating a log with a wooden mallet until the layers are loosened when they can be stripped and cut with heavy shears, a sharp knife, or a draw gauge such as that used for cutting leather (see page 154).

Long needles from the pine trees which grow along the eastern seaboard and in the southeastern states are not available commercially and must be collected by the basket makers. (See section on pine needle basketry, page 18.)

Commercially available materials include:

Reed, made from an imported tropical plant known as cane palm, is available in several sizes, the most generally used is round reed ranging from 1/64 to ⅛ inch. Flat reed or cane, which is used mainly for chair seats comes in sizes ¼, ⅜, and ½ inch. Reed which is flat on one side and oval on the other is also available in widths 5/16, 7/16, and ½ inch. This is used for chair seats as well as the construction of large baskets. The reed is made from the center or pith and the cane from the outside of the stem which has a hard smooth surface.

Willow is cultivated commercially for basket material, planted close together to avoid twig branching. Cut at different stages of growth, it is suitable for spokes and weavers.

Raffia made from the leaves of a tropical palm, which is split into varying widths and available in natural as well as dyed colors, is used for sewing and wrapping coils; it also can be used for the foundation coils.

All of these materials must be damp when woven. After dipping or soaking until flexible, it is best to wrap them in a damp cloth as the weaving is being done. Never leave them damp for any length of time. Store covered but only after drying.

Tools and equipment for basketry

Waterproof cover for table of workbench and a water pail. Sharp pair of scissors and a sharp knife.

Pair of round-nose pliers and flat-nose pliers to bend spokes.

An awl to make spaces in the weaving, or a knitting needle.

Rubber finger guards for right forefinger and thumb.

Useful but not essential is a smooth round metal bar for tapping willow weavers together.

A raised board attached to the table to slope toward the worker and support the basket is also helpful. The surface must be smooth to permit the easy rotating of the basket.

Basketry Terms and Weaving Patterns

Weaving terms, whether in fabric construction or in basketry are similar. The fabric term *warp* for the vertical threads and *weft* for the horizontal corresponds to the basketry terms of *spokes* and *weavers*. The terms spokes and weavers will be used in the instructions which follow, although the positions in basket weaving may be other than vertical and horizontal.

Fig. 6, sketches A, B, C, indicate weaving patterns in basketry.

Basket weaving patterns, also called wicker weaving (from the word for "willow or pliant twig"), are of three main types: used singly, sketch A; in combination: simple basket weave, over one, under one (spoke) with a single weaver; also over two, under two, with a parallel weaver. Three and four weavers may be paralleled in the same way or in combination. This weave is shown in sketch B.

Patterns of double or paired weavers in a twined or two-ply twist, sketch C, shows a clockwise and a counterclockwise rotation of the weavers between spokes to develop the twist pattern.

The pattern of triple or three-ply twist, sketch D, is the strongest construction and is used for edges or other sections which require reinforcement. The sketch detail indicates the process of twining in which the weavers cross between the spokes and also over them in rotation, passing under one, over two, and repeating as the weaving progresses.

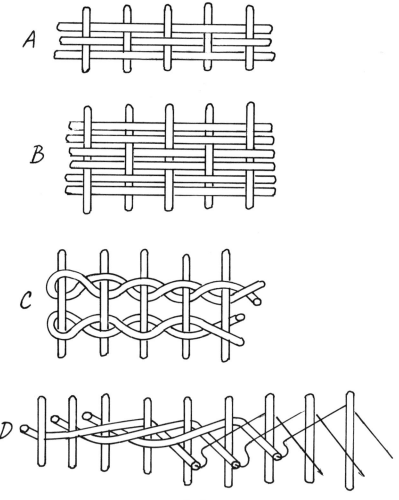

Fig. 6

Basic Wicker or Basket Weave

In the construction of a small mat or basket, the formation of the base requires that an odd number of spokes be used to provide the over one, under one principle in a regular pattern. This is used mainly when the spokes and weavers are nearly the same size and will not require the strength of a paired or triple twined element in the construction.

The method of inserting the odd spoke is shown in Fig. 7. Sketches A, B, C, and D and this base are examples of the start of a small mat, constructed of willow tips or cane.

Base construction

1. Cross an even number, 4 or 6 spokes at right angles, with the ends even and long enough for the selected size of the mat or basket and insert the extra spoke, Fig. 7, sketch A.

2. Encircle the crossed spokes twice with the first weaver, concealing the beginning end under the second circle or round (the usual weaving term), Fig. 7, sketch B.

3. Separate the spokes and tighten the weaver, continuing, over one, under one for the desired size of the mat or basket base, Fig. 7, sketch C.

4. The mat may be terminated with the finish shown in sketch D. Cut the ends of the spokes to a point and turn them back with a loop beyond the second or third spoke to the right or left.

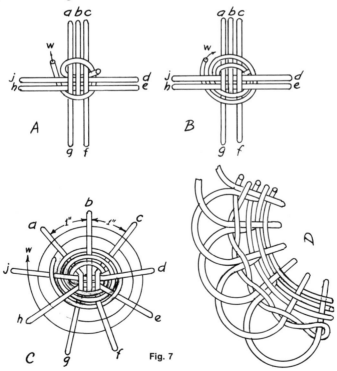

Fig. 7

Basket construction

    1. When the base is woven and the weavers tightened evenly to make it level, bend the spokes upward and intertwine a pair of weavers to provide added strength, Fig. 8, sketch A. Before the base dries, depress a slight concavity in the center.

    2. Continue the plain single basket weave forming the sides to the desired height, with straight, slightly rounded or concave shape which will be wider at the top if the spokes are spread. A rounded shape with smaller circumference at the top may be developed by narrowing the space between the spokes toward the top.

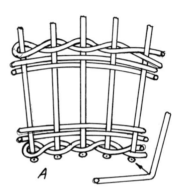

A

    3. Finish the top with a rim of two weaver lengths under which the spokes have been thinned, pointed, and turned down closely beneath the weavers below. Twine a pair of triple weavers over the rim lengths anchoring them to the two upper weavers. See Fig. 8, sketch B, for this and other rim finishes.

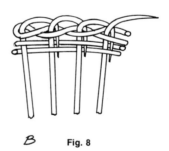

B   **Fig. 8**

Round Trays, Plate Holders, and Mats

    A combination of twined and plain wicker weave is used for the tray illustrated, Fig 9. It is made entirely of the same size of willow tips or reed, about 3/32 inch used for both spokes and weavers. All must be kept soft and pliable by moistening.

Material

    12 spokes, 20 inches long
    12 spokes, 12 inches long
    Approximately 60 lengths of weavers, 3 to 6 feet long

Weaving procedure

    1. Place 12 pairs of double spokes crosswise in the position shown in Fig. 10 and anchor them in a square formation as indicated with a pair of weavers, sketch A.

    2. Spread the 24 spokes radially, using the extra lengths of the anchor weavers to form a twine for the first circular weave. Pull these up closely to hold the spokes in position, Fig. 10, sketch B.

    3. Continue with a basket weave, over one, under one of the pairs of spokes, splicing the weavers under the spokes as required, for about two inches, Fig. 10, sketch B.

    4. Add the other 12 spokes to strengthen the base for the tray and permit the spreading of the spokes for the desired diameter of the completed project. Sketch C shows how the additional spokes are inserted between the separated pairs of the original spokes.

    5. Continue weaving over one, under one of the pairs of spokes for four inches, then separate them and hold with a pair of twined weavers, tightening slightly to start the angle for the rim.

    6. Continue weaving for 10 circles with the basket weave over and under the single spokes, spreading them equally toward the top of the sloping rim, then add a twined weaver to hold them in place.

    7. Finish the rim with a braid of three pair of weavers formed from the end lengths of the spokes, interwoven as shown in Fig. 10, sketch C.

Round Tray

Fig. 9

See Fig. 10, sketch C. The process is to carry each spoke successively over six spokes to the left as follows:

1. Carry spoke A over the next 5 and attach (with thread) to the weaver beyond.

2. Carry spoke B along spoke A over the next 5 and attach as before.

3. Weave spoke C over A, under B for the same distance.

4. Weave spoke D under A, over B, under C.

5. Weave spoke E under A, over B, under C paralleling A, then down under C and over B.

6. Weave spoke F under C, over the end of A, and parallel C under A and B, then over D and under C.

This completes the steps for the first group of six spokes. The edge for the remaining groups is formed in the same way.

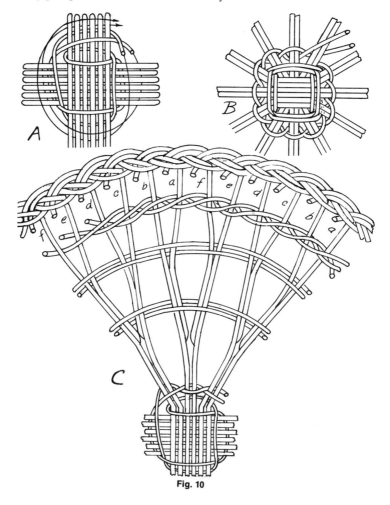

Fig. 10

Indian Coiled Baskets

The American Indian has created some of the finest baskets ever devised. In many tribes today the Indian still practices basketry. Typical examples are shown in Fig. 11. These are from the southwest Indian country in the United States where the same kind of plant fibers have been used for generations, even centuries. Close resemblance to techniques of prehistoric basket makers was revealed in remnants of their work found in excavated ruins.

These remnants indicate that building baskets with wrapped coils was probably the earliest method, so similar to coiled pottery that it cannot be determined which craft is the oldest. Both have been found in the same excavations of prehistoric settlements, and a practice seems to have existed of forming clay in a basket, which was then burned off in the firing of the pot, leaving on it the imprint of the basket.

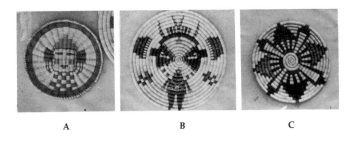

A   B   C

Fig. 11

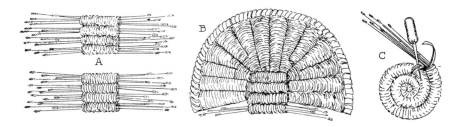

Fig. 12

Hopi trays and construction technique

The Hopi Trays or Plaques in Fig. 11 A, B, C were made of the fibrous leaves of the Yucca plant, which is shown on the first page of this section. It grows in many areas of America, particularly in the warm dry sections, where the rigid needle pointed leaves and spikes of white blossoms are a distinguishing feature of the landscape.

The Hopi basket maker develops the designs, which originated with her ancestors, using dyed strips of thinned Yucca tips to wrap and connect the grass or shredded Yucca filled coils. She may also use twigs from shrubs for the coils, and for the wrapping, sapwood strips from the "Rabbit Bush," a variety of sumac which grows throughout the Southwest.

The first tray in Fig. 11A shows a rare type of construction for a sacred design. It is called the "Spider Web" and the intricate formation is shown in the sketches of Fig. 12. Wrapped bunches of stiff grass radiate from the center group of four and increase in diameter as they form the widening proportions of the tray. The peeled sapwood wrapping strips are dyed for the colors of the design, which is perfectly balanced.

For this tray, the Hopi basket maker connects the wrapped coils with an invisible stitch or loop of the binding material through the edges, Fig. 12, sketches A, B.

For more common trays or plaques, Fig. 11, B, C, the Hopi basket maker uses the coil method, starting the foundation center or "button" with a pencil thin tapered bunch of grass or sumac twigs, which she wraps with Yucca strips or sumac sapwood.

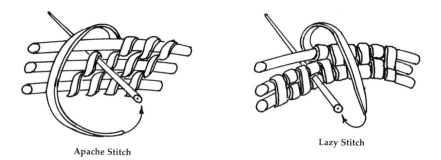

Apache Stitch

Lazy Stitch

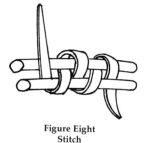

Figure Eight
Stitch

Fig. 13

Apache baskets and the Apache water bottle

The Jacarilla (northern New Mexico) tribe of Apache Indians make several kinds of deep and shallow baskets, including the famous Apache water bottle, which is illustrated in Fig. 14A. It is woven very closely of thin peeled strips from "Rabbit Bush," the same variety of sumac which the Hopi Indians of Arizona use.

A   B   C

D   E   F

Fig. 14

Twigs from the same plant form the coils which the basket maker shaped into the circular, rounded jar or bottle, with the strap attachment loops woven into the sides just below the neck. The woven binding strips connect the coils with the Apache stitch, Fig. 13, sketch A. The inside of the bottle is sealed with pinon pitch melted in the bottle with stones, heated very hot, and put in with fragments of the pitch, which is melted and distributed over the coils and all the spaces between them as the bottle is rotated and shaken until the pitch begins to harden. At this point the stones are removed.

1. Men are the basket makers of the Apaches, as was demonstrated to the author at the reservation near Dulce, New Mexico, in the construction of the tall basket in Fig. 14, D, E, F. John No Tongue took a green twig from the "Rabbit Bush" or sumac and separated it into three sections at the base. Then, holding one in his teeth, he pulled the other two with the fingers of both hands (a very efficient system!).

2. In this way an amazingly uniform width of strips was achieved, with a taper which followed the decreasing diameter of the twig. He removed the heartwood centers in the same way, leaving a thin strip about 1/32 inch thick, 30 inches long, and tapered from 3/16 to ⅛ inch.

3. After soaking the strips in water, he shaped the coil center of the base of the tall basket, Fig. 14D. As he wrapped and extended the foundation coils, he bound them together with the Apache stitch, using an awl to open up each stitch or loop, as indicated in the last coil forming the rim. He used two foundation lengths to finish the rim, wrapping them with strips over and through the

next two coils below, then over the rim lengths again, and back under the same two coils. This resembled a "herringbone" stitch, and made a very strong and durable finish, Fig. 14, E,F.

The bowl shaped tray is another type of Apache type coiled construction, built on a sumac foundation and wrapped together with narrow thin strips of sumac sapwood woven in the Apache stitch. A 3/16 inch coil forms the center from which the coils increase in diameter for 7 rounds to ⅜ inch for the base. The coils of the flaring sides remain approximately ⅜ inch for 12 rounds. The three center coils between the black triangles are wrapped with strips dyed red. The last round which forms the rim is wrapped with the one below in close tight weave of the herringbone stitch. The weavers are kept plain for a ½ inch space across the red bands to form a symbolic "Pathway for the spirit of the tray."

The group of Mexican made trays show the adaptation of designs and methods similar to those of the Hopi Indians to whom they are said to be ethnically related. The coil construction with a grass foundation and narrow thin sapwood wrapping strips is similar but the open effect between them, obtained by making a knot in each loop, as detailed in Fig. 15, is distinctively Mexican. Another name for this is the Lace Stitch.

 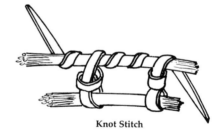

Knot Stitch

Fig. 15

Coiled Pine Needle Basketry

Baskets and other items, made with the long needles of the southern pine, are said by a basket maker of Georgia to have been devised of necessity during the Civil War, when everything had to be made of native materials. Hats for men and women were first made, then containers of various kinds. Later, when the necessity ended, pine needle basketry became a highly skilled craft, developed by individual basket makers of the southern highlands and taught in Settlement Schools.

The long needles from the southern pine and the shorter needles of other pine trees, combined with natural grasses or raffia, now the more commonly used material, make attractive and practical baskets and trays. Fallen needles which dry in shades of brown can be used without further drying. Green needles may be pulled from tree branches and will retain their color if dried in a dark place. Some basket makers cut the branches and hang them in the sun to dry the needles. The time required depends on weather conditions and humidity.

Fig. 16

1.   Soak the dry needles in warm water until pliable, and the little sheath which holds the bunch of needles, usually three, can be removed. Dip in hot water for a few minutes. This will soften the resin at the base so it can be wiped off.

The number required (for the small basket sketched) to show the formation of stitches, cannot be estimated, as the length and thickness of needles varies, also the length of raffia or other binding material.

2.   Method of making the Foundation Coil. Keep all materials damp while working. Place the strip of raffia or other binding material along two or three clusters of needles, with about an inch extending to form a loop as the strip is reversed. With this loop pointing to the left, Fig. 20, sketch 1, wrap the bunch of needles to the end as indicated, leaving just enough space to permit the insertion of the binding strip through the loop.

3.   Continue this process until the wrapped bunch can be coiled. Use a blunt needle with a large eye and avoid breaking the binding strips. Keep the coils straight and smooth, and keep the same diameter by adding a few needles at a time.

4.   Space the stiches equally as the coils are added, and keep the same tension on the loops of binding material. A radial or spiral design is thus formed as shown in the sketched basket, Fig. 16.

5.   Form the bowl shaped basket in a gradual flare. About 5 inches from the end of the coil or when the desired height is reached, cut off the extra length, then gradually reduce the diameter of the coil by cutting out a few needles at a time. Stitch the rest firmly to the underneath coil along to the end, and work the last few inches of the binding strip back between the coils.

Coiled Pine Needle Tray With Raffia Double Stitch

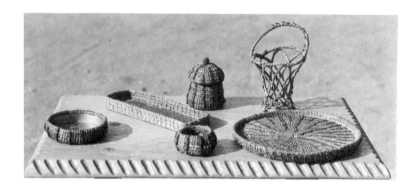

Fig. 17

Fig. 18

Pine Needle Tray

The tray illustrated was made of pine needles with the same kind of a foundation coil as for the basket, but of smaller diameter. Single binding stitches of the Figure 8 type are used for the first two circles or rounds. From this point, a decorative double stitch, formed like the opened enlargement in Fig. 19, sketch 5, holds the coils together and forms a spiderweb design. The method of building the tray coils with the double stitch is shown in sketch 7. The tray illustrated and other items made by the same method are shown in Fig. 17 and 18. The construction process follows:

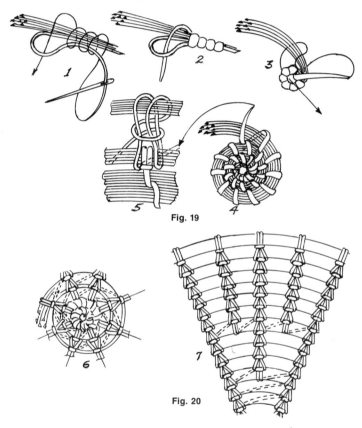

Fig. 19

Fig. 20

1. Form the center foundation coil with a bunch of needles about 3/16 inch in diameter following Fig. 19, sketches 1, 2, and 3, and using grass stems for the binding stitches of the first two coils to hold them firmly together. Turn the stitches back under or between the center coils.

2. The tray illustrated is 10 inches in diameter and approximately 32 inches in circumference. Five equal segments or divisions of the design, as shown in sketch 7, center the design as it starts from the second coil, with the double stitch of contrasting raffia detailed in sketch 6 at the 8 radial lines.

3. Continue the double stitched binding loops to hold the needle coils together. Note the connecting loop between the lines as it appears in Sketch 4 in the dotted lines. Build the needle coils by adding a few at a time as for the small basket. Keep the size uniform, and add the second set of 8 division lines as Sketch 7 of the segment indicates, making 16 at about the 1/3rd point on the tray.

4. At the 2/3rd point, add 16 lines of stitches and continue the 32 to the ⅜ inch rim, prepared with tapered ends and the right length to encircle the rest of the tray. Attach the rim with the binding raffia, wrapping it as indicated, Fig. 18, with the stitches drawn through and over the coil beneath to attach them firmly together. Weave the end of the raffia down through the third coil and back part way to anchor it. The overlapping ends of the rim coil should be concealed by the wrapping stitches.

This stitch, Fig. 20, sketch 4 and 7, is sometimes called the "pine needle stitch."

Willow Tray

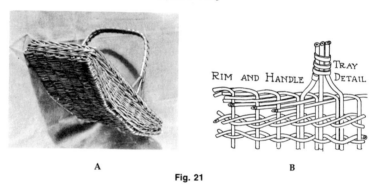

A   B

Fig. 21

The Willow Tray, Fig. 21, is made of willow tips and shoots, prepared as described on page 9 and kept soft and pliable by soaking in water at intervals. The rectangular base, approximately 8 by 18 inches is bent into three sections, the middle of which is the bottom as shown in Fig. 21A. This is constructed on 8 lengths of willow about 3/16 inch in diameter, 6 of which are spaced about 1½ inches apart for the parallel stakes, with the other two placed on either side to strengthen the base. The weaver lengths are smaller willow tips of ⅛ inch diameter which are woven back and forth to appear the same on both sides.

The double over and under weave for the base is done in two stages: first an over one and under one weave across the under side of the parallel stakes of the base, then up over the marginal stakes and back in the opposite direction across the top. The spaces between are then filled in with a second weaver length, so that the stakes are completely covered on both sides.

The side and end walls, or rim, of the tray are woven on extra spokes with tapered ends which are inserted into the sides of the base, in holes drilled into the doubled outer stakes about 2 inches apart, and at the ends placed along the parallel stakes and into the base for 2 inches, where they are held by the weavers. These wall stakes are then bent upright, 13 at the sides and 8 at the ends, with the side stakes graduated in height, so that the top of the tray is level.

The weavers for the rim are interwoven under and over the upright stakes in the same manner as for the bottom, with three-strand reinforcement weavers twined around the spokes at the bottom and at the top where one forms the edge of the rim, and a second parallels it an inch lower. The upper ends of the rim spokes are bent and twined with the top edge weaver, Fig. 21B.

A three-piece handle of larger willow lengths is made by wrapping 3/16 inch lengths together with ¼ inch strips of thinned sapwood which terminates and is fastened with a brad about four inches above the rim, where the sections are spread apart and inserted along the side spokes between the weavers as far as the base. These are held tightly when the weavers dry and shrink closely to the spokes.

After the willow tray is dry, it is protected with an application of white shellac.

Willow Basket with Decorative Rim

This basket, Fig. 22, may be made of willow tips or varying sizes of natural vine-type material such as the wild honeysuckle vine used for fine baskets in the Southern Highlands. There it grows to lengths of 15 to 20 feet which are wound in rolls, soaked in hot water until the bark can be rubbed off with a cloth, then rinsed in clear water, and hung in the sunshine to dry. It is possible to prepare other wild vines in the same way.

Fig. 22

Material requirements

The quantities of material suggested are approximate as the amount varies with the sizes of natural willow or vines.

For the base, provide ten 3/16 inch size 10 inches long peeled willow spokes or lengths of the same size vine, 40 weaver tips or vines, 24 to 36 inches long and tapering from ⅛ to 1/16 inch.

For the decorative rim, provide 100 lengths, 14 inches long of the same sizes.

The variations in size and color add interest to the finished basket. The sunshine will darken the material used for the rim, or it may be lightly stained.

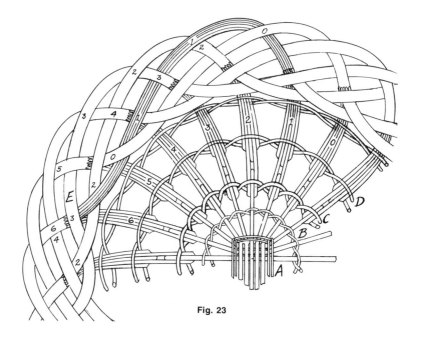

Fig. 23

Weaving procedure, Fig. 23

1. For the concave base, place the 10 larger spokes in a right angle position with 5 crossing the other 5 as indicated in Fig. 23A. Anchor the square center with a pair of weavers twined over and under.

2. Spread the spokes into a circle with the ends even and secure them with twined weavers, Fig. 23B, continuing with the same weave to the ends of the spokes, tightening the last 3 slightly to start the curve of the basket, and hold the spokes securely. Adjust for equal spacing and press together.

3. Prepare 20 lengths, 14 inches of selected finer weavers in strands of 5, and hold them in a flat position with strips of scotch tape, to be removed later.

4. Insert two of the strands along and on both sides of the spokes, Fig. 23C, of the base for about 1 inch as shown in Fig. 23D, then add the other three.

5. Using the strands as extension of the spokes, continue the twined or paired weaving until the outer circumference is a diameter of 8 inches. Tighten each of the circles of weavers slightly to develop the concave shape. As new weavers are required, conceal the ends under the spokes or strands.

6. Forming the decorative rim. The process of forming the interwoven curves of the rim requires that each band of 5, radiating from the woven section about an inch apart be carried successively to the next 5 in a pattern shown in Fig. 23.

7. Working with the dampened strands from the outside, curve band 1 up about 2 inches above the last weaver, carry it to the left, and attach the ends (temporarily with thread or tape) to the fifth band.

8. Weave band 2 under band 1 to form the next curve over to the next fifth band and attach as before.

9. Weave band 3 over 1 and under 2, then the same number of bands to the left to form the third curve.

10. Weave band 4 under 1, over 2, and then under number 3 to form the fourth curve.

11. Weave band 5 under 2, over 3, and then under 4 to form the fifth curve. This will be ¼ of the circumference of the rim.

12. Complete the rim by weaving the remaining strands in the same way. At this point all the ends should be anchored under other strands as shown in Fig. 23E. See anchor point where band number 1 rests on top of band number 6 and under band number 3, point E.

Splint Baskets

In eastern Canada and the New England States, the Indians are said to have perfected the method of making and using wood strips or splints for baskets. The practice may have been brought from England by the first settlers, or by those who became the mountain people of the southern highlands and shared their skill with the Cherokee Indians who became, and still are, expert basket makers.

Splints are made of hickory or ash, or other light woods such as oak, birch, and linden. Narrow splints are made from willow, by splitting peeled willow shoots, or from small bamboo lengths.

It is possible to make splints, Indian method, by beating a log with a large wooden mallet until the layers are loosened so they can be stripped from the log and cut into splints with a knife or a gauge similar to the draw gauge used for cutting leather straps (see page 154). Those used for spokes or "staves" (the Indian term), are ½ inch or more wide and cut thick enough to be rigid when dry. Weaving splints are thinner and flexible, cut into widths ⅛ to ½ inch. Both kinds are used for making the Adirondack Pack Basket described on page 34. The Round Splint Basket in Figs. 24 and 25A and B is a simple adaptation of this type of basketry.

Fig. 24

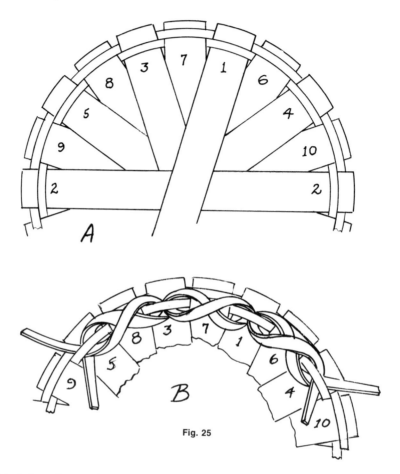

Fig. 25

Materials and procedure

1. Soak 10 splints ½ inch wide and 12 inches long in water until flexible, then cross them in pairs with the first or bottom pair at right angles. Spread the others radially into a circle drawn on paper with a compass or string and pencil.

2. At a point about 3 inches from the center where the edges of the splints begin to separate, turn them up to form the spokes of the basket with spaces between of about 3/16 inch, then twine a pair of narrow splint weavers, ⅛ inch wide at this edge of the base, Fig. 25B.

3. Continue weaving with pairs of single weavers to the tops of the spokes. Press the weavers closely together, adjusting the spaces evenly so that the inside and outside of the spokes are covered with the weavers in the alternate over one, under one, steps.

4. Evenly trim the ends of the alternate spokes and bend the others down on the inside of the basket. Cut the ends to a point and insert between the weavers for about 2 inches.

5. Place bands of 1-inch firm splints, which have been rounded and thinned to overlap about 3 inches at the ends, around the outer and inner circumference with the ends at opposite sides. Finish this rim edge with a pair of weavers crossed at the top and woven between the spokes as shown in the illustration, Fig. 24.

Fig. 26

Splint Basket with Handle

This basket is similar to some woven in the South. It is constructed entirely of bamboo wide and narrow splints and when finished is 5 inches deep and 12 inches in diameter, Figs. 26 and 27. These splints, made of the smooth outer surface of bamboo, have long sections between joints. The construction, except for the handle, is started like the preceding basket. Material requirements are:

10 splints 1 to 1¼ inches wide and 23 inches long; also a supply of narrow ⅛ inch weavers

2 handle sections, one 60 inches long, 1/16 inch thick, and 28 inches long, ⅛ inch thick. 1 reinforcing section, 21 inches long

2 splint bands for the top rim finish, ½ inch wide and 40 inches long

2 10 inch diameter wooden discs for a base form.

All materials must be kept moist and flexible. After soaking them for about 5 minutes, wrap in a damp cloth until woven (except the form).

Weaving procedure

1. Place the splint spokes on a flat surface in the order indicated in Fig. 27 of the base formation. Splint number 5 is extended to become the handle as shown in the cross section sketch, which also indicates the thicker reinforcing center splint. Point X must be placed at the center of the base, making the lengths from X, 32 inches from the right hand end and 28 inches from the left.

2. Five of the 21 inch splints should be crossed as shown below the long handle splint and four placed above as in Fig. 27. Fan the splints out evenly in slightly overlapping layers from the center to a diameter of 20 inches where they are about ½ inch apart, with the handle splint extended.

3. With a single narrow weaver start weaving from the point where the splints separate until a diameter of about 10 inches is obtained as shown in Fig. 27 of a section of the base. Tighten the weavers to hold the splint spokes firmly in position. Using a 10 inch wooden disc for a form, bend the moist, pliable splints upward, the sketch shows the outside of the base.

4. Remove the form and continue weaving from the outside, pressing the weavers closely together to cover the spaces between the splints to the 5 inch height. With the exception of the handle ends, carefully bend the ends of the spokes down and inward under the last three weavers. Have the spokes very damp, and if necessary cut a little V in the end so it will stay flat under the weavers. Loosen the weavers slightly with a round edge paper knife.

5. Place the two edge finish or rim splints around the inner and outer circumference of the top, thin and lap the ends at opposite points between the handle extensions. With two ¼ inch thinned and moistened weavers, wrap the

Splint Basket with Handle

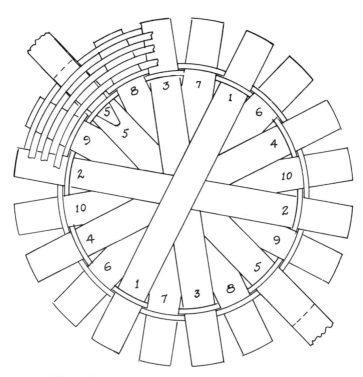

Formation of base with position of handle

Fig. 27

bands together as closely as possible, starting at A and B as shown in Fig. 28, sketch 2, and weave through the last two rounds of the weavers and beneath the down turned spokes. Insert a 3 inch length of the wrapping weaver down between the spokes and weavers.

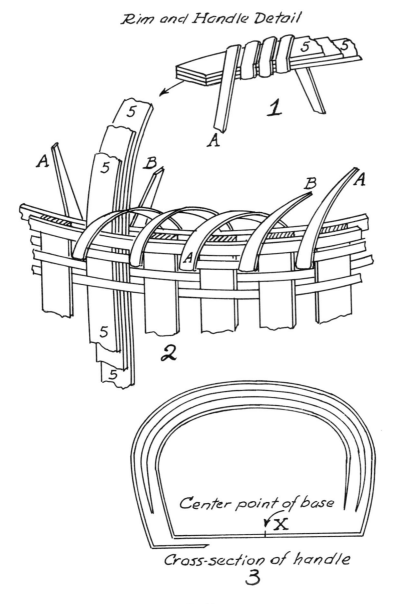

Rim and Handle Detail

1

2

Center point of base
X

Cross-section of handle
3

Fig. 28

Splint basket handle detail

6. As indicated in the cross section sketch, the 28 inch left-hand extension of the handle splint becomes the lower part. Moisten this well and bend into a curved position. Gradually insert the pointed end through the inside weavers for a depth of about 2/3rds of the distance from rim to base. Moisten the weavers so they may be opened slightly with a smooth paper knife. Bend the 21 inch center reinforcing splint, with ends pointed (dampened until flexible), into the handle position, and insert them between the weavers and on top of spoke number 5 about 2/3rds of the distance to the edge of the base, Fig. 28, sketch 3.

7. The 32 inch extension of splint number 5, as in the cross section sketch, becomes the upper section of the handle. Moisten well and bend closely over the other two parts of the handle, gradually inserting it between the weavers, over the reinforcing splint to the edge of the base for about 4 inches as in Fig. 28, sketch 3.

8. Wrap the handle sections closely together with ¼ or ⅜ inch thinned splints as indicated in the sketch of the handle detail, leaving about 3 inches of the wrapping strips to weave in with the binding strips of the rims, Fig. 28, sketch 1.

Oval Basket, Willow Splint Construction

The oval basket, Fig. 29, is another splint construction which is a good beginner's project. The shape is achieved by the selected size of the rim and the single basket weave method, which permits the depth of the basket to be increased or decreased according to the length of the spokes. These are narrow half sections of peeled willow, about 3/16 inch wide and the weavers are thinned willow splints ¼ to ⅜ inch wide.

Fig. 29

Materials required

11 spokes of unequal length, graduating from 16 inches at the center to 9 inches at the sides to conform to the shape of the oval rim. The extra inch at both ends permits attachment to the rim as shown in Fig. 30, sketch B.

Approximately 41 weavers divided for the 3 sections, 15 at the center and 13 for each end section.

For the rim, one 42 inch length of ⅜ inch diameter willow thinned on a bevel for about 5 inches at the ends to overlap without increasing the diameter, and leaving a perimeter for the rim of 32 inches. The ends are fastened together with a brad as shown in sketch A.

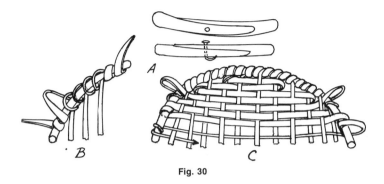

Fig. 30

The steps in the weaving are indicated in Fig. 30, sketch C.

1. Attach both ends of the thinned and bent short outside spokes to the rim with a length of moistened weaver splint wrapped over them twice, continuing ½ inch toward the center, and attach the second spoke in the same way, Fig. 30, sketch B.

2. Attach the other 9 spokes to the oval rim with the weavers, placing the 15 inch spoke at the center and the others on each side according to length. This makes the framework for the weaving.

3. At the opposite curved ends, weave a single length of weaver splint, over and under the spokes without going over the rim. See Fig. 30, sketch C. From here, pass the weaver splints evenly back and forth with a loop over the rim each time. Finish weaving each end section with the graduated weavers as divided, then weave the center section.

Oval Basket, Cane or Reed Construction with Handle

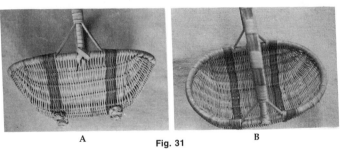

A   Fig. 31   B

The illustrated two color oval basket with handle and feet is made with reed or cane of the same size, 3/32 for both spokes and weavers, Fig. 31. Approximately twice as much material is required for the formation of this basket than was used in the first oval basket tray.

1. There will be required 22 graduated lengths of cane or reed ranging from 16 inches at the center to 9 inches at the sides in the same way as for the first basket.

2. 41 *double* weavers divided for the three sections, 15 for the center and 9 for each end section.

3. For the rim, two sections of ¼ inch split reed, 38 inches long with tapered 3 inch ends to overlap with a brad fastening.

4. Two 16 inch round cane lengths, ¼ inch in diameter to be placed along the sides of the base section and extending to the rim at each end to strengthen the base. There are 3 pairs of reed spokes between these. Use four "Turk's Head Knots" woven of reed for feet. This knot which is shown on page 312 is attached at four points of the base to the ¼ inch cane with a short length of reed as shown.

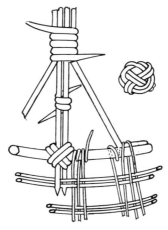

Fig. 32

5. For the handle, attached as shown in Fig. 32, 4 lengths of ¼ inch round cane about 4 feet long are required. These are wrapped together with a ¼ inch wide flat reed, leaving two 6 inch sections unwrapped at opposite ends, to be thinned, bent, and joined to the basket rim with the basket weavers which wrap the rim, as shown in Fig. 32.

6. Except for the handle detail, the formation of the basket is the same as in the preceding oval splint basket. The additional ¼ inch spokes along the sides of the base are woven in with the weavers, which loop over the rim as shown in Fig. 31A and 32.

Required for the handle wrapping is an estimated quantity of 5 yards flat reed, to cover all 4 of the handle sections to points where they separate, then to wrap the center cane lengths together and form the crossed fastening at the rim.

Covered Basket of Splint and Grass

The covered basket of thin splint and long grass, Fig. 33, is fascinating to make for a durable and attractive container. If lined, it is a useful holder for jewelry or trinkets. The basket is 8 inches in diameter and 2 inches deep. Larger sizes may be constructed with the material prepared according to the planned dimensions.

The natural grasses used as weavers combine with thin shaped splints, dyed a soft green to blend with the shaded grass stems. The splint forms the foundation of both bottom and cover of the basket as they appear in Fig. 33.

Fig. 33

Material:

A quantity of long grass stems will be required; also 32 splints, 12 inches long, of which 6 are extras to be used as replacements, if necessary. They should be ¾ to 1 inch in width. All material must be dampened enough to be pliable. The supply should be kept covered with a damp cloth.

The *construction process* is as follows:

1. Select 24 evenly thinned splints and one at a time cut them on a taper from each end to a center width of ⅛ inch. With care scissors may be used, but a safer method is to use a metal edged ruler and a sharp knife on a board. 12 are required for both the bottom and the cover of the basket. They are constructed in almost the same way.

2. Place 6 of the shaped splints, one above the other, in an evenly crossed position. Flare them into a circle, which may be drawn on a paper pattern and thumbtacked to the worktable or a board. Space them at the ends ¾ inch apart.

3. Start a basket weave of a long grass stem, over one, under one, of the crossed splint spokes, tighten as closely as possible to the center and continue to weave, with the spokes held in position until a diameter of 2 inches is formed. This is for either the cover or bottom of the basket. Turn the ends back under to fasten.

4. Reverse the work and place 6 more of the shaped splints in a crossed position directly over the woven center section and flare so that the spaces between the flared spokes or splints of the first circle are filled. Position them evenly with the pattern beneath. Any slight overlapping toward the ends may be trimmed.

5. Start a new weave with a long grass stem, over one, under one, of the combined splint spokes, keeping them flat and in position. Carefully tighten the weaver and press closely together with each round until a diameter of 5 inches is reached. Avoid folding or breaking the splint spokes. This will become the cover.

6. Reverse the work and finish the weaving from the outside. Prepare 7 strands of 3 braid grass stems at least 20 inches long. Weave 3 rounds with the braided strands, then turn down all of the ends of the splints to form the rim of the cover. Hold the splint spokes in position with 4 more rounds of the braided weavers. About 1¼ inches of the spokes should extend above the last round.

7. Cut an inch from every other one of the extended spokes, leaving ¼ inch above. Turn the alternate ones down at the same level and hold beneath the braided weavers. It may be necessary to split these spokes to overlap slightly and narrow the width. Fit a length of ¼ inch wide splint inside the ¼ inch space overlapping the ends about 2 inches.

8. For the outside make a straight strand of 6 or 8 lengths of grass stems, which will be the same width as the inside splint when compressed together. Cut out about half of each end for an inch, or enough for them to overlap and maintain the same size. Wrap the grass and splint together with an ⅛ inch strip of splint, passing it through the folded ends of the spokes. Conceal the end of the binding strip by weaving it under the inside weavers. This completes the cover.

9. Construct the bottom part of the basket in the same way and weave the grass stems over and under the splint spokes until a 5 inch diameter is reached. Then turn up the spokes to form the rim, overlapping the ends with enough tension to make the diameter small enough to fit inside the cover. Weave four strands of the braided grass over the base curve, leaving an inch of the splint spokes extending around the bottom rim.

10. Weave a band of splint ¾ inch wide over and under the turned up splints and overlap the ends to fit the smaller inside diameter. Cut off every other one of the splints except the last ¼ inch. Turn the others down at the same level and weave under the braided weavers. If necessary, split the ends to narrow them.

11. Finish the edge of the bottom of the basket with two bands of ¼ inch wide splint fitted inside and outside of the cut and folded ends of the spokes, overlapping them enough and with slight tension to allow the cover to fit closely over them. Bind these together with a ⅛ inch strip of splint woven over them between the spokes which were cut off, and through the folded ends of the others. Conceal the ends of the binding splint between the spokes.

Adirondack Pack Basket

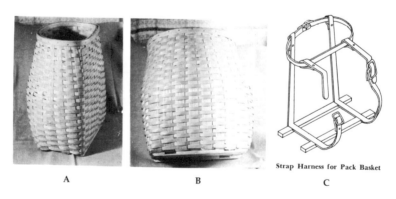

Strap Harness for Pack Basket

A   B   C

Fig. 34

The Adirondack pack basket, Fig. 34, has long been the back carrier of the Penobscot Indians of Maine and other tribes in the United States and Canada. The style has been adopted by the Boy Scouts and various hiking groups since straps of leather or webbing enable them to carry considerable loads on pack trips in the trail country without fatigue.

Splints are used for both the spokes (vertical) and weavers (horizontal) in a simple basket weave. The material requirements are:

13 foundation splints for spokes, 5 inches long and 1¼ inches wide. (If narrower splints are used 2 or 3 more are needed.)

40 or more weaver splints 4 to 6 inches long and ⅜ to ½ inch wide.

2 firm splints or lengths of ash for the rim, about 50 inches long, ¾ inch wide, and 3/16 inch thick, bent into an oval after soaking in water.

2 pair of wood cleats, slightly longer than the finished basket and 1½ inches wide.

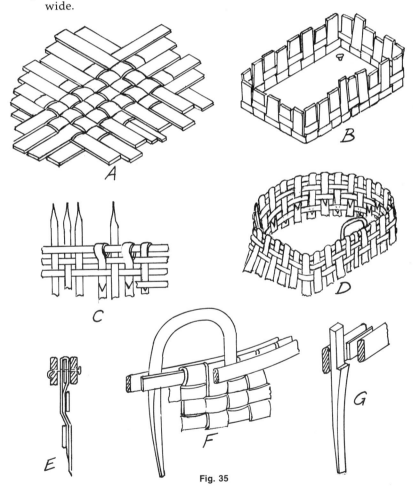

Fig. 35

Process of construction

1. Soak the splints in water until flexible. Wipe off excess water before weaving.

2. Form a rectangular base on a flat surface, 5 splints wide and 8 splints long, interweaving them as closely as possible. Split the fourth splint of the 8 on the side which will become the back, as an odd number is required for the basket weave, Fig. 35, sketch A.

3. Center a board, 8 by 12 inches, with slightly rounded corners on the woven base and fasten with screws at the corners which will come between the weavers, Fig. 35, sketch B. Using this as a form, bend all of the weaver splints upright, first dampening them to avoid splitting. Hold the splints in position and weave two or three rounds of horizontal splints as indicated in Fig. 35, sketch B.

4. Push these lower weavers closely together and proceed with the weaving of the body of the basket, developing the rounded front by spreading the vertical splints slightly and weaving a little more loosely. The wooden base form may be removed and a piece of cushion foam rubber braced against the front to help develop the rounded contour.

5. Maintain a flat surface for the back. Notice that the divided splint is on this side. When new horizontal splints are needed, overlap them and conceal under the vertical splints. Continue weaving until a height of about 20 inches is reached.

6. Toward the top, narrow the shape by bringing the vertical splints closely together, trimming them slightly on a long taper, if necessary, to fit them into the oval rim, after the top edge is formed by bending each vertical splint, cut to a V point down under the upper horizontal weavers, sketch C and D. (Keep the splints dampened with a wet sponge.)

7. Round and thin the ends of the inside and outside rim lengths and fit in place with the ends overlapping about 3 inches. Fasten them together at intervals with brads or small nails, driven through and bent down on the inside, sketch E.

8. Attach the inside and outside wood cleats to reinforce and support the base. See Fig. 34, sketch B and C, for insertion of the carrying straps through the recessed grooves in the outside cleats. The straps or webbing bands are buckled together below the rim of the basket and at each shoulder.

9. A handle for hand carrying may be attached as shown in Fig. 35, sketch F and G, which also shows the attachment of the rim. The handle is made from a piece of ash or hickory wood, ⅜ by ¾ inch and 15 inches long soaked in water, or steamed until it can be bent into the handle shape.

Split Cane Cherokee Basket

This diamond design basket, Fig. 36, is a typically fine basket of a type made for generations by the Cherokee Indians of North Carolina, who successfully defeated the efforts of the United States Government to move them from the Blue Ridge Mountains to Oklahoma.

The Cherokees use a split cane made from a strong native plant of the bamboo family, common to the South where it is used extensively by the people of the southern highlands as well as by the Cherokees. The design and the technique of weaving the bamboo cane or commercial cane may be adapted for different sized baskets by modern basket makers. The one illustrated is 12 inches in diameter and 8 inches in depth.

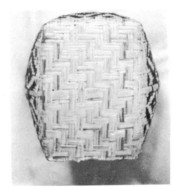

Fig. 36

The following materials are required:

Approximately 53 cane strips 36 inches long, averaging 3/16 inch for the width of the rectangular base and sides.

36 cane strips 40 inches long, averaging 3/16 inch for the lengthwise pattern of the base and the ends.

29 brown cane strips 42 inches long for the design and one firm length of cane, 40 inches for the top band.

A 50 inch length of hardwood shaped from ¾ by ⅜ inch at the center section and thinned to 1/16 inch for the 7 inch ends. Notches are cut at the points indicated in Fig. 37, sketch A, also the method of insertion in the basket.

Weaving procedure for the base, all materials well moistened

1. Start the herringbone design for the base with 3 bands of 3 cane strips or weavers in a horizontal position and 3 bands in a vertical position on a flat surface, woven in the pattern indicated in Fig. 37, sketch B.

2. Add bands of 3 alternately each way toward the ends and sides until 4 are woven, then weave 3 more bands at the ends to form the rectangular base, a total of 18 bands in length and 11 bands in width.

Weaving procedure for sides, all materials well moistened

1. Weave a single strip of cane around the base, over and under each group

of 3, then weave 4 more strips over 4, then under 4, carefully pulling them together to form the corners and a depth of about an inch as shown in Fig. 38. This shows the corners and the building of the design.

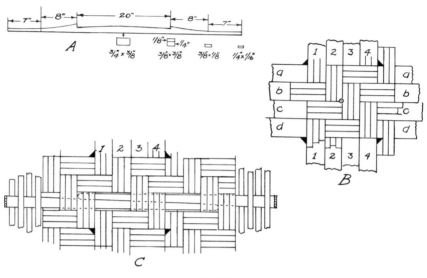

Fig. 37

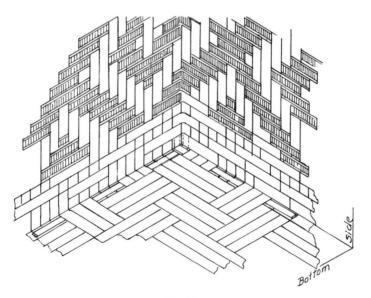

Fig. 38

2. Bend the thinned end sections of the handle and insert across the base, over and under the outer bands of 3, then under the fourth band on each side. Fig. 37, sketch C, shows the position of the handle.

3. From this point use the brown strips for weavers in the diamond design with the first one going over the handle. Build the pattern around the sides and ends, Fig. 38.

4. After weaving a depth of about 7 inches, tighten the last 3 horizontal weavers, Fig. 39B, over the vertical strips or spokes to bring the top into a circular form with a diameter of about 11 inches. Overlap these weavers through the spokes, then trim evenly *all except every fourth spoke.* These should extend about 3 inches.

5. Bend the extended spokes down closely to the left and weave a brown strip over and under the top weaver and between the groups of 4 spokes to form a firm edge as shown in Fig 39, sketch A.

6. Place the circular top band in position at the notches in the handle, holding it closely to the top edge. Overlap the thinned ends at least 3 inches at a point midway between the notches, and wrap firmly with a strip of cane ¼ inch wide, Fig. 39, sketch B.

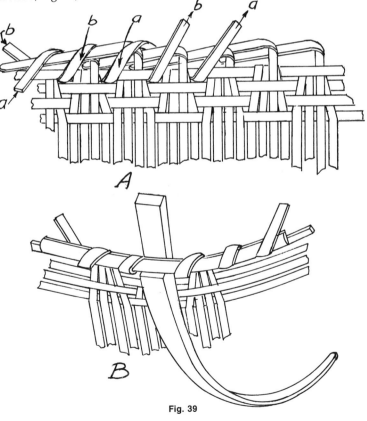

Fig. 39

CHAPTER 3

Bookbinding

The craft of bookbinding began about three centuries ago, during the period of the Guilds in England, when it became a highly skilled and respected craft. It is practiced today with little change, except for the introduction of machines, which have simplified some processes and made them more efficient.

The bookbinders of the Guild period originated a hand sewing method for a flexible binding of fine books, in which the distinguishing feature was the ridges across the backbinding under the cover or case. They revealed the position of the cords as sewn to the sections of pages, or signatures to hold them together with the so-called "kettle stitch," a corruption of catch-up stitch, which is still used in handbound books.

The cords, five to seven, depending on the size of the book, were carried over the edge of the boards (stiff cardboard which reinforced the cover), frayed out at the ends, and glued flat between the boards and cover or case. The interesting steps in the process are sketched in Fig. 40, which also shows the appearance of a leather covered cordbound book. Part of the decoration is the gold impressions which defined the cords.

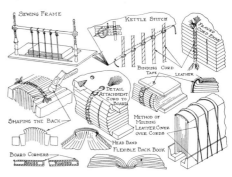

Fig. 40

40

A book is made up of a cover or case and the contents. The parts of the case are: the cloth, leather, or leather substitute binding, back stiffening, and lining, also the back headbands, a tape ½ inch wide with a woven cord selvage, two inner cover boards, a stiff interlining of thin bookbinders' "super," which is glued over the back and extends about one-third of the way across the boards, end-papers or "fly" leaves, and the lining papers for front and back.

The signatures or sections of the book contents are usually made up of 16 page forms, with the printing on both sides. As an example of the form of a signature as printed, before folding and cutting, fold a sheet of paper 8 by 11 inches crosswise 4 times. The position of the threads, 10 on the outside fold of a signature and 5 long stitches or loops on the inside of the center fold, is indicated in Fig. 41B.

The average modern book is machine sewed, with 3 to 9 double pages in a signature, depending on the size and number of pages. The edge folds of the forms are not cut until after the signatures are sewn together. The title page and other "fly" leaves are glued or "tipped" in separately.

The process of bookbinding is not difficult and with care can be success-fully done by hand.

Rebinding a Book

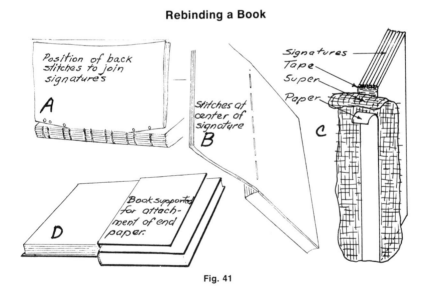

Fig. 41

The first step in rebinding a book is to remove the contents from the cover or case, Fig. 41A. Open the book and cut the lining papers and the super along the hinge groove without cutting the back of the case or the thread which holds the signatures together.

If the boards and back strip are in good condition, remove only the lining papers from the boards, and loosen the cloth super strips. Be careful not to tear or break the boards and trim closely any lining margins so that the inner edges of the boards are exposed. If the super along the back is loose in places but the signatures hold together, do not remove it or break any of the signature threads, Fig. 41C.

Preparing the contents for rebinding

When the signature threads are holding and the super is only loose in places, apply a thin coat of very hot glue to the entire length of the super along the back. This will permeate the open meshes of the super cloth and unite it more closely to the sewed signatures. Smooth the cloth in place with a bone folder.

Fig. 42

Restoring the binding threads

1. When the binding threads have been broken and the signatures are loosened, it may be necessary to resew them partially or all together, Fig. 42. The super and the old glue may be removed with a sponge, after softening with steam from teakettle of boiling water. Hold the back of the closed contents edgewise over the spout and gently scrape them with a case knife. A cloth wrung out of hot water and held against the back for a few minutes may soften it sufficiently to permit removal of the super and enough old glue to allow the retying of broken threads by the following method.

2. Open any loosened front or back signature at the center of the double pages and locate the part where the thread has broken or pulled out. Unravel or untie the ends, or cut, if necessary, to release the signature. Carefully move the threads through to the outer fold of the first firm section of the back and tie them in a hard knot, Fig. 42, leaving the ends along the fold to be concealed under the back papers, Fig. 41, sketch A. Do not cut them off.

3. Place the contents on a table with the back toward you and the loosened signatures on top. Open the signatures at the center, and hold one half at right angles with the left hand, or prop with a paperweight when necessary to use both hands. Tie a double length of new thread as close as possible to the knot ends, and with a blunt pointed needle stitch down through the knot to the center of the opened signatures. Note that there are two holes close to the fold

of the signature. If there is no perforation at this point, make one with a pointed needle, Fig. 41, sketch A.

4. Carry the thread to one of the next left hand holes and through the signature to the outside fold. Hold the loosened signature close to the one beneath, with the perforations in line, and bring the threads through to tie firmly in a bookbinder's knot. This is similar to a double buttonhole knot.

5. Bring the thread along the fold of the signature and through the next hole to the center, then along the back to the next holes through the fold of the signature. Attach to the lower signature as before with a firm knot. Continue this process through the line of holes, tying the loose signature to the lower signature at each perforated point. If any of the holes are broken out, make a new set as close as will hold.

6. When the last set of holes is reached, tie a firm knot without cutting the threads, then bring them back to the right, through the line of knots to the starting point, and tie firmly in a square knot. If the opposite end of the signature is loose, attach it in the same way, beginning at the right hand end and working to the next left hand firm section, making sure all knots are firmly tied. Leave the ends to be concealed and anchored in the back super with the glue. If necessary resew the signatures on the reverse side in the same way. When the resewing is complete, place them beneath a weighted board to compress them to the original thickness.

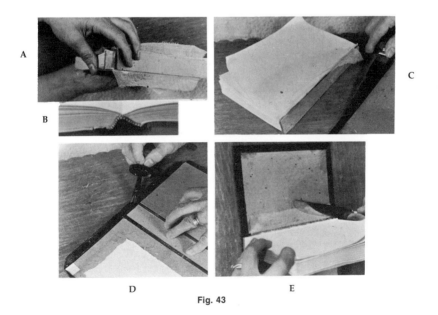

Fig. 43

Reinforcing the back

1. Cut a strip of bookbinder's super cloth or open mesh tailor's interlining 5 inches wide and one inch shorter than the signatures. Cut a strip of tough

lining paper the exact length and width of the signatures. Apply a uniform coat of hot glue to the folded edges of the signatures and smooth the super over them and the loose threads, with the extra width projecting evenly on both sides, Fig. 41C. These will be glued to the boards of the back later, Fig. 43C and 43E. Glue new headband tape, Fig. 43A, above the super with the woven selvage edge just beyond and even with the ends of the signatures. The head-bands are used in better bindings as they hold the signatures from separating and permit flexibility, Fig. 43B.

2. Apply a second coat of glue to the super and across the tape of the head-bands. Place the strip of lining paper evenly over the super and the tape with the ends coming to the selvage of the headbands and the side edges covering the signature folds, Fig. 41, sketch C. Smooth with the bone folder until the lining paper adheres to all edges of the signature folds, Fig. 43C.

Restoring the cover or case

1. If the signatures are intact and firmly attached to the super and lining strip along the back, and the original case is not torn or too heavy, with the boards in good condition, the new cover can be attached over it. Any blunted or bent corners of the boards may be flattened out and repaired with two strips of draftsmen's adhesive tape folded at right angles to make a square corner of two thicknesses of tape, Fig. 43D. If the corners are broken or torn, replace with new boards.

2. Cut the new cover or case of tooling calfskin, steerhide, or goatskin (Morocco, which is the most durable), large enough for at least ½ inch margin beyond the edges, ends, and sides of the lining boards, and in addition allow ½ extra length for the hinge that fits in against the sides of the signature folds, Fig. 43D.

3. Decorate the cover as desired. The steerhide may be either tooled, like calfskin, or stamped like goatskin which is more difficult to tool.

4. Lightly skive the ½ inch margins, which are to be folded over the boards. This process for leather is described on page 201. Crease a line along a straight edge to mark the position of the fold on the cover and on the inner margin, to indicate the position of the lining paper, about 3/16 inch from the fold. Crease also the front and back, where the extra space or hinge along the signatures will come, at the inner edge of the boards.

5. On the space at the center where the back or the signature folds will be attached, glue a strip of the tough lining paper, Fig. 43D. Fold the skived margins of the case or cover over the edge of the boards to determine the position, then apply a leather adhesive uniformly along the margins of the leather and out to the edges. First paste down the margins at both ends of the back lining strip, then over the boards and out to the corners, taking care not to stretch the skived leather, Fig. 43, sketch 2. Leave the corners until both the right- and left-hand side margins are pasted. Close the cover or case over the signatures, and crease along the inside edges of the boards to define the hinge sections and make sure the space is sufficient. If there is any tension, loosen the top and bottom margins and repaste smoothly.

6. Carefully miter the corners, after folding on the diagonal across each corner of the case to indicate the line to be cut. Apply adhesive and paste down the edges to the boards, fitting the mitered corners exactly together, Fig. 43E.

Attaching the new case to the contents

1. Place the contents or signatures on the cover so that they fit evenly into the back lining strip. Hold them vertically with the front edges toward you and the cover opened flat with the projecting strips of super in a position to attach Fig. 43E. Apply a coat of hot glue along the boards where the super strips extend from the back lining and smooth them in place, leaving sufficient looseness to fit the hinge. Reverse the position of the book and attach the strips of super to the other boards.

2. Close the book, then open one cover and prop it level with the rest of the contents, supported with another book, Fig. 41, sketch D. Place half of one of the cover lining papers and end pages which are (in one piece even with the cover margin, leaving a fold of about ¼ inch out) along the inner edges of the board next to the contents. Paste the lining paper smoothly on the board. Trim, if necessary, to leave the same margin of the cover which the original cover lining had. Crease the extra fold into the hinge and paste it down to cover the edges of the shoulder of the contents. If additional endpapers are needed, they may be "tipped in" or pasted in with the first endpaper.

3. Reverse the position of the book, supported with the other cover and book beneath, with the board open. Apply paste and follow the same steps to attach the paper lining and end pages as before.

Preparation of fabric covers

A heavy linen or a lightweight closely woven canvas is suitable for a book cover to replace the original case. The new cover may have the book title and any chosen design blockprinted, according to the instructions on page 118.

To prevent stretching or raveling of the bias corners of the cloth, it is suggested that they be machine stitched across before they are cut to miter over the boards. The margins, which should be at least ½ inch where folded over the boards, may also be stitched along the cover margins, where the lining papers end, unless they are selvage. Otherwise the process is the same as for the leather cover or case.

Binding a small book

Notebooks, program booklets, or other types of ½ inch thickness or less, may be bound flat, with double, four-fold or six-fold pages sewn together at the center and through a strip of cloth or tough lining paper. This should be cut about 3 inches wide and long enough to turn under for reinforcement at the "Head and Tail" or the top and bottom of the back of the book.

1. Perforate the pages at the center fold, through four or five at a time, on an unthreaded sewing machine adjusted for wide spaced stitches. The perforations will match if they are started at the same distance from the edge on all pages.

2. Prepare the binding cover or case of heavy paper or cloth which may be blockprinted or otherwise decorated. Cut the cover to extend about ⅛ inch beyond the pages when closed. A fabric may be used if lined with paper for stiffness, in which case the cover must be cut large enough to turn in all edges. These should be pasted down before the pages are sewn in.

3. With the stitched pages folded together, hold them on the cover at the center point of the back strip and paste down the extended edges of the cover along the front and back. An extra page or double page may be "tipped in" (glued) or stitched in with the others.

Scrapbooks or albums

Books into which film prints, clippings, or sketches are to be pasted may be made by a simple method. Cut the desired number of double pages or leaves of a good quality paper in a color which will be a good background. Cut enough pieces of the same paper the length of the pages and about 3 inches wide to insert between the double leaves at the center fold. These will provide sufficient back width to allow for the extra thickness of the prints or other items which are to be pasted on the leaves. Assemble the sections by sewing according to the method suggested for small books.

Fig. 44

Here is a small guest book with heavy cloth-covered boardbinding. The loose leaves are held with the binding boards in a channeled wood back. Leather thongs drawn through holes drilled in the back and tied together hold the pages firmly in the covers.

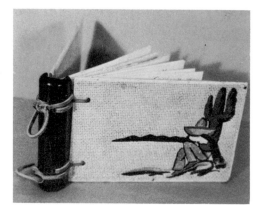

CHAPTER 4

Ceramics

Of all the skills which mankind has developed through the ages and employs in modern times, none is more ancient or practical than working with clay. Archaeological excavations of Egyptian civilizations 4,000 years ago prove that they had developed techniques of pottery making which are unsurpassed today. Earthenware, on baked clay tablets found with inscriptions, verify many periods of Biblical reference.

The Egyptians and the Persians decorated the walls of their buildings with color glazed scenes of religious or mythological significance. The glazing of baked clay is said to have been introduced into Spain by the Arabs and it was a Spanish friar, Don Juan de Quiroga, who taught the natives of Mexico the techniques which are shown today in the beautiful tile work of the Mexican cathedrals, public buildings, and private patio fountains. The similarity in form and design of pieces of pottery from Aztec and Mayan excavations in Central America and the clay work of the Indians of the southwest seem to reveal a connection between those great civilizations and the more primitive one of the Indians.

Pottery making is one of the skills in the art of living shared by craftsmen around the world. The potter works with earth, air, water, and fire. As he ex-

Fig. 45

The reverse mold serving plate, made in San Antonio, Texas, is decorated with a typically Spanish design, in brilliant blue, red, yellow, and green.

periments with them and acquires the skill to master them, he may express his own creative urge. He can begin with the simple tools used by ancient potters and like them may search out his clay, prepare and test it, or he can procure the tested and perfected "clay bodies" of the modern laboratory and start at the end of the preliminary process, which was the most difficult for his ancestors.

The Nature and Characteristics of Pottery Clay

Geologically, clay is a fine insoluble residue remaining from the decomposition of granite or feldspathic rocks over many thousands of years. Seldom is this residue found in the original location of the parent rock. North Carolina has a deposit of nearly pure *Kaolin,* as this residual clay is known and there is one in Cornwall, England. The name and the clay came from a hill in China, *Kaoling* (meaning high hill), and was first known by the rest of the world, when it was shipped to England and used for an ingredient of the fine porcelain made there, as it had been in China. Kaolin consists of feldspar (Aluminum-silicate in combination with water or hydrous alumina silicate).

The clay that has been moved by glaciers, wind, and water from its original source or sedimentary clay deposits may be found in lake beds — also as strata deposited between other formations, as frequently seen in banks or road cuts. Occasionally, this natural clay is found to have specific chemical properties, in the right proportions for a usable clay body, but a varying quantity of granular particles of quartz (silicon dioxide), are usually present.

The silicates, quartz and feldspar in crystalline form are necessary for the clay to fuse properly during the firing process. Ceramists have found that the quality of silica, which causes it to combine when heated with the alkaline earths and low melting oxides to form glassy substances, makes possible the development of ceramics, as now known, and the entire subject of glazes. Experimentation and research have revealed the chemical composition of the elements in clay bodies, and the formulas by which the vast number of glazes are now prepared. This is a study which advanced ceramists will find a challenge.

Mineral oxides or iron compounds frequently present in clay, as it naturally occurs, cause changes in color under heat, and these changes, often unpredictable, have a quality of mystery. Clay also contains the elements of hydrogen and oxygen, which unite chemically under heat to form water, which passes off as steam in what is called the "water smoking" period of firing, leaving the other elements fused into a dense hard substance quite different from the original clay.

Equipment and preparation for testing

The following instructions apply in the preparation and testing of natural and commercial clays. The equipment needed includes:

A piece of 2 by 2 inch hard wood at least 2 feet long with a smoothed end to use as a pestle.

An earthenware jar or large crock, with a tight fitting lid.

Two galvanized pails or other containers of two-gallon capacity.

A large sieve of ¼ inch mesh or a square of builders hardware cloth which may be tacked to a frame made to fit over a pail.

A second sieve of 1/16 inch mesh, and for finer screening a sieve of 40 mesh.
Several plaster of Paris "bats" as described on page 69.
A wooden spoon or rounded wood modeler, plastic sponge, also "elephant's ear" sponge.
A piece of sponge on a stick — to swab water from tall pots.
Potter's knife or a paring knife, also a sharp pointed tool.
Steel loop tool, also standard clay modeling tools.
A jar or other container for slip, also 2 or more plastic slip trailers.
Large plastic bag to keep pieces of clay and projects damp.
A rotating device for finishing and decoration.
Oilcloth covered or linoleum topped table.

Procedure for testing

1. Spread the clay on a wood surface or clean piece of canvas to dry out completely, after removing sticks, stones, and any foreign matter.

2. Crush large lumps and break dry fragments with the 2 by 2 held in both hands.

3. Screen into a pail through the large ¼ inch mesh sieve or screen.

4. Using twice as much water as clay, sprinkle into it by hand most of the clay, partially pulverized so that it will more readily soften. As the water is absorbed, a cone will build up to the surface, indicating sufficient clay for the first mixture. Leave this to soften and expand as the water permeates the clay for several hours, preferably overnight. Do not stir. Usually clay will absorb 30 to 40 percent of its weight in water.

5. Screen the mixture or "slip" through the second sieve of 1/16 inch mesh or a piece of nonrusting window screening to remove the larger sand particles. The softened fragments may be rubbed through with the wooden spoon or rounded stick. (The surface should be smooth so as not to break the screen.) Discard the last ½ inch which contains heavier sand particles.

6. After the slip stands another hour, mix it thoroughly. Experienced potters always do this by hand to determine the "feel" or plasticity of the slip. Then screen it again through the 40 mesh screen. Allow to stand overnight, pour off the excess water or absorb with a sponge, and spread out in a plaster container or "bat" to become dry.

Testing the quality of clay

Clay suitable for pottery making must have the qualities known as plasticity and porosity, and also the property of melting or fusing under heat. Another reaction to heat which should be predetermined by testing is shrinkage in volume. Plasticity is the quality which makes the clay pliant and responsive in the potter's hands. It depends partially on the texture or degree of grain, which is a determining factor, but also on the amount of water which the clay will absorb. The relation is the basis of a fairly accurate test for plasticity.

Water test for plasticity

A marble or glass base and glass graduate is needed.
The use of the metric system is advised to avoid involved calculations.

The unit of weight is the gram and the unit of volume is the cubic centimeter. One c.c. of water weighs one gram, so the volume of measured water that a given weight of clay will absorb may be figured as a percentage which is the index of plasticity.

1. Place 100 grams of dry clay on a glass or marble slab. Measure at least 50 c.c. of water in a graduate or glass graduated in centimeters and in tenths of centimeters. Slowly add the water to the clay while mixing with the hand until the clay becomes a stiff but workable mass of uniform consistency, with all air pockets removed.

2. Experience will enable the potter to gauge the "just right" quantity of water by the "feel" of the clay, but a beginner may test its plasticity by taking a small piece and forming a finger thick roll about 4 inches long. If this can be worked out to a pencil thin cylinder without breaking the clay, it may be considered sufficiently plastic to work and fire successfully.

3. The percentage of water absorbed by the clay is determined by figuring the actual quantity of water used, which is the difference between the original volume and that remaining in the graduate. If 100 grams of clay absorbed 40 c.c. of water, 40 percent is the percentage index of plasticity. It should be in the range of 30 to 40 percent.

Porosity and vitrification (fusing) heat tests

The porosity of clay depends on the presence of sand or insoluble particles which make it porous or pervious to the water which is chemically formed when the clay is heated. If the developing steam cannot be released from a clay body which is impervious or does not have the proper quantity of sand, this must be added. A plasticity index in excess of 40 percent would indicate the necessity for sand to provide porosity. Actually, plasticity and porosity are opposite qualities which must be present in the right balance to insure the successful working and firing of clay articles. A heat or experimental firing test is the best way to determine porosity, also the property of melting and fusing under heat.

The property which permits melting or fusion under heat is important. The degree of vitrification depends on the proportion and nature of the element of feldspar, also called a fusible sand. Ground feldspar is available from dealers in pottery or ceramic supplies, and the addition of small quantities may render a natural clay suitable for pottery by providing the property necessary for the fusing of clay particles into the required density for a usable piece of pottery. Otherwise breaking and distortion may result.

Firing test

This requires kiln props, pyrometric or test cones, a baked clay base, and kiln facilities.

1. Place one or more small flattened pieces of the dried clay on a baked clay base, Fig. 46, with the ends supported by kiln props, together with a "cone pat" of three or more pyrometric cones. (A patented device consisting of a partially baked clay pyramid which has been tested to establish a definite melting point and marked accordingly.) As these have a range of known melting

points, the temperature at which the test piece of clay begins to bend will be registered by the cone which bends at the same time. This is known as the maturing point when the clay has reached the highest degree of density and hardness without a change in shape. The actual firing of pottery made from the test clay would require a temperature and time limit just under this. The time required will depend on the kind of kiln and the nature of the fuel.

2. As proper porosity is essential to prevent breaking and distortion, it also determines the right degree of absorption necessary for glazing. A simple test is to apply a little water with a pad or sponge to the baked test tile and note the rapidity with which it is absorbed. An experienced potter will test the degree of absorption by touching his tongue to the baked or bisquetted piece and noting the "pull" of moisture.

3. The degree of shrinkage of the clay as it dries and is fired may be determined by placing a strip or slab of clay about 6 by 1 by ¼ inches, which is marked with a line exactly 10 centimeters long, on a flat surface to dry, after which the percentage of shrinkage will be found by a second measurement of the line. After firing measure the line again. A millimeter of shrinkage would be 1 percent. An example of shrinkage is shown in Fig. 48 (16% shrinkage).

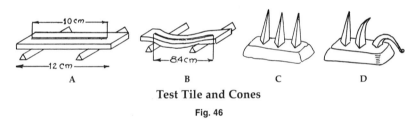

Test Tile and Cones

Fig. 46

The kiln fire and use of pyrometric cones

A new kiln should have a period of drying out at a low temperature before an attempt is made to fire pieces of clay. The time necessary will depend on the size and amount of masonry in the kiln. For the first test firing, small experimental plaques or slabs may be fired and their behavior observed and checked with the predetermined reaction of groups of pyrometric cones, the potter's timing and temperature gauge for all pottery firing. This device shown in Fig. 48, originated in one form in Germany and was perfected by Edward Orton, professor of ceramics at Ohio State University. His patented process of manufacture was given to the University with the provision that the proceeds from the sale of the cones, reasonably priced, be devoted to research in ceramics for the benefit of all potters.

The cones are slender pyramids made of clay with fluxes (minerals with known melting points) added so that each will melt at a known temperature. They are made in series of three, with a number indicating its temperature stamped on the side of each to indicate the range of the group, including one of the temperatures needed (one lower and one higher). The potter sets them in a "cone pat" or a small clay slab, at a slant tipping in the direction of the cone which will bend first. This is the signal that the temperature is nearing the desired point. When the second cone bends, the time to shut off the kiln is indicated. The cones in the sketch, Fig. 47, correspond to the numbers, 06, 05, 04.

Pyrometric cones are numbered from .022 to 19, indicating temperatures ranging from 1121° Fahrenheit (605° Centigrade) to 2768° Fahrenheit (1520° Centigrade). The maturing temperature of clay or glaze is designated in terms of the cone number.

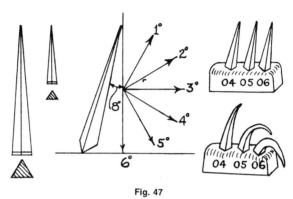

Fig. 47

Bisque firing

This firing is to harden the clay body by driving out the water in the first stage or "water smoking" period, which occurs within the temperature range of 500° Centigrade and 600° Centigrade or 935° Fahrenheit to 1112° Fahrenheit. The heat should be started at the low temperature and increased slowly to 1112°F where it is maintained for several hours until the moisture is all driven off. Condensation on a piece of metal or mirror held at the peephole indicates that moisture is still being driven off.

This first firing dehydrates or removes the water formed from the chemically combined hydrogen and oxygen between 350°C and 450°C. Organic matter in the clay burns at about 500°C. The heat should not be increased until all evidence of moisture has ceased. Just beyond this water smoking period, densification begins and a physical change takes place in the silica of the clay body making it expand, so that cracking may result if the heat increase is too rapid. Beyond 1112° Fahrenheit or 500° Centigrade, the bisque firing process can be hastened and the heat increased to the desired cone temperature. Average is about cone 010 or 1650° Fahrenheit.

The final stage in bisque firing at about 1840° Fahrenheit or 1015°C consists of melting and fusing the fluxes or minerals in the clay body, which is the process of densification and vitrifaction. This completes the maturing process, after which the kiln must be allowed to cool slowly, without opening for 8 hours or more. Some ceramists insist on 12 hours delay.

The total time of firing will vary according to the composition of the clay body and the thickness of the articles being fired, so that a record should be made and followed in determining the time and temperature required for each period.

Bisque or bisquette fired ware, except some kinds of stoneware, is porous and will not hold water, although some clay bodies with high silica content may fire to a glazed appearance. The discovery of colored glazes of different textures remained the secret of potters for countless years, until modern chemistry provided accurate means of achieving both color and texture.

A glaze is a surface application which melts and fuses like glass, and also acts chemically to adhere to the clay body or the bisquetted article. Tested clay bodies and corresponding glazes, clear and colored, are available from ceramic suppliers. The advanced potter or ceramist craftsman will want to study the chemistry of glaze composition and properties of firing, so that he may ultimately compound his own.

The materials and formulae, with instructions for mixing, are now supplied by dealers in ceramic equipment and supplies (several of whom are listed at the end of this section). An inquiry to a manufacturer will secure a reference to the nearest local dealer or distributer. In any metropolitan area, the local suppliers will be found in the "yellow pages" of the phone directory.

Drying pottery and ceramic forms

It will be found from the experimental test tile or slab that drying time varies with the humidity of the atmosphere and the nature of the clay. It requires at least twenty-four hours. Clays of very fine and plastic structures tend to retain moisture, which would cause the cracking of a finished piece. Fine sand or more sandy clays are sometimes added or a small amount of "grog" (a clay which has been fired and reground), and also crushed firebrick. Either should be screened through a thirty to sixty mesh screen, the size depending on whether a clay body with visible fragments is desired or not. "Terra Cotta," the term applied to a clay which is used for sculpture and commercial tile, has red grog added. Grog is handled by suppliers, or is easily made from brick and pieces of fired clay.

A surplus of sand makes the clay body soft or "punky." A proper balance can be determined by testing any required substance added to the clay body and thoroughly mixed in before the water is added. Ground feldspar may be added to "open the clay" for better drying. This also acts as a flux or fusing ingredient, which reduces the temperature required for vitrification.

Other special additives for a clay body are:

Bentonite, formed from decomposed volcanic ash or glass, is very plastic and is used to increase the plasticity of other clays and the adhesive quality of glazes. *Talc,* a hydrous magnesium silicate, which occurs in pockets or veins as a sedimentary deposit, is used to lower the firing temperature of "ball clays." (Ball clays are found deposited in swamps and so have more or less decomposed organic matter which results in a finer grain and greater plasticity.) *Flint,* a type of quartz, is also used to increase plasticity. *Grog* is added for texture, and also provides openings through which moisture can escape, making the clay more porous.

The preliminary drying of any piece of formed or cast pottery should be done in a cool place, free from drafts. The exposed edges, which dry more rapidly, should be protected with a slightly damp cloth. The drying process may be retarded by placing the "green" piece overnight in a box with an air moistening device, (such as a water saturated sponge or a piece of plaster), placed underneath the shelf of clay forms. A large breadbox may be adapted for a damp box and an old fashioned ice refrigerator with a water container in the ice chamber makes a good damp box or a place to store clay. Plastic bags closed firmly provide excellent protection for damp clay.

After removal from the damp box, a bone dry state must be reached before the first firing. This may take several days, in the open air. A simple test for dryness is to hold the piece against the face. If a cool sensation is noted, this is an indication that it is not sufficiently dry for firing.

Classification of ceramic clay bodies, according to density and firing temperatures

Earthenware clays are found in the Midwest, Northeast, and the State of Washington, less frequently in several other states. They occur in weathered rock, granite, and shale formations, and also to some extent in disintegrated glacial rock. The colors range from buff to red-brown and they mature at "low fire," 1859°F or Cone .06, but are porous unless glazed. Similar to the earthenware clays are the so-called *common clays,* used mostly to make brick. They are natural clays found throughout the United States, and so greatly varied in composition that they are a special challenge to the seeking ceramist craftsman or experimenting beginner, who wants to discover his own clay and method for working it. Firing temperatures range from low to high fire.

Natural stoneware clays are found in the Pacific Coast area and in the East from Missouri to New York. They are buff or grayish in color and quite plastic, indicating a high percentage of alumina and silica—also feldspar, which contains the alkaline fluxes, potash, soda, or lime in combination. They fire to a light buff color, with a range in maturing from cone 4 to cone 8 or 10. These are "high fire" clays and require specially insulated kilns. Stoneware is hard, dense, and strong when fired to high temperatures and will hold water even when not glazed. These clays are considered the most dependable for studio ceramic work.

Fire Clays occur in Colorado, the Pacific Coast states, and the Great Lakes region. Although commonly used for industrial products, fire clays can be substituted for stoneware clays, as they are usually sufficiently plastic for throwing. Some impurities, chiefly iron, give the clay a flecked appearance which can be lessened by the addition of stoneware clay, feldspar, talc, or silica. They mature between 2500°F and 2760°F. When modified by a stoneware clay, the maturing temperature is reduced and is between 2300° and 2400°F.

Porcelain Clay bodies are nearly always compounded, combining the less plastic but white firing kaolin with special pulverized ceramic raw materials.

It is translucent vitreous and strong when fired to maturity at high temperatures which range from Cone 8 to the very high Cone 16 at temperatures 2173°F to 2669°F. Only in Copenhagen, Denmark, is porcelain dinnerware produced at this very high temperature. Fig. 48 shows shrinkage of forms, 30 percent in firing.

Before — After Firing

Fig. 48

Glaze substitutes or natural glazes

When chemically compounded glazes are not available, some kinds of natural glazing slips from special clay or other materials can be obtained and used successfully as a substitute.

1. *Albany slip*, from clay found near Albany, New York, and a few other places in the United States contains the essential fluxes with the minerals, silica, and alumina in the right proportions to make a good glaze when fired at high temperatures. It is possible that there are similar bodies in the Southwestern U.S., known only to the Indian pottery makers, who use such a slip glaze and keep the source secret.

2. A mineral equivalent of some glazes is a crystalline substance called *Colemenite*, a hydrous calcium borate which occurs in borax formations. It makes a satisfactory glaze and is one of the elements in the manufacture of glass.

3. *Ground or finely crushed glass*, added to a clay base, is sometimes used for a glaze. This is available from suppliers or can be prepared, *with caution*, with a mortar and pestle. The process is hazardous, and experimentation alone will disclose the suitability for a glaze of the glass crushed from bottles or other glassware.

4. *Salt Glazing* has been used from time immemorial. It must be thrown into the kiln when the pottery forms are bisquited and when the temperature reaches the highest point. This must be done with caution as the salt volatilizes quickly and should not be inhaled. Special salt glazing kilns have an opening for the introduction of the salt. It produces a durable mottled glaze, especially attractive in modeled or sculptured clay. Colored stains and slips may be used on the pottery before firing and will remain under the salt glaze. This type of glazing is used in the manufacture of industrial tile and stoneware. As the salt volatilizes, it glazes the kiln as well as the pottery, making the kiln unsuitable for other pottery firing.

5. *Terra Sigillata* is a Roman term applied to an ancient way of producing a finish on pottery which resembles a glaze. It cannot be developed with all clays, so experimentation is necessary. This is a slip or engobe of very fine clay particles, which become suspended in water and forms a glaze solution.

A mixture of equal quantities of native clay and water, such as 1000 grams each, must be ground for several hours in a ball mill, then left undisturbed for twenty-four hours. Without a ball mill, the desired fineness of the clay (before mixing with water), can be obtained by pulverizing it in a mortar with pestle until it can be rubbed through a screen of 100 mesh. Then it must be thoroughly mixed with an equal quantity of water, shaken well in a covered container, and sieved again through the 100 mesh screen. A little more water may be required to make the mixture slightly more fluid than slip.

An alkaline substance such as sodium silicate, 20 grams to the 2000 of the mixture is then added (a water softener, such as Calgon has been used successfully), mixed well with the fluid clay and water, and left undisturbed for twenty-four hours. The alkaline substance causes an electrolytic action between the clay particles, making them separate into "Colloidal" particles and remain suspended in the water solution.

If the process for the kind of clay used is successful, a slightly gelatinous, colorless liquid appears at the top, with the remaining clay settled to the bottom. This liquid has become "Terra Sigillata," and when brushed or sprayed over unfired ware (green ware) and then fired will have developed a hard lustrous glaze.

Electric Kilns

With the development of electrically heated kilns, the whole process of ceramics has been greatly simplified. The studio type electric kilns are clean and easy to operate with no problem of air supply. The atmosphere is always neutral and the correct firing temperature is controlled by the amount of electric current in the heating element of the kiln. Formerly, electric kilns were wired for "low temperature" work, Cone .06 1859° Fahrenheit, but models are now being made with "Kanthal" elements which produce the "high temperature" required for stoneware and porcelain, Cones 5 to 10 or temperatures 2000° to 2350° Fahrenheit. Replaceable elements are available for electric kilns and the life of these elements depends to a great extent on the temperatures which are used, the higher temperatures shortening the life of the elements proportionately.

Good small kilns, with a firing chamber 9 by 9 by 9 inches (.432 cubic feet) also one with a firing chamber 11 by 11 by 11 inches (.775 cubic feet), which will operate on a house lighting circuit protected by a 30 ampere circuit breaker or fuse, are available from ceramic suppliers. This type is entirely suitable and satisfactory for firing tile, plates, coiled and slab built articles and ceramic jewelry.

A larger capacity kiln, 13½ by 13½ by 12 inches, operating on a 220-240, 20 ampere circuit (the service for an electric range), may also be purchased from ceramic suppliers or manufacturers.

A simplified type of homemade kiln may be constructed from the sketch and the specifications which follow. The potter craftsman, who builds his own kiln will not only have this satisfaction, but will save considerable part of the costs. Two types of electric kilns are shown in the sketches. Both are constructed with standard refractory and insulating materials, either brick or blocks and both will fire to a temperature of 2000° F.

Type A. Stationary Kiln, Fig. 49

The kiln base, 24 inches square, has a thickness of 5 inches in the two courses of refractory brick, 9 by 4½ by 2½ which are laid as indicated in the sketch. The kiln walls are then built and may be of three heights to provide a kiln chamber of as many sizes, using the same floor dimensions of 13½ by 13½ or 182 square inches. The sizes with required electric service are as follows:

No. of Bricks	Height, Inches	Volume Cu. ft.	Recommended Wattage (Kilowatts)
5	12½	1.3	4.5
6	15	1.6	6
7	17½	1.8	7.5

Either Armstrong N. 23 insulating brick or the equivalent Johns-Manville, N. 23 brick may be used. The overall dimensions will be 22½ by 22½ with the height varying in relation to the number of bricks in the wall as the table indicates.

Type A is a stationary kiln, built in one place, to be used permanently there. As it does not require venting, it may be placed near any connection for electric service, in studio or basement, or if protected it can be built outdoors. Type B is portable and built in two sizes. All electrical specifications, given in the wiring diagrams, conform to standards of the National Electric Code, and all heating elements, wiring detail, and controls comply with the requirements of the Underwriters Laboratories. (Fire Insurance Code).

The stationary type electric kiln shown with construction detail in Fig. 49 may be built upon a pedestal of four piers, brick or building blocks, topped with a concrete slab cast on a wooden base and troweled smooth. Upon this slab four pieces of lightweight angle iron, 24 inches long, placed as shown on the two top and lower edges with diagonal rod braces, support the brick structure, with allowance for the expansion and contraction during the firing operation.

CERAMIC KILN CONSTRUCTION DETAILS

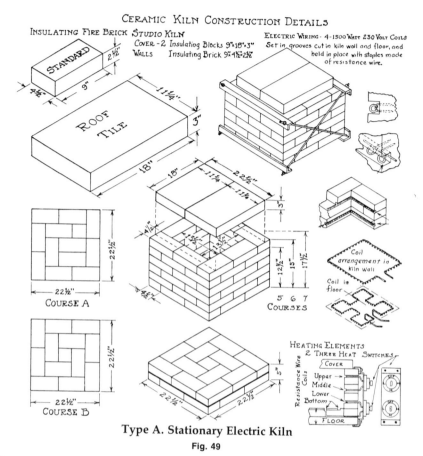

Type A. Stationary Electric Kiln

Fig. 49

Type B. Portable Electric Kiln, Fig. 50

This kiln is designed for use on an ordinary house lighting and appliance circuit of 110 volts, fused to carry a current not exceeding 20 amperes. It has a floor area of 97.2 square inches, and is large enough to fire a plate 10 inches in diameter. The height of 8 inches provides a volume of 77 cubic inches or .45 cubic feet.

The material used is standard insulating brick 9 by 4½ by 2½ and refractory slabs which are available in pieces 24 inches long and 9 inches wide in two thicknesses. The 2½ inch thickness is used for the Type B. kiln. This material cuts readily with a metal cutting hand or power saw, and since it cuts without waste, may be used economically to construct the hexagonal kiln, shown in the sketch with specifications. It is assembled in three separate parts, as indicated. The floor and cover are cut from slabs and the wall is built of bricks, saw-cut in a miter box at a 60 degree angle, to permit assembly in the hexagonal form. This shape permits effective use of all interior space in the firing chamber.

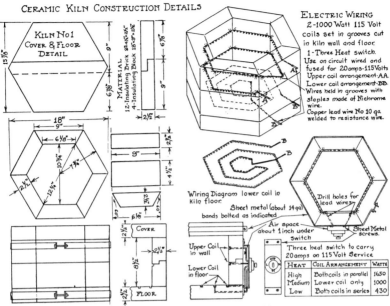

CERAMIC KILN CONSTRUCTION DETAILS

Type B. Portable Electric Kiln

Fig. 50

HEAT	COIL ARRANGEMENT	WATTS
High	Both coils in parallel	1650
Medium	Lower coil only	1000
Low	Both coils in series	430

Ceramic Decoration

Treatment for types of clay

The texture and to some extent the color of a ceramic article can be determined before the clay is put into water. Blended clays of different origins can be selected to increase the variety of body color and texture, especially in shades ranging from buff to red and brown. Grog, depending on the degree of fineness, can be mixed into the prepared dry clay to change the texture and add flecks of color. Crushed insulating brick is mostly buff. A good red-brown color can be made from old soft red bricks. Clay that has been bisque fired, but unglazed, can be crushed for grog. Depending on the size of fragments desired, the grog should be put through a 20 to 50 mesh screen. White grog is made from a bisque fired porcelain clay body.

The coloring oxides, red iron oxide and manganese oxide, are used most frequently as they are less expensive and more generally available in natural formations for the ceramist who is using a "discovered" clay. Ceramic suppliers can furnish a wide range of colors in prepared body stains for adding color to clay bodies.

Clay in the plastic state

After forming by any method, clay (whether coil built, thrown on the wheel or as a slab) can be decorated by finger ornamentation, such as indentations, ridges, circular or spiral lines which have a special natural character, revealing the plastic quality of clay. However, it should be firm enough to hold a clear impression.

Designs impressed in clay forms are thought to have been the first kind of decoration made by primitive man. Woven basket impressions have been mentioned. Another type of decoration, known to be of primitive origin, is that of applying designs to the plastic clay with stamps of baked clay. The practice existed among ancient Mediterranean cultures, and on this side of the world was developed during the Aztec and Mayan eras of Central America where they have been found in ruins. They were used in prehistoric old Mexico and continue to be used there for the decoration of pottery. See Enciso designs, pages 4 and 5.

Leather Hard Clay

At this stage in the drying process several types of decoration are possible, as the piece is dry enough to handle without injury, yet sufficiently pliant to permit various forms of decoration.

1. *Modeling in relief.* This is an effective type of ornamentation, similar to the process of leather tooling. The design outline is traced and modeled by pressing down the background along the lines, and slightly smoothing the margins of the design to produce a rounded raised effect, similar to that described for leather, Fig. 126B, page 159.

2. *Carving of leather hard clay.* Carving is another type of *relief ornamentation*, similar to leather decoration. The lines are cut with a sharp tool (old dental tools are good for carving and incising). Carving of leather hard clay is easier and more effective in curved designs. (See leather carving designs on page 160, also wood carving designs on page 411.) An adaptation of carving is to open the design outline and spread into the recess a contrasting strip of plastic clay, or partially dried slip, to form a high relief appearance. An example of an effective carved design is shown and described, Fig. 64B, page 76 (an original by Mrs. Clara Gloss). In this jar the incised lines are emphasized with gold.

3. *Incising.* Incising, or the slight cutting of the design outline, is more suitable for lineal decoration. *Inlay* or *mishima* is a process of defining and emphasizing the incised line with a contrasting underglaze color or slip, which is stippled into the lines with a fine brush and permitted to dry. When dry enough to handle, the excess slip may be removed with a flexible scraper, or by wiping with a damp sponge. *Mishima* is the term applied to the inlay process by the Japanese, who acquired the skill from the Koreans, with whom it was an ancient practice.

A transparent or semitransparent glaze, either clear or colored, may be applied to the clay form after decorating by any of these methods.

Decoration with slip or engobes

1. *Stenciling* on semihard pottery is a way of decorating with positive and negative patterns, cut from stiff paper and attached with an adhesive like rubber cement, which is easily removed.

2. Brush, stipple, or spray a contrasting slip over the entire clay form, and before this is entirely dry, carefully remove the paper pattern. *Incised* details may then be added.

3. The use of leaves for a stenciled effect is said to have been an ancient practice. Press the leaves smoothly into moist hand formed or cast pottery and before the clay is entirely dry, peel off the leaves and then apply the contrasting slip by any of the above methods. Redefine the outlines, if necessary. Incised details may be added.

Color Resists in design painting

Various materials are used as a *"color stopper"* or resist to outline or cover an area of one color and separate it from another. *Wax resists* are available as commercial compounds, or they may be made by mixing a little turpentine with heated beeswax. (Heat only in a container in hot water. Keep away from flame.)

One prepared wax resist is applied to the design areas on bisque ware. Colors are painted over the body of the ware or the design area before the application of wax, then another color may be painted over the wax in the adjacent design area. In the glazing and firing the wax burns out and the colors remain separate and distinct.

Another resist, called by the trade name "Water Carved" is painted over the design area previously traced on leather hard or green ware and permitted to harden. The entire area is then wiped with a damp sponge, removing the clay resist which is softened, to leave the design area in relief. The background or other areas may be lowered as desired by partial removal of the resist. The sponge should be rinsed in water frequently. When the ware is completely dry it is bisque fired and glazed, then fired again.

A third kind of resist, which some ceramists prefer because it peels off readily, is rubber cement. More care is required in its application than the others. See page 82 for "color stopper."

4. *Sgraffito* is a method of decoration, practiced by ceramists from ancient times and is still popular. In this country it was made famous by the "Pennsylvania Dutch." Both Mexican and Indian pottery have been decorated by this method.

Sgraffito designs (an Italian term, meaning scratched through) are applied when the pottery or ceramic form is leather hard.

(a) Cover the form with one or more contrasting colored engobes (a term for slip when it is used to cover a surface) or underglaze colors by dipping, brushing, or spraying.

(b) When the surface is firm, scratch, gouge, or incise the design through the engobe or slip to reveal the design beneath. The rose design platter by Evie Cremona, Fig. 67, page 78, is a beautiful example.

5. *Slip Painting or Trailing* is another method of ceramic ornamentation introduced in this country by the "Pennsylvania Dutch" in the early Eighteenth century. It was sometimes called "tulip ware" (this flower is a symbol of love, and appears on much of their pottery and household items as the Painting on Wood, page 113 shows). The method or a more modern adaptation is easily followed.

6. When the ware is slightly moist, apply the slip with a watercolor brush,

or "trail" the slip with a small syringe or pastry tube. This process is described under tile making, Fig. 71C, page 82. The clay green ware must not be too dry or the slip will peel.

An effective way of applying slip designs was used by the Pennsylvania colonists. A "slip cup," a small clay container which fitted into the hand had one or more quills in place of a spout, the flow of slip being controlled by opening or closing the hole in the top of the quill with the forefinger.

7. *Raised Decorations* may be applied with an engobe which is a prepared combination of slip and glaze, called a "self-glazing engobe" which requires only one firing. The method is as follows:

(a) Prepare a mixture of water and a self-glazing engobe or slip which is about the consistency of whipping cream and strain twice.

(b) Unless the ware is still moist, wipe it with a damp sponge, just before applying the slip. The self-glazing slip or engobe prepared from "Albany Clay," a fine natural clay with fluxes in the body, is applied with a pointed brush to the design which has been outlined with pencil or India Ink, both of which burn out in firing. A raised effect is thus developed.

(c) Lightly moisten the ware with a sponge, just before applying the coat of self-glazing engobe over the design. Build up successive layers as the slip dries or loses its shine. Model the entire design each time with a relief modeling tool.

(d) For a shaded translucent effect, apply the slip in thin coats, covering a little less each time. Several layers of different colors may be used, and the background left smooth, scratched, gouged, or otherwise incised to provide a contrast for the relief design.

(e) A bisque firing is sufficient for this decoration.

Underglaze decoration

Underglaze colors are prepared in liquid, semimoist, and crayon form, and may be painted on pottery in a *leather-hard or bisque state*. For the *leather-hard or "raw ware"* the design may be sketched with a pencil or India ink. Glycerine or the solution of gum tragacanth may be added to the colors when used on raw ware to lessen absorption by the clay, which should still be slightly moist.

An oil medium is needed when the painting is done on bisque ware. This may be a mixture of oil or turpentine and pigment. Combine this mixture with the underglaze colors. Ready to use underglaze colors are available for use, without additives, from suppliers of AMACO, American Art Clay products.

Underglaze crayons

The plate shown in Fig. 51 was designed and decorated by Mrs. Gloss, whose original work is shown on page 102. The underglaze crayon which was used is a new medium from AMACO. It provides a new type of decoration with many variations in design and color. Eight colors are offered by AMACO and their directions are as follows: "Crayon designs may be sketched on moist or dry bisque. For dense color applications, wet the bisque first to provide a rough surface "tooth." For subtle pastel effects, sketch directly on dry bisque or on a completely dry background of liquid or semimoist underglaze color.

Blend or shade with the fingers or cotton tipped swabs. Create watercolor effects by intermingling colors with a moist brush or sponge. For thin lines, pare crayons with a knife. Mix the leftover scraps with water for brushing or spraying on bisque or green ware.

Clear or transparent covering glazes may be sprayed over underglaze crayon decoration. Before glazing by any other method, spray the decoration with a fixative composed of one part gum solution to five parts water. When dry, the fixative coat prevents loose particles from being swept out of place.

Prepared glazes of many colors and textures are obtainable with directions from ceramic suppliers. Methods of application are many and varied and this is a study in itself. For the scientific description and methods of compounding glazes, *Ceramics* by Glenn C. Nelson, published by Holt, Rinehart and Winston is recommended.

Fig. 51

The use of iron oxides and other natural coloring minerals may be successfully used by ceramists, who experiment with natural clays. *Red iron oxide* produces tan and brown colors and manganese other shades of brown. Manganese will cause the clay ware to blister if more than 5 per cent is added to a stain mixture.

Copper oxide results in shades of green. Cobalt and vanadium with tin produces a bright yellow stain. Cobalt oxide in combination with alumina and zinc produces a wide range of blue shades.

It is recommended that the coloring oxides be applied when the clay ware is nearly dry but sufficiently absorbent that the coloring will not run. The bisque fire will cause them to adhere.

Some ceramists advise that the coloring oxides be mixed with water before adding to the clay as it is mixed for slip. Others find it easier and as uniform if mixed with the dry clay. This necessitates grinding the oxides with the clay, then screening them through a fine sieve. Proportions suggested are 1 teaspoon of oxide to 19 of clay, but more or less may be used. A small quantity of gum tragacanth, about a thimble full, dissolved in a pint of boiling hot water will add to the adhesive quality of the slip.

Hand Built and Modeled Forms

Ceramic items built by hand from flattened discs or slabs of clay are types which a beginner can undertake with confidence. This method provides knowledge of the nature of clay and its responsiveness, unlike any other material. With a supply of modeling clay (AMACO white modeling clay No. 25 is recommended) and some inexpensive equipment, many articles are simple to construct.

The *necessary equipment,* besides the fingers, includes: A well lighted table top, a drawing board or a breadboard covered with a pastry cloth, or the reverse side of a piece of oilcloth, a clean wooden rolling pin, a container for the clay, with attached wedging wire as shown in Fig. 52A, also two pairs of narrow pieces of wood, lattice or batten strips, ¼ to 3/5 inches sanded smooth on the upper side. The position of the rolling pin and wood strips is shown in Fig. 52B. A case knife, not too sharp, a knife with a sharp edge for cutting the clay, bone or wood creaser, modeling tools, and a small jar for the clay slip mixture, with an applicator (small watercolor brush).

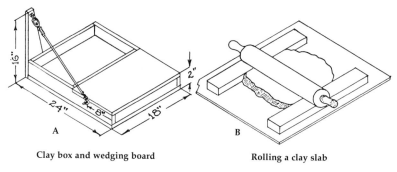

A
B

Clay box and wedging board   Rolling a clay slab

Fig. 52

To *prepare clay of modeling consistency* for any process, it must be made free of all air bubbles. The device called a wedging wire, shown in Fig. 52A, is a necessity. Hold the lump of clay in both hands and shape it like a loaf of bread. Cut it across the wire repeatedly and reform the segments, avoiding any folds. Alternately with the wedging, pound the clay on the table, knead it like bread, slap the pieces together. Inspect for air bubbles and continue wedging until all have disappeared.

A test for consistency before building a form is to wind a pencil-like coil of clay around a finger. If it starts to break, press the edges together with wet fingers, and work a very little moisture into the clay.

Hand Built Ceramic Projects

Free form modeling of clay develops skill and original creativity as the possibilities of developing ideas become apparent. The following projects are presented for practice and should suggest many adaptations.

As a first experience try forming a *"Pinch Pot"* or small bowl.

1. With the palm of the left hand as a mold, press a pancake size ball of prepared and well wedged clay into a 2 inch circle with a depression of ⅜ inch in the center. Gradually, work the edges upward with the thumb and fingers of the right hand, while keeping the thumb of the left hand in the center and rotating it to maintain the 2 inch base.

2. Turn the form clockwise and compress the folds to an equal thickness of about ¼ inch, at the same time working it up to as uniform a height as possible. Smooth and round the rim, also the outer and inner surfaces, leaving some finger impressions. Flatten the base inside and outside so the bowl will stand.

Pin tray or ash tray, Fig. 53A

Another simple project may be made from the ball of clay after it is shaped into the palm of the hand.

1. With the depressed disc on the wood surface or on a tile, flatten it smoothly to about ⅜ inch thickness with the fingers or a flexible spatula.

2. Work the edges upward into a rounded square about one inch deep.

3. Fold one side down and press the edge into the base as the illustration indicates. Shape the other three sides with slight indentations to permit the corners to round out.

Next try making simple animal forms or figures from little rolls and balls of clay. Leaves or abstract forms, rosettes, and wood carving elements, also several types of crosses or other church symbols are excellent practice items.

Relish dish

1. For the relish dish, Fig. 53B, flatten a ball of clay into a 6 inch disc and roll it into an oval form, 6 by 8 inches with a thickness of ¼ inch. As with piecrust, roll from the center outward rotating the disc to prevent folds.

2. With the thumb and fingers of the right hand, work the margins of the form, held between the thumb and fingers of the left hand, at the center of one end of the oval, upward and outward, sloping them to a thickness of about ⅛ inch around to the opposite end. Moisten slightly as needed with a damp sponge.

3. Reverse the position to permit working the opposite side into the position shown in Fig. 53B forming a slight indentation or curve inward near the end, which is narrowed for holding.

4. Make sure of a level base of 2½ to 3 inches in diameter by turning the form upside down over a pyrex or other dish with a base of this diameter. Smooth it evenly into a flat base, working any excess clay around and up on the sides.

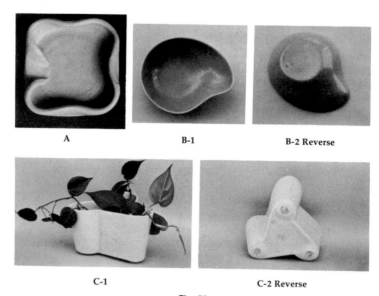

A   B-1   B-2 Reverse

C-1   C-2 Reverse

Fig. 53

5. While the form is supported in this position, level the top with the knife and smooth the edges. Reverse and carefully press with the fingers to round and even the rim.

Free form planter, Fig. 53C

1. Make a pattern from a piece of firm plastic for the bottom and a paper pattern for the sides, checking the contour of the bottom and the length of the side piece to be sure of agreement. Have ready a rolled disc of clay ¼ inch thick for the base, approximately 5½ inches in diameter, and a piece 3½ inches wide and 25 inches long and 3/16 inch thick for the sides.

2. Mark out the base piece to conform to the pattern, creasing around it lightly with the tip of a modeling tool or the wooden creaser. Remove the pattern from the clay and carefully cut through the creased line.

3. Cut from the remaining clay three small circles about 2 inches in diameter. Moisten them on one side with slip and apply a little to the rounded corners of the base. Place the circles on the base corners to form slight raised supports and let them stand until the circles are firmly attached and the clay base hard enough to handle, then bevel off the edges of the circles and apply a little slip to blend them into the base. They may be pressed out a little from the inside of the base with the thumb to increase the supports.

4. Compare the contour of the base with the length of the piece for the sides, and remove any excess from the ends with a knife or sharp pointed tool.

5. Roughen the margins of the base and the lower edge of the side piece, also the ends. Unite the ends of the side piece with thick slip. Weld them together with the fingers and modeling tool, smoothing the juncture until it is

invisible. Support the open ended cylinder by placing it over a jar or large milk carton until firm enough to hold its shape.

6. Prepare three little fillets of clay and moisten them with slip. Moisten likewise the edges of the base and the lower edge of the circle for the sides. Place this around the contour of the base and unite with a criss-cross pressure of the wood creaser inside and outside. Fill the angle of the inside juncture with the fillets and smooth into the seam with the flat modeling tool.

7. Press the outside edges together with the fingers and smooth into a united rounded edge with the flat modeling tool. Set aside to dry completely then bisque fire and waterproof by glazing later.

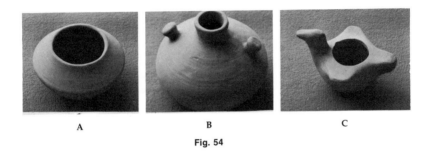

A   B   C

Fig. 54

Hand formed Indian type pottery, Fig. 54

Projects A and C in Fig. 54 were hand built and bisque fired. The Indian potter finishes similar articles with an all-over application of slip and designs painted with colored oxide stains as described in Fig. 88, page 107.

The water bottle, Fig. 54B, in the center, is practical and would have a strap or a plaited strand attached to the knobs for carrying water, if made for Indian use. The Indian potter would coil build this water bottle as is his method for many kinds of clay forms.

Hand Built Molds and Plaster Mold Casting

A *reverse mold* (see the plate in Fig. 55), can be made from a mound or hump of clay of slab consistency. It must be well wedged to eliminate air bubbles and in a pliant condition. Plates and shallow bowls may be made this way.

1. Form the mound of clay with the center about two inches high and sloping gradually to one inch at the margins. If a plate is to be built, make the center section a circle the diameter of the bottom of the plate, smoothing it with the scraper to make this as level as possible.

2. Press a plate similar to the one to be made, upper side down, gently over the mound, which has been covered with a damp cloth, in order to shape it to the inside contour. Let it remain a few minutes, then carefully remove. Allow the mound to dry slightly, Fig. 55A and B are from the Lewiston, Idaho ceramic workshop, pages 86-88.

3. Cover the mound with three layers of damp cheesecloth, then lay a disc of freshly rolled clay, about ⅜ inch thick over it. Press it gently into the form of the plate contour, upper side down, with a slightly damp sponge and the flexible scraper.

A   **Fig. 55**   B

4. Cut around the form with a downward motion, using the "fettling" knife, to remove excess clay from the edges of the form and mold. When the form will retain its shape but is still pliable, remove a thin layer of clay with the scraper from the center section of a circle the diameter of the bottom.

5. Define or outline the margin of the circle with a tracer, using a stiff paper pattern. Just outside this line, form a raised circle or support for the base about ⅛ inch high with a modler and loop tool, building it up from either side.

6. Smooth the surface inside this rim and even it with the end of a wood modler. If necessary, make a special wood tool like a wide creaser used in leather work.

7. When dry enough to hold its shape, reverse on a level surface to test and even any irregularities in the rim which prevents the plate from setting straight. Smooth the top of the plate with the flexible scraper and a slightly damp sponge.

Square or rectangular plates may be made by this method on a mound of the corresponding size, also saucers and bowls, or free forms.

If a more permanent mold for later work is wanted, it may be bisque fired. To prevent cracking or distortion, dry until leather hard, then carve out the inside leaving a wall about ½ inch thick. It will be more durable than a plaster mold.

Sandbox mold

For thicker free form pieces made of clay, with about one third grog or terra cotta clay such as is used for tile and sculptured pieces, this method permits a variety of forms. It has a rough texture and is more porous, so pieces of greater thickness may be shaped.

1. Half fill a box or large plastic container with damp sand and make a deep depression into which the shape will be pressed. Cover the sand with a damp cloth.

2. Roll out a slab of prepared terra cotta clay about ¾ inch thick on a damp cloth. Variations in thickness will add to the novelty of the form.

3. Cut out a curved shape with a knife and place it on the cloth in the

sandbox depression. Tamp the shape into the depression with a small sand filled bag. It need not conform exactly.

4. When the piece is dry enough to hold its shape, remove and attach short legs with slip, or shave off an indented area on the bottom, so that the piece will stand without tipping. Trim the contours with a flexible scraper.

One and Two-Piece Plaster Molds

Plaster of Paris is chemically derived from gypsum rock, a sulphate of calcium, and is produced by heating to drive off the water and reduce the gypsum to a dry form which is crushed to a fine powder. In this form, it has a chemical affinity for water and when mixed solidifies to the hardness of the original rock.

Slabs for dehydrating slip in preparing clay for pottery, as well as forms or "bats" on which it is built, may easily be made from plaster of Paris, Fig. 56.

A   B

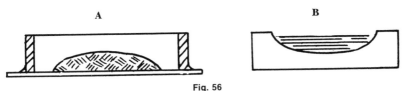

Fig. 56

1. To make a rectangular or oval container for dehydrating slip, form a mound of clay, hand building consistency, on a clean marble slab or piece of plate glass. The mound should be the size and depth the finished container is to be. "Bats" may be made in the same way.

2. Place sides and ends of wood around the model and a distance from each margin of about 1½ to 2 inches. Nail these together to form an enclosure which will be at least one inch higher than the model. Sand them first to a perfect smoothness on the inner sides.

4. Oil the wood with melted petroleum jelly or white vaseline. Wipe off any excess or guminess. Attach to the glass with clay fillets at the lower margins in (Fig. 56, sketch A). Plaster bats may be made in pyrex kitchen ware, round or rectangular.

Principles in mixing plaster

1. Procure the best quality fresh plaster. U.S. Gypsum pottery plaster is standard.

2. Accurately measure or weigh both plaster and water. 2¾ pounds to a quart of water are tested proportions.

3. Sift or slowly sprinkle the plaster into the water. If lumps appear, break or throw them out. If bubbles appear, puncture them with a pin.

4. Allow to stand *two minutes* undisturbed. If plaster comes to the surface there is an excess and a very little water may be added to absorb it.

5. Mix thoroughly to break up all lumps and release air. Many potters will use only the hand, held beneath the surface, but a slotted kitchen spoon will work. The important thing is to prevent the inclusion of air.

6. Do not withdraw the hand or spoon until it begins to thicken. It is then ready for pouring.

Mold making

When plaster is poured over any model made of plaster, wood, glazed and fired pottery, glass or metal, the surfaces must be "sized" to keep the plaster from adhering to the surface. Size makes a surface nonabsorbent. Size is never used on "green ware" as it would soften the surface. The following mixture is easy to prepare and can be stored and reheated many times before sizing any model.

1. Shave one large bar of castile soap into one quart of water and heat over a low flame until the soap is dissolved. Melt enough paraffin to make ¼th pint and pour into the water and soap. When about the consistency of thin syrup, it is ready to use. This solution is called a "separator." Other separators are available from suppliers. It should be applied immediately before the plaster is cast, as its sealing quality disappears with standing.

2. Apply the separator with a brush, evenly over the surface of the model, smooth the application with a damp sponge to equalize the separator.

3. Apply three or four successive coats of the separator, smoothing with a damp sponge each time. After the last coat has been smoothed, test the sealed surface with a few drops of water. If they do not roll off as from glass, additional size must be applied.

4. The final coating should be smoothed with a soft cloth, dipped in sweet oil, not in water. Smooth it evenly with the fingers.

Pouring the plaster

1. Place the model on a smooth surface, glass is preferable. Form an enclosure around the model with a 2 to 2½ inch space allowed around and above it. A strip of linoleum tied together is satisfactory. Flexible cardboard will answer. Size inner surface.

2. Seal the juncture with the glass or outer surface with rolls of clay as indicated in Fig. 57, sketches 2 and 3.

3. Pour the plaster in a continuous stream into the space enclosed by the wall. Allow it to set for 15 minutes. Note that as the plaster dries it takes on the appearance of cake frosting and has a matt finish. If this is not the case and the surface begins to solidify before it levels out, the plaster has not been poured soon enough. If poured too soon, it will seem to separate and water will appear on the surface.

4. Remove the enclosure and reverse the plaster mold. The model should remain on the glass or be lifted out as in Fig. 57, sketch 6 leaving the plaster mold. Trim off any fins of plaster.

Casting a bowl

The one-piece mold, just described, is called a drain mold, because excess plaster is drained away to leave the pottery form.

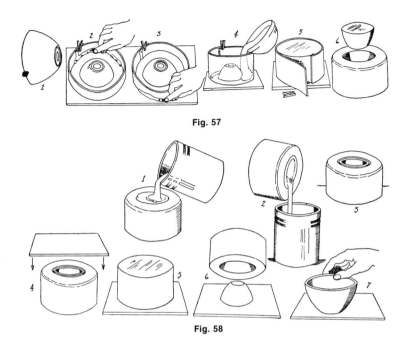

Fig. 57

Fig. 58

1. Prepare pottery slip as directed on page 55. For casting it should be a consistency that will pour smoothly. The addition of a little sodium silicate, or water glass (the solution of sodium silicate or potassium silicate in water), to a thick slip will make the clay more fluid and plastic. It is called a deflocculating agent which causes an electrolytic action, discharging the static electricity of the clay particles to make them less cohesive and more fluid.

2. Pour the slip back and forth to release air bubbles before pouring, then after pouring, jar the mold slightly to remove any lingering air bubbles.

3. Pour into the plaster mold sufficient clay to fill the cavity, Fig. 58, sketch 1. As the water in the clay is absorbed by the mold, the liquid pool will recede and the clay begin to stiffen and take form around the sides of the mold.

4. When the desired thickness of the bowl has been formed, ⅛″ to ⅜″, depending on the dimensions and shape, pour the remaining liquid clay back into the slip jar, Fig. 58, sketch 2.

5. Allow the mold, now lined with a layer of soft clay, to stand until the water is fully absorbed and the clay shrinks away from the mold as indicated in Fig. 58, sketch 3.

6. Place a thin cover plate of plywood or glass on top of the mold and reverse both together, Fig. 58, sketches 4 and 5. Remove the mold to leave the casting on the cover plate as shown in Fig. 58, sketch 6. Allow it to dry until it is leather hard before handling.

7. Trim the edges with a modeling tool and smooth out any fingerprints with a moistened sponge, Fig. 58, sketch 7. Set aside to dry as directed on page

53. Decorate and fire according to instructions for bisque and glazed pottery pages 52 and 55.

A plaster of Paris mold, constructed of two or more pieces, is necessary for the casting of clay articles of oval or other shapes in which both top and bottom diameters are at variance with the body of the article. This is in contrast with the principle of the one-piece mold in which cone or pyramid shapes are cast. The shape shown in Fig. 59, sketch 1, requires a two-piece mold.

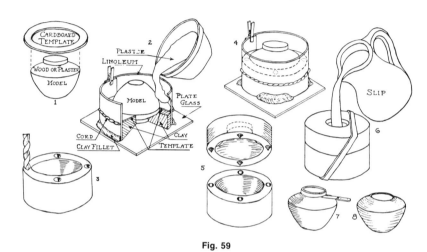

Fig. 59

Clayworking Tools

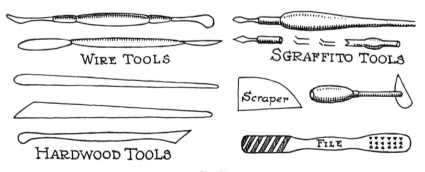

WIRE TOOLS

SGRAFFITO TOOLS

Scraper

HARDWOOD TOOLS

FILE

Fig. 60

Making a Two-Piece Mold

1. Prepare the model, either plaster of Paris or wood as directed in previous sections, and place it face down on a smooth surface, glass preferably.

2. Build into the space surrounding the lower portion of the model a sup-

port of moist modeling clay, extending at least an inch beyond the widest diameter, and level with it, Sketch 2. Smooth the surface and place a stiff paper template over the clay with the portion of the model which is to make the lower piece of the mold extending through and above it. Apply a size or parting compound to the surface.

3. Place a linoleum enclosure around the model and clay, allowing a space of 2½ to 3 inches on all margins and above the model. Remove any excess clay which prevents the enclosure from fitting closely against the template. Attach the linoleum to the glass with a clay fillet.

4. Mix the plaster of Paris for pouring and fill the space between the template and the top of the linoleum wall as indicated in Sketch 2. After the plaster has set about 30 minutes, remove the linoleum and clay and reverse the model partly encased in the plaster.

5. Remove the mold, which by this time has shrunk sufficiently to lift from the model and place it on a flat surface. With a twist drill or counter sink make four holes in the mold rim, about ⅜ inch deep. These have cone shaped points in the corresponding positions on the second piece of the mold when it is poured, and this makes it possible to fit the two pieces together accurately. These are called "joggles."

6. Replace the linoleum wall around the lower piece of the mold with the model again in place. Size the surfaces and pour plaster around the upper half of the model and just even with the top opening.

7. After the plaster for the second piece of the mold has set, remove the linoleum and separate the two pieces of the mold. The upper and lower portions appear as indicated in Fig. 59, sketch 5.

The casting of a bowl in a two-piece mold is done in the same manner as that described for casting in a one-piece mold. The two parts of the mold are held tightly together by wide rubberbands, which may be cut from a discarded inner tube, Fig. 59, sketch 6. Pour the prepared clay slip through the opening which is at the top of the bowl or jar. The model described was made with an additional top portion to allow for the shrinkage of the clay and permit finishing the edge to a uniform height by cutting away the excess Fig. 59, sketch 7 and 8. The edges then may be rounded and smoothed with modeling tools. Fig. 61 shows the parts of a two-piece mold, including the removable base of the bowl or lamp base which was cast in the mold. The illustration indicates the incised decoration on the blue underglaze, an adaptation of the sgraffito technique.

When fired the colors became a buff background (the natural clay color), with the blue glaze incised with the diagonal strips.

Fig. 62 shows a *three-piece mold*, with the original model made of plaster of Paris. The decoration was carved in relief, with a crosshatched background lightly incised before the plaster became entirely dry. The procedure in making this mold follows that for the other molds, but this was made in three pieces. A. is the plaster mold, B. the upper and lower parts of the mold, and C. the second half of the upper part.

Fig. 62A and B show the finished cast shapes, and together with a suggested adaptation. The addition of a handle, modeled from a strip of rolled clay and attached when the form was leather hard, made it a pitcher. The points of attachment were roughened and moistened with slip before the handle was pressed on the bowl. Fig. 63 shows a molded handle.

All of the castings were bisque fired, then glaze was applied inside for waterproofing. The outside of the bottle and cup (not illustrated), were finished with a light opaque slip and when dry, covered with a transparent glaze.

With a cup cast to fit the top and making a cover, Fig. 62A, it became a water bottle.

The carved decoration on the mold for the water bottle and pitcher is similar to the traditional "Plumed Serpent," a favorite motif of the ancient Mayan people of Central America, as well as of the Indian potters of the Pueblos. It will be recognized on the large jar displayed by Maris Martinez in her demonstrations, Fig. 86C, page 106.

Bowl   Mold

Fig. 61

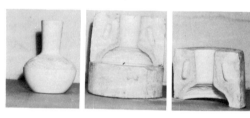

Mold

A   Castings   B

Fig. 62

Press molding a cup or pitcher handle

Place a coil of clay approximately the size of the handle to be formed into the cavity of one-half of the plaster mold. With the fingers shape the part of the coil remaining above the surface so that it will compress into the upper half when this is placed into position with the projections fitting into the corresponding holes. Bring the halves together as closely as possible.

Open the mold and with a knife blade remove any excess clay which adheres to the mold and handle. Replace the top half of the mold and compress again. Remove any excess clay as before and compress as many times as may be necessary to remove any clay or until the halves come completely together and the handle is evenly formed. Sketches 4 and 5 show the shaped handle. Allow this to partially dry.

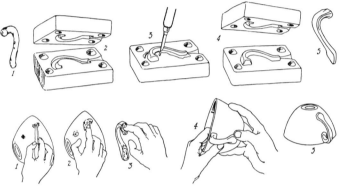

Fig. 63

To attach the handle to the cup, previously molded, roughen the contact points on the cup with a knife or a piece of abrasive paper. (This should be kept in the moist box until the handle is ready.) Cover these points with slip which is also applied to the ends of the handle. Join the surfaces of the handle ends to the cut and weld them together with the fingers. Set the cup aside to dry for firing.

Decorations for cast formed jars or vases (also slab rolled and coiled)

The three different kinds of ornamentation for the same type of jar were created by Mrs. Clara Gloss, a self-taught ceramist, who has achieved a wide reputation for her skill and original decorative designs for ceramics.

The slip cast jars of the same size were given a different form and ornamentation when in a partially dry or leather hard state. The photograph shows the appearance of the three jars, Fig. 64.

Jar A was decorated with an effective combination of gouged and scratched ornamentation. The upper section was gouged in three alternate rows of ovals in which a crosshatched surface was left. The area around the base was encircled with a row of similar round gouged elements. Around the center of the jar, a grooved or gouged space between parallel lines about an inch apart radiated from a slight raised line and curved toward the top and bottom of the jar as shown in the photograph. Shorter straight lines were scratched at the base. This jar was fired with a light green matt glaze at Cone 05.

Jar B was given a different appearance by the relief outline treatment of alternating scalloped design elements. These were drawn with a pencil and the lines incised or carved through the surface. The areas bordering the scallops were first gouged with a scraper, leaving the tops of the scallops in relief.

The jar was then bisque fired to Cone 05 and refired with a clear gloss at Cone 05. Later the entire surface was brush painted with China Painter's gold and fired to 019. The removel of the gold from the flat surfaces with #000 steel wool, left the gold in the incised lines.

A   B   C

Fig. 64

Jar C became a very unusual owl, created from sections of the third jar, cut to leave two of the feet on both sections and the circular base on one. The severed section was decorated upside down with simulated feathers, made of little balls of clay pressed on the surface of the owl body in sizes decreasing from the bottom to the top. Circles were carved out for the eyes and a little ball was shaped and attached for a beak.

The legs of the jar, now at the top of section 1, were pressed with the fingers into earlike flat protrusions and the bottom cut one-half circle to give a leg appearance.

The back of the #2 section was carved in an oval, as shown in the photograph, then the two sections were bisque fired to Cone 05. The #2 section was glazed with a special brown and tan glaze, and the owl section glazed with a clear glaze. Both were fired to Cone 05. Gold China paint was spattered over the front of the owl part, and the eyes were bordered with gold. It was then fired to Cone 019.

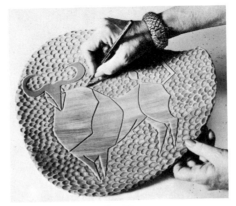

Fig. 65

Fig. 66

The *stylized Ferdinand,* a Marc Bellaire design, Fig. 65, is being incised by Mrs. Gloss with a sgraffito tool on the semihardened clay, which has been gouged with a wire loop tool, after the animal form was outlined on the smooth and burnished slab. When dry and glazed, he will be the decoration on the irregularly shaped dish. Underglaze animal colors in orange and a rich brown, with a wash of black and brown, will be added with a large sponge, making the strokes go in only one direction to give the appearance of a wood grain background for the animal. Clear glaze will be applied and fired to Cone 05.

The modified *Diamond Shaped Planter,* Fig. 66, is another example of the original designs created by Mrs. Gloss. Three-quarter inch clay coils from a rolled clay slab—nine for the planter and three for the base—were built as the photograph indicates. Refer to coil building method on page 84. The coils were smooth and pressed together on the inside, each one being scratched before a uniting slip was applied to insure a close joint. The rounded shape of the coils on the outside was left as part of the design, consisting of impressions made when the clay was semihard with the second joint of the right forefinger in a slightly irregular vertical pattern. Lines were traced to define them between the coils with a fingernail. The top coil was left smoothly rounded.

Sgraffito rose platter

The illustrated *Rose Platter* was decorated with an original design by Evie Cremona, Cremona Creations, Bay City, Michigan, who has generously permitted the use of her design and the photograph for inclusion here with the description, which appeared in *Ceramic Arts and Crafts*, May 1966. The procedure was as follows:

1. The green ware molded platter was first sponged with water over the top surface from the outside edge of the center, while the platter was spinning on a banding wheel or rotating support.

2. Apply a mixture of one part yellow translucent underglaze color and five parts water with the sponge in two coats, worked in from the outside edge. Then one coat orange, red, and maroon underglaze colors in the same way with the wheel spinning. Allow the colors to dry.

3. Sketch the design in position or transfer from tracing paper, taking care not to rub and smudge the colors.

4. Using the pointed sgraffito tool, incise around the stem and rose petal design lines; for the leaves, use a short push and pull stroke, making the edges look a little ragged. Sgraffito also a center vine line of about two thirds the length of each leaf.

5. Using a small texture sgraffito tool (a tool with about eight or ten stiff short wires that fan out at the tip), shade the design. When shading with this tool, apply the heaviest pressure at the start of the stroke and reduce pressure as you extend the stroke. This gives a feathery effect that will permit some of the orange and yellow color to show through. Shade the design with slightly curving strokes as indicated in the photograph.

6. Finish the edge of the platter with a band of maroon underglaze border while the wheel is spinning.

7. Bisque fire the platter to Cone 06-05, glaze with clear or transparent matt glaze and fire again.

Fig. 67

Lamp base

For the pictured lamp, Fig. 68, base a blend of native or natural clay from sedimentary deposits near Colorado Springs was used for the clay body. It became a rich brown when bisque fired. A turquoise blue glaze was applied to the pedestal and to the design areas which were thus given a relief appearance. A pattern with detailed designs is given in Fig. 69. This lamp base was cast, but may be coiled or thrown.

The base and shade were made by Lawrence Heller of the Heller Studio of Colorado Springs, who developed the stylized lily design to fit the contour of the lamp base. It is an excellent example of the principles of design, proportion, harmony and balance, as discussed in the section, "Design in Handicraft," page 2.

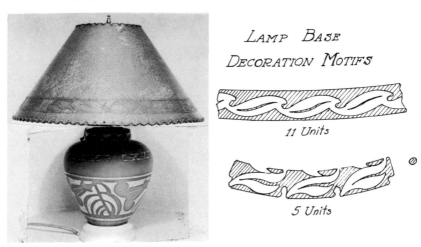

Fig. 68

LAMP BASE
DECORATION MOTIFS

11 Units

5 Units

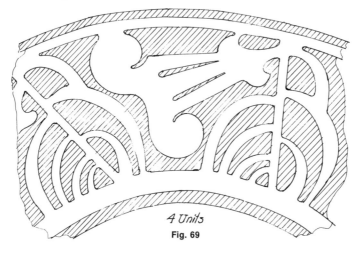

4 Units

Fig. 69

The lamp base is 9¾ inches high, 8¾ inches in diameter, shaped to the top rim which is 3½ inches in diameter. The separate pedestal, connected to the lamp base with the metal pipe, which carries the electrical cord, tapers from the lower edge 5¾ to 4¼ inches, to fit the bottom of the lamp base. A piece of felt distributes the pressure and prevents the base and pedestal from rubbing together, when held in place with a "hex" nut screwed to the end of the pipe.

The pipe with electrical cord extends through a copper disc fitted to the top of the base and terminates with the shade support and the lamp sockets.

The matching shade is made of parchmentized, translucent paper, decorated with a motif on a band similar to those on the base as shown in the sketches of Fig. 69.

Decorative Tiles

It is interesting to speculate on the origin of tile. Decorative plaques and glazed brick put together in a pattern to depict historical or symbolic scenes on the walls of ruined cities of the past have preserved for history much of the culture of that time. Customs were recorded on clay tablets and were called the books of ancient Assyria and Babylon.

Commercial tile has limitless uses today but the craftsman will want to make and assemble tile for a panel of decorative design or individual significance. Single tile with related designs in the same color are desired for furniture inlays, fireplace decoration, ornamental plaques, mounted in metal forms or in wood, comparable to the famous delft blue ornamental tile from Holland and scenic tile in this country. Typical Mexican scenes are reproduced in Fig. 73 page 84.

A series of four, six, or eight tile with a related or a pattern of designs, mounted on a wood base, with special tile cement, can be made into a practical and attractive coffee table with a metal or wood base, Fig. 72 page 83. An assembly of four or six tile can be mounted in a serving tray.

Tile making

Clay for tile should be tempered or modified to withstand firing with a minimum of warping, which is a problem with a flat shape. The addition of grog to the clay mixed for tile is recommended to correct this tendency. One fourth grog screened thru a 40-50 mesh screen is generally used. Grog may be made by pulverizing fragments of baked or bisque fired clay and is also available from ceramic suppliers.

1. If the tile is to be decorated with a *relief design*, an *incised mold* is needed. (See instructions for making plaster molds on pages 67-70.) The design must be incised ⅛ inch deep in the base of the mold to appear raised in the tile. Geometrical or other lineal designs may be drawn on paper, and blackened with a soft pencil so that it will clearly transfer to the mold.

2. Place the paper with design face down on the base of the mold, and with the broad tip of a modeler rub over the lines to transfer them to the mold. Remove the paper. Groove the lines with a V-shaped tool and round the edges with the modeler. The raised line design may be complete in itself or form the

border for a slip decoration. Fig. 71A shows a plain tile with the raised design, also the same design bordering a decoration.

3. For an assembly of two, four, six, or more tile a board frame can be made. A piece of ⅜ inch plywood large enough to hold the tile in squares or rectangles is made with a rim as high as the top of the tile, and ¼ inch larger than the fired tile to allow for grouting.

4. For either the single tile mold or the assembled form, waterproofed with 2 coats of shellac, sprinkle grog dust evenly over the plywood base after moistening it with water. Prepare tile clay in the proportions of clay for molds as described on page 64. It should be about the consistency of that for slab and coiled projects.

5. *The mold.* Fill the design area of the molds, Fig. 70A, *first* and stamp a strip of clay firmly into the grooves and over them. Continue adding clay, which has been kept moist under a damp cloth, wedging it closely together. Rolls of clay or strips from a slab of about tile thickness are best. Fill the entire mold, making sure the corners are an exact angle without crevices, gradually closing all spaces until the mold is filled with a unified mass of clay and it rounds up slightly above the top of the mold.

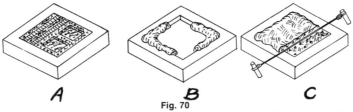

A   *B*   *C*

Fig. 70

6. Cut away the mound of clay and level the top with a stretched wire as shown in Fig. 70C. Remove shallow portions of the base about ⅛ inch deep in squares or lines. This helps to prevent warping. In the mold the tile will dry quickly so this must be done before it begins to shrink from the edges. To remove, hold a piece of plywood over the mold and reverse to leave the tile right side up.

7. *Assembly.* The tile molds can be filled with clay cut in sections from a slab rolled to a thickness slightly greater than that planned for the tile. Press all sections closely together moistening them, if necessary. As with the mold make sure the corners are evenly filled and pressed down.

8. Level the assembly of tile with a strong piece of smooth straight edge wood. Cut the clay into the planned number of tile, making allowance for the shrinkage, approximately one inch in twelve. Support the board at a slight angle until the tile is leather hard, then turn to release the tile on a level surface. Trim or smooth the edges evenly and set aside separately to dry.

Decoration of tile

The leather hard tile may be dried, see pages 60 and 62, and decorated by any of the methods described on pages 54 and 60 to 64 or the following modified methods may be used. Designs on pages 4 and 5 may be adapted for tile.

1. *Types of Underglaze Decoration* which are possible for tile include:
The *incising of a design outline* in the bottom of the tile mold.
Applying a "color stopper" or resist for the design outlines.
Outlining the design with slip to enclose the design areas.
Develop the design on slip covered tile by *sgraffito* process.

a. *Incised design outlines* in the bottom of the tile mold appear as raised or relief outlines on the surface of the cast tile. They provide the outline for the development of the design area filled with colored slip or underglaze colors. *Note.* White, buff or gray clay make the best base for colored slip decoration, as a dark firing clay will not be a clear base for colored slip.

b. *Bisquited tile* from the "Desert House Crafts" in Tucson, Arizona, were photographed as examples of incised mold outlines raised in the cast tile. Fig. 71A illustrates a design for a border with designs for two separate tile. A decorated bisquited tile is shown in Fig. 71B, and in Fig. 71C the use of a small syringe for the application of slip (regulated by pressure to produce an even inlay of color within the lines) is shown. Fig. 71D shows a drying and firing rack for tile.

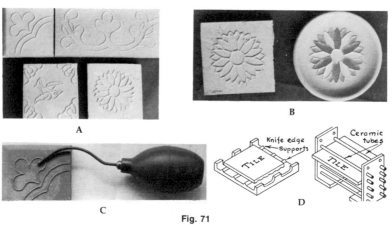

Fig. 71

To make a colored slip, take a portion of the dry prepared clay without grog and blend it with the chosen color in the proportions of three level teaspoons to one cup of clay. When this is thoroughly blended, apply a little to a sample of the moist clay and fire to determine the bisquited tint. Add more color or more clay if necessary to produce the right shade.

The addition of a little glycerine or gum tragacanth (½ teaspoon dissolved in a pint of boiling water and cooled), will give the slip an adhesive quality when it is brushed lightly over the design areas of the tile.

2. A *color stopper* or a commercial resist may be used for marking the design outline on the tile. A formula for a satisfactory color stopper, used by the Desert House Crafts in Tucson, is prepared as follows:
Mix a small amount of powdered manganese dioxide with a little glycerine in water contained in a small jar with a tight screw top. Try about a tablespoon

of water, a half teaspoon of glycerine, and a teaspoon of the powdered manganese dioxide.

Shake the jar vigorously to combine the powder with the liquid and test
it to determine the density of color. If the mixture does not form a distinct line,
add more glycerine, a drop at a time and more manganese dioxide. Frequent
shaking will be required to keep the powder in suspension.

An underglaze or slip color may be applied to develop the design areas
within the *color stopper lines* as the manganese solution dries almost immediately. The glaze can be applied with a small brush and the slip with the syringe
as in the incised outline method. Fill all colors having the same color before
changing to another. Clean the syringe by forcing water through it.

When the decoration is completely dry cover the face and ends of the tile
with a clear glaze and fire. The base should have a protective paraffin coat
before the tile is fired.

The matched tile for a wall hanging were made at the Desert House Crafts
in Tucson, Arizona. They depict the "Spirit Horse," a favorite subject of Indian
artists. The black and white horses were painted on a bisquited base with
underglaze colors, the Yucca plants a natural green and the earth brown under
the horses' hind feet (Fig. 26).

Fig. 72

The Spirit Horse design may also be applied by means of a stencil for the
horse outline and, if desired, for the "pinto" markings. The stencils should be
attached to the assembled tile with drafting or masking tape, and the animal's
form painted within the outline margins of the stencil pattern. For a natural
appearance, the manes and tails can be painted freehand, also the pinto markings, the grass, and the suggested ground.

3. The method using a line of slip, squeezed through a tube or the syringe,
on tile which has been bisquited can be used for a freehand decoration, applied
like the decoration of a cake with colored frosting. After the decorated tile is
dry, apply a transparent glaze and fire. This is an ancient method and still
used successfully.

4. A type of decoration, dating back to periods when baked clay forms
were first developed, is the *sgraffito or scratched design* on the tile dried to
the leather-hard stage. At that stage dip it, face down in an opaque slip of light
color. Buff makes a good background, also brown and red. Scratch the design
with a wooden modeling tracer when the slip is firm. After the slip has fully
dried, the design may be scratched with a metal scriber, like the method
described on page 60. Finish with clear glaze as before.

Mexican decorative tile

The separate square tile faithfully portrays the native Mexican, whose life in the villages has been improved by education and more modern community facilities, now made available to many of the people. The pair of single tile with a frequently used floral decoration was made for a tray. In sets of four, six, or eight, such tile designs make fine table tops. Many adaptations of the ancient designs found on baked clay tablets as described on page 9 may be seen as tile decorations in modern Mexico.

Scenic reproductions and religious motifs on tile are more likely to have been brought from Spain and methods of decoration taught by the friars when the Spanish church was in control. The tile in Fig. 73 came from a ceramic tile factory in Monterey, Mexico. The colors are brilliant blues, yellow, green, and orange on a white background.

Fig. 73

Coiled Pottery

The ceramist who has a studio equipped for building coiled pottery, also wheel thrown, modeled, and cast forms will choose the coiled, Fig. 89, sketches A to C, method for items of various kinds. If a beginner and not ready to purchase a wheel, he still can build experimental forms by the coil or slab methods, and derive satisfaction from the manipulation of the clay and the different kinds of articles he can make by either method.

The process he will follow in building a coiled piece of pottery is little changed from the Indian method. If he adopts their method of forming a base it will be stronger than the flat circle base usually used. While the Indian potter almost instinctively can coil build a perfectly shaped jar without preparing a pattern of any kind, the studio potter should make a full sized sketch on a stiff piece of paper or cardboard and cut out the shape to use as a template.

Some modern ceramists maintain that the method of coil building is preferable for all free form projects as well as for the forming of large jars and bowls. The continued use of coils for building the near perfect pottery of the Indians, from prehistoric times, seems to prove this theory, which was demonstrated by the famous Pueblo potter, Maria Martinez as photographed for the series of pictures on Fig. 85, page 104 and Fig. 75B and C.

Preparation and testing of natural clays

It is possible to use a "discovered" clay with the addition of essential minerals. The process of testing the qualities of clay requires time, patience, equipment for preparing the "slip" (pulverized clay in water), and facilities for firing an experimental project. The suitability for ceramics of any bed or strata of clay should be determined before any quantity is dug. A bucketful is sufficient for testing. See page 49-50 for the process.

Illustrating the rewarding possibilities of a "discovered" natural clay body is a report of the summer experimentation of an adult recreation group in Lewiston, Idaho, sponsored by the Y.W.C.A. and the City Recreation Department. The director of the project, Maxine Weber, gives suggestions helpful to any similar group or class:

"1. Keep varieties of clay (we had 7 or 8 varieties) separated in carefully labeled containers with notation of the source. We numbered our recipes and kept a notebook record of ingredients, characteristics, and results obtained.

2. Mix a sample of each clay alone, using ½ cup clay powder (prepared by the standard method), and ½ cup of water in a small covered jar, carefully labeled. Mix the clay and water thoroughly and let it age for several days.

3. Some of the clay will be crumbly, some oily, and some sticky. We started by combining 2 or 3 in different combinations. After a couple of trials we found we needed the crumbly and oily clays in a recipe, as each contributed a needed ingredient. Some combinations refused to work so were discarded.

4. When you have tested your recipes and have a finished product write the results in your notebook. Mark the stubborn ones that fail "no good" and discard. Be sure your recipe number follows the sample through the entire experiment.

5. We put all our discards in a bucket of water we used for washing our hands, then finding in it a lot of "settlings" decided to test the mixture. They made a very fine clay and a lovely large plate, Fig. 55, page 68.

6. When a sample proves itself superior, mark it "very good" and rush out to gather more of the clays used in the recipe. Our local firebrick plant provided a light bodied clay as well as grog (broken particles once fired).

7. Local clays make an inexpensive experimental material for any modeling work. We have used ours on the potter's wheel, for slab, coil, and pinch modeling. We found we had colors from white through the buffs, pinkish tan, and on to the medium and reddish browns."

Ceramic Projects — By the Lewiston, Idaho Workshop

In their experimentation with native clays, discovered in the vicinity of Lewiston, the director, Maxine Weber, emphasized originality in design and ingenuity in expressing the design in clay form. Seeking simplified procedures, they found it possible to devise methods and projects which were remarkably successful.

Students and members of the workshop learned and practiced the methods of building clay forms from slabs and the techniques of coil building and throwing on the wheel.

In the photographs, Fig. 74, taken in the garage workshop, a lesson in throwing, and demonstrations of the processes in throwing two kinds of projects are shown.

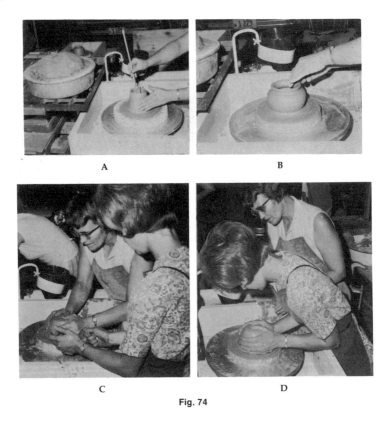

Fig. 74

The photographs in Fig. 75 show the coil building process as used by the Lewiston experimenters with native clay. Several of their projects are illustrated and described on pages 87 and 88.

1. Fig. 75A shows the use of the wedging wire and an air pocket in the clay ball, which this process will remove. Thorough and adequate wedging to

eliminate all air pockets is as essential for coiled pottery as for wheel thrown or other methods.

2. The splicing of coils and the start of a coiled bowl is shown in the photograph B, also two methods of forming the base, one with a disc cut from a rolled slab and the other built entirely with the coils which will form the bowl. Each coil has been roughened with slight crossway cuts, then moistened with slip, before the next one is coiled against it. Both are pressed together with the fingers and modeling tools. Not more than three coils are formed without an interval for partial drying.

3. Sometimes a continuous coil, with spliced sections as needed, is used and the spiral pattern of the coils modeled and left as a decoration on the outside, while they are smoothed and modeled for the inner surface.

Usually one coil at a time, with the length increased or decreased according to the desired contour, is considered the best method.

4. A shaped flexible scraper is used when the bowl is leather hard, to smooth it inside and outside. A template of stiff paper is necessary to guide in shaping the desired contour. Fig. 75C is a small coiled jar, set aside to dry before finishing is done. Fig. 75D enlargement to show detail.

A

B

C

Fig. 75

Lewiston workshop projects

The *Candle Holder* or *Lamp Base* in photograph Fig 76A...illustrates how effective a pierced or cut out design can be developed, using clear glaze over the openings filled with gleaming glass fragments which made this base so unusual and beautiful with candle or electric light. The processes for this and the other Lewiston projects were described by Maxine Weber, the instructor of the group.

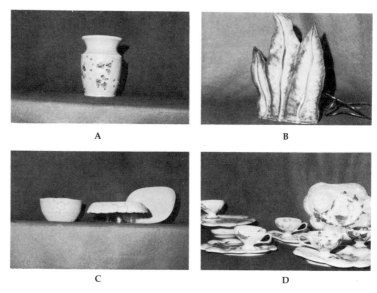

A   B

C   D

Fig. 76

"1. The base was made from a slip cast piece and removed from the mold as soon as it was firm, then the pattern of irregular leaves for the openings was immediately cut out with special care to make the edges straight. The little holes were cut with the top of a fountain pen.

2. After it was leather hard, any uneven edges were trimmed, and when dry the base was bisque fired and glaze applied to all surfaces except the inside edges of the openings. Masking tape was placed over all openings on the inside and attached with "poly paste" or resin glue, to which the catalyst, hardener provided with the resin), a small amount at a time, was mixed.

3. The openings and holes were filled with the resin mixture, then crushed green glass pressed into the resin, so that they were entirely filled with the colored glass bits. Be cautious about handling the glass and repeat the filling if necessary.

4. After the base was thoroughly dry, the masking tape was removed and a candle placed inside. If the base is made for an electric lamp, it will be necessary, to prepare holes in the green ware when removed from the mold, to

accommodate the light fittings, a small one to reflect the light from inside and a regular fixture with shade support above the base. A ceramic disc can be made to cover the base and enclose the fixture support."

The attractive T.V. Lamp, Fig. 76B, designed and built by Marguerite Thayer, was made of three different sizes of leaf forms simulating the tropical Ti leaves and glazed with a soft green underglaze which was shaded along the leaf margins and darkened for the center veins. Maxine Weber outlined the procedure as follows:

"1. The forms were cut from a slab, approximately ½ inch thick, which was rolled on the back of a sheet of oilcloth and left flat for a short period to firm up slightly, then lapped together and shaped into the Ti leaf outlines. Later, when the clay was leather hard, the center vein was traced, lightly incised and filled with a dark green underglaze, which was also used to shade the leaf margins.

2. When firm enough to hold their own wieght, the leaves were placed in position upright and propped with large newspaper wads. Close attention was given to the slowly firming pieces to keep them upright and the contour correct. Some remodeling with the fingers was occasionally necessary.

3. Rolled clay was formed into a housing to support the electrical fittings, using the fingers to model the clay. The housing rod for the electrical cord was attached to the center upright leaf with moistened clay. All edge junctures of the three leaves were roughened and slip covered to attach them in the unified position. When entirely dry the leaf forms were bisque fired, painted with underglaze and fired again.

4. The Tea Set Plates, Fig. 76D, were designed and hand modeled by Miss Thayer from sheets of clay, carefully rolled to a uniform thickness. The plate shapes were cut from a paper pattern and the edges propped up with rolls of newspaper to form the shallow bottoms. The indentations for the cups, which were cast in molds, were modeled on the plates, when they were dry enough to reverse.

Wild flower designs were hand painted on the plates and cups in a one-stroke underglaze and all were then bisquited, later a coat of luster glaze was applied and the set fired again. Cup handles Fig. 63A, page 75 were made in a press mold.

5. A *"Thumb"* Bowl, Fig. 76C, of which two small shapes are illustrated, is an interesting and easily built project as a first experiment in handling clay.

(a) A kitchen bowl or dish of any desired shape provides a mold. A thin coat of liquid detergent is first applied. This will aid in releasing the form when it has dried. Small balls of clay, made from identical strips of an evenly rolled clay slab, and shaped to the same diameter, are rolled in the palms of the hands, then pressed firmly side by side against the bowl bottom and sides.

(b) Each ball should form a seal with its neighbors when pressed with the thumb to flatten. When all the balls are in place, covering the inner surface of the bowl, they are gently smoothed to minimize the lumpy appearance on the inside.

(c) When the balls of the form have dried to the leatherhard stage, a coat of soft clay is spread over them with the fingers, to form a smooth lining for

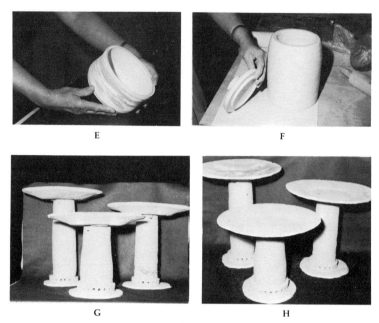

E

F

G

H

Fig. 76

the inside of the bowl. When this is dry, the bowl is reversed to permit the molded form to be removed, the detergent having been a kind of lubricant on the surface of the bowl mold.

(d) When the bowl is completely dry, the inner surface will be smooth and the outside will have a pebbled appearance. When fired the red-brown color of the native clay is evident. A colored glaze may be applied if desired.

6. *The Souffle Bowl,* Fig. 76E.

(a) This bowl was thrown on the wheel, using a mixture of local native clays, which fire to a soft buff shade. The shape, as the photograph indicates, was started with a ball of clay flattened to the diameter of the bowl, then controlled with the fingers held inside and outside to maintain the shape.

(b) When the form was completed on the wheel, and while it was still very wet, strips of a dark brown engobe, (creamy consistency), were spun slowly on the surface of the bowl. Maxine dipped the fingers of her right hand in the engobe then held them gently against the sides of the slowly spinning bowl, repeating until the strips were an irregular, yet symmetrical pattern.

(c) When the bowl was dry it was bisque fired, then glazed with a clear glaze."

The Cookie Jar, Fig. 76F, of native clay with coarse grog was thrown on the wheel and trued when it dried to the leather hard stage. The lid was also thrown, but upside down, so that the base made the top of the lid. When dry a knob was attached.

A *Dripping Water Fountain,* Fig. 76G and H, for the YWCA patio was designed by Maxine Weber, and made of three bird bath shapes, modeled on a hump mold, from rolled clay slabs, and three supporting cylinders, also made from evenly rolled clay ½ inch thick.

For the cylinders...

1. The slab consistency clay was rolled between leveling supports as described on page 64 on a large square of oilcloth, reverse side. A heavy paper core about 1¼ inch in diameter was slipped into a plastic bag, then placed on the rolled sheet of clay, which was wrapped closely around it. The oil cloth was held with the clay sheet and helped roll it smoothly against the core and plastic. All three cylinders were made in this way.

2. The edges of the seams were cut, to fit the core, cross hatched to roughen, then sealed by pressing them carefully together with the fingers and a modeling tool. The bottom edge was cut even with the core and the top to a line measured for the top of the cylinders.

3. The oil-cloth was kept wrapped around the clay wrapped cores to support them until they were firm. Then the cylinders were stood upright and when entirely firm, the cores were pulled out and later the plastic bags.

4. *A skirt and base* for the cylinders were modeled by hand, (they could be cut from a slab), and holes cut in them for bolting to a support in the bottom of the YWCA patio pool, (not a bathing pool). Slots were also cut in the top edges of the cylinders for use in fastening the plates safely to them. One cylinder, the tallest, had an opening at the base for the insertion of the water pipe and fountain fittings. The shortest cylinder covered the over-flow pipe.

5. A 2 inch opening, shaped to fit the inside dimensions of the shortest cylinder, was attached to the center bottom of the plate when it was leather hard. Holes were cut in the plates to hold the safety screws to correspond with the placement of the slots in the tops of the cylinders.

6. The inside of the plates were finished with a blue satin underglaze and the rest of the surfaces glazed in a clear matt to preserve the soft brown color of the native clays which were used. A circulation pump was installed to keep the water clear and conserve on water use.

Throwing on the Wheel

This is the phrase that means pottery to many people, and to the throngs sembling at potteries where the process is demonstrated. Evidence of the existence of a kind of wheel and even of kilns and finished pottery has been found in the excavation of ancient Egyptian ruins together with clay tablet records of the date 4000 B.C.

The direct kick wheel, operated by kicking a heavy flywheel, is probably the oldest known form still used. Once the potter learns to coordinate the hands as they control the clay and the kicking action of the foot, the process becomes almost instinctive. This is also true of a later development of the treadle kick wheel such as is used in the Van Briggle pottery in Colorado Springs. The illustration in Fig. 78 shows the potter Fred Wills demonstrating the process of throwing on a treadle kick wheel built by Artis Van Briggle, the founder of the pottery over fifty years ago. The scale drawing, (Fig. 77) duplicates this wheel on which Mr. Wills throws hundreds of bowls and vases displayed in the showrooms. He says that it is easy to operate as the initial kicking often sustains the momentum through the entire process of throwing a piece of pottery. The articles shown in Fig. 81 were thrown on this wheel by Mr. Wills and finished with a turquoise glaze.

The mystery and romance connected with the historical and prehistorical development of the potter's wheel, lures those who have endeavored to learn the art and those who can only watch the potter at work.

At the famous Van Briggle pottery in Colorado Springs, the tile decorations inside and outside of the building, designed and built by Artis Van Briggle, an artist-potter trained in Holland, intrigue and amaze the visitors who are further enthralled by the skillful demonstrations of Fred Wills, the master potter.

In Fig. 79, Mr. Wills demonstrates the principal steps in throwing, a cylinder which becomes a vase.

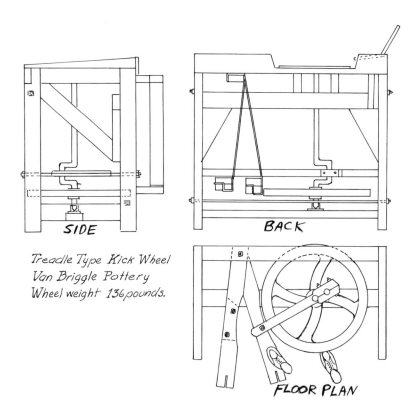

SIDE

BACK

FLOOR PLAN

Treadle Type Kick Wheel
Van Briggle Pottery
Wheel weight 136 pounds.

Fig. 77

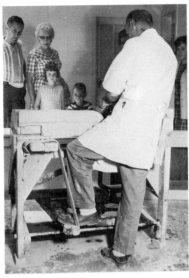 

A   B

Fig. 78

1. Of all the steps in throwing on the wheel, the first one is most essential, that of thoroughly "wedging" the well mixed clay. A wedging wire is always a part of the wheel structure, as is the wedging board. The process consists of cutting the ball of clay on the wire, slapping it on the board, kneading, cutting, and reforming until all air bubbles are removed. The wedging also makes the clay more flexible and more responsive to the potter's control during the throwing process. See Fig. 52, sketch A, page 64.

2. Equally essential for successful throwing is the actual throwing and centering of the ball of clay on the plaster "bat" or other disc mounted on the wheel head at the top of the shaft, which the potter operates with his foot, as shown in photograph A of Fig. 78. Beginners are urged to practice this step before attempting to throw a piece of pottery on the wheel.

3. Photograph A (Fig. 79) shows Mr. Wills centering the ball of clay which he has just thrown on the disc or "bat." While the wheel is rotating he regulates it, with his foot on the treadle, to move slowly until the ball is centered. B. shows how the clay is permitted to rise in a cone, then is pushed down. The potter repeats this step until he feels that the clay is perfectly centered and sufficiently pliable with all air bubbles removed.

4. C. shows how the ball is opened and the cylinder started for a vase. The potter's thumbs press from the inside, while the fingers control from the outside. Photographs D,E, and F show the position of the hands in raising and forming the cylinder, F and G, forming of ring, H in cutting from bat with wire. Mr. Wills keeps the wheel head rotating rapidly during these steps.

In A of Fig. 80, Mr. Wills is spreading the ball for the formation of a low bowl, starting from the step shown in C, Fig. 79 and continuing to shape the contour as it appears in B and C. After the bowl has partially dried, he turns the top down over wedges of clay and forms the base with a scraper, held as in D, E, and F. During the entire process of throwing a piece of pottery, the wheel is kept continually moving at the rate the potter controls with his foot. Fig. 81, G and H are Van Briggle Pottery.

Pottery Demonstration — Fred Wills

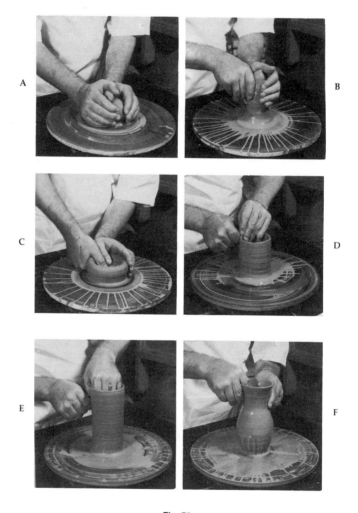

Fig. 79

Throwing a Low Bowl

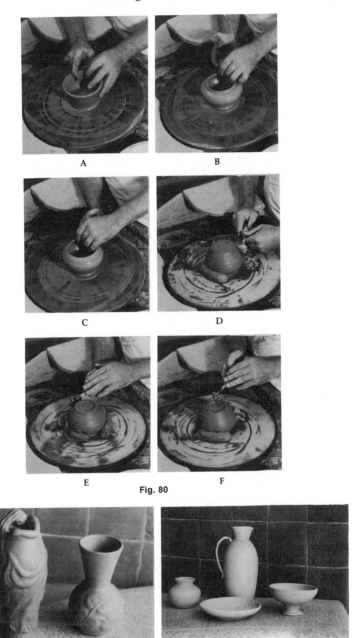

A

B

C

D

E

F

Fig. 80

G

H

Fig. 81

Mosaics

Excavations of ancient ruins of Babylonian cities reveal the artist crafts-men's mastery of the art of building scenes with fragments of marble, bone, ivory, and colored stones, with which some precious and semiprecious stones were combined. Panels or murals, according to dates on ceramic tablets, were created in 3600 B.C.

Techniques perfected by the Greeks and Romans enabled them to build mosaics which have survived until modern times. They learned to make tesserae or tiles from glass and clay in the Fifteenth century, and then aban-doned the use of marble and stone pieces.

Biblical pictures in mosaics, as decoration in the churches of Italy, pre-ceded the murals painted by the great Italian artists. In modern times some of the finest mosaic work has been done in Mexico. The library in the University of Mexico is the outstanding example. Decorations in public buildings, churches, and in the patios of private homes, amaze the visitors to Mexico with their beauty and perfection. It is generally assumed that the friars from Spain, where the art was highly developed, brought the techniques to Mexico and taught them to the native Indians at the time of the conquest by Spain in 1520.

Sources of glass and ceramic mosaic tile

Venetian and Byzantine glass tesserae is made in Italy and imported by dealers in mosaic supplies in the United States. The Venetian glass tesserae is mostly made in the vicinity of Venice, where the availability of natural mineral components make it a famous glass producing area.

In the manufacture of Venetian glass tesserae, special minerals are added to molten glass to give it strength and color. The molten glass mixture is cooled in molds divided into tiny ¾ inch squares. As required, they may be cut with mosaic nippers. They retain their brilliant colors, are stainproof and waterproof. When set in a special cement, they are practically indestructible.

Mosaics of Venetian glass tesserae, designed and made by Clara Gloss, are described on page 100.

Mosaic canes or small rod shaped glass, made by Venetian glassworkers, are effective when used for accents or strips for outlining.

Byzantine glass tesserae in thousands of color shades is made at the famous Murano glassworks on the island of Murano, near Venice, Italy. In the molten state, it is poured on a flat surface in ⅜ inch thick circles, which are scored with narrow irregular lines when cooled. This permits their breaking into pieces with light reflecting surfaces. Some beautiful marble for mosaics is also imported from Italy.

Recently the *Venetian* type glass tesserae has been developed in Juarez, Mexico. It is an excellent quality, and may be obtained from the producers listed at the end of this section.

Paladiano tesserae is similar to Venetian glass. It is made in sheets, like window glass, which can be broken with a rubber tipped hammer and cut with mosaic cutters. It is usually sold broken by mosaic suppliers.

Pieces of stained window glass or ordinary bottle glass can be used effectively in some designs.

Ceramic Tile for mosaics is imported from Puerto Rico, Italy, and Japan, where the base material is porcelain, which is impervious and more durable than the ceramic tile made in the United States. The United States tile comes in many colors and is satisfactory for use in pieces for indoors, where moisture cannot affect it.

A project for making ceramic tile

Tile for mosaics can readily be made in the studio or school shop, and is an excellent project for a group. Selected clays and glaze colors should first be tested and chosen in relation to the plan of the mosaic design, prepared on paper in advance. The first experiment should be a small and simple design.

1. Indicate the position of each color and the form of the mosaic elements on a tracing of the plan. Mix a portion of clay for each color to a slab consistency, wedged with extra care to eliminate any bubbles.

2. Roll the prepared clay on the reverse side of oilcloth to an exact level between ½ inch or ⅜ inch thick battens (see page 64). Permit it to dry to leather hardness and square all corners.

3. Prepare and stain the glazes, unless the ready mixed types are to be used, adding a little gum tragacanth for strength and smoothness — or use a self-glazing engobe.

4. Brush the separate colors of the glaze or engobe evenly over the damp slabs. Brush in the reverse direction when the shine leaves the surface.

5. Slice the slabs almost through when firm. Cut straight down in squares or rectangles, about ¾ inch wide, with several extra pieces in each color for reserve. The slabs may be sliced in strips to be broken after firing for irregular tesserae. Slabs rolled 3/16 inch thick are best for such strips.

6. Detach the separate tesserae after firing, or hold to separate during the setting process. When dry enough to handle, transfer them to the shelves of the kiln *without heat* and let them dry slowly to prevent warping. Fire according to the temperature required for the glaze, or self-glazing engobe.

7. Slide the fired tesserae color portions on to the design tracing with a spatula and transfer to the prepared backing when completely dry. The method for setting tesserae is described on page 98.

Setting mosaics

The *adhesive* used in setting mosaics should be selected for the porous and nonporous, or impervious, mosaics with which they are to be used. Water soluble cements, such as Elmer's, can be used for items which will not be exposed to weather; but the rubber base nonporous cements are preferable for almost all mosaics. The ceramic adhesives for ceramic tesserae permeate porous surfaces and make a permanent nonporous setting.

Impervious glass adhesives dry slowly and so permit the changing of positions or replacement of mosaics. Avoid getting it on the fingers. Lighter fluid or nail polish remover will remove it, but must be used with caution in a ventilated place. These adhesives are obtainable from tile contractors and mosaic stores. A slow drying "floating type" cement, used for tile, is recommended for mosaics set on a horizontal surface.

Setting procedure

Setting mosaics has been termed "composing with color chips."

1. Waterproof the backing with shellac on both sides. Use the rough side of tempered masonite, or marine ⅝ inch plywood. Have frames prepared and braces (if required on the back to support large, heavy backings) attached before setting tesserae. Protect the frames with masking tape.

2. Use a sketch as a general guide. Wipe all surfaces of the tesserae. Start from the center if the design is circular. Remember that the tesserae must not touch or it will bend as the cement dries.

3. The tesserae should be embedded in the adhesive first. After it dries, a special cement, or grout, available from mosaic dealers, is used for a filler. This can be dyed to match to harmonize with the mosaics. Mix samples first to be sure of the color.

4. Reshape tesserae as needed for the design by nipping with the mosaic cutters. Smooth any projections with a file or rub on medium rough sandpaper. If irregular pieces are required for the design, hammer the tesserae between pieces of cardboard. Be careful not to break into pieces to small to handle.

Methods of applying tesserae

Direct method

The direct method is required for tesserae which are supplied on foot square paper, glued face down.

1. Soak the paper until it can be peeled off. A wet paper towel, followed by a damp sponge will loosen it.

2. Spread adhesive on as much of the backing as can be set in 30 minutes or less. For ceramic mosaics, magnesite cement mix, which can be tinted with magnesite colorants, is recommended. Add about ¼th magnesium chloride to obtain a workable consistency.

3. Spread the cement over a small area at a time, varying the depth so the bed is twice the thickness of the tesserae and embed singly or in sections. It may be kept level or tilted slightly to catch the reflected light.

4. Apply grout to the cracks *after 48 hours,* then cure under damp paper or cloth for 72 hours.

Indirect method

1. Place the tesserae face down on kraft paper in accordance with the design previously sketched *in reverse.* The paper may be cut in strips or sections for easier handling.

2. Apply mosaic adhesive to the entire surface of the backing. Let it stand until it becomes tacky, 6 to 8 minutes, then pour a "slow setting floating type" of cement lightly over the adhesive with a pallet knife. Do not touch the adhesive.

3. Set the sections or strips of paper, holding the mosaics, on to the cement and tamp lightly into it. A rolling pin may be used to even the surface and press the cement up between the cracks after all sections have been placed.

4. Let them dry for an hour, then remove the paper by dampening with a wet cloth or sponge. When the cement is partially dry, remove any particles and fill in holes or open places. Permit the mosaic to dry for 12 to 20 hours, then pour a little water over the top surface. Remove all particles of paper and clean with fine steel wool, 000 size; then polish with a silicone polish.

Mosaic Wall Hangings

The beautiful examples of mosaic wall hangings, shown in the photographs are the imaginative and skillful work of Mrs. Clara Gloss, whose ceramic designs and pottery were described on page 75. The brilliant colors, which the photographs do not reveal, range from ivory and white through rainbow colors to gold. Venetian glass tesserae was used for the greater part of the design with ceramic tile where indicated.

Colors for the swan

1. Breast and wing strips, irregular ceramic gold
2. Eyes and beak, red glass
3. Spots on wings, deep blue cut from bottle glass
4. Wings shaded blue, green, and gold
5. Neck and upper breast, mosaic ivory tile
6. Shield shaped part of the back, soft orange, Venetian glass
7. The white Venetian glass on breast and gold ceramic tile on lower breast grouted with white mosaic cement

Fig. 82A

1. *The Swan Hanging* (Fig. 82A) was built on ¼ inch masonite, waterproofed with two coats of shellac and cut to the pattern outline, which was bound with brass edging. All design areas were outlined or divided with similar brass strips, attached to the backing with a special glue, which was applied on both sides of the strips at the lower edge.

2. After the glue became "tacky," these edges of the brass strips, 1/16 by ¼ inch were pressed along the design outline, marked on the masonite with a pencil, and held a few minutes to let them adhere firmly.

3. The Venetian glass tesserae in the colors listed, and cut irregularly with the mosaic "nippers" were fitted into all the design areas and pressed into the colorless mosaic glass cement, spread over the masonite. This permitted the light to penetrate the reflect from the irregular surfaces of the glass tesserae.

4. Ceramic tile circles, recut to have straight edges, were fitted into the lower breast and grouted with light yellow grout, similar in color to the gold. These were cut with a small cookie cutter from clay, gold glazed and fired.

Fig. 82B

Colors for the compote
Bowl and pedestal, gold Venetian mosaic, colors from the bowl upward and left to right
1. White ceramic for grapes
2. First group, maroon, green, orange
3. Next, green, tan, yellow
4. Next above, blue, turquoise, red
5. Then yellow, green, blue
6. Followed by gray, red, green, and blue, capped with gray

1. *The Compote Hanging* (Fig. 82B) required a base of 1¼ inch thick beveled Philippine mahogany. A simulated weather grain was produced by sanding the surface, spraying it lightly (or brushing) with a thinned flat white paint.

2. The surface was wiped up and down in long strokes with a cloth, after the white paint had soaked into soft portions of the wood. After a few minutes drying for the paint to adhere a little, the board was lightly rubbed with a piece of lintless cloth. The beveled edges were painted with a solid white matt.

3. The segments of color, representing different kinds of fruit, were outlined with the brass strips, attached to the wood with glue in the same way that they were attached to the masonite for the swan. The fruit shaped designs were formed of Venetian glass mosaic tesserae, pressed into the colorless glass cement, which had been spread over the wood backing. Irregular sizes, handmade with the nippers to fit the design areas and cut to shade toward the brass

Fig. 82C

edges, were placed in slightly uneven levels to reflect the light and emphasize the colors.

The mosaic topped table (Fig. 82) of wrought iron in two tiers, was inlaid with irregular smoky white mosaic tile, set into a grout with mosaic tile adhesive, on a waterproofed base of ⅜ inch plywood on both levels. The elongated, modernistic star, shaped to center the curved oval of the top, was built with the lower part of the "star burst" in two shades of blue, and the top in two shades of purple. The grout was tinted blue and purple.

Porcelain flowers

The porcelian flowers, Fig. 83, created by Mrs. Gloss are exact replicas of the originals. The perfection of some of these, an orchid, a gardenia, a carnation, and a rose, attached to the porcelain trays, and a porcelain box, is shown in the photograph. Bell's colored porcelains were used on the roses and carnations with the leaves in green tones.

1. *Mrs. Gloss demonstrated* the steps in her procedure in the photographs. A rose petal was used in Fig. 83B to show the technique of coating a leaf or petal with liquid porcelain. The petals are first lightly rubbed with the fingers dipped in the porcelain slip, to remove the natural oils in flowers that resist the porcelain. The porcelain is applied starting from the tip of the leaf or petal.

2. Mrs. Gloss has applied the porcelain to the three parts of the rose leaf, carefully repeating the applications several times to obtain the right thickness of the porcelain coating. The stiffening becomes evident as the applications are repeated. Each coating must be allowed to become leather hard, before another can be applied. Three or four coatings are necessary depending on the type of flower, Sketch C.

3. *The process of removing the petal* from the porcelain rose petal formed on it is shown in photograph D. The very delicate process of peeling it from the fragile procelian is done with a needle-like tool. This must be done while the porcelian slip is still in the leather hard stage. If they are left to dry, the real petal dries and shrinks causing the porcelain petal to crack to pieces. A bisque firing follows when petals are entirely dry.

4. In Fig. 83 Mrs. Gloss demonstrates the process of making flower petals of porcelain, such as were assembled for the natural size blossoms on the trays and a box lid in A. The removal of the finished petal of a poppy is shown in B. C is the process of coating the underside of a rose leaf, and D the process of removing the leaf from the formed porcelain petal. E shows the assembly of petals on an unfired porcelain tray. When completely dry a second bisque firing for the tray and attached porcelain flower will result in a soft translucent appearance. No glaze is used on the porcelain flowers. F shows porcelain poppy leaves, the center and stamens made from partially dry slip rubbed through a fine sieve.

Porcelain Flowers — Clara Gloss

Fig. 83

Indian Sources and Preparation of Clay

Pueblo women potters must seek clay in one place, find sand to mix it with in another, get the oxides for paint in still another. Each village usually has its own clay pit and the color is often considered identification of their pottery.

In former days the digging was done with a stick and the clay carried in a basket or a hide. Always while digging, she spoke to the earth, asking permission, and perhaps leaving an offering, for Pueblo people feel that clay and rocks, like animals and plants have their own feelings and that man must live on friendly terms with them. Today they dig with a metal pick and carry the clay home in gunny sacks, but many still speak to the earth as they used to do.

The Indian potter must work for days preparing the clay, first pounding the lumps to pieces and taking out the pebbles, then grinding it to a fine powder on a stone metate, just as she grinds corn for cornmeal. If she does not plan to use it at once, she wraps it in a damp cloth or buries it in the ground to keep it form forming lumps again.

Experience has shown her just how much temper she will need. The women of the Tewa Pueblo use volcanic sand, others pound up volcanic rock, which they find at places along the Rio Grande River. Some pound up pottery scraps and in the Pueblos of Taos and Picuris, the potters have clay which does not need any temper.

Indian pottery with coil formed clay

Records of primitive people in nearly every part of the world reveal their skill in making vessels of clay. Their method of coil building, unchanged over the centuries, is still used wherever pottery is now made. In the modern studio it has been found that nearly every form of pottery can be made by the coil method, which permits the building of free form shapes as well as vases and bowls.

The Indians of the Southwest and Mexico still use the coil method of building the pottery for which they are famous. Clever processes their potters have learned from experience enables them to produce the finest ware with primitive tools and equipment.

The Indian potter does not start her coiled pottery with a flat circular base piece and build the coils from there, but forms a mold in the supporting piece which may be part of a hard gourd or the bottom of a broken pot, Fig. 84. This is placed on a flat stone where it can be rotated and is deep enough to permit her to mold the base and several inches of the upper part of the new bowl or jar, Fig. 84.

Maria Martinez, the famous potter of San Ildefonso Pueblo, demonstrates her traditional method of forming a pottery jar for the New Mexico Tourist Bureau to which we are indebted for this series of pictures. First, the ball of clay which she has worked to perfect smoothness without air bubbles, then the shaped piecrust like base for the coiled pot. She has built the sides with coils and then smoothes them in a perfectly even contour with a treasured bone or shell tool.

Maria grinds clay
in her metate.

A

B

C

D

E

F

G

H

I

Fig. 84

Before Maria starts the coiled part of the new form, she pinches the top of the molded base section, now partially dry, until it is thin and irregular, making a base for the first coil and the irregularities which help them to stick together. She then rolls a handful of clay like a sausage, Fig. 84E, elongating it from the center to make a coil of even diameter, which she places within the thin top of the base, and unites them evenly with wet fingers.

As she continues to add coils she turns the support, so that she is always working on the near side, which enables her to keep the curves regular. Usually she works on several jars at once, alternating as she forms and builds the coils, frequently moistening her fingers to keep the coils smooth and to unite them. Her tools are pieces of hard gourd shell, cut so their edges have different curves.

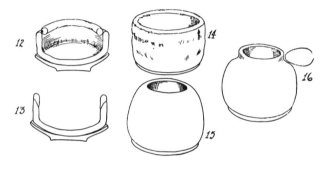

Fig. 85

Maria's method of shaping the large jar, which she displays, Fig. 84I, with some of her black pottery, is shown in Fig. 86A.

Before decorating with a design, Maria and other potters apply a thin wash of a special clay slip, white or red. This is found in only a few places and is highly prized, both for decoration and to give the pottery a smooth lustrous finish. Several coats may be applied with an interval for drying in between, and for the polishing of the slightly damp clay with a smooth water worn stone.

Her set of stones have been collected over generations and are of all sizes and shapes needed for every contour of her pottery.

Unless the piece of pottery is to be quite large, she does not attempt to shape or bulge the sides until it is the desired height, Fig. 84F. The wide part of a large jar may be formed before it becomes too high. In a smaller jar, the coil formed irregularities in thickness have been left to be equalized in an even thinness, which she achieves by scraping and shaping with her gourd tools. At the same time Maria widens the jar to the distinctive shape, see Fig. 85, sketches 14, 15, and 16, with the left hand supporting the outside while the right hand slowly and gently presses the inside outward, Fig. 84G. Fig. 85, sketch 16, shows a scraper used to form the neck on a pot. After becoming completely dry the pottery is decorated and fired in a primitive kiln, Fig. 89, page 108.

Indian pottery and method of decorating

It is an interesting fact that the Indians of the Southwestern United States and Mexico have always been able to find sources of almost pure iron oxides, occurring in tiny nodules in some formations of the mesa country, also natural ocher and copper in combinations with iron oxide. From these the Indians can produce the shades of brown, yellow, orange, red, and green, used to decorate their pottery.

They grind the fragments or nodules to a fine powder in a cavity of a flat stone or in their metates, the hollowed out stone in which they also grind corn, then mix them with the clay and enough water to make a slip with which to paint designs on the dried pottery before firing.

Another pigment used by Maria Martinez is made from the juice of the "bee plant," concentrated by boiling to a charred mass. This is ground into a water solution which produces the matt or dull finish on her black pottery. Before applying this substance to the design area, usually a background for symbolic designs, the rest of the pot is rubbed with a smooth stone to a soft shine. Sometimes two or more coats of the clay slip is applied and each one rubbed when dry.

Originally Maria's black pottery, Fig. 86A, was a reddish brown, the color of the natural clay she uses. The iron oxide in the clay causes it to become black when exposed to the fumes from the bee plant pigment and the nitrogen released from the animal manure mixed with the firewood (also the carbon from the slow burning wood). These fumes are kept from escaping and the fire is partly smothered by a covering of ashes, broken pottery pieces, and old metal roofing sheets. Pottery of the Hopi Indians is shown in 86B and C.

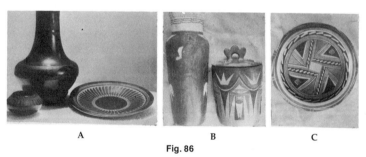

A   B   C

Fig. 86

Indian design method

The marking out of a design on a pot is an ingenious technique of primitive origin, and is largely a freehand process. The Indian potter blocks out the areas of a design, which he develops as he works. Formerly charcoal or some chalky substance was used, but now he uses a pencil as in Fig. 87, sketch 1. The size and number of the design areas are laid out by sight, freehand or by the aid of a twig or piece of string. A freehand stroke is sometimes made by pressing the arm against the body (when crouched over the pot), placed on the knee, Fig. 87, sketch 7. The lines are drawn from point to point as the body is straightened up.

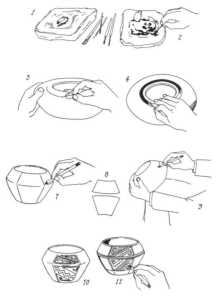

Fig. 87

When the boundary lines are horizontal, they are drawn freehand with one or more fingers overhanging the top or bottom of the pot to serve as a distance gauge. This method is shown in Fig. 87, sketches 3 and 4.

The pigment is applied to the pot with a brush or applicator made from Yucca leaves, Fig. 87, sketches 1, 2, and 3. Short sections of the leaf are flattened at one end with the teeth, and reduced to the desired width by stripping off part of the fibers. Sometimes turkey leg tendons are used for brushes, the width of line on the pot is controlled by the number of fibers left in the brush. The moisture absorbed from the pigment makes the parallel fibers of the Yucca leaf more flexible. This brush is not used like the ordinary commercial brush. The back and forth sweeping motion is not the Indian technique. He charges the fibers with pigment by drawing the brush through the little pool of pigment toward himself, sketch 2. Lines are made on the pot by holding the fiber brush flat against the surface and drawing the brush from point to point in one direction, toward himself. This method of using the fragile fiber brush produces very uniform width and density of line and insures comparatively long life to the Yucca brush.

Pieces, which have been found in ruins of the Southwestern Pueblos, indicate that the prehistoric basket making people may have learned to mold their pottery jars in woven baskets and to fire them in the basket form, both to partially protect the clay and to develop the imprint of the design. This practice may have been the origin of designs applied with mineral or vegetable dyes, which persist in some of the Pueblos of New Mexico today.

The Pottery Maker of Santa Clara

The picture of Silva Nestor was taken at Tewa, which means, "Where the Roses Bloom beside the Water." As she stirs the fire that is firing her pottery, it seems that she is stirring up memories of the past.

The mystic smoke seems to form the warriors of the past. The mesa on the horizon is the famed "Black Mesa of San Ildefonso," the last battleground of the Indians where they fought the Spaniards until driven back into the desert. This battle occurred in 1690 under the leadership of Don de Vargas, the Conqueror.

Picture, Courtesy Talmadge Chilson

Fig. 88

Firing of Indian pottery

How the ancient potter discovered that a soft, fragile, and water absorbing piece of clay would become hard, durable, and also hold water after exposure to continued heat, will ever remain a mystery. Certain clays develop a finish in firing that resembles a glazed surface and is almost as hard. This may have been the accidental discovery of the Egyptians which led them to the development of the beautiful colored glazes which have survived the centuries.

Primitive people from prehistoric times down to the present use an open fire, with the piece of pottery either buried under some slow burning fuel or encased in a larger piece for protection from smoke and flames. A modern variation of this protective covering is made of clay which will resist high temperatures. This is called a "sagger."

The primitive kiln, still used in the Pueblos of New Mexico and on the Hopi Mesas of Arizona is little more than a hole in the ground, filled with pieces of wood, dried leaves, bark, and bits of broken pottery. The pottery is covered with sand, more broken pieces, then more fuel, scrub oak branches, and dry cakes of manure, which are held in place with stones and old pieces of sheet iron.

Maintaining the fire at the right temperature for the required period, often several days, is a test of the Indian potter's judgment and skill which enable her to produce near perfect pottery, such as that made by Maria Martinez.

Fig. 89

A firing of Maria's black pottery just uncovered.

The Colorado State Museum in Denver and other Art Museums have collected and preserved many examples of prehistoric pottery as well as that of Maria Martinez and other expert potters of the Southwestern United States. Examples of old Pueblo Indian pottery are shown in Fig. 91. Those in Fig. 90 are reproductions of the traditional Hopi designs and shapes of pottery made by J. B. Breslin, a rancher of La Junta, Colorado.

Fig. 90

Fig. 91

CHAPTER **5**

Decoration of Fabrics, Paper and Wood

Design printing on fabrics came into practice as an adaptation of the wood engraving method of printing manuscripts in the Twelfth century. It was about that time when paper was introduced into Europe and hand-lettered scrolls of parchment were replaced with the less costly method of printing. Centuries later as the industrial era began, wood blocks for the printing of fabrics were developed. Woodcuts were used by the Romans to print letters on leather, wood and cloth.

In the Orient, the independent development of printing letters and illustrations from woodcuts dates from earlies times. The Chinese used woodblocks to print fabrics, as well, and for many years block printed silks were imported by England from India, Persia, and China. When the government banned importations in order to stimulate the silk industry of Britain, the process of design printing on silks and other fabrics became highly perfected.

Over the years, design printing on fabrics has become an intricate machine process of printing from engraved rollers, but the making of hand blocked fabrics of individual design remains a field for original and exclusive expression.

Other methods of design printing on fabrics will be given for the beginner, and block printing described later. For any method the following precautions will help insure satisfactory results:

1. Wash the fabric if it contains any size or starch.

2. For the first attempt, light colors should be chosen. Smooth cottons, linens, rayons, or nylons are easiest to work on.

3. Use a blotter or absorbent paper between the material to be printed and the surface on which the work is done. A large bread or drawing board makes a good work surface.

4. Always test paint on a scrap piece of material. Keep a clean paper or cloth available to wipe excess paint from the brush before applying it to the fabric.

5. Do not wash the fabric for at least 10 days after printing, as the paint must first become thoroughly dry. Follow directions that come with good quality paint. There are many good brands of textile colors on the market and it is recommended that a beginner start with the ready mixed colors.

Design Printing

Stencil method adapted from demonstration by Mary Francis Bunning, at Northland Recreation Laboratory of 1954.

The tools and materials include: transparent stencil paper, stencil knife or razor blade in a handle, masking tape, oil type brushes with tapered points, and stencil colors.

Process for printing a fabric with a stencil

1. To cut a stencil, lay a piece of transparent stencil paper over the design to be reproduced. Mark a guide line around one corner if more than one color is to be registered, then prepare the stencils for each color.

2. With a pencil, draw around all portions of the design which are to be of one color. Fit a piece of stencil paper for each color into the corner guide, then make an outline of each successive color. Write in the color and a check mark to indicate the upper right hand corner of the stencil.

3. With a stencil knife or safety razor blade, cut out the portions of each stencil for the indicated design color to be used. When these are complete for all the colors or design elements, stack the stencils together, right side up and right hand corners together, and hold them up to the light to check the total design.

If the stencils for the total design are complete and correct, cut a key in the upper right hand corner through all the stencils, held closely together.

Method of stencil printing on fabrics

1. Lay the first stencil on the fabric, smoothly stretched over a piece of blotting paper or other absorbent paper. Note where the key comes and stick a small piece of paper or masking tape directly over the key, on the fabric. Draw the outline of the key on the paper with a pencil. Do this with each subsequent stencil to be assured of perfect alignment.

2. Dip a stencil or oil type brush into the first color and work it on paper to remove excess paint. Apply the color from the edge of the stencil to the center of the design, rotating from the stencil edge until the opening is painted, with the centers light or unpainted.

3. Continue to place the prepared stencils in order according to the key, and apply the selected color from the edge of the stencil toward the center as before. Leave the set of stencils in position until the colors are dry, to avoid any blurring of the design. Then remove the stencils and touch up any places that were missed.

Color printing freehand

1. Many simple and beautiful freehand designs can be developed with freehand brush strokes. Interesting patterns may be made from the torn edges of paper held on the fabric or attached with tape. Apply the color from the edges of the paper on to the fabric. Gold textile paint is especially effective on colored fabrics. Gold outlines on a fabric previously stencil printed will emphasize the design.

2. After experimenting with freehand borders, such as scallops and zig-zags, on a trial piece of material, try applying freehand or make a design pattern and transfer them to the fabric. This may be done with a charcoal pencil in the same way as the method used for transferring a design to wood, described on page 115.

Observe color combinations that are pleasing in printed materials, or adapt a design with details and colors different from the originals.

Early American designs

The colorful, gay and whimsical painting which once decorated nearly every household article in the homes of the German folk, who came to Pennsylvania at the invitation of William Penn, is the inspiration for many decorative arts as applied to fabrics, pottery, printing on paper, as well as wood. Designs developed by the Pennsylvania Dutch have been aptly called "the only truly American Folk Art."

A stylized design for note paper and a reproduction of Pennsylvania Dutch figures and flowers from a calendar are shown in Fig. 92 and Fig. 93A and B.

Fig. 92

A   **Fig. 93**   B

The Plate and Covered Bowl in Fig. 94 are good wood projects. The designs, painted with shades of brown dyes, resembles carvings that have been stained. The undecorated items may be obtained from suppliers, or turned on a home or cabinet shop lathe. Those shown in Fig. 94 are approximately one-half actual size.

Fig. 94

Tinware, earthenware, dishes, glassware, ornamental pottery, and more enduring pieces of furniture, now displayed in museums or held in treasured collections, are evidence of this unique folk art, which is perhaps more admired and appreciated today than when it was commonplace to the Pennsylvania Dutch.

Carved and brightly painted furniture, including dressers and chests, especially dower chests provided every daughter, occupied the men in the "off seasons" or the time between the seasons of farmwork. Meanwhile, the women made the elaborate coverlets and embroidered linens to fill the dower chests.

Decoration of wood

The decoration of wooden trays and plates with some of the typical motifs of the Pennsylvania Dutch, Fig. 94A-B-C-D, and the Scandinavians, who perfected the art they call "Rosemalerie," and beautify their homes with painted designs of typical charm and artistry, is a practical and enjoyable craft.

The process which follows was demonstrated at the Northland Recreation Laboratory, near Minneapolis, By Mrs. Harris (Chris) Jesperson. Mrs. Harris listed the following materials as needed:

"1. Tempera paints, poster paints, or any water-soluble paints to use on raw wood or wood that has been given a thin coat of shellac and rubbed down well. Artist oil paints, the basic colors or as many as wanted — to use only on a finished surface, since the oil will bleed into raw wood.

2. Two sizes of round sable brushes, perhaps a size 1 for finer lines, a medium soft charcoal or carbon pencil for transferring the designs, art gum or soft eraser, very fine sandpaper, and 000 steel wool.

3. White shellac to be diluted with denatured or wood alcohol, equal parts of each, and a brush to apply it, also a good clear quick drying rubbing varnish. If an article will have much wear, use spar varnish. Apply with a brush, and remove excess with old nylon hose.

4. Paste wax, tissues, and soft cloths for cleaning, brushing, dusting, polishing. Turpentine to clean varnish from hands."

The wooden household articles, Fig. 94A, decorated in the Pennsylvania Dutch style by Mary Francis Bunning, who demonstrated the methods of fabric decoration, described on page 111, Fig. 94, are typical of both the floral motifs and the lettering in German that is characteristic of this art. Similar designs may be used for the decoration of such articles, or original ones, with English sentiments, adapted for more modern forms of painting.

The first example described by Mrs. Harris was a wooden tray or plate to use as a decorative piece and for serving. The following instructions were given:

"1. Sand the tray very thoroughly, even though it seems smooth to the first touch. Rub always with the grain of the wood, using a fine grade sandpaper to smooth down the wood. Rub lightly, do not bear down on it. The more you sand the wood, the easier it will be to paint on the surface. When you have sanded enough (as you may think), repeat the process and finish by smoothing one way with your hand.

2. The design. We must remember that the popular hand decorated wooden articles from former days, whether they are Scandinavian or Pennsylvania Dutch peasant designs or from any other national source, were surely done by amateurs and not skilled artists. Don't try to copy their ideas but study and absorb and appreciate their work, then draw from your own resources.

3. Know your designs and keep them simple and pure and consistent. For example, one should not mix geometric or abstract designs with the simple curves of a peasant flower or figure." (The ancient naturalistic and symbolic designs of old Mexico, described and pictured by Senor Jorge Enciso are suggestive for modern abstract development, Fig. 3 and 4, pages 4 and 5, also Fig. 95A.)

4. Above all, do try a simple design first. Remember that the simple things are the most beautiful; and the little touches that you give express you. If you are not familiar with sources of design suggestions, or do not have a notebook of design motifs, this is the time to start one. Embroidery designs in color, as given in different pattern books, are often suitable for a first effort in wood painting. These include designs similar to the types of animal, bird, and flower motifs which are typical of the Pennsylvania Dutch and Scandinavian wood decorations.

5. When you are satisfied with the design you have chosen, draw it on a piece of tracing paper, exactly as it will appear on the plate, then proceed as follows:

6. Outline the design on the *back, or wrong* side of the tracing paper, with a carbon pencil. Be careful not to make the lines too heavy and leave the fine lines to be filled in freehand, also some of the details. It is easier to paint these later than to have many lines in the carbon pencil impression.

7. Lay the design on the tray or plate, carbon side down, and rub with a smooth round surface, such as the back of a spoon or your finger. Be careful and do not let the paper slip. This should transfer the design clearly enough to follow when painting the wood. If you have left the background a natural wood, it is easier to paint with show card watercolors. They are easy to blend, quick drying, and after being protected with varnish, are just as durable as with any paint. Always paint *from* the design outline, the larger areas first.

8. If you have used a background color, oil paint, or enamel, it is necessary to use oil paints for decoration. Thin the oil paint with equal parts of turpentine and varnish. Your design will be more interesting if you dip into a color, such as blue, then a touch of white with as few brush strokes as possible, but letting the brush do its own shading. Leaves are more interesting if you combine green with a touch of red and yellow. Outlining makes a design more distinctive."

Ancient Mexican Designs

Fig. 95A

Fig. 95B

The photographs of tray designs in Fig. 95B are from modern Mexico, painted with the vivid bright colors that the Mexican artists use. The beautiful sky blues do not photograph well, and shades of gray, as the blues appear, must be imagined in blue.

9. When the paint is entirely dry, remove any pencil marks or smudges. Apply three coats of varnish (pads made of nylon hose make good applicators). Wipe the first coat on carefully and *quickly* to avoid any "bleeding" of the colors previously painted. Hold the plate up to the light and *smooth the finish coat in one direction only, with the grain.* Remove, with the nylon pad, any dust particles, air bubbles or ridges of varnish.

10. If a skin forms on the varnish, strain it through a piece of nylon hose. Heating with a little turpentine will restore varnish that has thickened to the right consistency. *Caution. Put the varnish mixture in a small can or jar and heat it in hot water. Do not put it on a burner.*

11. Rub each coat down with 000 steel wool, carefully wiping away any of

the particles with a clean cloth. Finish the last coat with powdered pumice and paraffin oil. A final coat of polished paste wax will protect your plate and "make it last forever."

Clean your brushes immediately and *never let them* stand, brush end down in water or a cleaner. Always put them away in a jar or can brush side up.

The linoleum block

Printing fabrics, paper and cards with individually created designs is easily possible with the modern linoleum block, which may be obtained from craft supply houses or made from plain color remnant pieces of the heavier grade of linoleum mounted on a ¾" piece of plywood.

Preparation of the linoleum block

1. Clean the surface thoroughly, then coat it with a film of white lead paint which is a little thicker than for usual painting. White surface blocks in a limited assortment of sizes are available from suppliers. Plain linoleum squares and rectangles are supplied in a wide variety of sizes.

2. Mix the paint, about a tablespoon full for a block, from the bottom of the can where it is thicker, with a few drops of drier in a small glass jar. Spread this with a fine brush in an even smooth film across the surface of the linoleum block, brushing it lightly in one direction, then crosswise. Allow the film of paint to dry several hours or until no longer tacky.

3. Trace the design drawing with a medium hard pencil on good bond paper with all details, as it will appear in the impression. When ready to transfer it to the prepared surface of the linoleum, place it for a moment on a damp cloth to slightly dampen the back of the paper.

4. Place the drawing face down on the linoleum and attach to the sides with scotch or drafting tape so that it cannot slip. Hold the paper firmly against the linoleum with the left hand, rub the entire surface with the flat side of a bone folder or the handle of a knife. Make sure no portion of the design is left unrubbed in this way.

5. When the paper is removed the pencil design will be imprinted on the white film on the surface of the linoleum, in the reverse position as required for the correct "right side up" printing, according to the original plan of the design.

Cutting the linoleum block

1. Several of the standard wood carving tools are useful for cutting a block. It may be necessary to shorten the handles for this work. These are shown in Fig. 96 as B, the veiner which makes the V cut; C, the short radius gouge which cuts a U-shaped groove; and D, the long radius gouge which is used for shallow grooves. E is a straight chisel for beveled lines and F the incising knife with which the outline is cut.

2. For the fine detail of design outlines, use the short, sharp V veiner, held between the thumb and first two fingers so that the tool may be guided and a light pressure maintained. This permits the cutting of lines and curves

on a slight slant which leaves a stronger margin to support the edge of the design outline, than a straight vertical cut would. Place the block so it may be turned when cutting the curves. Do not cut the lines but keep the edge of the tool just outside them at all times.

3. After the design outlines have been cut, remove the background areas with the gouges. These must be carefully held and the pressure controlled to avoid cutting into the design margins at any point.

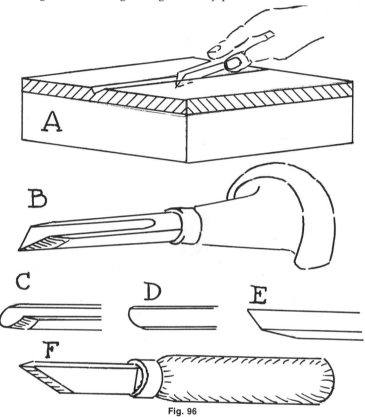

Fig. 96

Printing fabrics with the linoleum block

The photographs in Fig. 97 show three designs for Boy Scout neckerchiefs, insignia representing troop or patrol emblems, which were made on a linoleum block according to the method given below:

1. Aniline dyes and prepared textile paints which are waterproof and flexible are available from suppliers for linoleum block printing on fabrics.

2. Spread a film of the coloring medium on a glass slab or palette. Ink the roller or brayer by rolling it through the paint until it is evenly coated. Avoid any excess as the color may spread beyond the design areas and into the background and cause blurring. Fig. 98, sketch B, shows the inking of a block.

3. Stretch the fabric to be printed in a frame over a pad consisting of newspaper and four or five sheets of blotting paper. Form guide lines by stretching strings as shown in Fig. 98, sketch D. Try the impression of the inked block on remnant pieces of cloth, then carefully position the block on the fabric.

4. Exert sufficient pressure on the block, Fig. 98D, to slightly indent the blotting paper beneath the fabric. Ink the roller as before and repeat the printing in all design areas.

5. The linoleum block method of design printing is especially practical for the application of unit designs with a variety of colors, as different inked rollers are impressed by turns. Borders on all kinds of household items and children's garments add a distinctive and original charm. Repeat designs on fabrics for sport clothing can be printed from blocks designed to symbolize the sport in many kinds of design adaptation.

6. Textile paints have special directions for setting colors. Aniline dyes are usually steam set by hanging the fabric, pinned open to a support, above a container of boiling water until it is damp heated through but not wet.

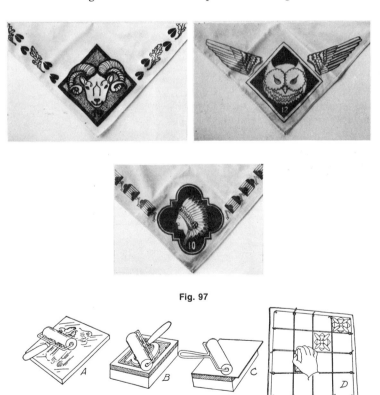

Fig. 97

Fig. 98

Printing cards with the linoleum block

1. In printing cards with a linoleum block, the process requires that the card be pressed on the inked block, as shown in Fig. 98, sketch C in which a clean roller is used to exert equal pressure. It is necessary to wedge the block in a fixed position. Watercolors or special inks for card printing are available from suppliers, also cards and suitable paper for use with the different inks.

For schools and organizations (also individuals making a quantity of cards or paper folders), a special block printing press saves time and insures uniformity of printing. Such presses are available for sizes up to 9" by 12".

2. The *space requirements for lettering* cards and folders usually necessitates a design arrangement that allows space for lettering. The decoration motiff and lettering are more effective if they harmonize in simplicity.

3. In cutting a linoleum block for cards or folders which requires the lettering of a name, message, or sentiment, such as a bookplate, birthday or Christmas card, a plain form of lettering can be cut as well as the design, but this must be in reverse to read correctly when printed. Prepare the design with lettering on firm copy paper, then turn the paper over, and outline both the design and the lettering in reverse, as they now appear.

4. Transfer the design and lettering to the block as directed in the section on page 117 and cut with special care for the alignment of the letters.

Depending on the form of letters desired, it may be best to plan space for them and cut only the design. After the cards or folders are printed, draw or paint the letters in any desired form.

For easily followed instructions on a great variety of lettering designs, as well as suggestions for posters and cards, the *Speedball Text Book,* published by the Hunt Pen Company, Camden, N.J. is recommended.

Silk screen printing

Silk Screen Printing is a method of imprinting designs on textiles in a process developed in this country, an adaptation of the stencil method with which it is used. It enables the craftsman to print larger areas than is possible with blocks and permits identical duplication with less expense of time and effort. The screen is a piece of porous cloth attached firmly to a wood frame.

The material originally used was silk, hence the name of the process. Fine cotton cloth, organdy, or muslin will be satisfactory for limited use, if washed to remove all starch or other filling.

Preparation of the screen

Stencil screens (with or without the special silk screening materials mounted in the stencil screens) are available from suppliers, and can be obtained with a base to which the screen frame is attached with hinges having removable screws. The sizes offered correspond to the average size of cards, letterheads, double letter sheets, and posters. The poster size, 16 by 28 inches is the maximum size. The average size of 10 by 14 inches can be used for cards, folders, and smaller sizes, besides the regular letterhead size.

The average size frame for silk screen printing, which is supplied in kits, is 10 by 14 inches, inside dimensions. This size may easily be constructed in the school or home woodworking shop. The following materials are required:

For the frame,
>   4 pieces of selected straight grain pine or other soft wood.
>
> >   2 lengths for top and bottom ends, ¾ by 1¼ by 16½ inches
> >   2 lengths for sides, ¾ by 1¼ by 12½ inches
> >   1 piece for the back bar, ¾ by 1¼ by 12½ inches

For assembly, as indicated in Fig. 99, sketch 1.
>   2-¼ by 3 inch bolts
>   2-¼ inch wing nuts
>   2-¾ inch diameter washers for ¼ inch bolts
>   1 pair 2½ or 3 inch loose pin butt hinges, bright metal or brass pierced for wood screws and 12 No. 6 by ¾ inch countersunk wood screws to match.

For the base, a drawing board or other level smooth board, at least 4 inches wider and 6 inches longer than the screen frame which is hinged to it.

For the screen, 1 piece of screen silk, number 12 mesh, with sufficient margin to tack to the frame as shown in Fig. 99, sketch 2. The screen silk should be preshrunk, then dampened after being tacked in place so that it will become perfectly tight when dry. For preshrunken cotton materials this is not necessary.

Tack the sides of the material first, starting at the center and completing one, then stretching the opposite side taut while tacking it, from the center to each corner as before. Tack the ends from the corners toward the center, stretching out all the wrinkles in the process. Cover all the tacks with screen masking tape, Fig. 99, sketch 3. Extend the tape over the inside edge and the inner margins of the frame.

Make sure the base or table for the screen is level so that the frame will set closely against it, preventing any variations in the pressure against the cloth in the printing process. Fig. 99, sketch 1-2-3, shows the construction of the frame and method of attaching the screen cloth.

Silk screen stencils

The preparation of a paper stencil:

1. Draw an original design or trace from a sketch or picture on bond paper. Choose a simple design for the first experiment.

2. Place the drawing on the base between the guides beneath the silk screen, and cover with transparent tracing paper, held in place with removable tape.

3. Holding the stencil knife like the tracing pencil, cut carefully through the tracing paper, without cutting the design drawing.

4. Transfer the design stencil to the silk screen, now lowered against it, with the drawing still in place, by applying the stencil paint across the screen with the squeegee as indicated by Fig. 99, sketch 4.

5. Remove the drawing from the base and place the card or paper to be printed directly beneath the design outline, now held to the screen with the paint.

6. Lower the stencil frame and screen against the card and squeegee more paint evenly across the screen with enough pressure to imprint the design on the card or paper. After printing the desired quantity, remove the paper stencil and clean the screen with a paint remover or thinner.

(A special "printmaker's tape" or mat is available in sheets 8½ by 11 for screen stencils on which the design can be traced directly.)

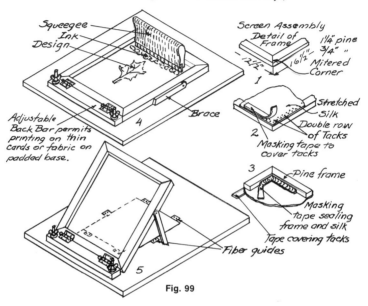

Fig. 99

Preparation of a lacquer film stencil

Since the paper stencil cannot be cleaned and reused after serving for one lot of printing of a single design, the lacquer film stencil is preferable. The lacquer film stencil as well as the screen may easily be cleaned and used as many times as desired as long as it remains intact. Remove film with lacquer thinner when no longer usable or wanted.

1. Prepare and place the design drawing on the screen base within the guides directly beneath the hinged screen.

2. Cover the drawing with the same size piece of lacquer film, which is a thin layer of film backed by a layer of transparent paper which must be placed against the drawing. The lacquer surface may be identified by its glossy appearance, which is uppermost.

3. Attach the layers of film to the base with tape, so they will not move. With the special stencil cutting knife, cut the design outline through the film layer, leaving the paper intact to hold the parts of the design until the film is attached to the silk screen.

4. With a little lacquer thinner on a cloth pad, used as an adherer, rub the surface of the screen over the design until complete contact has been made with the film, which is thus transferred to the screen.

5. Wipe with a dry cloth to remove all thinner from the face of the screen, and peel off the paper backing from the lacquer layer which is now attached to the screen.

6. Protect the marginal areas between the design area and the edges of the screen frame with strips of masking tape. This is to prevent any of the paint from seeping through to stain the paper or fabric being printed.

Design printing with the silk screen film stencil Fig. 99

For fabrics, excellent textile paints in paste form are available. Dyes are sometimes used, but these require some thickening such as dextrin or starch, (in a thick cooked form). An advantage to dyes is that they are partially transparent and one shade or color may be applied over another to produce a third shade.

1. Apply the color medium or paint to the screen with the squeegee, (a piece of rubber held in a grooved piece of wood), which is without a handle so it can be used with one or both hands. Spread a small quantity of the color paste along one end of the screen, closed over the paper or fabric to be printed, and push it with the squeegee across and through the screen to the opposite end. Push any remaining paint back to the other end. Add more paint paste and repeat the process if necessary to imprint the entire design in every detail. *Printing on a fabric* with the silk screen requires that a pad be placed under the fabric to obtain the best imprints.

1. Prepare the printing pad by placing a piece of unbleached muslin or old sheet over a double thickness of flannel or a felt table protector. Stretch the material to be printed carefully over the padding with the margin parallel to the edge or guide marker. Pin or baste the material with needle and thread to the padding.

2. With the screen in place and the frame closed over the material, spread a little of the textile print paste just beyond one margin of the design and quickly smooth it with the squeegee over the entire design area. Work the squeegee back and forth as many times as is necessary to obtain a perfectly even spread of color. More paste may be added as needed, but be careful not to have an excess.

3. If a series of design motifs are to be printed, lift the screen and place according to the desired positions, which may be indicated by thread or colored chalk markings. To avoid smearing, it is a good plan to print every other design, then go back after the first have dried, and print those in between.

It is possible to print a design with several colors, but a different screen will be required for each color. The first color must have completely dried and the area of this impression blocked out on the screen with masking tape, unless a new stencil has been prepared. Clean the paint from the screen and film stencil with a paint remover.

4. Permit the colors in the finished work to become entirely dry and then set them by steaming as described under block printing. If the fabric is washable, it may be hand washed with mild soap.

1. Batik, Javanese wax resist method

Batik is a form of design printing, used primarily in the decoration of fabrics. The correct word is *battik,* a Hindu-Javanese term which is applied to textiles decorated in successive stages by the wax resist method on the island of Java, where the art is developed to a high degree of perfection. Little is known of its origin, but it is said to have been practiced in Java by the Hindus, who were among the first people to learn the art of textile decoration centuries ago.

When Indonesia (then called East Indies) was occupied by the Dutch in the Sixteenth century, the colonists were fascinated by the beautiful fabrics which the natives used for garments and for religious vestments. Books on the batik art of Java have been written by Dutch authors, but none have been translated into English as yet.

The Javanese batik designs consist of a wide range of floral and geometric motifs. Fantastic animal and bird forms are depicted, also allegorical figures, somewhat similar to those found in excavations of prehistoric Mexico, shown on pages 4 and 5, Fig. 3 and Fig. 4.

In parts of Europe, Easter eggs are decorated by a batik or wax method. In Czechoslovakia, elaborate designs and symbols are used in painting the eggs, and similar decorations are applied to woodenware articles for household use.

The Wax Batik method, along with simplified methods, will be described which will make it possible for the beginner to enjoy this fascinating craft with minimum equipment and with the assurance of success.
The tools required are:

Tjanting tool, prepared batik wax (or 4 parts liquid wax and 5 parts paraffin blended together). Glass or tin for melting wax.

Design and coloring brushes.

Small deep pan, candy thermometer.

Graphite paper, drawing board, tracing tool.

Adjustable frame, dye bath (aniline-alcohol solution), gas line.

Rubber gloves, paper towels, thumbtacks, pressing iron.

Materials:

Unloaded or pure dye silk is usually selected. Cotton fabrics are satisfactory if first laundered to remove any starch. Light shades only are used, and very heavy materials are difficult to handle.

A margin of at least one inch should be allowed for tacking or sewing the material to the frame.

Transfer the design from a blueprint or sketch on tracing paper.

1. Trace the design on a thin fabric from the tracing paper placed underneath. Thumbtack both to a drawing board and use a fine pencil, such as a colored Mongol pencil of a color similar to the design outline.

2. On firm materials, place graphite paper against the cloth with the tracing on top and tack all to the drawing board. Be sure the cloth is perfectly smooth and evenly placed with relation to the design (vertical with the weave of the cloth), before tracing the design outline with a fine pencil or tip of the tjanting tool, Fig. 100.

3. Remove the fabric and tack it on the frame as indicated in Fig. 100, sketch B.

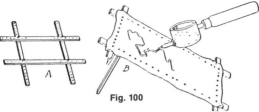

Fig. 100

Preparation of the wax

This step is most important as success depends on the correct temperature and mixture of the wax.

1. If prepared wax is used, put it in a glass or tin container and heat in a pan of water. Use cold water which should fill the pan to the level of the wax, and heat slowly.

An electric plate is desirable, but a gas or bunsen burner may be used if care is taken not to permit any of the wax to come in contact with the flame. Heat to a temperature of about 160 degrees or until the wax is entirely liquified.

2. If a mixture of wax and paraffin is to be prepared, melt both separately, before mixing so that the exact proportions may be determined. Heat to 160 degrees. Allow the wax and paraffin mixture to cool to 140 degrees, then fill the reservoir of the tjanting tool which should be heated in water and dried. Test the tool on a scrap of the material and if the wax does not run readily, clear the spout with a fine wire.

3. Follow the design outline with the tip of the tool, permitting the wax to penetrate the fabric and form a line on both sides of the cloth of about 1/16 inch. Hold in the position of sketch B and proceed as rapidly as possible. If necessary to lift the tip of the tool from the fabric for an instant, hold a piece of blotting paper under the tip to prevent a drop of wax from falling in the wrong place.

4. Leave a continuous line of wax on the fabric, otherwise the dye will run into the design area. If a wider line is desired, heat the wax until the line spreads slightly. At 160 degrees, the line will be 3/32 inch.

Brushes may be used instead of the tool for applying wax to large areas which are not to be dyed. Wax all parts that are to remain the original color, and all that will later be dyed other colors.

Dyeing the design

1. Dampen the material with *lukewarm* water, (cold water may crack the wax and hot water will melt it), and dip it in a *cool* dye bath of the lightest color of the design. When the color is uniform, remove the cloth from the dye and rinse in cool water until the dye ceases to run. Pin it on the stretcher and pat gently with paper towels to hasten drying.

2. When the fabric is thoroughly dry, cover all parts which are to remain the first color with an application of wax. Again dampen the fabric in lukewarm water and immerse in the second dye bath. Remove, rinse, and dry on the

stretcher as before. Several dips may be made, but it is best to restrict the coloring to three or four harmonious shades.

Removal of wax

Two methods of removing wax are possible:

1. Place the fabric between blotting papers and press with a moderately hot iron. Move the paper frequently so that the wax can be absorbed in the clear spaces of the paper. Remove any remaining traces of wax by dipping in gasoline.

2. Immerse the fabric directly in gasoline and stir until the wax is absorbed. It may be necessary to change the gasoline several times if a quantity of wax has been used.

2. Batik, dye stopper or gum arabic method

The same principle as that employed in the wax method is used, in that the outlines or other parts of the design and fabric are protected by a dye resisting agent, when the color is applied. This is a simplified process but color effects as beautiful as the wax batik can be secured.

The tools and equipment required includes:

Two ounces gum arabic dissolved in about 6 ounces of water.

Flat liner or pointed brushes for outline.

Round watercolor brushes for backgrounds, one of each for as many colors as are used.

Two medicine droppers, drawing board, paper towels.

Adjustable frame, thumbtacks, small piece of glass (about 4 by 6 inches).

1. Transfer the design to the cloth, using graphite paper between the tracing and the material, or trace directly from a blueprint or sketch. The drawing board or other firm level surface should support the fabric underneath.

Use silk or cotton fabrics, same as for wax batik. Pieces must be large enough to allow a margin for tacking to the frame. For large areas such as pieces of a garment, it is possible to attach one end to the edge of a table with thumbtacks pressed through a folded strip of the material on a straight edge of the fabric, while applying the color resist. Keep the tension equal during the application of the dye stopper.

Application of Dye Resist.

2. If the outline is to remain the color of the original fabric, apply the clear gum arabic solution with a fine pointed brush along the design tracing.

Experiment on a piece of fabric before touching the design outline, to test the consistency of the solution, and the method of controlling the width of line, by varying the pressure of the brush and the rapidity of motion.

3. The solution should seem like syrup and flow from the tip of the brush in a line about 1/16 to 3/32 inch in width. If it does not penetrate the fabric, it is too thick and may be thinned with a little water. If too thin, it will run and spoil the outlines in the coloring process. The solution will thicken by evaporation if left exposed a few minutes in an open dish. All areas which are to resist color, as well as the outlines, should be "stopped out" with the Gum Arabic solution. The fabric must be entirely dry before coloring.

Color Outlining of the design may be readily done with the Gum Arabic solution to which a little of the concentrated dye has been added.

1. Mix only a small quantity as needed and combine exactly as directed. *First* put about a teaspoonful of the Gum Arabic solution in a small container and *second* add very slowly, with a medicine dropper, a few drops of the dye, stirring gently until the shade is uniform. *Caution:* If the process is reversed or excess dye added at one time, the mixture will coagulate.

2. A small quantity of the solution may be prepared on a piece of glass. Drop on the glass a very little of the Gum Arabic syrup, which will retain a globular shape. Add a drop of dye with the dropper or a fine brush, and mix carefully with the outline brush before applying. If it dries, mix in a little water to restore the right consistency.

3. Outline the design as directed in Step 2, also apply the colored solution to any areas that are to resist further coloring.

Design coloring

1. After the Gum Arabic has thoroughly dried, carefully flow the dyes, which have been diluted or mixed to the desired shades, over the design areas and along the outlines. Use the round brush.

2. Start about ¼ inch from the outline, as the color will flow toward the line. Any excess may run across it to the next area. Direct the brush strokes with the thread of the material, except near the outline, where the stroke must parallel the line. Use the liner brush for flowing the dye up to the outlines. Shaded effects may be secured with one dye by brushing the surfaces which are to appear lighter with clear alcohol before applying the colors.

3. If a crackle effect is desired, coat the entire surface of the fabric with the clear Gum Arabic solution, after the colors have been applied and the material entirely dry. When this coating is dry and stiff, crush the surface in the hands until the desired crackle lines have broken through the gum.

Then paint on a light wash of the color desired for the crackle lines. This should be a shade darker than the design colors, and if carefully rubbed into the crackle lines will result in a delicate webbed effect, which is characteristic of true batik.

4. Removing the Gum Arabic solution. Immerse the fabric in *cold water* or hold under the faucet and strip it with the fingers until all the gum has been dissolved. Place between paper towels and pat gently to remove as much of the moisture as possible. When nearly dry, press between a fold of dry paper towel or cloth with a moderately hot iron.

Fabrics decorated with batik coloring may be adapted to many purposes: scarfs, neckerchiefs, pillow tops, table runners, wall panel hangings, as well as motifs on sections of garments (before they are sewn together).

CHAPTER **6**

Lapidary Craftwork

The quest for precious and semi-precious gem stones has led men to search the far corners of the earth from time immemorial. The art of the prehistoric gem cutter and his fascination with the beauty and value of his polished jewels is evident in the museum collections found in ruins and excavations. ...This fascination still leads the searcher and he may be rewarded by finding stones of gem quality in the form of crystals or rock fragments in sedimentary deposits.

The ceaseless action of water in riverbeds and along the ocean shores often reveals pebbles of gemlike quality, which it has polished through centuries of time, as nature's forces have combined to bring these treasures from their original sources deep in the earth to places of access to all.

Tumbler Polished Stones
Fig. 101

Mrs. Lillian Hemmie, of the Rock Creek Lapidary, Colorado Springs, whose accomplishments, as a finder of gem stones and as a skillful worker who transforms them into perfect gems, has brought her a nationwide reputation, writes of her hobby with enthusiasm. With her permission the following quotations are included in the intriguing story of the lapidary art.

"The aim in Lapidary is to bring out all the hidden beauty of a piece of rock....The modern idea of free form and abstract design is all there, in the form of Malachite, Verisite and similar stones, deposited by Nature millions of years ago. Why break up and try to confine in tight rounds or ovals, the grace of line, form, and color that can be enhanced by grinding and polishing?

128

"After I rough grind a slab or rock, or a gem stone, I can see what the possibilities are for the size and shape of the finished stone, and for the best use of the natural pattern and design, the combinations of line and color that can be revealed. Remember that it is impossible to get a high polish on a scratched surface. I use a hand lens to be sure that all scratches are sanded off before I start to polish.

"The present demand for mounted semiprecious stones for accessories to costumes, stress color and texture interest. In Colorado petrified, (agatized) wood. The range of pattern and color are limitless, as the cells of the fallen trees were replaced with the minerals common to opals, agate and other silica. Over 200 million years ago these were all living trees.

"It is much more exciting to go rock-hunting and find material for cabochons than to buy them, so if you have the urge to become a rockhound, a good way to start is to join a local mineral club. I know of no craft or hobby that holds more satisfaction, a day out of doors, searching for nature's treasures, then cutting and polishing them to bring to light all their hidden beauty. This is a soul satisfying experience."

A — Arizona Agatized Wood   **B — Geode with Crystallized Agate**

C — Polished Agate Slab Specimens — Banded Agate

Fig. 102

Classification of Gems

Gems will be recognized as belonging to groups that are mainly opaque and translucent, with few but the diamond being transparent. The beauty of opaque stones depends on color, such as the lapis lazuli, opals, torquoise, and some jade. Translucent gems have depth color and light values which add to their charm. Amethysts, aquamarines, and topaz are among these.

A few gems are of organic origin: The precious pearl formed by the oyster is well known. Others are coral, the accumulated skeletal material of tiny marine animals; amber, a fossil resin from early coniferous trees; and jet which is a compacted black variety of lignite coal.

Lapis lazuli is a gem rock of metamorphic origin and is said to be the gem mentioned in the Bible as sapphire. Marco Polo in 1271 visited mines in Afghanistan, which had been worked for centuries, and are still said to be working. Other famous lapis lazuli deposits are in Chili and Siberia.

The diamond consists solely of crystalized carbon. Most gems are complex silicates, others are oxides, carbonates, and phosphates, of which the turquoise is the most famous.

Petrified or more correctly, agatized wood, such as the Arizona "petrified Forest," Fig. 102A, and wood, found in a few locations in Colorado, Oregon and Washington, is a source of a variety of beautifully colored and marked gems and specimens. As the tree cells became impregnated with minerals deposited from water, this carries away the woody fiber, leaving the tree structure of agatized cells.

The following table lists the main groups of semiprecious gem stones. They are available from dealers as preform, rough, and also as finished Cabochons, the term used for convex, half-round polished gem stones.

Amber	Moonstone	Amethyst
Azurite	Garnet	Jasper
Beryl	Jade	Onyx
Aquamarine	Jet	Rock Crystal
Golden Beryl	Lapis Lazuli	Rose Quartz
Bloodstone	Malachite	Smoky Quartz
Chrysoberyl	Obsidian	Topaz
Coral	Opal	Tourmaline
Feldspar	Petrified Wood	Turquoise
Amazonite	Quartz	Verisite
Labradorite	Agate	Zircon

Moh's scale of hardness, which follows, indicates rank of hardness, but not degree of difference in hardness, the diamond being more than ten times harder than talc.

Diamond	10	Apatite	5
Corundum (Ruby-Emerald)	9	Fluorite	4
Topaz	8	Calcite	3
Quartz	7	Gypsum	2
Feldspar	6	Talc	1

Gem Cutting Procedure and Equipment

The popularity of modern gemology and the art of lapidary has greatly increased in the last decade, with the scientific and industrial utilization of gems and more specific knowledge of gem sources and qualities, as well as a corresponding development of improved equipment for cutting and polishing.

Equipment has been standardized in different sizes and range of prices, from small units which are portable to sizes for industrial production, so that the individual, the school workshop, and commercial lapidary can obtain the minimum equipment or units designed for extensive work. A list of suppliers of guaranteed equipment will be found on page 454.

With access to a well equipped machine shop, the assembly of parts for lapidary equipment can be undertaken. Excepting the special devices for specific processes, and the diamond saw blades, essential parts may be procured from local suppliers. A source for usable motors and some parts can be found in dismantled washing machines and other household appliances.

Before attempting to procure and assemble lapidary equipment, it is recommended that a careful study be made of standard equipment and methods of operation, to determine the requirements for each unit and whether practical to assemble.

Dividing a Slab with a Diamond Trim Saw

Fig. 103

The process of cutting with a diamond saw

Diamond saw disc blades are available in diameters of 4 to 14 inches for the average workshop. (Larger diameters, up to 36 inches, are made especially for industrial work.) For the average diameter diamond blade one manufacturer, Craftools, Inc., lists the following rules for their proper use:

1. Use with a coolant at all times. Coolant must be kept clean and not allowed to heat.

2. Reverse the blade regularly for longer life and better cutting.

3. Use collars at all times. (These are washers which support the saw unit and hold it in position.) A safe rule for speeds, when cutting agate or similar material is to have the blade rotate at approximately 3,000 surface feet per minute. Use the following formula to determine correct shaft speed to provide 3,000 SFPM, 11,460 divided by the diameter of the blade in inches equals the R.P.M. or revolutions per minute of the blade shaft.

The maximum safe speed for the manufactured diamond saws is usually indicated.

Other precautions are:

It is important to have a switch control that will stop the motor when the cut is completed; it is also important to have the stone in contact with the saw when the motor is started.

The oil lubricant or coolant which has been developed for lapidary use is water soluble, noninflammable, and nonrusting. It should be wiped from the stone immediately with a cloth dipped in a detergent solution.

Grinding and Shaping a Cabochon Gem

Standardized cabochon shapes for opaque stones, such as the turquoise, agate, and malachite are illustrated in Fig. 104. The outline shapes, both surface and side view, may be used to make templates from which the roughly shaped or slab cut stone may be marked for finishing.

A   B

Fig. 104

Fig 104A indicates shapes preferable for opaque stones. Fig. 104B shows shapes more suitable for stones like the translucent moonstone or jade in which the beauty depends on depth and color play. These are cut to develop the angles of light refraction which will reveal them to the best advantage.

The grinding of the cabochon is shown in Fig. 106. This operation forms the rough gem stone into the approximate shape of the cabochon template. It may have been cut from a section or slab, called a cabochon blank, which requires shaping to conform to the selected template, or is a single piece like a water worn pebble, in which the natural freeform can be preserved with only slight shaping.

The recently developed process of grinding and shaping single stones in "tumbling" machines or power rotated drums, provides a wide variety of "baroques" or polished stones of various shapes and sizes. This process is described more fully on page 139.

The shapes shown in Fig. 105 for which templates may be secured from lapidary suppliers, are designed for gems which are to be mounted for rings or other pieces of jewelry in which the round, oval, and square shapes are preferable. As Lillian Hemmie recommends, the "chosen shape and size should make the best use of the natural pattern, with the combination of line and color that can be enhanced by grinding and polishing."

The grinding wheel, mounted on the arbor which operated the diamond saw, consists of grains or grit of *silicon carbide,* a product of the electric furnace, which are bonded together in rubber or a resinoid substance. For stones of average hardness, as given in the table on page 130, two wheels are required. These wheels, 8 to 10 inches in diameter and 1½ to 2 inches thick are suggested for the small experimental school, lapidary workshop, or the individual studio. They are necessary for the stages of grinding, sanding, and polishing and should be of 100 to 220 grit, adjusted to run at 1,000 RPM or less according to the manufacturers specifications.

They are mounted on the same arbor.

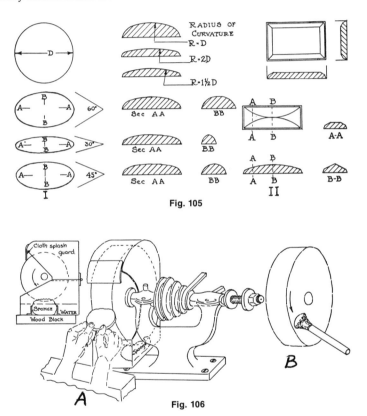

Fig. 105

Fig. 106

The *position of the lapidary worker,* as shown in Fig. 106 and 103, page 131, is directly in front of a wheel which is enclosed in a splash guard of sheet metal or plastic. The small sketch of the outer side view of the wheel shows a moistening sponge in a reservoir of water. An alternate way of moistening the wheel more uniformly for the grinding operation is to provide a continuous drip of water on the wheel from a faucet or a container mounted above the grinding wheel. With this a drain from the splash pan is necessary.

Caution. Never permit the wheel to stand in water. Remove the sponge and container, or turn off the drip of water as soon as the rotation of the wheel is stopped.

In the *process of grinding,* the worker's arms rest on the table or a support, so that a steady pressure can be maintained without undue fatigue. This pressure may vary according to the hardness of the stone, but should be as light as possible to prevent excessive wear on the wheel or the breakage of the stone.

To secure an even well-rounded contour, *keep the stone moving* across the face of the sheel and turn it frequently. Shape the stone close to the aluminum pencil marking for the finished outline of the base of the stone and grind it so that there is a slight slope toward the top and a small bevel for the mounting around the base edge.

A *holder for a segment of stone* or a small pebble *is called a "dop stick".* Select a stick which corresponds in diameter to the stone, 3½ to 6 inches long. Apply a special lapidary cement or a mixture of sealing wax and stick shellac, either of which has been melted over the flame of an alcohol lamp in a small container (a juice can is suitable). Dip the stick in the cement and coat the bottom of the stone, repeating the process until a partially hardened cushion of cement is built up for the base of the stone. Shape the edge of the cement (with wet fingers) around the stone, after pressing it firmly into the soft cement, to secure adhesion. Permit the cement to harden before using the stick. Fig. 107A and 107B show the hand sanding and polishing of a turquoise on abrasive cloth, and buckskin charged with jewelers rouge. In Fig. 107C the turquoise were polished by this method, as described on page 141.

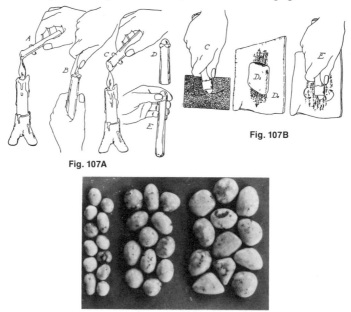

Fig. 107A

Fig. 107B

Fig. 107C

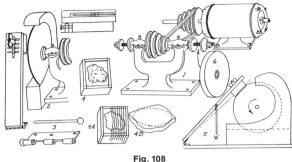

Fig. 108

Equipment for gem cutting

Figure 108 shows an assembly of essential equipment for slicing or leveling a gem stone or specimen. With the addition of different sizes of grinding wheels, abrasives, and polishing agents, it can be used for grinding, sanding, and polishing.

1. Fig. 108, sketch 1, shows the arrangement of a motor (1/4 to 1/3 horsepower) driven arbor with step pulleys adjustable for speed variations according to the position of the belt. Manufacturers of standard lapidary equipment stipulate "the maximum safe speed" for diamond saw cutting and also provide tables for the selection of grinding abrasives and polishing agents for specific stones.

2. Sketch 2 shows the diamond saw mounted on the arbor and partially protected by the removable sheet metal splash guard. The stone cutting diamond saw unit is a mounted blade of a special steel alloy impregnated with diamond dust by a manufacturing process.

Note: Prior to the development of the modern diamond saw blade, an experimental process to incorporate a diamond dust mixture in the cutting surface of the blade, was suggested by writers on gem cutting and suppliers of material. Now that manufacturers have perfected the diamond saw blade, which is available at a reasonable cost, no attempt should be made to prepare one in a home, school, or commercial shop.

3. Sketch 3 shows a loose pin hinge with which the arm for holding the stone is adjusted to the proper angle for the specified gravity pressure against the cutting saw blade. The reverse of the holding arm, or carriage, with the adjustable set screw is shown by the wheel in sketch 2 and as it operates in sketch 5.

4. Sketch 4 shows the gem stone with markings for the cuts, as held in a bed of plaster of Paris, secured to the bottom of the box with the bolt head of a set screw, inserted before the plaster is poured. An aluminum pencil is recommended for marking the stone as it will not wash off. A vise attachment for holding the stone in the carriage and in the right position for cutting is available from manufacturers and suppliers.

The plaster of Paris bed is prepared as follows:

Mix 1 cup of plaster in 1-1/3 cup of water. (It is important that fresh plaster be used.) Sift the plaster into the water slowly and stir to a creamy consistency. Let it stand about 2 minutes before pouring into the box, made to permit a margin of about ½ inch around the stone, previously placed in the box. Leave the box and stone undisturbed until the plaster is set and hard.

5.   The other method of holding the stone, clamped in a vise, requires that the jaws are lined with hard wood. Maple at least ½ inch thick makes a durable lining. Make sure that the stone is held rigidly by the pressure of the vise jaws, with the sharp surfaces embedded in the wood.

6.   Start the saw by hand pressure, then adjust the weight, as indicated in Fig. 108, sketch 5, to maintain the pressure. A power feed attachment is available for the carriage, and this has the advantage of being adjustable for the degree of hardness of the stone, and of maintaining a strong steady controlled pressure for the entire distance of the cut.

7.   Control the last ½ inch of the cut by hand pressure, after releasing the tension of the weight or disengaging the power driven feed, as excessive pressure at this point may damage the blade or break off a fragment of the edge of the stone. Avoid an irregular protruding edge which can be trimmed after the stone is removed from the vise or the plaster bed.

In Fig. 108, sketch 5, the position of the drip pan in relation to the saw blade is shown. The approved level of the oil lubricant (a mixture of kerosene and lubricating oil), or the special coolant recommended by the manufacturer, is high enough to submerge ¼ inch of the rotating blade. This is essential to keep the blade from becoming too hot from the friction of the sawing operation.

The position of the arm holding the plaster embedded stone, after the cut is completed, is indicated by the dotted line which shows that the blade has cut through both the box and the stone.

W. indicates the attachment of a weight to maintain the pressure. With a power driven feed attachment for the arm or carriage, the weight is not necessary.

Caution. Should the saw blade jam, quickly disengage the power feed or release the tension of the weight. Inspect the saw blade to make sure it is running in alignment with the carriage feed. Certain stones, like agate may dislodge particles of the diamond dust, or drag the blade over the embedded fragments. To restore the blade, first make sure of the position of the stone, bring it into the exact alignment required, then clear the surface of the blade by running it into a "blade dressing brick" which is clamped in the vise and several cuts made in it.

Sanding and polishing a cabochon

The sanding operation which follows the grinding, completes the shaping and smoothes the surface of the cabochon. There are three types of sanders now available: *drum, disc, and belt sanders,* all of which are fitted with *silicon carbide sanding cloth.* The drum sander is a cast aluminum drum with a cushion rubber or felt covered with a strip of silicon carbide sanding cloth around the rim and locked into the drum. The sanding is done on the rotating outer surface of the drum.

Disc Sanders which run either vertically or horizontally have one face surfaced, with the sanding cloth over a cushion of felt or rubber. In Fig. 109A the drum grinder or sander, depending on the abrasive used, is shown with a specimen held against the surface. A disc faced sanding wheel which rotates, as the arrow indicates, Fig. 109B, is shown with a cabochon mounted on a dop stick in position for shaping. Fig. 110A shows the arbor with disc covered with the abrasive cloth.

The *belt sander* is an endless strip or belt which runs over pulleys. Types for both wet and dry sanding are available. The belt sander yields slightly to the shape of the cabochon, thus preserving the template or freeform outline, while developing a satisfactory polish. The sanding operation should be continued until all bumps and scratches left from the grinding are removed.

Dry and wet sanding with the silicon carbide sanding cloth are both used. Caution is necessary with the dry cloth to keep the stone from getting too hot, which may cause it to crack. For this reason, and because of the dust from the dry sanding operation, the type of sanding cloth which can be used wet is preferable. This requires a device for a fine spray on the cloth and for a splash drain pan, as in grinding.

It is recommended that, before sanding a stone, new sanding cloth has the sharp silicon carbide grains smoothed by sanding a rough stone, kept for this purpose, for about 20 minutes. When the cloth is ready for use, apply the stone or cabochon mounted on a dop stick in a circular and side to side motion to prevent wearing grooves. Keep the stone in contact with light pressure, working from the lower edges toward the top. Compare frequently with the template or the aluminum pencil outline marking.

When the desired shape is obtained, Fig. 109A, and the surface of the stone free from scratches, it is ready for polishing. Make sure of this by examining with a hand lens, as a good polish cannot be secured if any scratches remain. Wash all particles, left from sanding, from the stone, dop stick, and the hands. Wear a clean apron for the polishing operation, also when changing grits or sanding wheels. Even one piece can ruin a stone. The *polishing operation,* Fig. 109B, is not difficult, if the sanding has been completely done.

Shaping a Specimen by Grinding   Polishing a Cabochon on Leather Disc

Fig. 109A   Fig. 109B

Felt surfaced wheels of different degrees of hardness, according to the stones to be polished are available from manufacturers, the sizes 6 to 8 inches in diameter being recommended for general use. The thickness of one inch is designed for stone polishing with a dop stick on the periphery of the wheel.

Many kinds of buffs are now available; muslin, cotton flannel, chamois skin, which are made up in several layers, laminated, and stitched together. Muslin is recommended for the softer stones, such as turquoise, malachite, and verisite. All buffs must be treated with polishing agents and many kinds are made by manufacturers of optical and lapidary equipment. Some of these will be listed below.

As illustrated in Fig. 110A and B, the *vertical disc type polishing wheel* is used in many lapidary shops. A wooden disc surfaced with leather over foam rubber is shown in Fig. 110A. Elk or heavy steerhide is stretched in place while damp, so that the leather shrinks taut when dry. Two other disc types of polishing wheels are shown in Fig. 110A. These are faced with canvas or a special cloth treated with a polishing agent. One is held in place with a rubber-band and the other a clamped metal ring. Fig. 110B shows a wooden wheel adapted to polishing cabochons on an internal surface.

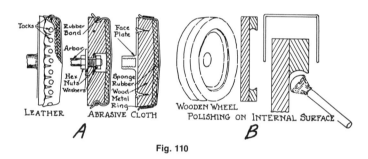

Fig. 110

Polishing agents for cabochons

Only one type of polishing agent should be used on a buff; separate buffs are thus needed if more than one agent is used. These are usually applied in a paste made by mixing the polishing powder in water. A paint brush makes a good applicator.

Tin oxide and tripoli are recommended for hard materials.

Cerium and Zirconium oxides are widely used. *Cerium oxide* is an optical polish.

Fine rouge powder is considered best for final polishing and makes a high gloss on most cabochons.

An aluminum oxide in the form of a powdered or levigated alumina is satisfactory for polishing most gem stones and is widely used.

In addition, manufacturers of lapidary equipment supply special polishing agents.

Note: It is recommended that the final polishing of soft stones be done on a soft muslin buff with a very little polishing agent, so the buff will be almost dry. Intermittent periods of polishing may be necessary because of the tendency for heat to develop. This sometimes cracks the stone.

Synthetic gems

Synthetic gems, products of specially constructed furnaces, are indistinguishable in appearance and identical in physical and chemical composition with natural mineral stones. They are grouped as *Corundum* or *Spinel,* being similar in chemical composition to these minerals. Both are extremely hard, ranking next to the diamond on the Mohs scale; they are 9 and 8 respectively.

The process of fusing the powdered alumina of the mineral *Corundum* with coloring (red oxide) was discovered after years of experimentation by the French chemist, Auguste Victor Louis Verneuil. Under the intense heat of an inverted oxyhydrogen blow pipe, which he invented, the components of corundum are melted into liquid form.

A catalyst causes this liquid to drop and solidify, with its natural crystalline structure, into cylindrical forms known as "boules," (a French term) which are later sawed or broken for shaping into cabochons or faceted gems. The process is still used, with some improvements, in the factory manufacture of synthetic rubies, sapphires, and other fine gems. Besides ruby, the colored gems or *boules* of the *corundum* group are made in a wide range of sapphire colors, duplicating the natural gems, including garnet and other precious stones. The *spinels* are similar and formed by the process of Verneuil, who added magnesium to secure a slightly less hard gem ranging in blue and green shades of sapphire and emerald. Later other French chemists developed a *synthetic tourmaline* with shaded and blended colors of the entire spectrum. The hardness of tourmaline is described as moderate.

Lapidarists and students are urged to read the fascinating descriptions of the natural gem stones as given in the technical gemology references. These are listed on page 453.

Cabochons formed by the tumbling process are available from suppliers as pre-forms in flat, semioval, or round, partially polished gem stones. Equipment for shaping and polishing stones by the tumbling process may be assembled in a studio or school shop, and is also available from suppliers in sizes for individual or commercial work.

As quoted in the instructions in the booklet, *So You Want to Cut Gem Stones* by Jack R. Cox, issued by the Covington Lapidary Eng. Corp., "A tumbler has a special type barrel which revolves at a slow rate of speed. In this barrel are put stones (of more or less similar hardness and size), with silicon carbide grit and water. After being tumbled in coarse grit, the stones are run in medium and then fine grits. Finally the stones are polished in a polish powder and water solution, then burnished in a detergent and water mixture."

The mounting of tumbled gems (also hand shaped and polished gem stones) has been greatly simplified by the availability of many kinds of mountings, plated, sterling, and gold from suppliers in equipment—especially for the tumbled freeform or irregular gems. A cap and attachment eyelet in various sizes makes possible attractive and practical settings with *epoxy* cement. Accurate and easily followed detailed instructions for tumbling and mounting gem stones are given in *Gem Tumbling and Baroque Jewelry Making* by Arthur Earl Victor and Lila Mae Victor.

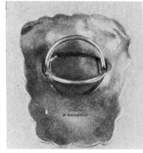
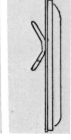

Bola Slides and Tips. Tumbled – Polished

Bent Ring Slide Soldered on
Cabochon Bezel Plate for Bola tie.

Fig. 111

Pendants Tumbled and Polished

Polished Agates mounted with chain
Bell Caps attached with
Epoxy Cement for a pendant.

Ear Pendants
Tumbled Polished
Agates mounted
in Bell Caps.

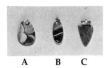

Other Types of Pendant Mountings
A – Tumbled stone Drilled for Ring
B – Cabochon-Ring on Bezel Plate
C – Flaked Arrowhead Band with Loop.

A   B   C

Cabochon Agates – Bezel Mounting for brooch and tie clips.

Brooch   Tie Clip

Fig. 111a

Sanding and polishing turquoise

Reference was made to the use of the dop stick in the grinding and sanding operation, where it was used to hold the gem stone against the abrasive wheel. Fig. 107A and B, sketches A to E, on page 134 indicate the hand method of sanding and polishing a rough cut turquoise held in sealing wax on a dop stick. Here the wax is softened in a candle flame and the stone attached as in D and E sketches while the wax was soft. After the wax hardened and the turquoise firmly held, it was sanded on abrasive paper in Fig. 107A, sketch C, to the desired shape. Polishing rouge on a piece of leather is shown in D and D1 and fine pumice powder for the final polish, also on leather in sketch E.

The turquoise is not usually shaped to an exact contour, but sanded and polished individually to retain color markings. Because of the matrix composition of the turquoise, *wheels must be used with special caution,* to avoid loosening matrix particles (see Fig. 104A and 107C).

Turquoise cabochons are shown in Fig. 107C in the actual sizes and typical shapes available from suppliers. This stone, which the Indians of the Southwest have cherished for centuries, is still shaped and polished by them in a primitive but effective technique. They shape the stones by rubbing them in a groove in a fine sandstone cliff formation, then polish on buckskin with a paste of sifted wood ashes. The Indian method of drilling turquoise for beads will be described later.

Making of spheres and beads from gem stones

In the Orient a craftsman of ancient time is said to have discovered that small spheres of quartz carried in the hand would cool the palms. This is a practice still continued in some Far Eastern countries. Crystal spheres have been found in excavations of the habitations of prehistoric people, and are thought to have been used for kindling altar fires. Over many ages and even to the present day, "crystal gazers" seek mystic power from the mesmerizing visions produced by continued gazing into a crystal sphere.

Some of the harder gem materials make colorful spheres for decorative use or for mineral exhibits. Agates, onyx, agatized wood, and some garnet and quartz crystals, may be formed into beautiful and perfect spheres. Agates, like the "thunder egg," are found in nodules of nearly spherical form.

A sphere cutting tool can be made from a short length of iron pipe of slightly less diameter than the sphere by the following method:

1. Bevel the inner edge of the pipe with a file, close the other end with a pipe cap. Fill with an abrasive compound and attach to the shaft of an electric motor.

2. Prepare a rough cut sphere, shaped from a cube by grinding off the corners and edges, hold it against the abrasive on the beveled edge of the pipe, and rotate it with a second length of pipe.

3. Repeat the process with three or four grades of silicon carbide, progressively finer. Thoroughly clean out the pipes between grades. Be sure all scratches are removed from the sphere and a perfectly curved surface developed with the application of the finest grit silicon carbide.

4. *Hold the sphere by hand* on a felt buffing wheel for the final polish, rotating it to retain the spherical shape.

5. *To form bead-size spheres,* attach the stone to a dop stick and rough grind and sand to the approximate size and shape of the desired sphere on felt wheels treated with the abrasive grits in grades medium coarse to fine, changing the dop sticks and cleaning the surface of the stone between grades.

Finish by polishing on a felt buff polishing wheel. These final steps may be deferred until the bead is drilled. Then it can be attached to a stick with a pin on which it will rotate, and in this way be held against the polishing buff.

Bead drilling

The spherical gem may be drilled for beads with a fine metal tube drill.

1. Rub an abrasive mixed with oil on the end of the drill and add a little to the hole as the drilling progresses. Hard stones may require a diamond tipped point for drilling. Fig. 112 shows the position and operation of the tube drill.

2. Hold the sphere or rounded cube in a pyramid shaped hole machined in the top of a metal block, which is screwed to the table of the drill press. As shown in Fig. 112, sketches C and D, this hole should extend down into or through the block.

3. Place the bead sphere in the center of the drilled hole with a tiny spot or starting hole for the drill scratched with a pointed tool. Drill the bead about two-thirds of the way through, then reverse its position, holding it exactly in line for the rest of the drilling with a pin which extends from the block rest (up into the previously drilled section, as shown in Fig. 112, sketch D). The gem drill moves up and down and also revolves.

4. Smooth the roughness in the completed hole by pushing the bead back and forth on a piece of stranded wire (like picture wire), charged with an abrasive paste. Pumice powder is suggested for the final smoothing of the hole. Wash any remaining particles of the abrasive from the bead before the final polishing.

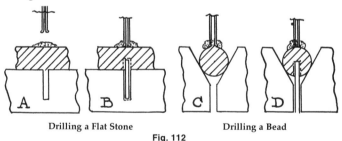

Drilling a Flat Stone   Drilling a Bead

Fig. 112

Bead making, Indian method

The *primitive Indian Pump Drills* were ingenious inventions, which employ mechanical principles of a high order. This interesting method of making beads or drilling gem stones is entirely practical for any shop.

1. The pump drill shown in Fig. 113 consists of the following parts: A drill shaft counter weighted near the lower end by a disc of wood. A cross stick which fits loosely around the drill shaft and is attached to the shaft by a leather thong. The thong passes through a slot in the top of the drill shaft and is attached to each end of the cross stick.

2. Operation of the pump drill is indicated in Fig. 113. The position of the thong, under tension, is shown in sketch A, twisted tightly around the drill

shaft, with the cross stick raised, in sketch B. As a downward pressure on the cross stick revolves the drill shaft, the thong unwinds.

The weighted drill shaft will continue to revolve for a moment after the pressure on the cross stick is removed. This rotation is sufficient to rewind the leather thong around the drill shaft while the cross stick is lifted to its upper position. Downward pressure again exerted on the cross stick revolves the drill. The direction of rotation of the drill changes with each downstroke, which operates the drill point in the stone. A little practice will develop the necessary skill to use this primitive type of drill which cuts with surprising rapidity.

Regular sustained up and down pressure as indicated in the sketches of Fig. 113 maintains the momentum of the weighted shaft sufficiently to keep it revolving to drive the drill point through the stone. Drilled pieces of turquoise to be made up in a necklace are strung on a cord of thong and ground to the desired shape by drawing the strand back and forth across an abrasive cloth stretched over a cavity. The beads are polished with rouge on leather.

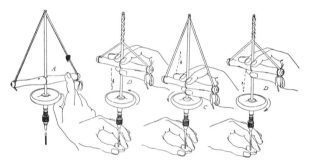

Drilling Turquoise with Pump Drill

Fig. 113

Stone sculpture

Hand carving of some of the softer stones, which can be cut and shaped with a few tools, is a rewarding craft for the beginner or persons who do not own or have access to shop equipment. Some of these are *marble,* of the less hard variety, *jade,* and *alabaster. Marble,* which was originally limestone, is chemically calcium carbonate and known as a metamorphic rock or one changed by the earth's internal forces; heat, pressure, and water. It has a wide range of density, hardness, and color. There are famous marble quarries in all parts of the world—those in Greece and Italy are associated with the names of famous sculptors.

In the United States, quarries in Georgia, Vermont, and Colorado are among those producing the finest building marble. The former Yule quarries at Marble, Colorado, no longer operating, produced some of the largest perfect pieces ever quarried, which were used in the Lincoln Memorial and the Tomb of the Unknown Soldier.

There are several varieties of *jade* or of stones resembling jade. The "true jade" is either the least common *jadite, a silicate of sodium and aluminum, or nephrite a silicate of calcium and magnesium*. The Chinese sculptors, whose carvings range from the most fanciful and intricate statuettes to utilitarian pieces, considered jade the most precious of stones. Although of medium hardness, jade is a "tough" stone, with a structure which makes it nearly impossible to break, it is a very satisfactory stone for carving.

Alabaster is a finely grained variety of gypsum, often white and translucent. Mention in the Bible of "alabasters" referred to containers for ointment. Historically, the ancient Assyrians were said to be the first to sculpture alabaster. Similar stones, often under other names such as the "image stone" in India and the "pagoda stone" in China are of the same mineral formations.

A form of alabaster found extensively in Colorado is a stone ranging in hardness from gypsum (calcium sulphite) to that of marble (calcium carbonate), and in general is a composite of these minerals. The hardness in different pieces varies considerably, as will be detected by hand tools, also by difference in color. The base color is cream pink or gray, with iron oxide markings which range from light to dark brown. A reddish veining is sometimes intermingled with the brown.

Alabaster carving, hand method

The beauty of alabaster is best revealed in simple and graceful shapes, rather than in more elaborate sculpture. Its translucence is particularly beautiful in cylindrical forms which can be made into lamps. Fig. 114A and 114B shows two such lamps and a clock base. The cross and bookends in Fig. 116 were hand carved.

Fig. 115 shows types of bookends, letter holder, and picture frames with a bookend. Its surface decoration is engraved. The use of the right and left wing forms with the suggested primary and secondary feather arrangement, are placed together in the proportions of width and height as well as depth. The side view indicates the length of the base, Fig. 115, and the end view the relative width and height.

1. Cover the piece to be sawed with damp sand for 24 hours before starting to work. For the wing type bookends, cut two pieces of alabaster 3 by 4 by 6 inches with a hack saw, then shape them to the approximate size and shape of the wings with the saw and a wood rasp. For this rough cutting, wedge the piece between blocks of wood nailed to the workbench.

2. Dip the stone in water before starting to shape the wing and moisten frequently with a sponge. This will keep the dust to a minimum.

3. Trace the outline of the wing design on both pieces and shape the edges with a wood rasp. Define the feather form with an engraving tool and bevel the outlines with a pocket knife or rounded skew chisel, as in wood carving.

4. Shape the base in the same way. Carve the front and reverse sides of both pieces with the feather design, and mark the book supporting side with vertical lines to be cut with a V chisel or engraving tool, as extensions of the markings on the front of the wings. Engrave similar lines, closer together on the ends between the wings.

5. *Apply fine sandpaper* dipped in water to remove tool marks along the lines and smooth the surface between them with No. 000 sandpaper dipped in water. The wet or dry type of abrasive is required. Careful finishing with the fine sandpaper should produce a smooth scratchless surface.

6. *Dry the bookends overnight* in a warm place, then apply mineral oil to all surfaces. After ten to fifteen minutes for the oil to be absorbed, wipe the surface with a dry cloth to remove any remaining oil.

7. *Polish with a dry soft cloth* or a piece of leather, sprinkled with a little pumice powder. This will produce a mat finish. If a high gloss is desired, use jeweler's polishing rouge. Glue a piece of felt to the base surfaces.

The projects indicated in Fig. 116 are carved in the same way, also the cross and styles of bookends and jars.

Since possession or accessibility to a lathe is not possible for all persons interested in the carving of alabaster, the author has made arrangements with Lloyd's Art Shop, 1505 N. College Street, Fort Collins, Colorado, to supply preform shapes, cylinders, and discs, also blocks, selected for carved projects.

Alabaster carving, machine method

Cylindrical forms like those illustrated in Fig. 116 can be turned on wood or metal working lathes. To restore natural moisture and facilitate machining, leave the piece covered with damp sand for 24 hours.

1. Attach the block of alabaster to the lathe face plate with screws or wedge in place with the chuck. Turn as large a cylinder as can be made from the rough block and true up the ends. Adjust the position of the cylinder in the lathe and hollow it out with a wood turning tool. Work at slow speed, 300 to 400 R.P.M. until the cylinder is running true between centers. Protect the lathe base plate and other parts from the fine dust by covering with a damp cloth or newspaper. Where much alabaster lathe work is done the installation of an exhaust with blower fan is desirable to catch the dust in an enclosed box or carry out doors.

2. Wet the turned piece of alabaster with a sponge and rub with fine sandpaper to remove tool marks. Polish with fine pumice stone or abrasive powder applied on a moist cloth. Follow with jewelers rouge, tripoli compound or crocus powder, applied with a clean cloth. Burnish with a strip of moist canvas.

3. Water proof vases or bowls by heating them in an oven temperature of 110 to 120 degrees Fahrenheit. Pour melted paraffin inside and rotate until the surface is well coated. Pour out any excess.

4. Polishing may be done on cloth buffing wheels or discs, as described for stone polishing on page 137.

Alabaster with cedar

Fig. 114 illustrates several projects in which an alabaster base, carved or turned, provides a stable support and an attractive color contrast with the red-brown cedar. These are cemented to pieces of felt or leather to protect the surfaces from being scratched by the bare stone.

Cedar-Alabaster Candlesticks and
Electric Clock

A

Cedar-Alabaster Lamp base,
Candlestick and Photo Holder

B

Alabaster Photo Holder.
Dimensions given
in sketch 114F.

C

Lamp Base and Shade

D

Bookends Cedar Burl mounted
on Alabaster base

E

Photo Holder Pattern

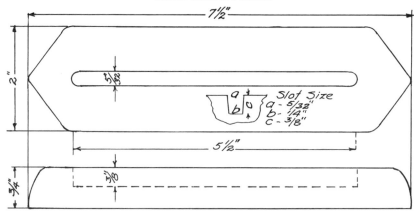

7½"

2"

5/32

Slot Size
a - 5/32"
b - ¼"
c - 3/8"

a
b
c

5½"

¾"

3/8

*All edges sanded
Top and sides beveled
Print size - 3½" x 5"
2 pcs- Glass - 4"x 5½" Double Strength*

F

Fig. 114

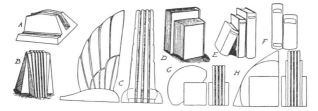

Fig. 115

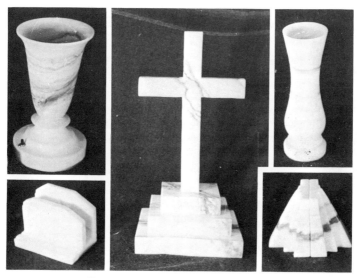

Vases — Cross — Envelope Holder — Bookends

Fig. 116

Silver Beaver — Scout Award.
Mounted on Hewn Cedar and Alabaster Base

Fig. 117

1. *The cedar wood mounting* for the electric clock movement, Fig. 114A, is hand carved, the candlesticks and lamp base hand turned. The unusual pair of bookends, Fig. 114E, were made from a large cedar burl, divided into approximately equal sections and cut across one end for the base. The cut surfaces are sanded and polished but the surface of the burl left in its natural form. Wood screws attach the alabaster bases to the wood sections.

2. *The picture holder*, Fig. 114C, is simply an oblong piece of alabaster with a channel, about ⅜ inch wide, cut with an electric routing tool or removed with a chisel, Fig. 114D, after the sides are saw cut. The photograph is held between pieces of plate glass.

Alabaster and cedar make excellent bases for awards or other metal figures. Fig. 117 shows the Silver Beaver, Boy Scout leader's award thus mounted.

3. Alabaster is an excellent material for wood lamp pedestals, as it is heavy enough to balance the rest of the lamp. The pedestals illustrated were made from discs of alabaster ½ to 1¼ inches in thickness and about 6¼ inches in diameter before being carved in the forms shown, Fig. 114.

4. All three lamps were made of cedar fence posts which were thoroughly dried. Lamps 1 and 2A and B were lathe turned. C was hand whittled for a hewn appearance. Holes in the alabaster pedestals and the cedar lamp sections were bored in the center for the electric wire conduit, connections, and assembly of the socket, all held together with a nut recessed into the base of the pedestal. A groove deep enough for the cord was cut in the base and covered with a layer of felt glued to the surface to hold the cord in place and keep the base level, also to prevent scratches on a table surface.

Bas-relief figure carving

The carving of figures in relief on a flat plane follows the same procedure for stone as for wood. With skill developed by carving figures in relief, the carver will be enabled to successfully carve busts or complete figures.

Practice on one of the varieties of gypsum or jade will make it possible to sculpture marble. As a beginning, experimental carving of cast plaster of Paris, such as is used for making ceramic models develops familiarity with the planes and surface areas of a figure or design.

The designs on postage stamps may serve as models for bas-relief stone carving. Others will be found in studies of Egyptian, Greek, or Gothic art, as well as in modern sculptured forms. Silhouette types of designs may also be developed in stone. An outline of the procedure follows:

1. Transfer the outline of the figure, sketched on drawing paper, to the block of stone with carbon paper. As with alabaster, dampen the stone by storing overnight in damp sand.

2. With the skew chisel or engraving tool, cut a slight beveled line just outside the marked outline. Working from this line and away from the figure, remove the background stone to a depth of about ⅛ inch, using a U tool and the skew chisel to chip away small fragments. Keep the depth as uniform as possible. The background may be left slightly rough in a stippled effect or smoothed down with the wood rasp and sandpaper.

3. Shape the edges of the marked relief figure into the appearance of the original model, using a sharp knife and a chisel. With the U and V gouges (engraving tools), cut and define the natural lines. Be careful not to cut too deeply or mar the design lines.

4. *Finish the bas-relief figure* with 000 sandpaper. Wash off all loose dust. After the carving is dry, apply mineral oil to bring out the color. Polish with a soft cloth and a little pumice powder or jeweler's rouge.

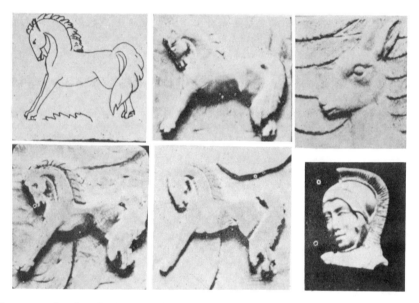

Some examples of carving in Steatite or a form of jade is reproduced through the courtesy of the Far Eastern Sculpstone Company. The horse paper weight is made from a slab of material 3 inches square and ⅜ inch thick and the stages in carving the background and forming the relief figure are shown.

Stone flaking

Stones must have special characteristics to flake successfully. Not every stone can be made into an arrowhead, but only those which break under pressure into spawls and flakes with thin edges can be shaped into arrowheads and other weapons or tools which the Indians used. Arrowheads today are part of the sport of archery. Occasionally a sportsman hunter emulates the Indian in his big game search.

All flaking stones are identified by the geologists as those which have a "conchoidal fracture" or break into flakes of different sizes, leaving shell shaped cavities of glass like smoothness. Obsidian (volcanic glass) and flint are the main rocks having this type of fracture. The structure of manufactured glass is similar and this also will flake.

In the classification of arrowheads known to have been used by primitive man, as recorded in the Bureau of Ethnology reports, the nature of the parts as made by different groups or tribes were given a terminology for identification as follows:

As indicated in Fig. 118, sketch A, A is the point, B the edges, C the face, D the bevel, E the blade, F the tang, G the stem, H the base, I the notch, K the neck, M the barb or shoulder. Sketches B and C show how the beveled edge of an arrowhead appears when flaked first from one side then the other.

As the Indians learned, a piece of bone (preferably the point of an antler) makes the best flaking tool. Fig. 118, sketch E, indicates by the dotted line the shape of an arrowhead which can be flaked from the larger piece of spawl (the geologists term for such a fractured piece of stone); the cross sections D1 to D6 shows, in the relative positions of the flaking tool, the method of applying pressure to the spawl with the tool.

Hold the spawl firmly, as shown in sketch G, with the top of the bone tool pressed downward and against the underside of the stone, sketch D. (The broken chip is caught by the leather palm protector which takes up the impact of the tool.)

Turn the spawl over and remove another flake, sketch D2, then break off the thinned and beveled edge (sketch D3). Continue the process of alternately chipping the top and bottom corners, then breaking the edge until the spawl is reduced to the desired shape (sketch F).

Keep the spawl on the base of the thumb, supported as in sketch G. *Do not* let it shift into position H, with the center unsupported as the arrow indicates. Pressure at this point may break the spawl instead of chipping a flake as desired.

Apart from the satisfaction of acquiring the skill of stone flaking or the making of arrows for archery, collecting arrowheads from areas previously occupied by Indians, or in places of suitable stone deposits, is an interesting hobby.

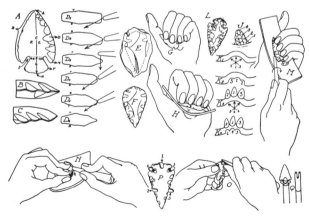

Fig. 118

CHAPTER **7**

Leather Work Processes and Projects

Early Egyptian records give us the knowledge of the first uses of leather as clothing, furniture ornamentation, shields, and coverings for ships.

From the Hebrew Talmud we learn that the Babylonians knew how to make leather. The story of the founding of Carthage has preserved the legend that Queen Dido, when promised land that could be covered with a bull's hide, cut it into a thin strip and encircled the land on which the city was built.

Classification of Leather

Leather is classified in two ways, first by the name of the animal from which it was taken, and second by the kind of tanning process used to produce it.

Skins from domestic animals are the chief source of present day commercial leathers. These are: cowhide, calfskin, horsehide, sheepskin, goatskin, kidskin, and pigskin. The game animals, which the hunter uses for the leather he tans, are the deer, elk, and moose.

Cowhide is the leather most readily available in present-day markets in weights processed for strap leather, mineral tanned or vegetable tanned, which is the quality required for tooling, carving, and stamping. A thinned top grain cowhide or steerhide, as it is termed, is tanned especially for decorating and is available in natural, also in dyed shaded green and brown.

Fig. 119

The illustrated chair back of natural tooling steerhide, Fig. 119, is an example of skilled decorating by Eva Clark Keller, the artist whose sketches

151

and demonstrations illustrate many processes in this book. The design represents an allegorical, heraldic decoration with floral elements.

Cowhide, suitable for belts, camera, briefcases, and similar articles which are to be decorated by stamping or carving, is designated by the weight per square foot and priced accordingly. The range of weights for this so-called strap leather is light, 3 to 5 ounces; medium, 6 to 7 ounces; and heavy, 8 to 10 ounces per square foot.

Steerhide is the commercial term used for a thinned outer or "top grain" surface leather made from cowhide. It is used for handbags, billfolds, purses, cases, and similar items and is especially good for decoration by tooling, modeling, and some forms of stamping. Steerhide is a very durable leather and will retain its finish and a decoration almost indefinitely. Its weight varies from 2 to 5 ounces per square foot. Cowhide and steerhide are processed in sides, 20 to 28 square feet.

Veal and calfskins, from half grown and young cattle, provide a fine grained smooth and lightweight leather which is used for shoe uppers, also for many kinds of tooled and otherwise decorated items. Veal or kip is available in weights 3 to 5 ounces and in entire skins, 14 to 18 square feet, also in half and quarter skins.

Calfskins are thinner and lighter, range in weight from 2½ to 5 ounces and are sold in whole skins, 8 to 12 square feet, and in half skins. These skins are softer than cowhide or steerhide, and they tool more readily. As they show scratches or tool marks more readily, greater care must be taken in decorating and making up articles from veal or calfskin.

Horsehide is a durable, nontooling leather used mainly for garments such as jackets, chaps, vests, moccasins, shoes, and gloves. *Pigskin* is another very durable leather with a characteristic grain. It is especially popular for gloves and for some types of purses and billfolds.

Sheepskins are porous and soft textured. Finished on the flesh side by buffing, they are known as velvet or suede sheep and used for linings, also for some bags. Skivers are thin lining leathers made from the grain surface of sheepskin.

Goatskins are mostly imported from the Alpine countries, where the cold endured by the animal results in the toughest and tightest grain leather known. Morocco, the European term, is still preferred for fine handbound books, and in Italy, is used for fine stamped and gilded leather items. Goatskin is excellent and long wearing for lining, lacing thongs, and fine leather work. Kidskin and young goatskins are used for fine shoe uppers and for gloves. It is the lightest leather available commercially, average weight 1½ ounces.

Genuine alligator and ostrich are rare and high priced leathers, used for fine luggage and bags, also for shoe uppers. They are distinguished by the grain and markings of the surface, which are imitated in cheaper embossed leathers of different types. Embossed leathers, calf and sheepskin, are produced by means of a process of running the skins between steam heated rollers, the upper of which has a design engraved. The design thus imprinted on the leather may simulate alligator, lizard, pigskin, and other natural grain leathers.

Finished commercial leathers are also divided into top grain and splits. Top grain leather refers to all kinds which have retained the outer or top surface of the original skin. Much of the strength of the leather as well as the characteristic finish depends on the preservation of this top grain. *Splits* are leathers from which the top grain surface has been removed. They are used for work gloves and similar items.

Leather as classified by tanning process

Leather is tanned in two main groups, vegetable and mineral or "chrome" tanned. Only *vegetable tanned leather* can be successfully decorated by the methods of tooling, stamping and carving, because it retains permanently a design thus impressed upon the moistened surface. The basic element in *vegetable tanning* is tannic acid which is derived from the bark of certain trees and shrubs.

Leathers tanned by the *mineral or chrome* (potassium bichromate) process are not toolable. They are rendered tough, firm, and water repellent. The mineral renders the cut edges a bluish green, by which the leather is readily identified as chrome tanned. This method is generally used for all skins which are to be finished as shoe leather as well as for garments and gloves.

Homer's *Iliad* describes a tanning process in which the thoroughly washed skin is softened with oil beaten and rubbed into the stretched hide. The essential procedure is still followed with modern machinery and is called "Shamoying."

The Romans knew how to tan hides with barks and roots and the word tan comes from *tanare*, meaning oak bark.

The early colonists were surprised to find that the Indians were very skilled in the art of tanning leather, but it never has been determined whence this knowledge came. The process which the Indian still uses when the animals, chiefly deer, are obtainable, is called "Buckskin or Indian Tan." Manufacturers have adopted the method with little modification except in equipment. The Indian women, whose task it has been, loosened the hair with a solution of wood ashes, and scraped the hide with a section of sharpened bone to remove both hair and all flesh tissue, and then rubbed into it a mixture made from the liver and brains of the animal. Finally it was hung for days in a small tepee constructed over a fire made of rotten wood, so that the hide would be throughly impregnated with smoke which kept it soft and pliable even after wetting.

Selection and cutting of leather

Firm calfskin and steerhide, also cowhide or strap leather of uniform thickness are required for successful tooling, stamping, and carving. The less firm sections may be used for gussets and pockets. It is an economy to buy calfskins in whole skins and plan the cutting of several projects at one time in order to utilize the firm back and the softer body sections to the best advantage. Steerhide is available only in sides, unless cut to order for separate projects.

The essential leather working tools and equipment are as follows:

Awls; Sadlers, Harness, Shoemaker's curved Sewing Awls

Barbours Linen No. 12, Beeswax

Cutting Block-Knot free pine

Designs and Patterns

Dividers, Compass or beam type

Draw Gauge — for cutting strap leather

Edge Beveler, Creaser, Metal and wood

Edge Burnishing Wax, Colorless, brown, black

Findings; snap fasteners, rivets, eyelets, buckles, swivels, rings, dees, snaps

Marlin Spike — Knives; Incising, Swivel cutter

Modelers, Tracers, Creasers, Deerfoot, Spoon

Needles; Glovers, Harness, Egg eyed, Blunt Leather lacing Needle

Oil stone, Coarse and fine surfaces, Oil Leather strap with Jeweler's Rouge

Punches; Drive punch — sizes 1-2-6-8

Punching Block — Hardwood end grain

Shears — 8 inch

Skiving stone, 8" x 10" marble or plate glass

Stamping tools

Stitching wheels, 5-6 and 7 stitches per inch

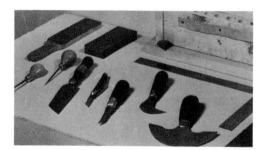

Fig. 120A Cutting tools and use of ½ round rocker knife

Fig. 120B Sharpening the ½ round knife

The equipment required for cutting leather includes:

1. A large cutting board of soft end grained pine.

2. The two styles of rocker or "head" knives, half and quarter round blades.

3. A square or straight edge for marking corners and the straight margins of patterns, which may be cut with a rocker knife or

4. A knife with removable extension blades.

5. A pattern of stiff paper to permit the exact tracing of the design outline with the tracing tool.

The equipment and tools required for the decoration of tooling leather:

1. Piece of marble or plate glass
2. Single or combination tracer and edge creaser
3. Hard wood creaser
4. Set of modeling tools which include the spoon and deer foot ends.
5. For stamped background: a stippler and crosshatched stamping tools
6. A clean sponge for moistening the leather
7. Suitable designs sketched or printed on lightweight bond paper
8. Patterns for the articles selected

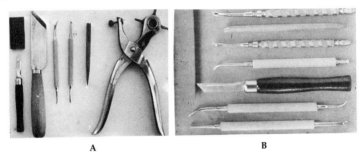

A   B

Fig. 121 shows a 4-tube Rotary Punch with spacing gauge, Skiving and Thong Knife. Modeling Tools: Metal and Wood Edge Creasers, Beveling Tool, Tracer, Spoon and Deerfoot Tools, Bone Folder.

Fig. 121

Selection of lining and attachment process

Some articles made of calfskin, such as small purses without gussets need not be lined, as the flesh or inner surface is usually buffed to a suedelike finish, with the color nearly the same on both surfaces.

Articles in calf which require lining: billfolds, keytainers, cases, and bags may be lined with the thinner, softer sections of the skin, or with suede or skivers. Skiver linings are not thinned by skiving, but the other lining leathers should be reduced in thickness at the edges as previously described.

The grain surface of tooling steerhide is colored by a spray process, but the flesh side, from which the extra thickness has been removed or split off, is left rough and light colored. Suede sheepskin or skivers (a grain surface split from sheepskin), thin goatskin, or lining calfskin may be used for lining steerhide articles. Goatskin is the most durable and is especially satisfactory in articles subject to a great deal of wear.

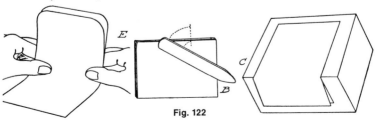

Fig. 122

1. *Cement the leather and lining* together, first along one side or end, applying the adhesive over two or three inches at a time. Smooth the parts together, before applying more cement.

2. Smooth out any wrinkles which develop, with the bone folder, working toward the edges as indicated in sketch B, which shows the flat part of a small purse. In order to prevent a wrinkle at the fold of the flap, apply the cement along the sections to be folded, and out to the margins, sketch E.

3. Before the cement dries, bring the folded part, or flap, down over the front, and trim any edges of the lining which may extend beyond the leather.

Preparing a gusset for an envelope purse

Fig. 123A, sketches B, C, D, and E indicate the process of lining a gusset for an envelope purse, such as the one shown in sketch A. B shows the shape of the outside piece of leather with the edges skived along the margins from the dotted line. Note that the top is skived back farther than the rest, and that the lining in sketch C is shorter. The process is as follows:

1. Apply cement to the edges and along the line of the fold, then place the lining in position as shown in sketch C and fold the top edge over it as in sketch D. Press all edges smoothly and firmly together, holding the gusset in the folded position, sketch E. Place the gusset in position in the purse and cement the edges together for 3/16 inch of the margins, to hold them in place as the edges are perforated and laced. See assembly detail, page 195.

2. After the edges are cemented, trim any uneven margins which may have developed. This can best be done by cutting with a sharp knife, extension blade type, along a straight edge or metal edged ruler on a block of wood.

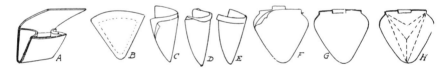

Fig. 123A

Envelope Bags, Brief Cases, Portfolios, and other projects requiring straight folded corner gussets are punched and laced as indicated in Fig. 123B.

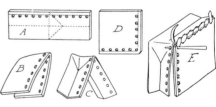

Fig. 123B

Preparation of leather for modeling or tooling

1. Moisten the leather just sufficiently to make it pliable. Rub or pat the damp sponge over the flesh side first, then apply lightly to the grain surface until the color darkens uniformly. Do not have the leather wet enough for any moisture to ooze out when a tool is applied.

2. Let the leather stand a few minutes, until the moisture is distributed evenly, while testing tools, condition of leather, and designs on a scrap piece similarly moistened.

3. Remoisten the leather occasionally as the tooling progresses. Permit it to dry completely before doing any assembly.

Transfer of design

Prepare a suitable design for the area to be decorated and make a pattern of tracing paper. Secure the pattern at the corners with drafting tape in an area which is not to be decorated. Paper clips may be used to hold a pattern in place if pressure is avoided.

Go over the entire design with the tracer tip of the modeling tool, using a uniform, continuous stroke for each line section. Hold the tip at an angle which will not tear the paper.

Remove the paper pattern and go over the lines carefully, retracing them until a bold distinct impression is obtained.

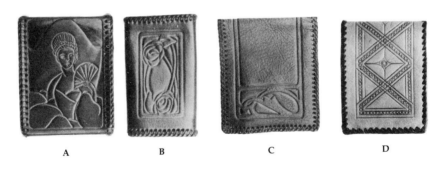

A   B   C   D

Fig. 124

Forms of leather decoration

A. 1. *A design in outline* is the simplest form of leather decoration. It is merely the deeply creased outline of the design with all details uniformly and clearly defined. A design suitable for this development should be chosen. A good design for outlining is shown in Fig. 124A. Smoothly burnish all lines with the tracing tool or the single end of the wood creaser.

2. A design in outline may be emphasized or given the effect of relief, by slightly rounding off or beveling the margins along the design lines as will be apparent in some of the illustrated projects to be described.

B. 1. *A double bevel outline* has the appearance of a raised line, Fig. 128C2, as illustrated in Fig. 127 and other designs. The method requires practice and a steady hand to follow exactly the first outline by sight, an ability that can be acquired. For parallel or straight lines, a thin ruler may be used.

2. After the first line has been traced and deepened as for simple outline, trace a second line about 1/16 or 3/32 inch inside or outside the first line and deepen as before. Both lines should be slightly beveled on the outside. A small deer foot is the best tool to use and the leather must be moist, Fig. 127.

3. An effective adaptation of the double bevel outline is illustrated on the billfold in Fig. 124D. A continuous line of small rosette stamped impressions between the lines adds to the appearance of the design.

C. *Flat modeling* refers to the depression or leveling of all background areas of the design. Rub these with the flat surface of the spoon modeler, or the deer foot first, then slightly bevel the design outline with the same tool, smoothing *from* the lines, so as not to obliterate any part. The address book in Fig. 126C is an example of flat modeling.

D. *Relief or Repousse modeling* is the process of raising the leather in portions of the design from the reverse side. The outlining of the design on the surface usually makes an impression sufficiently distinct to be followed on the flesh side.

 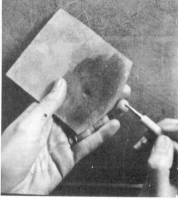

A   B

Fig. 125

1. Place the piece of leather, on which the design has been traced, on a smooth surface (glass or marble), and carefully redefine any lines which are not clear, taking care not to make an impression which would blur the marginal lines on the back or flesh side.

2. Hold the piece as shown in Fig. 125A, so that pressure can be exerted on the portion to be raised, or place it face down on a piece of double corrugated cardboard, which will yield slightly without breaking. Use the deer foot modeler or one with a round ball end to press down the parts of the design which are to appear raised on the surface or grain side of the leather.

3. Again place the leather right or grain side on the marble or glass and retrace the outline, rounding up the margins of the raised design.

4. To retain the raised or relief appearance, pack the areas with cotton or modeling clay, which will harden into permanent form, or use several layers of plastic tape. If the leather is to be assembled over a metal form, as for a book end, cement a piece of cotton, shaped to fit the depression, on the flesh side. A lining is necessary with the other methods.

A stamped or stippled background may be applied for contrast in design elements and is especially effective when insignia, initials, or monograms are used in a decorative design.

An example of a stippled design background is shown on the purse in Fig. 126E. This is produced by tapping the leather lightly with the stippler or the end of the raising tool.

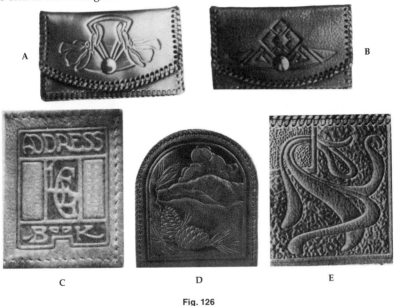

Fig. 126

Photo A shows four steps: 1—Traced outline, 2—Double bevel process, 3—Relief effect inside outline, 4—Outside margin defined. The deerfoot and tracer modeling tools are used.

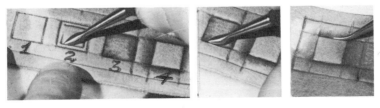

Fig. 127

Designs for Leather Tooling

Assembly process for tooled leather, calfskin or steerhide

The tool requirements include: Skiving knife and a piece of marble or smooth plate glass, flexible leather cement, bone folder or other spreader; edge creaser, tube punch and drive punches for perforating the leather; a spike or other tool with smooth tapered point.

Edge skiving is necessary where the thickness of the edge of the leather requires thinning for a folded and cemented margin. Both outside and lining to be laced together may require thinning to reduce thickness.

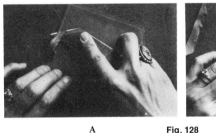 

A   Fig. 128   B

Place the leather, grain surface down on the skiving surface, mark the line of fold and incise lightly. Start the skiving at the left side on the line about one fourth inch from the corner in the position shown in A of Fig. 128, with the cut toward the edge as indicated. Reduce the thickness, with caution not to cut the edge and carefully taper it from the line. Practice on a piece of scrap leather before skiving a part of a project. Note that the point of the knife rests on the stone surface, making a guide for the width of cut. Remove thin layers in successive cuts and keep the edge of the knife very sharp.

Rotate the piece of leather until all edges, *except the corners,* are skived. Skive the corners in a series of cuts with the position of the knife as held in B of Fig. 128.

Fig. 129

To cement the skived edge, moisten it and press down with the fingers or the bone folder, smoothing from the incised line and fold to the edges. Apply cement after the folded edge dries and firmly press it into place. Crease with the wood creaser for a finish. The process is shown in Fig. 129.

Methods of perforating leather

For assembly with edge lacing, a leather punch, Fig. 130, with a hole spacing gauge fitted with a suitable tube, is the simplest tool to use. The holes made with a punch permit a more rapid lacing operation than other methods of perforation.

Fig. 130 shows a single tube punch with the spacing gauge tip inserted in the first hole punched in the corner of the leather and touching the creased guide lines.

For narrow lacing thongs, 3/32 inch wide, a double naught (00) should be selected. Wide lacing thongs (¼ inch or ⅜ inch thong widths) used for Florentine wide lacing, requires naught (0) or Number 1 size tube, depending on the thickness of the thong.

Keep the marginal space even by following the creased guide line as the punching progresses. At a point about ½ inch to ¾ inch from the corner Fig. 132B, observe the intervening space, and if necessary increase or decrease the spacing slightly in order to make the corner hole come in the right position.

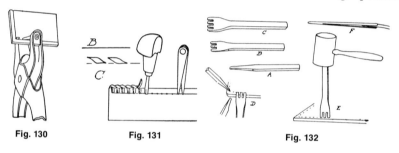

Fig. 130   **Fig. 131**   **Fig. 132**

A good practice is to estimate the spacing, and mark lightly the position of the holes necessary for equalizing the space, before punching independently of the gauge. If the anvil becomes rough from use, the under margin of holes may be marred. Prevent this by smoothing the anvil occasionally with a fine file. In any case, it is desirable to punch with the outside of an article uppermost.

Fig. 131, sketches B and C show the method of perforating leather for edge lacing, using an awl instead of a punch with a spacing gauge. Place the awl holes in the position shown in sketch B to preserve the strength of the margin. Mark the spacing with the dividers before the awl perforations are made, as the lacing progresses. It may be necessary to spread them with a marlin spike or end of the tracing tool to receive the end of the lacing.

Fig. 132, sketches D and E show another method of perforating the leather for edge lacing, using the thong chisel. These are available with one, three, and four prongs as indicated by sketches A, B, and C. The single prong chisel is useful for punching corner holes. The three and four prong chisels are used as indicated in sketches D and E. The hole spacing is controlled by placing one prong of the chisel in the last hole punched. Sketch F shows a Thong Lacing Tip or Needle which holds and carries the lacing through the awl or chisel cut perforations.

Leather Thong Cutting Methods

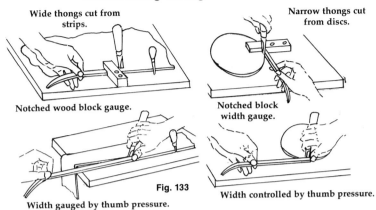

Fig. 133

Width gauged by thumb pressure.

Hand methods of making lacing

Wide and Narrow Lacing Thongs can be made of steerhide and goatskin, when it is not possible to obtain a commercial product. Narrow lacing can be cut by hand from discs of leather as shown in the sketches of Fig. 133. Goatskin makes the best lacing for calfskin articles as it retains its surface finish and is most durable.

Skiving or beveling the edges of narrow lacing thongs is necessary to limit the bulk of the edge lacing and the light-colored margins. Thinning is not usually necessary as the full strength of the thong is needed. Fig. 134A shows the thong beveling process according to the following method:

1. File a flat groove, the width and depth of the thong to be beveled, in a hardwood block. Cut another groove on a slight slant from the right hand edge of the groove, deep enough to permit a knife blade *to be held at the angle shown* in the illustration of the process. The knife, which must be sharp, held in this position cuts a triangular shaving to make a beveled edge as the thong is pulled through the groove by the left hand.

When one edge is beveled, reverse the ends of the thong, and bevel the other side of the thong in the same way.

As the beveled edges are usually light in color, they should be dyed by dipping or by the application of dye on a swab.

A

B

Fig. 134

A hand gauge method of cutting wide lacing thongs from a strip of steerhide is shown in Fig. 134B. B shows the thinning process, accomplished by means of a knife blade held *across a flat* groove in a hard wood block, as the wide steerhide thong is pulled through the groove from right to left, flesh side up.

Success in skiving or thinning a wide thong requires a steady hand, a sharp, thin bladed knife and a correctly sloped, perfectly level groove. The skill is easily acquired with practice.

Florentine Wide Lacing, so-called because it is used almost altogether on the embossed Morocco leather articles, made in Italy, is best for many tooled steerhide and carved strap leather projects.

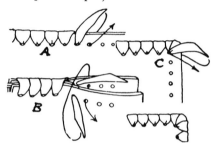

Fig. 135

The sketches in Fig. 135 show the appearance and method of whip lacing edges together with a wide thong. In lined articles, short lengths of thong can be used as the method of splicing is simple, the thong ends being concealed as in Sketch B.

For holes ⅛ inch from the edge and spaced ¼ inch apart, thongs approximately 2½ times the edge to be laced will be sufficient. The holes should be spaced so that the thongs, ¼ inch wide, conceal the edge of the leather. It is usually necessary to lace through the corner hole two or three times to cover the corner edges, as shown in Sketch C.

Pattern and design for desk sets to be assembled with wide facing book end appears on page 160 in examples of tooling.

Fig. 136

Principles of lacing assembly

With any of the types of lacing to be described, the following principles must be observed to insure neat appearing work:

1. Keep the margin between the holes and the edge exact by following carefully the creased line, as a guide in punching with any of the tools described on page 162.

2. Do not permit the thong to become twisted. This can be prevented by running the thumb and forefinger, with the thong between, back from the last stitch to the point of the thong, before inserting it for the next stitch.

3. Do not try to work with too long a thong. A two yard length is as long as can easily be handled. If care is taken in splicing, the ends will not be noticeable.

4. Most important is the caution against pulling the lacing thong too tight. The finished lacing should lay along the edge and not slant to either side, or pucker the edge of the leather.

5. In finishing the lacing, the end may be concealed by trimming it to a narrow point and pulling it back under several stitches on the inside of the leather. This can easily be done if the last three or four stitches are left loose and tightened after the end of the thong has been drawn through them.

Pull up and tighten the separate loops in succession, taking care not to break the thong.

6. The final step in edge lacing is to flatten the laced edge of the leather by carefully pounding it with a smooth wooden mallet.

Styles and methods of edge lacing

Three styles of narrow edge lacing, in the so-called layover stitch are shown in Fig. 137. To start lacing, by any of the methods which will be described, study the position, in which the article to be laced is held with the outer or right side away from the worker, and note that the direction of the lacing thong is toward the worker and the process is from left to right.

Single	Double	Triple

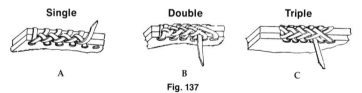

A   B   C

Fig. 137

1. Take one whip stitch to anchor the end of the thong as the lacing continues. Leave about two inches of space for splicing or for concealment between the lining and the outside, or beneath the stitches which follow. This ending is usually sufficient at the end of a gusset.

2. Note that the single lay-over lacing is similar to a buttonhole stitch used in sewing. Lay the thong back over itself after each loop through the punched or chisel slit hole in the leather parts which are being laced. Fig. 138, sketches A to F indicate the process and direction of the lacing thong. Sketch E shows reverse appearance.

Edge Lacing Methods

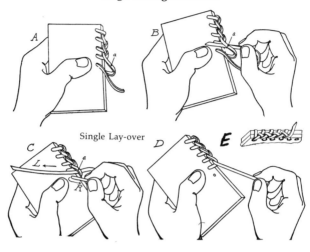

Single Lay-over

Fig. 138

3. Tighten the loops of the lacing every three or four stitches, keeping the thong vertical or at right angles to the outside of the leather with an even slope on the inside. A thong approximately 4½ times the length of the edges to be laced is required for single layover stitch.

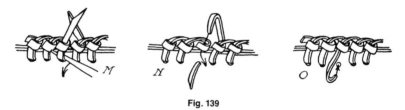

Fig. 139

4. To splice a thong follow the sketches in Fig. 139.

a. Draw the thong through the last three loops formed by the preceding thong and between the lining and the outside leather.

b. Form the next stitch with the new thong as indicated by the arrow as it passes under the preceding loops of the old thong and continues through the next hole. Tighten the loops to hold the new thong between the layers of leather or the leather and lining.

5. End the lacing as shown in Fig. 139, sketches M, N, O. This method is used for an article assembled with edge lacing which is joined at the starting point to make it appear continuous. Pull the end of the thong down through the loop and as the arrow indicates, pull the other end through the same loop and both back between the lining and the leather on the outside. Adjust the tension of the loops with a marlin spike to give a uniform appearance to the junction of the thongs.

6. *Double lay-over lacing* as shown in Fig. 140, sketch D, differs from the single only in the fact that as the lacing progresses, the looped stitch is taken through the preceding stitch as well as around and over itself.

Fig. 140

(a) Take the first looped stitch around the thong as in simple lay-over and leave it loose to permit the insertion of the spike. Pass the end of the thong through this space, after pulling it through the third hole. *Note* that the second loop is formed at the point where the first lay-over or looped stitch crosses back over itself. Sketches B and C show the next steps.

(b) Tighten the double lay-over stitches progressively so that the appearance becomes the same on both sides of the leather, with the loops seeming to run in opposite directions. The vertical or right angle of the stitches should be on the outside with the slant coming on the inside.

(c) To facilitate the lacing operation, cut the thong to a taper point and skive the ends. Glue this to a portion of a toothpick or use a lacing needle. An application of soap to the flesh side of the ends will temporarily stiffen them but must be repeated frequently.

A metal thong tip with special pliers made to grip it on the thong is available from suppliers.

As compared with single lay-over, the double style more nearly covers the edges of two or more pieces of leather which are being assembled. It is especially suitable for lacing bags or other articles with gussets.

The width of the finished lacing, as Fig. 138, sketch D, is approximately three times the width of the lacing thong, and the appearance is that of a three plait braid or weave.

A thong approximately six times the edge to be laced is required for a double lay-over stitch.

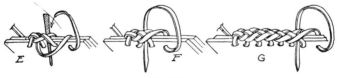

Fig. 141

7. *The Triple Edge Lacing* as shown in Fig. 141, sketch G, is begun as shown in sketch E. The difference between this style and the double lay-over is that each time a stitch is taken through the leather, the thong is carried back under the last and the two preceding loops at the point of crossing. This is indicated by the position of the spike which permits the thong to be pulled through and tightened as the stitches are taken.

Triple edge lacing has a top or edge appearance of a four plait flat braid, and is approximately four times the width of the single thong. The amount of thong required for triple lay-over lacing is approximately seven times the length of the edge to be laced. It will completely cover several thicknesses of leather.

8. The Four Plait Round Edge Lacing shown in Fig. 142, sketch A to H is made with a single thong and resembles a strand of four plait round. The process is as follows:

(a) Pass the lacing thong through the first hole in the edge of the leather pieces to be laced together in the direction of back to front, sketch A.

(b) Carry the thong over the edge and pass it through the fourth hole, then over the edge and through the second hole, again from back to front.

(c) Next carry the thong over the edge and pass it through hole 5 as indicated by the arrow in sketch B. Sketch C shows the thong protruding from hole 5.

(d) Carry the thong back to hole 3, passing it over the thong in holes 2 to 5 and under the thong extending in holes from 1 to 4. See sketch C.

(e) Carry the thong under the thong extending from holes 4 to 2, then over the thong extending from holes 5 to 3, then through hole 6 as in sketch E.

(f) Again carry the thong over and under a thong as before and through hole 4, as shown by the arrow in sketch E. This indicates that the thong is to pass over and under a thong, over the edge and through hole 7.

Repeat the process described in step d, carrying the thong over one and under one, then back through hole 5. The appearance of the four plait round edge lacing is shown in sketch H. Allow ample time for this kind of edge lacing and use a thin edged thong for best results.

Four Plait Round Edge Lacing

Fig. 142

Tool Making for Stamped Leather Decoration

A great variety of leather working tools for stamping, carving, and modeling are available commercially in sets with other tools or singly. Nonrusting chrome plated tools in minimum and maximum sets can be obtained from suppliers, such as those listed at the end of this section.

As a project, however, or in situations where there are no supplies of tools, the basic set of leather stamping tools can be made by a group or an individual, with access to a bench vise, hammers, center punch, and an assortment of files.

Lacking a vise, a good substitute is a section of log, with a pair of pliers to hold the nail or steel rod firmly in place while being filed to develop a tool design.

Nails of untempered steel, sizes 16 or 20 penny, are used for the set of five or six tools, with which the stamping examples in Fig. 144 are shown. The sketches, Fig. 143, indicate the stages in the shaping and filing of nail heads for *making the one and three dot background tools and the design tools*, star or rosette, basket weave, horseshoe, and pine tree tools.

The necessary files are:
        1 10 or 12 inch rough, flat file,
        1 3-sided tapered or 3-square file,
        A square file, also a rat-tail or tapered round file,
        A few jeweler's needle files, No. 4 cut,
        A center punch and hammer.

1. The first operation is to file the head of the nail with the large flat file or shape it on an emery wheel until the approximate shape and size of the specific tool is obtained. This step is indicated for the set of 5 tools.

2. After shaping the nail head, make the reference or base lines by filing them lightly with one edge of the three-sided file. If this line is not in the proper place, file the head smooth and try again. From the base line or lines, space the other lines or cuts by sight, judging by the number to be cut and the space between them.

3. The sketches, series 3 to 7, indicate the stages in the making of five of the tools, from the shaping of the nail head. Detail shown in Fig. 144, tools B, C, and D.

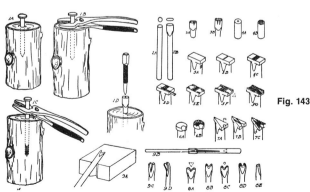

Fig. 143

Making Tools for Carving and Stamping

1. To make the background tools of the set, shape the nail head to an oval and make the dots with the center punch. Clamp the nail securely in a vise, mark X with an awl for the position of the dot for the one dot tool and make it with the center punch. Make the three dot or additional dots in the same way, forming them with the center punch.

For the one dot, file the oval end to a point as indicated, Fig. 144, sketch 5. File the surface of this end so that it does not make an impression.

The dot series of tools are used to depress the background along design margins as will be noted in the carved leather examples and projects.

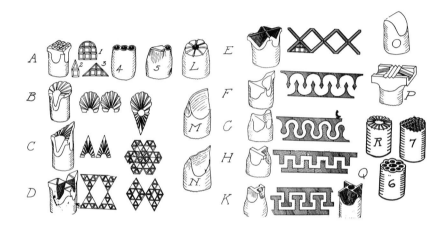

Fig. 144

2. Other background tools are the series in different sizes: rosette, star, margin shader, and the round, oval, and triangular shading or depression stamps. Some of these are crosshatched or filed with vertical lines, others are left entirely smooth. Fig. 144, sketches A1, 2, 3 and 7 show part of the cross-hatched background tools. Sketch O shows a margin beveler or shader. Sketches 6 and R show the rosette and star tools.

3. To define or emphasize floral elements, the tools called the horseshoe, the leaf and margin veiners, and the scallops are most frequently used for the combined carving-stamping process. These are designated in a section of a carved case in Fig. 150, page 175.

4. The tools shown in Fig. 144, sketches D, E, F, G, and H, are border stamping tools, also used effectively for panel designs in combination with the basic set, sketched in Fig. 143, also shown in Fig. 144A, B, C.

5. The basket weave, Fig. 144, is made as indicated in the steps 5A to 5G in Fig. 143. Steps 6 and 7 of Fig. 143 indicate the making of the horseshoe and pine tree stamps.

Background tools such as the rosettes and stippling tools, similar to those used in the carved designs, are required to depress areas around design motifs or initials.

For covering a considerable area the basket weave tool, Fig. 144, is frequently used, in the following order.

1. Develop the design by applying the basket weave tool first at a lower corner of a panel to be decorated. Make the next impression one line above, to the right or left according to the direction. Slightly overlap the upper edge of the first impression. Continue in this manner until the space is filled. If the space is not square-cornered, stamp the graduated impressions across a center section and then stamp in the opposite direction, decreasing or widening the impressions as required.

2. Slightly round all corners and remove wire edges with a file, taking care not to change the shape. File the cuts and keep them perfectly regular.

Cut off the point of the nail, slightly bevel it, and smooth the top to make a flat striking surface for the mallet or striking stick, Fig. 150B.

3. Fig. 143, sketches 8A to 8E, show the steps in making a creaser from a nail head and a beveler, sketches 9A, 9B, 9C, and 9D, from a length of drill rod or a nut pick. These and discarded dental tools (usually obtainable for the asking), make good modeling tools. Any piece of metal round pointed (like a tapestry needle) and bent to a 30 degree curve makes a tracing tool.

The decoration of various cowhide or strap leather articles with stamped designs in combination with creased lines and carved elements is effective when done with accuracy in the spacing and arrangement, also in the exact alignment of the impressions, stamped along the border lines. *Note:* For all tooling, carving, and stamping leathers, creasers of hard wood and its substitute, plastic, are excellent. They do not leave any stains when the surface of the leather is too moist.

While the leather is not cut as in carving, it is depressed to a depth that makes a clear and lasting impression of the stamping tool designs. With practice, the ability to position, hold, and strike the tools is easily acquired, and a wide variety of design motifs can be developed.

Fig. 145

The illustrated Belt sections, Fig. 145, show a few of the many styles of decoration which may be stamped or carved on belt straps of natural, unglazed cowhide, 6 oz. weight, or vealskin, 4 oz. weight. For a beginner, stamping a simple design with one or two stamping tools, may be undertaken as a first project.

Methods of Decorating Leather — Carving — Stamping

The selection of suitable leather is important. Cowhide or strap leather is generally used, although a grade of vealskin, known as Kip, is satisfactory for some lightweight projects. Both should be vegetable tanned, with the natural grain unglazed. This leather is flexible and sufficiently soft to take tool impressions readily. Various cases and sheaths can be made of the 4 to 6 ounce weight. The 7 to 8 ounce weight is generally more satisfactory for belts, holsters and large articles.

The preparation of leather to be stamped or carved

To be sure the leather is uniformly moist, immerse it in cold water for about 10 seconds, then blot between paper towels or wipe with a soft cloth to remove excess moisture.

Before starting to decorate, let the leather stand for a few minutes covered with a damp cloth until the surface color appears nearly uniform.

Bend or flex the surface slightly to hasten the distribution of moisture.

The tools required for Leather Carving and Stamping are:

Edge beveler, edge creaser, swivel cutter or incising knife
Tracer, modeling tool with spoon and deerfoot ends
A piece of heavy plate glass or marble slab with a smooth surface
Background and design stamping tools
Wood mallet or hard wood striking stick, covered with rawhide

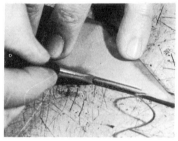

A   B
Beveling   Creasing

Fig. 146

After skill in the use of stamping tools is acquired with practice on scrap leather, a combination of more intricate designs can be successfully stamped.

The technique for carving leather requires more skill. For a beginner, the carving of a belt design in outline with a stamped background can be undertaken first. Later, as he develops the necessary skill, he will want to adapt or perfect carving designs with all possible variations. Repeat or continuous designs from those illustrated are examples.

Procedure in carving and stamping vealskin and strap leather

1. *Beveling.* Remove the edges, both top and bottom, or grain and flesh sides with the beveling tool, held with the V shaped and at the angle shown in Fig. 146. This controls the depth of cut which is regulated by the position of the third and fourth fingers, resting on the glass or marble, Fig. 146A.

Complete the beveling operation in one continuous stroke as far as possible in order to avoid any irregularities in the cut.

2. *Creasing.* Round the beveled edges with the creasing tool or the wood creaser. This smooths and rounds the beveled edges and provides a guide for the placing of the design, Fig. 146B.

3. *Transfer of Design.* If the leather surface has started to dry, as the color may indicate, moisten it again with the damp sponge and wipe as before. Prepare the design on tracing or bond paper, or use a section of a design sheet. Hold the design pattern with the fingers or attach it with drafting tape which is easily removed. Trace the design with even pressure to transfer or imprint it on the leather (Fig. 147A). Remove the paper and deepen all lines with the tip of the tracing tool, Fig. 147B.

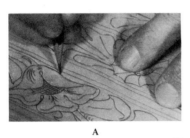 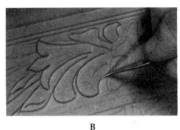

A   B

Fig. 147

4. Incising or carving of the design

The appearance of the finished decoration depends on the care and exactness of this operation. On a piece of scrap leather, practice the position of the hand, pressure, and depth of cut, until perfect control of the swivel cutter is achieved.

A   B
Shows incising of design outline.   Stamping background.

Fig. 148

a. Grasp the swivel cutter between the thumb and third finger with the forefinger pressing against the saddle or top, so that the slant or cutting edge can be guided while the necessary pressure is exerted, Fig. 148A.

b. Regulate the depth approximately 1/32 inch by the angle at which the cutting edge is held, Fig. 148A, and pull the cutter toward the inner edge of the leather. Guide and support the moving hand with the third and fourth fingers. Lift the cutter where design lines cross.

c. After the design outlines are incised, open and·spread them with the tracer to bring the design into clear relief. Avoid blurring the lines at any point. Use the deerfoot end to model the overlapping elements so that contrast and depth is produced.

5. Applying the background and design tools

Note the design elements and detail of border lines which must be even and clearly defined, as in Fig. 150A. A mallet or a cowhide-covered striking stick may be used.

a. Outline the background area by stamping a single line border, with the three or four dot stamp along the design margins. Be careful not to blur any design lines, Fig. 148B.

b. Continue to stamp the larger areas of the background with the different rosette stamps. Do not crowd them together but keep separate and distinct. The striking stick allows a more uniform balance in the pressure on the stamp than does the mallet.

c. Apply the selected border scallop, floral, and depression tools to complete the design motifs and emphasize elements in the decoration.

6. In some designs, a flat modeled background with relief modeling of the carved margins is effective. The spoon and deerfoot tools are used.

7. Finish the carved article after it is assembled and laced, unless a belt was carved. This can be finished at once with an application of saddle soap and leather dressing.

Carving Designs for Panels, Straps, and Other Items

Fig. 149

Use of tools for stamping and carving

Fig. 150, a carved leather music case shows the impressions of the background and floral element stamping tools which are used in carving. The dot series, used to form a stippled background, are indicated as A and B. Four veiner impressions, left, right, and the tip of a leaf, are indicated as C, D, E and F.

The leaf margin scallops are indicated by G, the oval depressions by H, and the sunburst or rosette by J. These elements and the tools for making them, also the crosshatch tools and impressions used for backgrounds, will be recognized in the photograph of tools, Fig. 151.

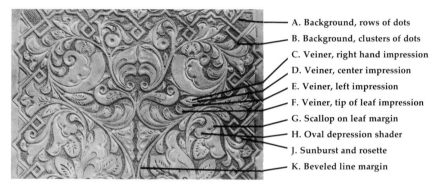

A. Background, rows of dots
B. Background, clusters of dots
C. Veiner, right hand impression
D. Veiner, center impression
E. Veiner, left impression
F. Veiner, tip of leaf impression
G. Scallop on leaf margin
H. Oval depression shader
J. Sunburst and rosette
K. Beveled line margin

Fig. 150

Background and Design Tools

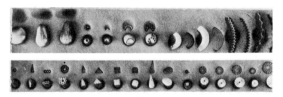

Fig. 151

Basket Weave Panel and With Carving

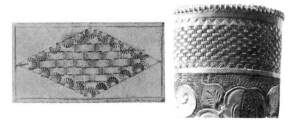

Fig. 152

Leather Craftwork Projects, Patterns, Decoration, and Assembly
Keytainers

Unlined Key Purses may be made of heavy calfskin or vealskin and these are not necessarily laced. Then the key plate is attached directly to the leather.

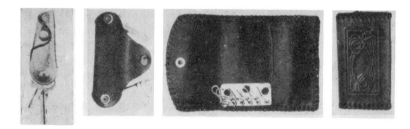

Fig. 153

The pattern sketch ½ size keytainer is an average size for the four key hook type. It may be enlarged to take additional keys, and the plates are available. The process, similar to that for other tooling projects, follows:

Dampen, crease and apply a suitable design. A panel, monogram, or conventional design on the center of the three fold pattern is the usual decoration. A small design or symbol may be tooled on the flap, if desired.

If the keytainer is not to be laced, crease the edge and stain, then polish with spoon tool or burnisher. The wood creasers often have a groove wide enough for this smoothing and polishing. The key plate and snap fastener may be attached either before or after the design is tooled. It should be done last if it interferes with the design.

The keyholder of the swivel plate type, made of steerhide or calfskin, should be lined with goatskin. Cut the outside and lining leathers the same size, apply the design and attach the key plate to the lining as directed and sketched in Fig. 152. Lace the lining to the outside without folding. The edges of the two pieces may be lightly cemented to hold together.

Attachment of snap fasteners

As a rule the snap fastener should be attached before a project is laced. If it is necessary to attach it afterward, lay it on a smooth surface and insert a firm heavy piece of leather which will prevent the drive punch from perforating the outside leather. Leave the leather in the same position for the attachment of the fastener. For a lined keytainer, if a concealed type fastener cap is used, it is necessary to leave this part unlaced until the cap is attached.

Keytainers – Three Styles
Patterns One-Half Actual Size

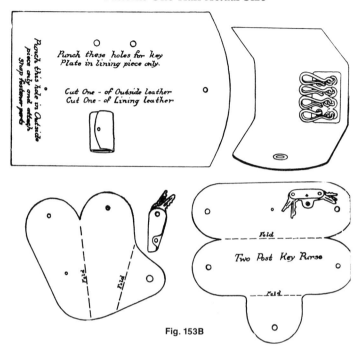

Fig. 153B

Snap Fastener Tools and Attachment Process

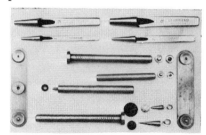

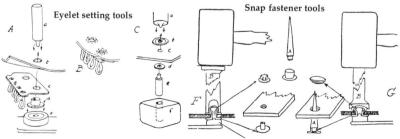

Fig. 154

1. Use a drive punch to perforate the leather to receive the post. The tool parts in Fig. 154, and in the sketches are: needle, setting tool, and anvil. The small end of the setting tool fits over the spring of the lower part. The larger end sets the cap as indicated in sketches F and G.

Drive punches of the sizes which are used are also shown.

2. Insert the post in the leather for the lower spring part of the fastener. Place it on the anvil with the small tip in the center of the post and the spring above as shown in sketch F. With the setting tool over the anvil, strike it lightly with the wood mallet.

3. To attach the cap and eyelet, press the leather down over the needle and the eyelet, remove the needle, place the cap over the eyelet, and cover it with the setting tool. Press the cap in place or rivet it firmly by striking with the wooden mallet.

Tooling steer and calfskin coin purses

Examples of the decoration of a coin purse are shown in the description of tooling on page 186. Patterns in Fig. 156.

Both leathers may be used unlined but the inside finish of the steer is neater if lined. A single coin purse involves less assembly detail than other purse projects and is desirable for learning and experimentation.

The process for a single calfskin coin purse:

1. Dampen by immersion in water for a brief time, or until the color changes uniformly, then lay the piece or part face down on a level absorbent surface until partially dry.

2. Flex the leather slightly to distribute the remaining moisture. Crease the edges and transfer the design.

3. Apply the tooled decoration and permit the leather to dry. Cement the front and back together *along the edges only* and deepen the edge crease as a guide for the lacing assembly.

4. Start at one corner and punch the holes or perforate by any of the methods shown on page 162. Estimate the holes and space near the corners to bring the holes at that point in each corner.

5. Stain the edges if the leather shows a light edge, dry, and start lacing about three holes below the top edge of the front.

The same process is used with steerhide except that the front is cut long enough to turn under at the top. If a lining is desired refer to the detailed procedure on page 155.

6. *Double Coin Purses and Coin Case Purses* are constructed in about the same way except for the insertion of the additional pocket and flap. These must be skived thin at the edges so that the combined thickness will not be out of proportion with the single thickness of the flap. Cement carefully in position before punching and trim along the edges to remove any unevenness.

Use a straight edge to mark and cut this away with an extension blade knife. The dimensions are optional. An average size is 3 by 6 inches for the one-piece back, allowing for the fold of the curved flap, the part usually decorated.

7. A practical type of coin purse with an outside pocket which expands is sketched in Fig. 156 with the approximately one-half actual size pattern.

Stamped design

Tooled designs

Fig. 155

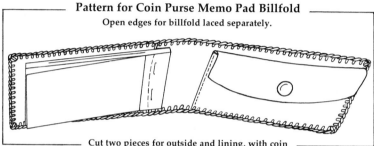

Pattern for Coin Purse Memo Pad Billfold

Open edges for billfold laced separately.

Cut two pieces for outside and lining, with coin
purse of corresponding size. Pocket for memo pad as indicated.

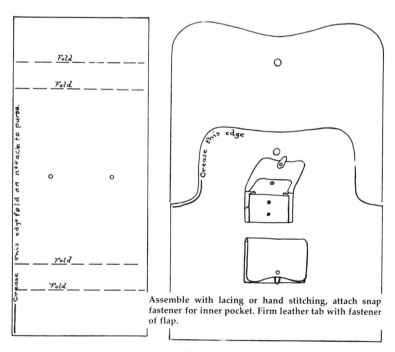

Assemble with lacing or hand stitching, attach snap
fastener for inner pocket. Firm leather tab with fastener
of flap.

Fig. 156

Billfolds

Two styles of billfolds are sketched for the patterns below. If to be decorated by tooling or modeling, firm steerhide or calfskin should be used.

Nontooling leather, goatskin, or pigskin may also be made according to these patterns. The construction detail is indicated on the patterns in the following order.

1. Plan a design for decoration and cut the pattern pieces. Calfskin need not have an attached lining and vealskin is also smooth enough so it can be used without a lining. A stamped or carved decoration is suitable for vealskin, tooled decorations for calfskin.

2. Follow procedure for preparation of leather and decorating as given on pages 158 to 159.

3. Skive lightly and carefully the edges of steerhide which are not to be laced. (These must be cut ⅜ inch longer than for calfskin.) Crease and burnish the lines for a finish on these edges. Crease edges to be laced as a guide for perforations.

4. Assemble the parts, cement the edges lightly to hold in position for lacing. Use wide steer or narrow goatskin for either steerhide or calf. Self lacing can be used for pigskin or goatskin. Start the lacing at a point that will permit the end of the thong to be concealed.

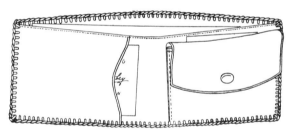

Fig. 157A

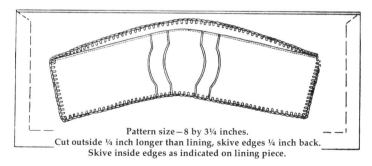

Pattern size—8 by 3¼ inches.
Cut outside ¼ inch longer than lining, skive edges ¼ inch back.
Skive inside edges as indicated on lining piece.

Fig. 157B

Methods of decoration — tooled leather projects

Notebooks may be made of tooling vealskin, tooling steer, or 4 ounce cowhide.

The illustration, Fig. 158, shows 4 ounce cowhide, A, with a modeled decoration. A carved design would also be suitable for this weight leather. The others are vealskin, B, with Girl Scout emblem tooled and steerhide, C, also tooled. The cowhide is unlined; the vealskin and steerhide notebooks are lined with goatskin. All three are laced with wide steerhide thongs.

1. Bevel and crease the edges, then moisten as for other projects. Trace the design from a pattern or design sheet while the leather is moist. Carefully redefine the outlines and relief model of the elements of the designs, adding details freehand in the emblem and the Indian head decorations, if either is selected. The cowhide cover, Fig. 158A, is decorated with lettering developed with the double bevel line design.

2. After the decoration is applied, fold the cover over a pad of paper or cardboard about the thickness of the notebook leaves until the leather dries.

3. Attach the notebook metal to the cowhide with rivets inserted in the base plate metal. The album, Fig. 158D, is described on page 182.

Fig. 158

The Photograph Album in Fig. 158 is steerhide with a relief modeled decoration. The edges may be creased and stained to leave as in the illustration, or they be whip laced with wide steerhide lacing. The covers and album leaves are punched for assembly with a plaited thong strand and sliding knot. See pages 312-313 for plaiting and knots.

Bookends — steerhide or calfskin

A pattern for bookends may be cut according to one of those illustrated in Fig. 159. The leather pieces must be cut ⅜ inch larger than the metals, and the outside piece ½ inch longer to allow for bending over the metal form. The process follows:

Fig. 159

1. Cut a pair of rust resistant 18 gauge metal forms from a paper pattern, ¼ inch smaller than the inside leather pattern, using metal snips. Remove the rough edges with a file.

2. Mark the position of the bend for the L-shaped metal, according to the leather pattern. Place the upper part between two woodblocks with the line of bend just visible above the lower block. Clamp the blocks in a bench vise.

3. Bend the protruding end as far as possible by hand, then shape to a right angle bend with a metal hammer or rawhide mallet.

4. Decorate the front section with a suitable design. Relief or repoussé modeling is effective, since a padding over the metal will prevent the flattening of the raised elements of the design. Pad the section of metal with sheet wadding, adding slightly thicker pieces in the raised parts. Attach with a little cement at the edges, keeping below the creased line margin, so as not to interfere with the lacing.

5. Cement the lining to the metals, smoothing out all wrinkles. Suede or a thin section of steerhide is suitable. Place the outside in position over the wadding, cementing it at the fold and edges. Cement the outside to the lining margins which extend beyond the metals. Keep the design or border lines even with the margins, allowing space beyond the metals for the perforations and lacing.

6. If necessary, trim any uneven places in the edges of the lining. Punch carefully, within a margin of ⅛ inch and avoiding any contact with the edge of the metal. Lace the edges together with wide whip lacing.

Camera cases

Cameras of periods before the importation of other models with cases to fit, are still in use and cases may need replacement. The illustrated models made of durable top grain cowhide in lighter weights may be adapted for these earlier models.

The sketches show a style of carrying strap and method of making the knot which was used on the strap. The detail is sketched and can be followed in tying the knot in Fig. 160B, 1 to 6, which is a two-strand Turk's Head.

In lacing the gussets it is essential that the two thongs from the edges of the front be started and continued together, with the direction indicated from the sides underneath and up on the front, repeated at the same rate to the bottom of the oval gussets. These must be punched with the same number of holes as the outside and so must be closer together on the semicircular gusset edge. The method of marking and punching these holes is indicated in Fig. 160D, sketch C.

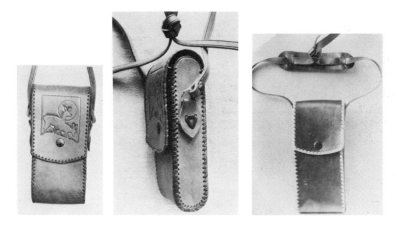

Fig. 160A

Carrying Strap Detail — Two-Strand Turk's Head

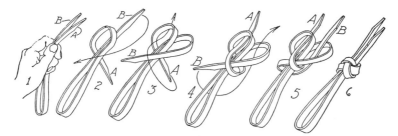

Fig. 160B

Attachment of notebook metals

For Style C, attach the metal to the lining before it is cemented in place. Assemble with wide lacing starting near the top of a pocket.

A slip over style notebook cover is illustrated in Fig. 158B. This is suitable for stiff paperbacked notebooks, manuals, and some other book covers. Pockets are laced to the outside pieces and the original covers slipped into them. This style cover should be cut ⅜ inch larger than the cover which is to be inserted, with an additional width for the fold.

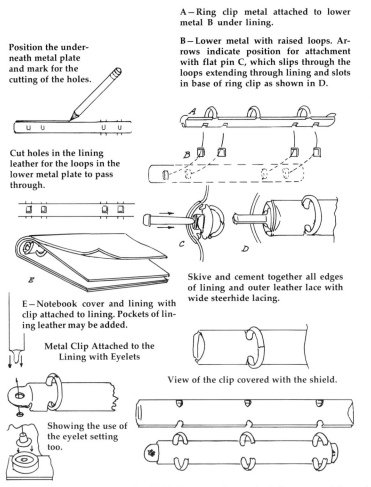

A—Ring clip metal attached to lower metal B under lining.

B—Lower metal with raised loops. Arrows indicate position for attachment with flat pin C, which slips through the loops extending through lining and slots in base of ring clip as shown in D.

Position the underneath metal plate and mark for the cutting of the holes.

Cut holes in the lining leather for the loops in the lower metal plate to pass through.

E—Notebook cover and lining with clip attached to lining. Pockets of lining leather may be added.

Skive and cement together all edges of lining and outer leather lace with wide steerhide lacing.

Metal Clip Attached to the Lining with Eyelets

View of the clip covered with the shield.

Showing the use of the eyelet setting too.

Slip the shield down over the attached clip to conceal the eyelets.

Fig. 160C

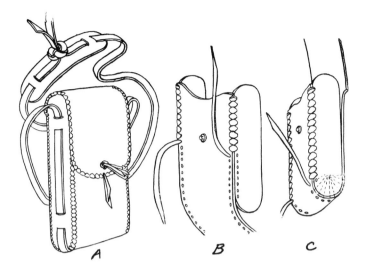

Fig. 160D

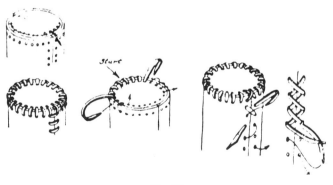

Fig. 161

A circular base for a quiver or other case is laced as in Fig. 161, starting at the arrow point. The side closing may be laced with crossed thongs on the outside or inside.

Folding coin purses

A popular type of gusset purse, which is an adaptation of the English stitched coin purse, is carved in Fig. 162 and sketched to show the pattern outline and method of assembling in Fig. 163. Pigskin is commercially used for this purse and is very durable. The types shown are vealskin carved and stamped.

The procedure follows:

1. Prepare a pattern in proportion to the parts shown in the sketch. The dimensions of this purse are 3 by 4 inches which is a practical size. Also select a carving or stamping design and sketch both on tracing paper.

2. Trace the pattern outline on moistened leather, which must be firm, and carefully cut the parts so they will fit together *exactly*.

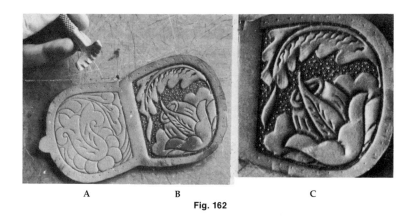

A   B   C

Fig. 162

3. Trace the design for carving on the outside piece and practice the carving elements on a scrap piece of leather before attempting to carve the purse. Refer to page 173 for instructions in carving. (Do not bevel vealskin.)

4. Incise the outline with the swivel cutter or an incising knife, keeping the depth of cut even and not exceeding one-fourth the thickness of the leather. A safe rule for vealskin is to cut only just through the grain surface of the leather.

5. Open the incised lines by spreading them apart with the tip of a modeling tool. Develop a background for the carved motif by depressing the area with the round pebble dot tool, using a rawhide striking stick or hard wood mallet to lightly hammer the tool head, while moving it in irregular contours without overlapping.

6. Depress all design elements where the pattern indicates an overlaping. Use a modeling or shaped beveling tool which rounds and deepens the margins.

7. In turn, apply the scallop shaped tools and the horseshoe shaped tools, then the oval depression tools along the floral outlines to give relief to plain areas. Design and background tools are shown in Fig. 144, page 170.

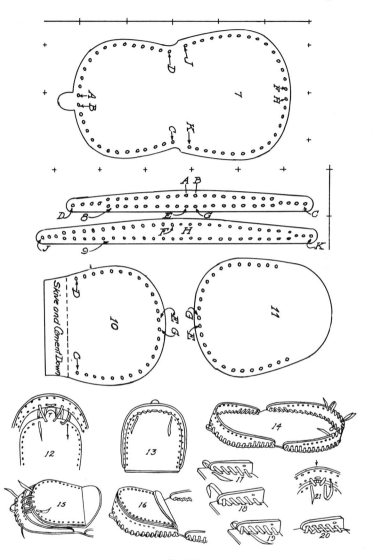

Fig. 163

Folding Coin Purse

Punching and lacing procedure

The success of the purse assembly and the finished appearance depends on the accuracy of the punching and the order of lacing the parts together with an even whip stitch. The parts of the purse are shown in the pattern outlines, Fig. 163.

1. Starting at the center points F and H of the upper section, mark with

pencil dots the position of the 15 holes required in each side. These are approximately 3/16" apart, but the slight variation on the curves precludes the use of the gauge punch. Note that the space is left for the fold at points J and K. Punch the holes singly with a hand punch or drive punch.

2. Starting at the center points A and B mark 14 holes on each side to D and C as indicated in the pattern. Mark the gussets with corresponding holes and punch singly as before.

3. Mark and punch the holes for the pocket sections E to D and G to C as indicated. Skive and cement down the top of the outside pocket over which the flap of the inner pocket folds.

Folding coin purse, lacing process

1. Start at the middle points of each gusset, Fig. 163, parts 8 and 9 and lace the edges to the purse, part 7. Lace gusset 8 with center point marked A-B to part 7 starting at the corresponding points A-B. Note that the lacing thong is passed through the two center points of the gusset 8 to the middle of the thong and each end then laced toward the points C-D using a Whip stitch. One end of the lacing moves to the right while the other moves to the left alternately. Gusset 9 is attached to part 7 in the same manner, starting at points F-H and moving to points J and K.

2. Lace the parts 10 and 11 to the upper edge of gusset 9 as indicated in Fig. 163, sketch 15. Start the lacing at points E and G. End the lacing as shown in sketches 17 to 20.

3. Lace the upper edge of gusset 9 as indicated in Fig. 163, sketch 13. Two short thongs may be used and the ends left protruding to serve as finger hold opposite the tab at A-B, Fig. 163. These two extensions are a convenience in opening the purse.

4. End the lacing at the gusset tip as shown in Fig. 163, sketch 18. Pass the lacing through the last hole in the gusset twice as indicated in sketch 19 and carry the end under three or four loops as shown in Fig. 163, sketch 20. Tighten the lacing before cutting off the end.

5. In Fig. 162A the lower half of the traced design has been carved and design tools applied. A leaf design stamped with the stamping tool is shown. In B margins have been beveled down to produce a relief effect. The enlargement Fig. 162C shows detail of background and design stamping.

Hand purses A and B

The small hand purses of vealskin, shown as A and B, Fig. 164, with carved designs, are cut according to the scale drawn pattern and dimensions shown in Fig. 164 and 165. Light weight strap leather or cowhide, carving quality, may also be used. This permits deeper carving. These leathers, which have a smooth flesh surface, need not be lined, unless to provide a base for a stitched pocket. In this case, goatskin is preferable for the lining and lacing. Suede may be used for the lining and pockets, if desired, but with narrow goatskin or wide steerhide lacing thongs.

A

Fig. 164

B

Either purse illustrated is constructed as follows:

1. Cut the lining, if required, then the outside from selected vealskin, steerhide, or 4 ounce weight cowhide. Dampen, edge crease, and trace the design shown, or one adapted from other carving designs shown on page 160. If vealskin is used, the design may be tooled or carved. Steerhide can only be tooled. Follow instructions for tooling or carving on page 158 and 173.

2. Cut the gussets from the thinner sections of the leather according to the dimensions given in the patterns, Fig. 165. Calfskin or steerhide pieces should be cut long enough to skive, cement, and fold down at the top. Purse A requires a shaped gusset for ends of folded purse, purse B, a straight gusset with zipper opening at rounded top.

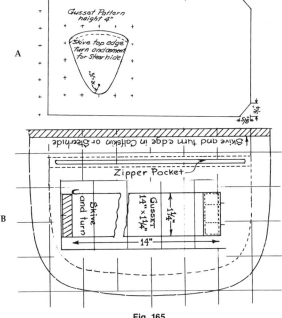

Fig. 165

Purse B includes a zipper closed pocket, stitched to the lining as indicated. Dimensions of the gussets are given. The loop handle can be a straight piece 1½ by 14 inches skived, folded together and cemented. Attach to gusset with 3-hole fastener or hand stitching. The gussets for both purses are laced to the outside with narrow lacing in any of the styles of lay-over stitch.

Hand Purse C

The unusual combination of tooling and plain calfskin used for the hand purse in C of Fig. 166 is especially suitable for a tooled monogram decoration as shown on the shaped handle, which conforms to the flap of the purse. This is proportioned as sketched in Fig. 167. The construction process is as follows:

1. Cut the front and the back sections of selected colored calfskin (not tooling calfskin) according to the planned dimensions, using a pattern with which the shaped hand strap will conform. The width or height of the closed purse should be about two-thirds of the length for good proportions.

2. Cut the straight gusset in one piece or in two pieces, sewn together at the center of the bottom. Use a thin section of calfskin. Cut the lining of a matching or contrasting suede with pockets for front and back. This purse may have a zipper closing, if desired. Stitch the zipper to the lining before this is cemented in place. Trim ¼ inch from the top of the gusset ends and front lining parts to permit the outside margin of the calfskin to be skived and turned down over them.

3. Cut the shaped handle of tooling calfskin, from the pattern given in Fig. 167. Crease the edges for the lacing and tool a monogram or decorative design on the front. Lace with narrow matching or contrasting goatskin thongs in the simple layover style, starting at one corner of the straight strap end. Continue lacing around the shaped front and back to the opposite corner of the strap end which will later be laced in with the center of the gusset and the back section.

Attach the base or cage of the snap fastener to the purse front in line with the plate post to be attached to the flap, under the handle.

4. Place the front of the handle in position above the curve of the purse flap and hold with cement while marking through the lacing holes with a pencil to indicate where corresponding holes are to be punched in the flap. Remove the tooled front of the handle and make the perforations where marked with a 3/32 inch drive punch.

C   **Fig. 166**   D

Hand Purse C Pattern

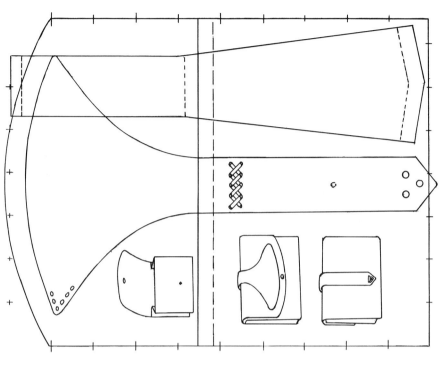

Fig. 167

5. Cement the handle section along the lacing in the same position with the holes corresponding. Attach it to the front of the purse with a thong drawn up from the back of the front, at one corner of the curve, then down and up through the holes in turn around the curve to the opposite corner. Weave both ends back through the last 3 loops of the thong stitches, then carefully tighten them to hold the ends securely.

6. Attach the handle strap at the top and center of the flap with a lacing thong brought through two parallel rows of holes, centered and punched with the 3/32 inch drive punch, so that a firm crossed attachment secures the handle to the purse flap.

7. Lightly skive the top margins of the front and gussets, cement the lining in position, and turn the margins down over it. Cement and crease the folded tops for a finish. Cement the assembly margins of the lining and outside to-gether, trim any uneven edges and crease for the lacing guide line. Punch with the gauge punch and lace together with the same narrow lacing as for the shaped handle. Cement the unfinished end of the handle strap to the back of the purse at the center, before punching and lacing this section.

Style D. Underarm

This underarm purse with a zipper or slide fastener closing is a simply constructed one piece style of steerhide decorated with a monogram in one corner. Two pockets, front and back, are stitched to a suede lining. The outline pattern for the outside and lining of the purse, also the gussets, is sketched in Fig. 167. The position of the pockets is indicated by dotted lines. The steerhide facings which cover the curved tops of the purse above the slide fastener are also indicated. The depth of the finished purse at the center is 6½ inches, width at the bottom, 10½ inches, and the rounded corner top is 8½ inches wide at the point of the fastener closing.

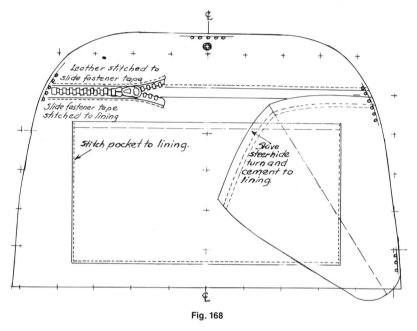

Fig. 168

Construction procedure

1. Cut the outside from selected firm steerhide and the gussets from softer thinner sections, also the facing pieces, according to the pattern in Fig. 168. Cut the suede lining for the outside, gussets, and pockets. Allow ⅜ inch margins on the tops.

2. Lightly skive the lower edge of the facing pieces, also skive the top edges of the gussets. Construct the gussets as described on page 156 with the top edges turned down and cemented to the lining.

3. Skive the top edges of the lining, turn under ¼ inch and cement to the underneath side of the fastener tape, leaving 1/16 inch space along the fastener metals. Turn under the skived lower edges of the steerhide facings and carefully cement to top of the fastener tape exactly in line with the suede cemented underneath. The opening should be from the left.

4. Machine stitch the edges to the tape, with the slide fastener now open. If necessary to keep margins straight, hand stitch the end sections (about 1 inch) turning the tape ends in between the lining and steer facings.

5. Cement one edge of the gussets to the outside from the curve at the narrow bottom ends, punch and lace with wide steer lacing or narrow lay-over lacing of goatskin. Instructions for lacing styles are given on page 137. Start lacing at the bottom curve at the center of a thong long enough to lace to the top of the gussets and leave an end to be concealed. Avoid making a hole on the fold of the gussets, and space according to the width and style of lacing.

6. Cement the opposite sides of the gussets, punch and lace as before. If there is difficulty keeping these edges together, insert and tie a piece of thong to hold them at the top until this can be laced.

7. With separate thongs, punch and lace the tops of the bag, cementing the facing and the outside together. Attach a bag plate at the center.

The purses A and B in Fig. 169A are shown to illustrate the type of decoration possible with stamped designs and creased lines. Background types of stamping are shown in the corners of purse A. 169B is an enlargement of a tooled calfskin purse, showing both relief and repousse decoration.

Fig. 169A

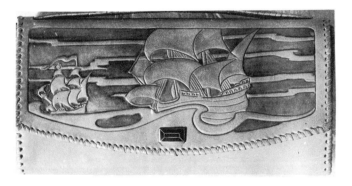

Fig. 169B

Envelope purse

This practical style of envelope purse may be made of calfskin, vealskin, or steerhide, in natural or dyed colors, and decorated with the tooled design shown in photographs, Fig. 169, or with other selected designs. An embossed leather, colored calfskin or morocco may be constructed in the same style, but without ornamentation.

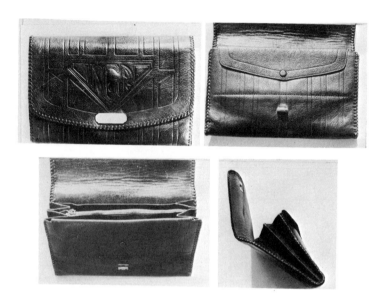

Fig. 169

The purse illustrated was made of black steerhide, lined with black morocco and laced with narrow goatskin thongs, six times the edge length, dyed to match. The size: 9 by 5 inches finished. Evenly spaced vertical parallel lines, creased with a tracing tool, relieve the plain surface of the front, back, and flap, which also has a tooled monogram decoration. The construction process is as follows:

Cutting the parts

1. Cut from selected firm leather the outside piece 9⅝ inches wide and 15¼ inches long, for the front, back and flap. For the gussets, cut a pair from the softer, thinner leather, 5½ inches deep and 5½ inches wide at the curved top. For the front outside pocket, cut one firm piece of leather 8 inches wide and 4½ inches deep, with lining cut the same size.

2. Cut lining leather for back and front inside pockets 2¼ inches deep and 8 inches wide. Cut two linings for the zipper fastened pocket 5½ inches deep and 8¼ inches wide. For the lining of the zipper pocket, cut thin suede or goatskin, the same width and 5¼ inches deep. For the gussets, cut lining leather ¼ inch shorter than the gusset pieces.

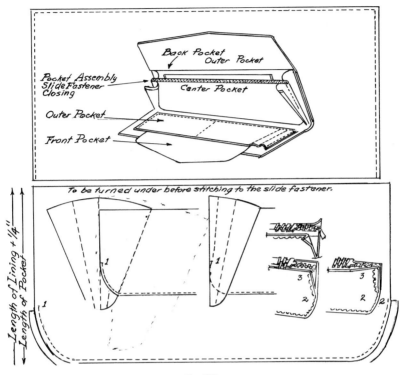

Fig. 170

Assembly process

1. Dampen the outside leather evenly with a sponge, then permit it to dry partially, so that no moisture appears on the surface and it is uniformly darkened. Crease the measured lines, then tool the monogram or design on the flap. Fold the leather over a pad of paper towels and permit it to dry in this position.

2. While the outside is drying, assemble the lining. Skive slightly and turn down the top ¼ inch of the inside back and front pockets, cement and smooth in place. Cement together the parts for the front pocket and crease the margins. Cement the inside sections, about 2½ inches to the lining and stitch this part to it.

3. Construct the zipper pocket: Skive, apply cement to the edge, and turn down ¼ inch along the tops of the pocket and their lining pieces, then cement the pocket lining pieces along the underneath sides of the zipper fastener, leaving a margin of 3/16 inch on each side of the closed metal slide. Machine stitch in place, then attach the outside pocket pieces to the top of the slide fastener in the same way, stitching the folded edge the same distance from the metal. Stitch the lower edges to the lining at the line of the fold of the bottom of the front.

4. Assemble the gussets, skiving the top margin and cementing it down over the lining. Apply cement lightly to the rest of the inner surface of the gussets and smooth the lining to them. Fold the gusset from the top down at the center and slip over the ends of the zipper pocket. Cement them close to the center, then stitch the gusset folded with sufficient margin to securely hold the ends of the zipper pocket together.

5. Skive the front top edge of the outside leather; cement the lining to it, smoothing out all wrinkles toward the sides. Turn the top skived edge down over it and cement in place. Trim off any uneven edges of lining and then cement the gussets to the outside along the margins, as directed for gusset assembly on page 156. Punch holes with a 00 tube for narrow lacing 3/32 inch, adjusting the spacing so that ⅛ inch remains at the top corners.

6. Start lacing at the top of the front with a double stitch through the first hole, and the end concealed between the outside and gusset lining. Continue around the gusset and take a double stitch through the last hole. Cut the thong, if the end is too long, to conceal as before. Tighten the last 4 or 5 stitches.

7. With a new thong, lace the flap of the purse around to the top of the second gusset. Conceal two or three inches under the gusset lacing at both sides, after tightening the last four stitches; others, if necessary.

8. Attach the snap fastener and bag plate. Finish with a light coat of leather dressing.

Writing portfolio

The writing portfolio sketched in Fig. 171 and illustrated in Fig. 172 is made of steerhide in a two-tone brown and laced with matching wide steerhide thongs. While it is an advanced project, the craftsman, who has mastered the tooling and assembly process, will have no difficulty if the directions are carefully followed.

The materials required are:

A selected firm piece of steerhide, 12½ by 28½ inches for outside cover
2 4 by 5 inches of firm steerhide cut diagonally for blotter corners
2 pieces of firm steerhide, 6 by 2½ inches shaped for fastener strap
1 bag plate or portfolio lock for fastener
3 pieces for overlapping pockets, cut from thinner sections of steerhide:
   1 piece 12 by 7½ inches, 1 piece 12 by 5½ inches, 1 piece 12 by 3½ inches
2 gusset pieces of thin, soft steer, 7½ x 1 inch tapered to ¾ inch with this end rounded, and wide steerhide lacing 2½ times the edge margins
1 piece of suede lining 12½ by 28½ inches
1 piece skiver lining for base of the blotter pad 9 by 11¾ inches
1 piece of blotting paper or smooth writing surface
1 piece of buckram or firm, flexible interlining, 11½ by 26 inches

The equipment needed includes:

Cement, bone folder, modeling tools, rocker knife, skiving knife, gauge and single punch, mallet, moistening sponge and cutting block.

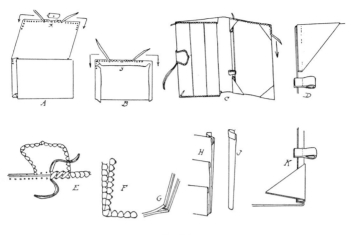

Fig. 171

The construction process:

1. Dampen the surface of the cover piece, crease the edges for a punching and lacing guide and trace the chosen designs for back and front, as described on page 157. Test the method of decoration and tools on a scrap piece of leather, then apply the decoration. When complete, fold the steerhide cover over a pad of paper towels or newspapers and permit it to dry.

2. Skive all the edges of the pocket pieces, turn the top edges under, cement the fold and crease for a finish. If a division is desired in the inner pocket, stitch in position to the suede lining, with the three edge margins even. Place the other two overlapping pockets together and cement at the side, top and bottom, then cement the assembled pockets to the lining in the position shown in Fig. 172, sketch C.

3. Cement the pieces for the fastening strap together, and trim one end in a rounded or shaped form similar to the one illustrated. Position the parts of the bag plate or portfolio lock and attach the cage to the lower pocket, in a perforation through the pocket and lining. Adjust the post to correspond to the fastening strap and attach. See attachments, page 177. Edge crease and lace the sides and shaped end.

4. Cement the ends of the overlapping pocket assembly to one side of the gussets, then punch and lace (holes ½ inch apart), sketches A, B and E. End the thong at the center of the tapered gusset, laced through the corner, by inserting the last inch through three loops.

5. Skive all edges of the blotter corners. Turn the edge of the diagonal under, cement down and crease for a finish. Hand or machine stitch the longer outside edges of the right hand blotter corner and the pencil loop to the skiver base of the blotter, sketch D. Turn the seam inward and cement it to skiver base, to be covered with the blotter or other writing surface later, sketch K. Cement the other outside corner edges to the blotter base.

6. Pad with cotton the backs of any raised parts of the design. Cement a piece of buckram or stiff tailor's interlining over them and also cement the ½ inch margins to the steerhide cover. Smooth the suede lining over the interlining, attaching it with cement along the back fold of the portfolio, then along all margins for 2 inches from the edge of the steerhide. Trim any extended edges of the lining even with the cover. Keep in the folded position as in sketch D.

7. Cement the other edge of the gussets, previously cemented to the overlapping pocket assembly, to the lining and steerhide cover.

8. Using a ruler or straight edge, mark any uneven margins and trim. Crease the guide line, ⅛ inch from all margins and punch the holes ¼ inch apart for wide lacing, avoiding any perforation on a fold of the pockets or blotter corners.

9. Start the lacing, Fig. 172, about an inch from the diagonal of one of the outer blotter corners, concealing the ends under three loops before proceeding. Continue lacing to the upper corner of a pocket gusset, then lace it to the outside, and around the lower tapered end as in sketch F. Lace from the corner of the outside to the center, where the fastener strap is to be attached. Lace the other margins, along the side, ends, and opposite gusset corner to end at the center as before.

10. Punch and lace the fastener strap, except the end which is to be inserted at the center of the lower pocket as in sketch E. Insert the strap between the lining and the cover, adjusting it with the position of the cage part of the bag plate, so that the fastening will leave about an inch space, when the portfolio is closed.

11. Center the strap and mark two rows of holes as indicated in sketch E, then remove and punch the holes as marked. Replace the strap with the holes coinciding, and lace in place with the ends of the strap and edge lacing thongs, forming a double cross lacing. Insert the thong ends between the lining and lower pocket, tighten the loops and cement any loose end to the lining. Insert the blotter or writing surface under the corners.

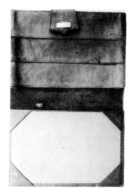

Fig. 172

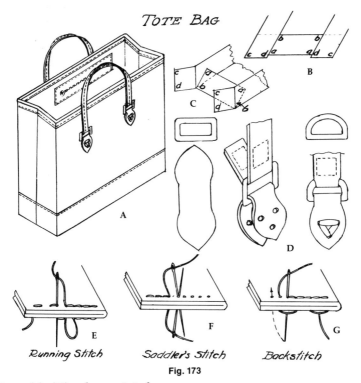

Running Stitch   Saddler's Stitch   Backstitch

Fig. 173

Utility and knitting bag or tote bag

A practical all-purpose bag is shown in the sketch and pattern of Fig. 173 also the assembly detail for the three parts, the one-piece lining, the fabric sides, and the base of leather or a leather substitute. The construction process follows:

1. Cut the lining of suitable cloth, or a lightweight lining leather substitute, which is flexible, in one piece 32½ inches wide and 29½ inches long or deep. Cut the ends of the lining as indicated at A-B, 2½ inches deep at each corner, sketch A.

2. Cut a piece of the lining material for the pocket, 8 inches long and 4½ inches wide. Stitch a slide fastener, Fig. 173, sketch A, 7 inches long in the position indicated, one tape to each side of the fastener opening in the pocket. Stitch the pocket to the lining. Conceal the ends of the tape between the pocket and lining and hand stitch in place.

3. Form the bottom of the lining by folding the corners, where cut, toward the center, Fig. 173 B and C. Stitch the edges c-d together. Fold the projecting base part upward on the seamed side of the corners and cement the stitched corners to it. Hand stitch the juncture for added strength, if desired. Fold the lining along the ends as indicated in sketch C. Hand or machine stitch edges d-b to base ends b-b. Fold the corners b-e vertically to form the base. Use Barbour's linen thread, size 12, for hand stitching.

4. Cut a piece of heavy linen or homespun fabric for the center section,

33½ inches by 9 inches. Cut a piece of tailor's interlining or firm lightweight cardboard the same size as the lining. Cut an additional piece 4¼ inches by 11 inches, for extra stiffness on the bottom.

5. Construct the base of a piece of firm steerhide or leather substitute. Slash and fold it to form the shallow box base in the same way the lining was cut, folded, and stitched, Fig. 173B and C. Skive the edges, if steerhide is used, fold the top edges under ¼ inch and cement down. Hand stitch the vertical edges together with needle and thread from opposite sides to form a double or harness stitch, Fig. 173, sketch F.

6. Place the base over the bottom of the center section for a depth of ⅜ inch. Apply cement along both edges and smooth evenly together. Hand stitch together with two threads and needles, using the harness stitch.

7. Fold the ends of the interlining or cardboard to fit between the lining and the outside, center section and base. Insert the extra base piece of the interlining. Hand or machine stitch the ends of the center section together. Fit over the lining and interlining.

8. Construct the handle as sketched, a piece of the base material 18 inches by 1¼ inches stitched as indicated and attached to the center section with dees and separate ends, cut double and cemented together for the three hole fastening to attach the handle to the bag. The fastening ends are stitched to the handle, with the juncture concealed by the dees, and the three hole fastening made of a goatskin thong, tied through the outside and the interlining.

9. Trim any protruding edges at the top and baste together. Finish with a binding of the base material or the lining, using a piece 32 inches long and 1¼ inches wide. Fold over the top with the margins even on both sides and cement in place. Stitch through both edges with the double harness stitch to hold the binding firmly in place.

Leather Box — Style A

Leather boxes may be made entirely of cowhide in a medium heavy weight, of steerhide or of Morocco, lined with goatskin. Patterns are given in Fig. 174 for a hand sewn style and for one assembled by means of the three hole fastening device, Fig. 182. One half of each style is shown and the dimensions may be followed in cutting the leather. Both boxes may be decorated by carving or with line creased panels.

Tools and equipment for hand sewn box
    Woodblock 1¼" by 3" by 5½"
    Rocker knife for cutting saddle skirting on soft pine board
    Skiving knife
    Overstitch wheel with 6 stitches per inch
    Harness awl and curved stitching awl
    Harness needles
    Linen thread, Barbours No. 12
    Edge beveler-edge creaser, tools for decoration
    Edge stain, leather dressing
    Spring type catch

Cutting and preparation of leather

1. Lay out the pattern according to the outlines for the style chosen, making an allowance for the thickness of the leather, that is a margin equal to the thickness of the leather for the folds. This step would not be necessary for steerhide or Morocco.

2. Cut the leather to the pattern outlines, as adjusted for thickness. Bevel strap leather and crease the edges. Cut the grooves for the folds as indicated in the pattern, taking care not to cut deeper than one half the thickness of the leather. Skive the edges to miter together on a 45 degree angle as indicated in the sketch of the corner detail, Fig. 174, A and B.

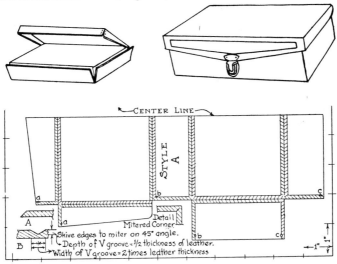

Fig. 174

Assembly Procedure

For the hand sewn box, Style A, Fig. 174, a waxed thread assembly is necessary. The making of waxed thread is described on page 211. The tools required include: incising knife, skiving knife, creaser, beveler, stitching wheel, awl, and wood block.

1. Immerse the leather for a minute in cool water. Place it flat on a paper towel and wipe off any excess of water that may cling to the surface. If this does not appear uniformly darkened, wipe over the surface with a damp sponge.

2. Mark the hole spacing, 6 stitches per inch, marked with the over stitch finishing wheel, Fig. 175, sketch E. Pierce holes with the awl along lines creased at the points marked as shown in sketch F. Keep a soft pine board or cutting block under the leather during this process.

3. Allow the leather to partially dry before sewing the box over the wood-block. Sew with waxed Barbour's linen thread, using two needles as indicated in sketches J to N. Shape the stitches with the overstitch finishing wheel as each part is sewn together.

4. Start at a lower corner of the box, sketch I. With a needle at each end of the thread, pull it to the middle point. Pass the needles through the next hole above in opposite directions. Use a curved awl to open up the holes as shown in sketch J.

5. The formation of a locked stitch is indicated in Fig. 176. Make one turn with the loop of thread around each needle, then pull the needle through and the thread taut. The direction of the turn around the right-hand needle is clockwise and that of the left-hand needle is counterclockwise. The formation of the locked stitch is indicated in sketches L and M. Shape the stitches with the finishing wheel as shown in sketch N.

6. Attach the catch or lock according to directions. Apply burnishing stain to all edges and leather dressing to all surfaces. The finished box may be lined with skiver, or a water proof oiled silk.

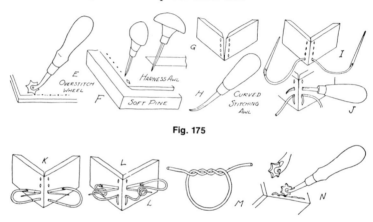

Fig. 175

Fig. 176

Leather Box — Style B

The finished appearance of the carved style B box, Fig. 177, depends on the accuracy of the cutting of the fastening projections and the spacing of the holes, as well as the perfection of the carved decoration. All holes, in the ends and in the projections, must match exactly. Mark them before cutting the leather.

1. Prepare the leather as for style A and allow to partially dry. Crease all edges for a finish.

2. Decorate the lid of the box with a carving design, first outlined from a pattern, with a tracer.

3. Carefully incise the outlines of design elements with the swivel cutter or incising knife. Do not make the cuts deeper than the grain surface of the leather.

(a) Open the lines to a groove with the special outline beveler.

(b) Apply background stamps, then the depression stamps, veiners and scallop stamps to define and emphasize the floral elements, as directed in the section on the carving process, pages 172-174.

(c) Crease a panel line on the sides, ends, and flap.

4. Dampen the leather again and form the box over the woodblock. Make sure the marked holes are in line and punch with a driver punch before removing the leather from the wooden form. Let the box dry on the form with the fastening projections lightly cemented in place.

5. Assemble when dry with goatskin thongs, 3/16 inch wide, following the steps of the three-hole fastening sketched on page 209, Fig. 182. Attach lock or metal clasp. Burnish the edges and rub lightly with leather dressing to finish as suggested for the hand-sewn box.

6. The steerhide box, shown in the photograph is decorated with a simple creased line design. This and other effective designs for this project are reproduced on page 160. It is lined with firm goatskin and laced with narrow contrasting goat lacing. Wide Florentine lacing of steer would also be suitable. The box illustrated is 4 by 6 inches with a depth of 2 inches. Other proportionate sizes can be constructed and assembled in the same way.

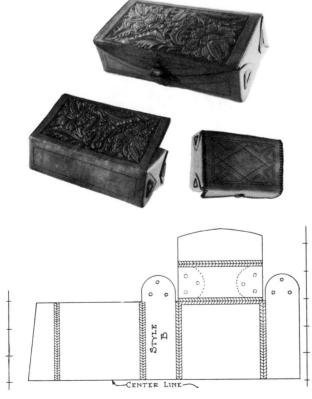

Fig. 177

Combination brief case and notebook

This briefcase, with or without the notebook ring binder is a neat and practical carrying case for a student or secretary. The closing slide fastener, which permits the case to open flat, may have a lock, if desired. The over-all size of the finished case is 12 inches by 13 inches. A larger case, 14 inches by 15 inches may be constructed with proportional pocket dimensions.

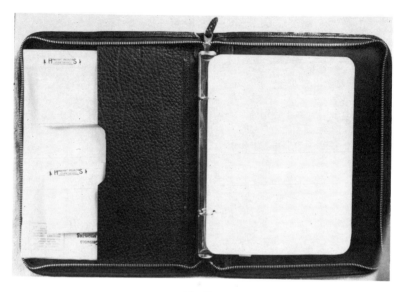

Fig. 178

Suitable Leather includes a nontooling cowhide with a boarded or textured surface, such as the case in Fig. 178, which is a 3 ounce weight. Also, tooling steerhide in 2½ to 3 ounce weight or medium weight strap leather, 4 to 6 ounce, which may be decorated with a carved or stamped design.

All of these should be lined with skiver or goatskin. The steerhide requires an interlining of buckram for stiffness. The parts or pieces to be cut are:

1 piece of outer leather 24 inches long and 14 inches wide of any of the kinds suggested. Steerhide or strap to be decorated should be firm and without blemish.

1 piece of lining leather, skiver or goatskin, the same size.

1 pocket piece 10¼ inches by 6⅜ inches.

1 pocket piece 15½ inches by 8⅝ inches with fold for expansion 9 inches by ½ inch.

1 pocket piece 14 inches by 8 inches. 2 for a flat pocket.

1 slide fastener 36 inches long and facing strips 38 inches by 1 inch with 2 end pieces 2 inches by 3 inches and 1 cover strip 3½ inches by 13 inches. Cut all these pieces of goatskin or thin firm steerhide.

Brief Case – Slide Fastener Assembly

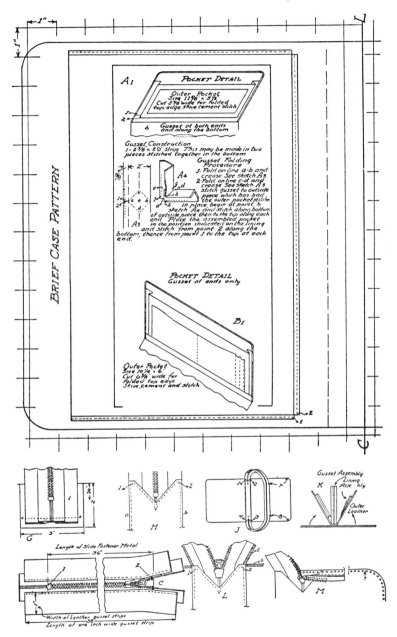

Fig. 179

Construction Procedure

1. If tooling steerhide or strap leather for carving or stamping has been chosen, prepare the design on tracing paper and apply the decoration.

2. Prepare the pocket pieces: If steerhide is used, skive lightly all the edges, turn under, cement and crease the tops for a finish. Goatskin and skiver may be turned under with little or no skiving. Stitch the small pocket to the larger one with the pencil pocket section stitched, also the center divider line.

3. Make and crease the expansion fold at the ends of the large pocket and stitch to the lining at the bottom. Cement the ends to the margins of the lining and crease for the punching guide line. Stitch the flat pocket to the lining at the bottom and cement the ends to the lining on the opposite side.

4. Attach a ring notebook metal to the lining, if desired. See page 184 for attachment instructions.

5. Cement the lining assembly to the outer leather, smoothing it from the center to the margin. Trim any uneven margins, crease the outer leather.

6. Stitch the facing strips of gusset leather to the slide fastener tape on both sides. Place the ends at the center of the lined cover as indicated in sketches G and J. Stitch the short cover sections underneath the ends of the tape as in sketch G and the long cover strip across the center and over the ends. Cut back at the center to permit the corners to be turned as in sketch H and L, showing the slide open. Stitch to the lining leather and across the ends as indicated.

7. Open the slide fastener and evenly cement the leather facing strips to the margins of the lining and outer leather of the case, from the center around the opposite ends, measuring the distance and the facing first, so that the corners may be rounded for an exact fit. Punch for wide lacing as indicated in sketch M.

8. Lace from the center of both sides around the ends in opposite directions so that the lacing is completed at the center of the ends and all lacing ends concealed under the center cover strip. Machine or hand sewing may be used.

Brief Case

The finished size of this strap leather brief case is the regulation 19 by 14½ inches. It may be constructed with a center divider and two full size compartments, requiring two gussets, or as illustrated in Fig. 180 with a single compartment and double pockets front and back.

Medium weight, 6 ounce cowhide is the quality for carving or stamping, and either decoration may be used. Fig. 180 shows a simple stamped border.

Fig. 180

The materials for this size brief case include:
  1 piece of firm smooth strap leather, 4 to 6 ounce weight, 36 by 14½ inches for the back and flap which is narrowed to 13½ inches from the top of the case. Lining leather the same size, preferably goatskin, but firm suede may be used.
  1 piece of the same quality leather and lining for the front, 19 by 14½ inches. If a divider is used it is the same kind and size. It may be thinner.
  1 or 2 pieces of light weight strap or steerhide for the single or double compartment brief case gussets, 36½ by 2½ inches.
  1 Firm length of one inch strap leather for the handle and closing strap attachments.
  An estimated quantity of wide lacing, at least 2½ times the edges to be laced together, also the flap and handle. It may be hand sewn by the method given for leather boxes on page 201.

The construction process
    Prepare the leather as for other strap leather projects and decorate as desired. If a divider with two compartments and double gussets is used, skive it lightly along the bottom and side edges. Cement both gusset pieces to the divider with leather cement and perforate the lacing holes ¼ inch apart with point. The folding and lacing of a gusset is described on page 156. Follow this detail in assembling the parts.
    Punch the lacing holes around the flap, back and front, making the front holes correspond to those in the divider gussets and lace together, starting at the center point of the flap as shown in Fig. 182, sketch B. The front slits or holes for the attachment of the lock and buckle straps should be made before the parts are assembled. Mark them carefully from the lock base metal.

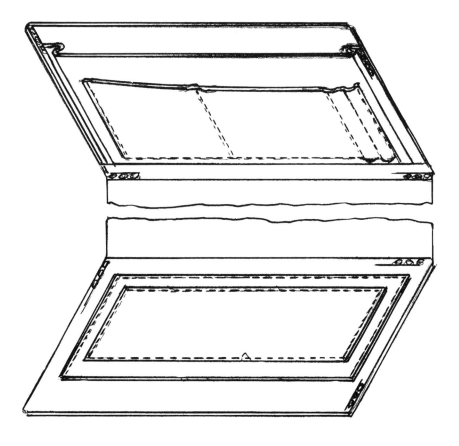

The single compartment brief case pockets are detailed in Fig. 181. Cut the pockets from the lining leather in the proportions indicated. One or two flat pockets may be used on one side. The opposite side has the expandable pockets with space for paper, pen and pencil and must be sufficiently longer to allow for the stitched spaces. Skive and turn under all the top edges, then stitch the pockets to the lining.

Fig. 181

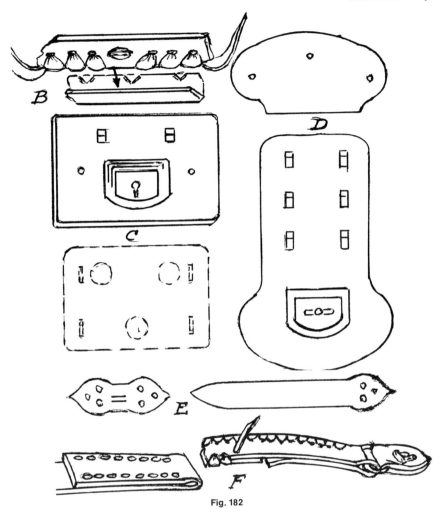

Fig. 182

Fig. 182 shows the lock, strap and handle details for the single or double compartment sizes, with the attachment dees and buckles. Place the top of the lock at the center of the flap over the lacing, sketch B with the triangular prongs beneath. Press the sides together, forcing the prongs into the back of the leather and crimping the front securely over the lacing.

Place the base part of the lock under the front and the openings that were previously cut. Center the front part over the base with the prongs extending through the openings in the leather and the metal. Bend them down toward the center.

The handle, sketch F, shows the detail of folding, attachment to the case with dees and the three hole fastening device. Lace the handle folds together as indicated and fasten it in place at the top fold of the flap.

Western Riding Bridles

Two types of western riding bridles are sketched in Fig. 183 as shown in the photo. Light skirting cowhide or strap leather should be used for the headstall and reins. Eight ounce strap leather is best for the curb strap and throat latch.

The complete specifications for the parts of bridles A and B are:

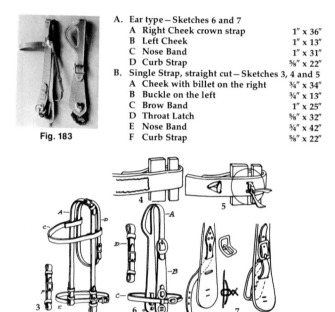

Fig. 183

A. Ear type — Sketches 6 and 7
   A Right Cheek crown strap   1″ x 36″
   B Left Cheek   1″ x 13″
   C Nose Band   1″ x 31″
   D Curb Strap   ⅝″ x 22″
B. Single Strap, straight cut — Sketches 3, 4 and 5
   A Cheek with billet on the right   ¾″ x 34″
   B Buckle on the left   ¾″ x 13″
   C Brow Band   1″ x 25″
   D Throat Latch   ⅝″ x 32″
   E Nose Band   ¾″ x 42″
   F Curb Strap   ⅝″ x 22″

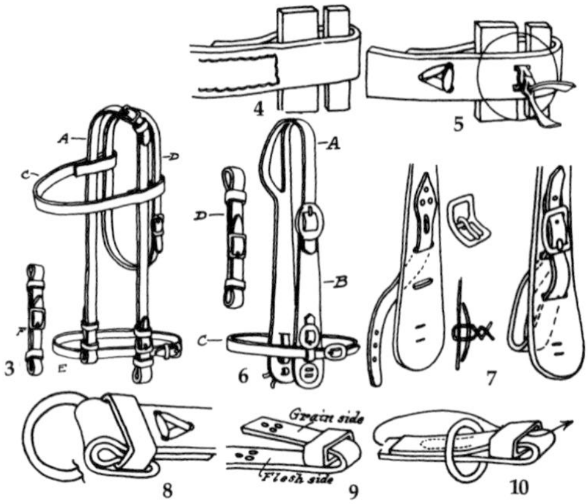

Fig. 184

Devices and fasteners are sketched in 4 and 5 of Fig. 184 with attachments sewn with waxed thread or held with the three hole fastening. The rein attachments, sketches 8, 9, and 10 may be with a ring, held in place with a leather loop, or a single loop held with the three hole fastening. Sketch 10 shows the rein attached to the bit ring or chain.

The straps are prepared in the same way as the belts on page 145 and the assembly is as shown in the sketches. A stamped or carved decoration may be applied before assembly and edges stained.

Ornamental conchas may be used for the attachments, as appear in the photo. Conchas can be purchased or made according to the instructions on page 288.

An application of saddle soap will clean, polish and preserve the leather in bridles and other riding equipment.

Making waxed thread

1. Pull out from the ball a length of about 6 feet of No. 12 Barbours linen thread. Untwist without tension for a space of about 3 inches. Hold the thread as indicated in Fig. 185, sketch A. Note that the fibers are released and enlarged in diameter.

2. Give the untwisted strand a quick jerk to separate the fibers, and pull gently about 2 inches into elongated and tapered points, as shown in sketch B. Repeat this operation for three or more strands, according to the strength of thread desired.

3. Make a three or four ply strand with the lengths of tapered thread, with the ends spaced about an inch and one-half apart, as indicated. Wax the strand into a ribbon, as shown in sketch D. Roll the waxed ribbon into a round thread, saddlers' method, by rolling it on the thigh with slight tension to prevent kinking.

4. With one end in the left hand, roll the strands with the palm of the right hand, taking successive lengths of about 3 inches at a time, sketch E. A palm's length roll puts 15 to 20 twists per inch in the 3 inch sections of a three strand thread. Attach the harness needle to the waxed thread as, indicated in sketches F, G, H.

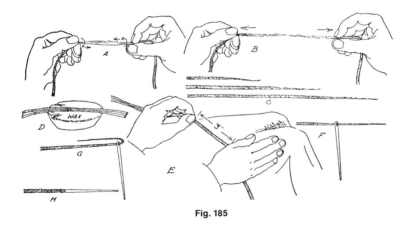

Fig. 185

Moccasin pattern development

This process for making a moccasin pattern has been developed from foot measurements. The craftsman should be able to plan a pattern to fit any foot measurements taken, as described.

Tools: Pencil, heavy paper, scissors, pine board, ¾ inch for foot forms, ruler.

1. Make a straight line on a piece of paper about two inches longer than the foot length. Place the bare or stockinged foot on this line which extends beyond the heel and toes, Fig. 188, sketch A. Center the heel on this line. Position the foot to bring the second toe directly over the line.

2. Mark the foot outline with a lead pencil. Keep the pencil in a vertical position and mark a complete outline as indicated in Fig. 188, sketch C. The second line, marked with the pencil held in the position shown in sketch D, makes the original foot outline conform to a shoe last size from which the wooden moccasin form is constructed. Correct any irregularities in curvature after removing the foot.

3. Take a girth measurement at the ball of the foot (widest part), as indicated in Fig. 188, sketch E. This measurement does not need to be accurate to a fraction of an inch, and may be taken with a strip of paper as indicated in sketch F.

4. Mark the length W (width of foot outline at ball) on the paper, sketch F. Divide W into length of ½, ¼, and ⅛ by folding the end back on the paper strip as shown in sketch G. This subdivided length, W, is the unit of measurement which will be used to develop the tongue and vamp patterns. Example Fig. 189 is for a size 6 moccasin. Fig. 187 shows hand sewn heel and tongue. Sketch shows awl perforations for tongue.

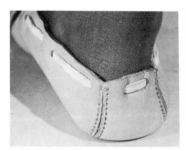

Fig. 186

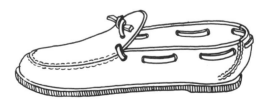

Fig. 187

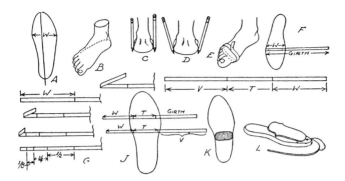

Fig. 188

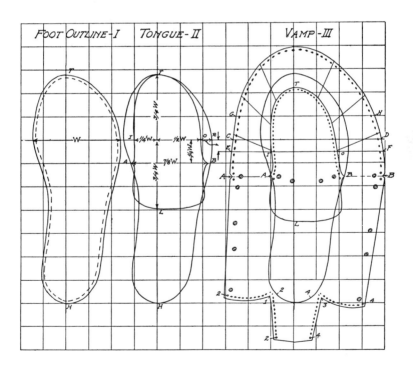

Fig. 189

Develop the tongue pattern, No. II

1. Redraw the foot outline as shown in the sketch of pattern, Part No. II, Fig. 189. Mark the vertical line (toe to heel), also the horizontal line (through the ball of the foot), in their porper positions.

2. At the point of intersection, lay off the tongue length, ¾W above and ¾W below the horizontal line. Lay off ¼ inch to the left of the vertical line and ½W to the right. This determines the location of points I and O. The distance between is the tongue width.

3. Draw another horizontal line ¼ inch below line I-O. Locate point A where the line intersects the foot outline, and lay off a length of ⅞W to the right of point A. This locates point B. The length A-B is the tongue width at the notches or instep.

4. Cut a paper pattern of the tongue. The six points I-L, I-O, and A-B define the length and width for the tongue pattern. Sketch pattern freehand.

Develop the vamp pattern

1. Redraw the foot outline, with the vertical and horizontal C-D lines shown in the sketch, Part III, Fig. 189.

2. Draw another horizontal line E-F across the foot, outline the distance O-R below C-D. O-R is the distance between the tongue, Part II, Fig. 189, and the foot outline. Slide the tongue pattern along the vertical line T-H until line I-O rests upon the line E-F.

3. Draw the outline of the tongue pattern in the new position and another horizontal line through points A-B. Extend this line a couple of inches beyond points A-B. Scale of pattern, Fig. 189—one inch squares.

4. Determine the width of the vamp by measuring the girth of the foot on a strip of paper through points A-B. Since the girth measurement, G, includes the width of the foot outline W and the width of the tongue, T, Fig. 188, sketch J, these two lengths must be subtracted from G. This is indicated in Sketch J. The remaining length V is added to the width of the foot outline at this point to give width of vamp, line A-B.

5. Add one-half of the length V to each side of the foot outline on the line A-B. This locates the points on the vamp marked A-B where the notches are cut to receive the corresponding points on the tongue. Locate points C-D and G-H on the vamp by a similar procedure, using girth measurement less foot outline and tongue width.

Make a Wooden Form. This may be hand sawed or cut by hand with a fret saw.

1. Make a paper pattern corresponding to the last form, outline Fig. 188, sketch K.

2. Cut the form from a piece of ¾ inch wood (pine). Round the edges as shown in Fig. 188, sketch K.

3. Cut the leather to size and shape of pattern parts, A vamp and B tongue. The pattern shown is for the right foot. Turn the pattern over to cut leather for the left moccasin.

4. Pierce the holes for the toe and heel seams as indicated on the pattern

following carefully the spacing shown. (See Fig. 190, sketch M, for the method of piercing a skived edge.)

5. Sew the heel seams. Moisten the edges to be sewn by dipping quickly in and out of water. Begin sewing at points 1 and 3. To facilitate sewing tie both points 2 and 4, Fig. 189 together and start sewing as indicated in Fig. 190, sketch F. The first stitch is taken through holes pierced below points 1 and 3. (See sketch F.) Rather the leather is folded and the awl pierces the fold as indicated in sketch G.

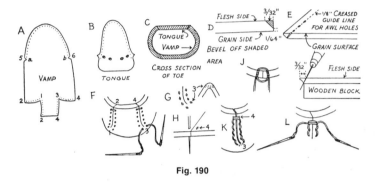

Fig. 190

6. Crease a line on the grain side of the leather ⅛ inch from the edge to guide in piercing awl holes. Crease a line about 3/32 inch from the edge on the flesh side of both vamp and tongue as indicated in Fig. 190, sketch E and M.

7. Skive the edges of the vamp and tongue between points a and b as shown in sketches D and F. Also skive the edges of both heel seams. All edges to be skived are shown in sketch D as shaded margins. Slightly moisten with water before skiving. Refer to use of skiving knife, page 161.

8. Sew the Moccasin Toe Seam. Wet the vamp part A, by soaking it in water. The edges of the vamp must be sufficiently pliable to permit compressing between the holes. Wet the tongue (sketch B) slightly by dipping it quickly in the water. The edges of the tongue must be almost dry, and firm enough to support the compressed edge of the vamp without stretching.

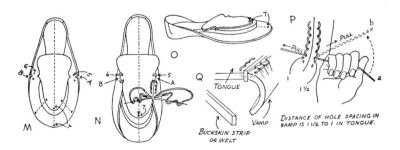

Fig. 191

9. Insert one of the two needles in this hole and pull the thread to its middle point. Use the locked harness stitch, Fig. 191, sketch N. Open the pierced holes with the curved awl before inserting the needles. The locked stitch is formed by wrapping the thread around each needle as shown in Fig. 191, sketch N. Fasten the thread at the top of the seam by forming two transverse locked stitches across the seam. See sketches J and K for method of making this transverse stitch. Finish both heel seams before starting the toe seams.

10. Place the wooden foot form on the vamp with the heel contacting the leather. Shape the moist leather, cupping it around the curves of the foot form.

11. Place the tongue on the wooden form in the position shown in Fig. 188, sketch L, and bring the V notches in the vamp into contact with points A and B by shaping it over the form as indicated in Fig. 191, sketch M. Sew the vamp and tongue together with two transverse locked stitches on each side of V notch A.

12. Remove the wooden form and sew the opposite points together on each side of V notch B with the same locked stitch. Replace the wooden form and press it firmly against the moccasin heel.

13. Stretch the vamp and tongue along the foot form and drive a small nail through the hole in the end of the tongue at point 7, Fig. 191, sketches M and N. Proceed with the sewing along edge 5 to 7, using the locked harness stitch as shown in Fig. 191, sketch M.

14. As the vamp edge must be compressed to fit the tongue, the space holes in the vamp must be one and one-half times that of the tongue. Pull the lighter stitches uniformly to pull the fullness into position as the sewing progresses. Keep both threads in tension while drawing the stitch. The edge of the vamp must be wet enough to permit a slight folding as the stitch shortens and the hand is moved from position a to b, Fig. 191, sketch P, as the final pull is exerted on the thread. The preceding stitches indicate the appearance of the compressed vamp edge.

15. Shape the moist moccasin to the foot and either dry it on the foot or fill with crushed newspapers to retain the desired form, and dry overnight. Insert ankle thong.

16. Apply leather dressing to the outer surface of the moccasin, and colorless burnishing wax to all edges. Polish when dry with a cloth. This treatment is recommended for moccasins to be worn indoors. The dressing preserves the light russet or natural color.

Moccasins to be used for outdoor wear should be oiled. Any waterproof boot oil is satisfactory. Neat's-foot oil is excellent. As a precaution to insure watertight seams, a piece of soft smoked buckskin strap may be inserted as a welt between the edges of the tongue and vamp during the sewing operation as indicated in Fig. 191, sketch Q. This strip of buckskin fills the space, and being absorbent may be impregnated with waterproof oil or wax, thereby rendering the seam water repellent.

The detail for adding an upper to the moccasin, Fig. 192, is shown in Figs. 193, 194 and 195.

Fig. 192

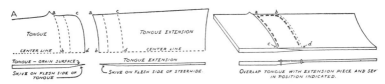

Fig. 193

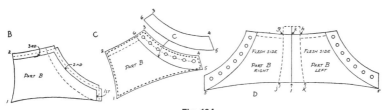

Fig. 194

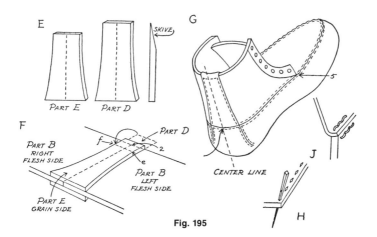

Fig. 195

CHAPTER **8**

Metal Craftwork Processes

Metal Work

The word *metal,* derived from the Greek, *metallon,* originally meant "something diligently sought", and was applied to gold, silver, copper, iron, tin, and lead, all of which were known in prehistoric times. Relics prove that gold, silver, and copper were known to metal workers of the earliest civilizations and thousands of years later, about 2000 B.C., they discovered the secret of making bronze of steel hardness by a method of fusing copper and tin.

Many centuries later, antimony, bismuth, and zinc were discovered, then in modern times, methods of extracting cobalt, manganese, platinum, and other rare metals from ore bodies were developed and many uses for them were found. Gold, silver, platinum, and copper are found in their metallic states, but all the rest are found in "ores," where they are chemically combined with metals or other substances, and must be extracted by reduction processes.

The craft metals are: aluminum, copper, brass, bronze, nickel silver, and silver. Gold, because of its cost, is prohibitive for the craftsman and restricted to the professional manufacturing jeweler. Silver, the most beautiful and adaptable for all hand processes, is also costly but not prohibitive for the skilled metal worker, who can undertake projects in silver, after mastering the techniques for working a less precious metal.

Hammered and Chased Design for Aluminum Tray with Fluted Edges.
Project described on page 256.

Fig. 196

Aluminum, which has rightly been called the wonder metal, does not occur in a pure state, but in combination with other elements. It is said to be more plentiful throughout the earth than any other metal, but metallurgists did not succeed in extracting it until 1886. Earlier its existence as a metal was known in its combinations with oxygen, silica, and phosphate as jewel stones, which are described in the chapter on lapidary.

A combination of *aluminum* with water (aluminum hydroxide), iron, and some impurities are found in the mineral *bauxite* and in *cryolite,* a mineral composed of *sodium aluminum fluoride.* These two minerals are the source of industrial aluminum at this time.

In 1886, American and French metallurgists, working separately, discovered an electrolytic process for the separation of aluminum. Research and experiment since have developed, with alloys of copper, iron, zinc, and chromium, the inexpensive, adaptable and indispensable metal.

As a craft metal, aluminum has become increasingly popular. It is soft enough to shape by molding into wooden contour blocks, yet sufficiently hard to shape by planishing with a ball-peen hammer. Designs can be applied to aluminum by chasing or engraving, with stippled or textured backgrounds, also by etching, which is effective in contrast with either a plain or hammered background.

A recently developed nonacid etching powder, which is mixed with water, for aluminum makes the process easier as it requires fewer safety precautions than the acid etching process required for other metals. Aluminum can now be soldered with a rod type which needs only to be rubbed on the metal when it has been heated to a 500 degree temperature, Fahrenheit. No flux is required. This solder is available from agents for Dixon Tools and Supplies.

Aluminum for craft work is available from suppliers in a wide selection of flat sheets, rectangles and circles, 16 and 18 gauge, or thickness, also in pre-formed rectangles and circles, shaped for trays and ready for decorating.

Brass is an alloy which contains copper and zinc. In its oldest use, alloys of copper and tin were called brass, but these are now known as bronze. The brass of Bible reference was probably bronze, as there are records of its use in ancient times by the Assyrians, Egyptians, and other nations.

The first positive evidence of the manufacture of brass was in England in the sixteenth century and until 1810, brass sheets were hammered out by hand. Then the rolling mill process was developed. All brass alloys containing 55 percent or more of copper are malleable, either hot or cold. It is only slightly harder to work than copper, and the same methods are used.

Brass in combination with copper or nickel silver, as well as alone, is an excellent craft metal. Its golden yellow color, when highly polished or when etched, pierced, or hammered, as well as chased and engraved, is suitable for many projects. It is especially attractive for the embellishment of small walnut or mahogany boxes, as corners, edge moldings, and pierced ornaments. It is used extensively in Asian countries and is a feature on the intricately carved chests of the Japanese.

Brass is available in rolled sheets 10# minimum quantity, which is approximately 4.5-5.6-7.1-8.9 square feet for gauges, 16, 18, 20, and 22. The foil or tooling brass is approximately 45.4 square feet in the 10# roll. Brass wire in gauges, 14, 16, 18, and 20 is also available from suppliers.

Bronze, the oldest alloy known, was developed to perfection and used in the early culture, called the bronze age, in Asia Minor about 2500 B.C. This ancient bronze was of a fine quality, said to be unmatched since. The process of hardening, discovered about that time, enabled the metal worker of the Bronze Age to make the sharpest edged tools, the equal of steel tools made today. The process is still unknown.

Bronze has a reddish yellow color and is harder than brass or copper. It can be hammered, pierced, and etched like copper, but is most satisfactory and widely used for cast figures, award statuettes, and the like. It is available in sheets, circles, and in round wire, 8 to 24 gauge, but is not carried by all suppliers.

Copper, considered the best craft metal by some workers, was discovered and used by prehistoric man, long before he knew what it was. An imaginary explanation of his first discovery may be correct. The story depicts him as finding a molten mass in his fire, which was very hard when it cooled, although he had only put around the fire pieces of reddish rock. He soon replaced his stone ax and other tools with the metal and progressively learned about other metals which could be fused or alloyed with it, and so brass and bronze were made.

In the prehistoric ruins of Egypt, estimated as from 4700 B.C. to 3800 B.C., objects of copper and copper alloys have been found. The name comes from the Roman name for the Island Cyprus, Cuprium, where mines were worked from a very early period. The Spanish conquerors of Central America found the natives skilled in the use of both copper and bronze and the Mound Builders of North America made implements of copper which they found in the Great Lakes region, still a source of copper from mines which existed before the Jesuit missionaries came.

Copper occurs in all soils and ores. Huge bodies of copper, in widely separated areas in the United States, have been mined from the beginning of American history. As a craft metal, it is unsurpassed in possibilities. All kinds of shaping and decorative processes can be used on the 16 to 26 gauges available in 12 inch, 10# rolls and 4 to 12 inch circles, paper thin foil (36 gauge) and soft wire, 14 to 20 gauge.

Nickel or German Silver from its first recorded development, was produced by two different German scientists in 1824, although it was first made in China, from an unknown date earlier. The alloys of nickel silver vary in the percentages of nickel, copper, and zinc. It does not contain any silver. The alloy which contains 18 percent nickel is used for inexpensive tableware and as a base for the best silver plate.

Nickel Silver is harder and tougher than brass, and takes a high polish. It can be pierced, etched, or hammered, and resembles silver in color to an extent that it is an excellent material for beginners in the design and making of silver jewelry and tableware. It does not tarnish.

Nickel Silver is available in the 12 inch rolls 10# weight in the gauges, 16, 18, and 20. The corresponding sizes are 4.3, 5.4, and 6.9 square feet. A soft roll nickel silver, 6 inches wide in 16, 18, and 20 gauge, is also available. It can be soldered, formed, and annealed like brass.

Pewter was known to the ancient Chinese where its use was recorded 3000 years ago. Japanese pewter ware in an English museum is known to be 1100 years old.

In the time of Julius Caesar, household utensils of pewter were in demand by the Romans. The art of working pewter was said to have been lost in the Dark Ages, but was revived in Europe in the fourteenth century and by the Craft Guild of Pewterers in England.

Modern Pewter or britannia metal, as it is sometimes called, was developed during the middle of the eighteenth century. It is an alloy containing 91 parts tin, 7.5 parts antimony, and 1.5 parts copper. Pewter is malleable without annealing, and may easily be hammered into a desired shape by means of tools and methods similar to those employed by the Guild pewterers. The melting point of pewter is lower than any of the other craft metals and a special pewter solder has been developed for it. Unlike other metals, pewter does not harden under hammering and so annealing is not necessary. It retains its dark silvery luster and its satiny surface is beautiful without any surface decoration. However, it can be chased and etched with the same mordant as the other metals, except aluminum. Pierced designs and light hammering are suitable for some articles. Pewter is available in sheets 18 by 24 inches and 12 by 12 inches in gauges, 14, 16, 18, and 20, also in circular discs, 6 to 12 inches diameter, gauges 16 and 18. In 3, 4, and 5 inch discs pewter is available in 16 gauge only.

Silver, unlike gold, is rarely found in the pure state and must be extracted from other metals, with which it is chemically combined. Silver occurs in volcanic or igneous rocks, but infrequently, and was possibly discovered first when these rocks were broken or eroded away. It is mentioned by Homer and in Bible references before the Christian era.

Knowledge of the refining of silver ores to extract it from other minerals was probably of Egyptian origin. Later the Romans passed on the skill to Europe and from there it went to England.

For centuries, the silver of India, China, Mexico and other widely separated countries, has been refined and fabricated for coinage, jewelry and in more recent times, for tableware of finer quality. In the pure state, silver is very soft, so for commercial and craft use, also for coins, it is alloyed with copper to harden it. Sterling silver, which is the degree of purity required for the British shilling and pound is 92.5 percent pure silver and 7.5 pure copper. Silver is available in gauges 14 to 20 (Brown and Sharpe or B. and S. standard) sheets or blanks, circular, and square, also wire in round, half round, square, and rectangular.

The beauty of silver, as well as its adaptability for many projects and its ease of manipulation, makes it a superior choice for the craftsman, but its value and price are closely related to monetary fluctuations. The craftsman who truly appreciates the value of silver will perfect his skill on less precious metals before trying silver projects.

Craft Metals	Melting Points	Forms Available	Gauges	Remarks
Aluminum	1220°F.	12" rolls, 10 to 140' foil	36	For tooling
		Circles, 10 diameters		Used for all metal work
		from 4" to 20"	18	processes.
		Rectangles, 6 x 9", 9 x 12"		Used for all metal work
		and 12 x 18"	18	processes.
		Preformed discs and		Ask supplier for roll and
		rectangles	16-18	sheet price for other
				gauges.
Copper	1481°F.	Foil 12",16",20" rolls	36	For all copper work, ask
		1 to 9' and also roll of		for "cold rolled" or soft
		10' and up — 148' or less		rolled copper, gauges
				16-24. — less depending
				on width.
		Discs, sheets and wire	16-26	Sheets in 10' rolls
		Many shapes for enamel-		Wire 14 to 20 gauge.
		ing, preformed bowls,		Large bowls are 16
		trays, rectangles, free-		gauge. Ask dealer about
		form shapes, also circles.	all 18	availability.
Brass	1751°F.	Foil in 10' rolls, approx.		
		45.4 sq. ft. 12" wide	36	For tooling.
		Soft roll brass, similar to	16-18	Brass is somewhat
		copper for same projects	20-22	harder and stiffer than
		12" widths — squares and		copper, can be worked
		rectangles, 1 x 6 to		same way. Wire 14-16-
		12 x 12		120 gauge.
Bronze	1866°F.	Produced by T. B. Hagstoz		Information on forms
		(see list of suppliers)		and prices on request.
Nickel Silver or German	2030°F.	Product of T. B. Hagstoz, available in 10# rolls also discs and wire.	16-20	Contains 18% nickel, varying quantities copper and zinc. Can be formed, annealed, and soldered like brass.
Pewter	550°F.	Available in sheets,		Hoyt's Pewter recom-
		12 x 12", 12 x 24", 6 x 6",		mended. Hoyt's Special
		6 x 12". Circles, 6-9-10-11-	14-16	solder required.
		12" diameters.	18-20	
Sterling Silver	1640°F.	Both supplied direct or through dealers by T. B. Hagstoz		Inquire gauge available and price — these vary according to market or
Fine Silver	1761°F.	Available in blank shapes, discs and wire.		government price changes.

Equipment and tool requirements for metal work
listed by processes and materials

Minimum Workshop Facilities:

Workbench or sturdy table of proper height, well lighted, electrical and gas connections, cupboard and containers for materials — ventilating fan, materials for finishing and polishing.

1. *Metal Cutting Tools:*

   Shears shaped for straight and curved cutting.

   Jeweler's or fret saw frames, with blades in sizes numbered from 1, the finest to 5, the coarsest. The difference is in the thickness of the blade and the size of the teeth, which are formed in a slant downward. The Nos. 2 and 3 blades are usually used for copper and silver sawing.

2. *Hammering Tools:*

   Smooth metal block and anvil, with flat surface, vise and pieces of wood to support rim of metal circle while being hammered.

   Round and oval ball-peen hammers with double ends.

   Chasing hammer with flat surface and small rounded end.

3. *Tools for Mold Formed Metal and Fluting:*

   Hardwood molds in shallow and deep forms, in diameters needed for sizes to be made.

   Wooden hammer and wood stake. For pewter, leather tipped or one face rawhide.

   Smooth planishing hammer and metal stakes of different shapes.

   Wooden fluting tool, fluting hammer, and fluting stakes.

4. *Equipment for Raising a Bowl:*

   Anvil or pedestal for holding stakes.

   Assortment of anvil heads or stakes: flat, round, dome, square, sloped, and T-shaped, others available as needed.

   Chasing hammer, planishing hammer, ball-peen hammer.

   Wooden and rawhide hammers for pewter work.

   Sand filled bag.

5. *Annealing and Pickling:* Copper, Brass, and Silver.

   Asbestos Mat with baffle of asbestos or firebrick to protect metal and concentrate flame of electric or gas fired blow torch.

   Pickling Solution—15 parts water to 1 part (one) sulphuric acid is added. *Caution:* Always put water in container, glass, porcelain, or copper, then add acid carefully—*do not inhale* or permit to touch hands or clothing. Copper pickling pans are supplied by metal-craft dealers. Wooden tongs for handling, rubber gloves for protection. Container for clear water, wiping cloths.

   Note: A commercial pickling material, *Sparex No. 2*, a granular dry acid, is recommended by the manufacturer for all metals. *Follow directions.* Aluminum may be cleaned with a solution of caustic soda (sodium hydroxide). Pewter does not require pickling.

6. *Tools for Pierced Metal Work:*

   Jeweler's saw, 5 inch with 00 and No. 1 blades, hand drill with set of twist drills; files: square, half round and triangular, scraper, burnisher, tracing paper. Metal carbon paper, chinese white or show card white paint.

7. *Chasing and Repoussé:*

Chasing tools, available from suppliers or made according to directions page 239.

Metal scribe and engraving tools, also outline tool and stippling tools.

Piece of heavy linoleum or slab of soft lead, as substitute for jewelry makers pitch pot and material for making "chasers pitch," prepared pitch from suppliers.

Chasing Hammer (flat end for hammering tools only, not on metal) small round end may be used on metal to texture background.

8. *Etching Equipment and Materials:*

Special dry acid powder for aluminum and pewter. Mordant for other metals.

Etching resist (Dixon's) substitute for asphaltum, easier to apply.

Turpentine for resist or asphaltum removal.

Chinese white or show card white for transfer of design.

Carbon paper.

9. *Bending Metal Shapes:*

A vise, woodblock, and pieces of smooth hard wood to protect and hold metal in vise. Wooden mallet and mandrel or length of round hard wood for shaping bracelets, also ring mandrel.

10. *Soldering:*

An acid core hard solder, with self contained flux is recommended for beginners, such as "SWIF'S" tube form, also Dixon, "Solderall" which is similar.

Special solder for aluminum and another for pewter (Hoyt's Pewter Flux and Solder for Hoyt's Pewter), is recommended.

The solders must have a melting point below that of the metals. Soft solder with a low melting point has a limited use. It is a tin-lead formula for sheet metal and tin shop work.

Three types of silver solder are used for silver jewelry and sterling ware, and may also be used on copper, brass, and nickel silver. The melting points for the three silver solders are: No. 1 solder, 1425°F., medium silver solder, 1390°F. and for Easy silver solder, 1325°F. degrees.

Cutting metal for projects

The softer and less expensive metals, aluminum and pewter, are also easier for the beginner in metal work to practice the processes of cutting, sawing, bending, and finishing, and to make a sampler of the decorative processes: hammering, embossing or chasing and etching.

The process of cutting requires first: That the metal be perfectly clean.

1. Immerse in a pickling solution, if stained or oxidized, otherwise clean with fine steel wool and a recommended cleaning solution.

2. Flatten out any irregularities by placing the piece of metal between two boards and pounding the upper one with a wooden hammer.

3. Use a cardboard template for a pattern of the selected article and mark around it with a pencil. Define the outline with a metal scriber. If the article is irregular, the outline may by cut more accurately from a piece of metal, rectangular or square of the same approximate size.

4. Curved metal shears, or a type adjustable for straight or curved cutting may be used. These are best for thinner pieces of metal, gauges 20 or 22. Snips may be necessary for heavier gauges.

5. Rest the lower blade of the metal cutting shears against the surface of the workbench. Hold and operate the blades with the right hand while pressing the piece of metal into the open blades with the left hand.

In cutting large or irregular pieces, it may be necessary to bend a part of the metal and flatten it after it is cut. File any sharp edges or metal burrs, then rub smooth with emery cloth or paper. To round corners, wrap the emery cloth or paper around a manicure or other stick.

Sawing for pierced designs

The process of sawing removes areas of metal for pierced designs and is also required for making ornamental overlays or attachments of a contrasting metal.

1. Draw the design on tracing paper for the pattern and attach it with rubber cement to the surface of the metal, which must have been carefully cleaned and without finger marks, or if possible scribe it directly on the metal freehand.

2. A recommended method for transferring a design to metal, is to place a sheet of heavy metal carbon paper face down on the metal, with the design tracing over it. Go over the design outlines with a hard blunt pointed tracing tool. *Note* that the metal must be absolutely clean or the carbon paper will not leave an impression.

3. After removing the carbon paper, go over the design lines with a fine sharp scriber to define them. To make sure of obtaining an accurate impression from the carbon, a light coat of Chinese white or show-card white watercolor paint may be applied with a small brush. When dry it will take the carbon impression perfectly. After the design lines are clearly incised, the white paint can be washed off.

4. Drill holes for the insertion of the saw blade in each area to be removed. There should be sufficient metal between parts of the design and the margins of the pattern to prevent any part being so thin it will break out. To mark the spot for the hole, use a center punch and make a slight dent inside the design, but not too close to it, for the drill point to enter the metal. Use a fine drill for the first perforation, then enlarge it with a bigger drill, so it will admit the saw blade.

5. Insert the saw blade, No. 1 or 2, from the under side and make sure the teeth point downward. To secure the upper end of the saw blade and give it the necessary tension, brace the top of the saw frame with the body against the edge of the table. Put the end of the blade in the frame and tighten the screws. Fig. 197, sketch D, shows the method of attaching the blade and process

of piercing. (A very light application of oil or wax will help lessen the friction and the heating action of the blade.)

Practice in drilling the hole and sawing a piece of scrap metal is recommended before the piercing of a design is attempted.

6. With the metal supported on a bench pin or a V notch cut into the end of a block of wood, and the saw held vertically with the blade inserted in the hole in the position shown, Fig. 197, sketch E, push upward to start the cut.

7. Hold the handle lightly to permit free movement of wrist and elbow. Saw exactly on the line, so as to leave no uneven margins which will require file corrections.

8. Position the metal with the left hand, turning it as required to keep the angle of the saw blade vertical and at right angles to the metal. Do not exert any forward pressure, but make short quick strokes, using about two inches of the saw blade.

9. In approaching a corner, which is less than 90 degrees, remove the saw at the end of the first cut toward the corner. Draw the blade downward and release the screw holding it, so that it can be backed out. Complete the cutting of the corner by sawing from the opposite direction.

10. When the sawing or piercing of the design is completed, remove any burrs of metal from the edges with a fine file. Burnish to round the edge smoothly.

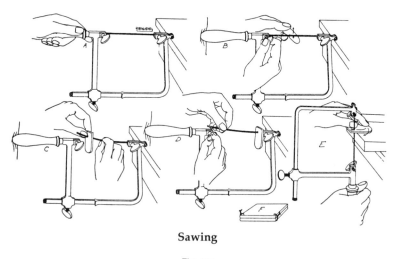

Sawing

Fig. 197

Bending metal forms

Craft work metals may be bent on straight lines without difficulty although it may be necessary to anneal the harder metals after the initial fold.

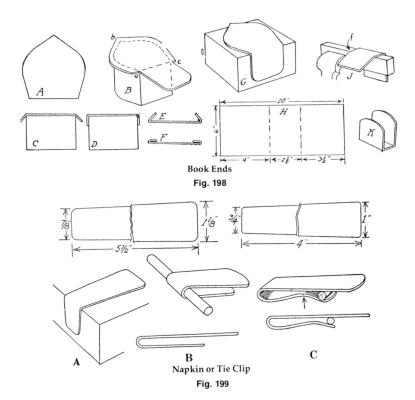

Book Ends

Fig. 198

A   B   C

Napkin or Tie Clip

Fig. 199

Figure 198, sketches A, B, and G, also J and K, indicate the bending of a right angle or less, also a reverse bend. The steps are as follows:

1. Draw lines on both sides of the metals to indicate the bend and place it between two smooth pieces of wood, held in a vise, with the line for the bend exactly even with the top edges of the wood and the end to be bent extending up.

2. Small forms may be bent to a right angle with a piece of wood long enough to extend beyond the metal about an inch at all margins. Press the wood, held in both hands firmly against the metal until the desired curve is formed. If a completely flat base is required, as for a bookend, flatten the angle with a wood mallet.

3. When a second bend is required, as for a letter holder, place a wooden block of the correct size in the angle of the first bend. Place the metal and piece of wood on a smooth wood surface with the completed angle underneath.

4. Hold the metal and block in place with the left hand and strike the metal in a succession of quick blows with the flat end of the wooden mallet along a line about one inch above the edge of the block or the position of the fold. Continue striking the metal, working evenly across the form and closer to the bending line each time, flattening the bend until the right angle is completed. See Fig. 198, sketches J and K.

5. *Metal which is to be curved,* as for bracelets, may be rounded over a mandrel held in a vise. A rolling pin, a piece of pipe, or a length of hard wood of the required diameter may be used. Strike the metal along the area to be curved with the wooden mallet until it conforms to the shape of the mandrel. The smooth horn of the anvil can be used, but as the diameter tapers the metal surface will follow the shape and so must be evened up on a circular surface later.

Hammered metal

Aluminum, copper, brass, and pewter surfaces in both horizontal and curved planes are often decorated by hammering, either alone or in combination with pierced, embossed, or repoussé designs. *Note:* A wood or rawhide hammer must be used for pewter, which is softer and more malleable than other craft metals.

1. Cut the metal slightly larger than the pattern (outside the design lines), clean it thoroughly with fine steel wool, 000, and lay it on a smooth metal block, or the flat surface of the anvil.

2. Except for pewter, use the round or oval ball-peen hammer, (available in different sizes of heads), which must be perfectly smooth and heavy enough to produce the desired hammered effect by weight alone, when dropped 2 to 3 inches. For pewter, a wood or rawhide tipped hammer is required.

On an oblong shape or margin, such as the sides of a tray, follow the margin in parallel lines. On a circular shape, start at the center and work to the edge in concentric circles to cover the area. Perfect regularity is not necessary in filling the spaces, but the hammer impressions should be kept approximately even in the same direction, just touching, but not overlapping.

3. The knack is to develop a rhythm of wrist movement, with a light grip on the handle, which allows the hammer head to rebound after each stroke. Force is not necessary. Avoid any tipping of the hammer face, causing a deeper indentation on one side, which detracts from a uniform appearance.

Something like a honeycomb or hexagonal effect results from the even close hammer impressions, alternating in position with successive rows. Note tray illustration, Fig. 196.

The metal is hardened by this process and must be annealed at intervals to restore the malleability, also before any shaping can be done. This is not necessary for pewter and soft aluminum.

Mold formed metal

The amazing qualities of malleability and ductility of most metals, although in varying degrees, makes it possible to form them into trays, bowls, and plates by pressing or hammering them into hard wood molds, which may be turned on a lathe or obtained from dealers in metal work supplies. Also available are reversible molds of a hard aluminum alloy with different sizes of trays or bowls on both faces or both top and bottom surfaces. A depression carved in a block or end of a log is satisfactory for small round items.

The sketches in Fig. 200 show, first, a crossection of a mold and bowl which have been formed in a block mold, sketch A and B. Sketch C shows the truing of the edge on a wood or metal stake. The steps are as follows:

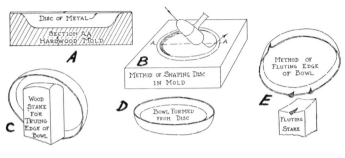

Fig. 200

Procedure for mold formed metal

1. Thoroughly clean the metal circle, slightly larger than the bowl outline, with fine steel wool, center it over the mold and gradually shape into the contour of the mold.

2. Starting at the center, gradually form the base by hammering in concentric circles with a wooden hammer, shaped as indicated in Fig. 200, sketch B. Rotate the circle or disc after a few hammer strokes to keep the expanding and stretching of the metal uniform. If it ceases to "give" or stretch, or seems to be heating, stop the hammering and *anneal* the metal to restore malleability. Avoid overheating at all times by waiting periods at intervals. The process of annealing is described on page 233.

3. After the metal has been cleaned or pickled and becomes entirely cool from the heat of the annealing process, continue the hammering until the contour of the bottom is the desired shape. Then place the form on a depression made by packing slightly damp sand in a canvas bag, and proceed to lightly hammer the sides, rotating the bowl form to keep it evenly stretched. It is suggested that the rotating be done regularly every three hammer strokes.

4. Straighten the edges, which may have become buckled in the hammering process, over a stake or hard wood shape, corresponding to the desired contour of the bowl or tray, Fig. 200, sketch C. After the sides are evenly shaped with the planishing hammer, use the flat end to smooth out the surface, supporting the metal on the sand bag.

5. In all the hammering steps, the blows or strokes must be kept regular and light, stretching the metal in a different spot each time. When the metal is carefully planished, only faint traces of the hammer marks will be discernable.

6. Finish the bowl inside and out with very fine steel wool, followed by fine pumice powder on a damp clean cloth for a matt surface. If a high luster is desired, apply rouge on cloth or buckskin. Wash with detergent and water

and apply a protective lacquer with a spray. Some metal craftsmen prefer an application of paste wax on the *heated* metal surface. A dip in very hot water, followed by a thorough drying, will leave the surface sufficiently warm for the application of wax.

7. After the bowl has cooled completely, wipe and polish it with a clean soft cloth. An occasional application of paste wax on the heated surface, polished when cold, will preserve the finish indefinitely, unless removed by washing in the meantime. This treatment, however, will not withstand hot liquids or acids. Lacquer is preferable if the metal must be so used.

Raising a metal bowl

Raising is another way of forming a metal bowl or other shapes from a flat piece of copper, brass, or silver. Copper can be raised more easily because of its pliability. Raising is the term used for the process by silversmiths which is applied to many possible forms or shapes. Twenty gauge copper is the thickness suggested for the process of raising a small bowl. The sketches in Fig. 201 show the equipment: pedestal, stakes, and raising hammers, and indicate the process as follows:

1. The size of the metal disc required may be determined by adding the height and the largest diameter of the design of the chosen form. The example of a bowl 3 inches high with a diameter of 4 inches is made from a 7 inch Circle or disc.

2. Mark a circle for the base diameter and as a guide line to be followed in raising the bowl over the metal stake, Fig. 201, sketch A.

3. Place the stake on the pedestal, sketch B, and hold the disc against the stake as indicated in sketch D with the guide line in contact with the curve of the stake. This type of pedestal is bolted to the workbench, but the stake may be held in a vise.

4. Strike the metal with the raising hammer just outside the guide circle. If the metal seems hard or does not respond it should then be annealed. Cool it gradually before continuing the raising process.

5. It is recommended by experienced metal workers, to crimp the sides of the disc to make the raising process develop faster. Do this by placing the disc sides against a groove in a block, like the fluting block shown in Fig. 200. With the block held in a vise, depress the sides into the block at regular intervals with a metal creasing tool.

6. Place the crimped disc on the anvil stake and rotate it with the left hand while hammering with light blows around the circle until the base is clearly defined. The experienced metal worker maintains a rhythm count of three consecutive slightly overlapping blows at a time, continuing the process until the curve is established, as shown in sketches F and G.

7. Correct the tendency of the base of the bowl to cup at the bottom by placing it on a flat surface and straightening it with the flat surface of the ball-peen hammer, as shown in sketch H. When the desired form of the bowl has been obtained and the crimp marks smoothed out, place it against the stake, sketch J, and use the planishing hammer to reduce or press out the raising hammer marks.

Planish the inner surface with the bowl held against the sand bag, until only faint traces of the marks remain. Use a fine half round file to remove any irregularities from the top edge of the bowl.

Caution: It must be remembered that annealing and cleaning or pickling, page 233, is required whenever the metal loses its ductility and does not respond to the strokes of the raising mallet or hammer. This is always the last step before the final finishing. See metal finishing, page 245.

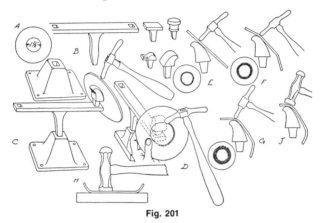

Fig. 201

Edge finishes

1. If a textured rim is desired, place the metal between two pieces of wood, held firmly in a vise, with the edge extending about 1/16 inch. Tap lightly with the small end of the ball-peen hammer. This treatment is effective as a finish decoration and also hardens the rim. A variation is to stamp the edge with one of the background tools. Regular placing of the tool and light pressure of the stamping hammer is essential.

2. A turned or fluted edge may be formed on the rim or edge of a tray with a hard wood "turn-up stick" or a commercial fluter. The making of a stick is a simple process. It requires a piece of hardwood 10 inches long, 1½ inches wide and 1 inch thick, saw cut at both ends, as indicated in Fig. 202. Note that one saw cut is 1½ inches deep and the other ⅝ inch deep. Taper the end with the deeper cut to a width of ⅞ inch. Smooth with emery cloth or fine sandpaper. This tool can be used on round, square, or rectangular metal shapes.

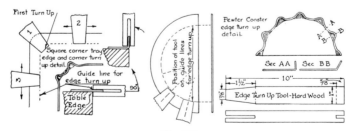

Fig. 202

This method of fluting the softer metals, especially *pewter*, was developed by Mr. Louis J. Haas, director of occupational therapy, Bloomingdale Hospital, White Plains, New York. He describes this method of making ornamental rims in *The Fold-ups, Art Metal Work with a Stick,* published by the author, White Plains, N.Y.

Method of using the stick fluter

1. Insert the metal in the wide saw cut, with the piece to be fluted supported on the table or a block of wood in a fixed position. Turn the metal with the stick to a 90 degree angle. At this point shape the corners of the fold with the small rounded end of a wooden ball-peen hammer. If necessary to increase the height of the rim, make a second turn-up with the rim in the shorter cut.

If desired, roll the rim inward and downward.

Use of fluting jig

2. Another fluted or rolled rim may be formed on a *fluting jig,* as shown in Fig. 203, indicated by the crossection and the AA—BB lines, which correspond to the edge shapes. These are turned in at the AA point and the top edge at BB folded slightly backward and upward.

3. A hard wood block or stake shaped at the top in a curve to correspond to the contour of the bowl shaped metal, either convex or concave, and grooved to hold the rim section, is the recommended device for this kind of fluting.

Make the stake from a block of hard wood, 4 by 4 inches or 6 inches and long enough to be held in a vise. Shape the top as required and sand it smooth. File the groove 3/16 to ⅜ inch deep and taper it to ⅛ inch on one side. Smooth it with fine folded sandpaper, Fig. 200, sketch E.

4. Mark the bowl at the points to be fluted and space these evenly by dividing the circumference or perimeter into sections. Keep these symmetrical with the spaces between. A division into 3, 5, 6, or 7 is a good balance. The flutes may be increased by odd numbered spaces for larger sizes.

• 5. Hold the edge of the article firmly against the stake in the position to be fluted inward or outward, and hammer with a fluting hammer or the narrow end of a riveting hammer.

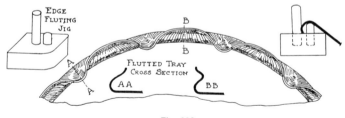

EDGE FLUTING JIG

B
B

FLUTED TRAY CROSS SECTION
AA   BB

Fig. 203

On pewter a wooden hammer is required. Hold the hammer at a right angle to the arm, so that a rhythmic wrist motion can be maintained in striking the metal. Begin toward the front and work gently back to press the metal into the groove as far as desired.

Annealing copper, brass, and silver

Hammering to shape, raise or otherwise re-form metals, especially when a metal surface tool is used, will make all metals, except pewter, and to a slight extent, aluminum, unless this is the soft rolled quality, lose their malleability and become hard so that the forming cannot be continued. The softening process, or annealing, consists of heating the metal as in the first stage of tempering tools.

1. Place the metal article on an asbestos mat with a surrounding baffle of asbestos or firebricks to concentrate the heat. Apply a soft bushy flame of the blow torch (low pressure), until the annealing temperature is reached and the area glows with a dull cherry red color. This requires only a few minutes, two to five, depending on the size of the article. Only experience will enable the worker to determine the right annealing temperature for specific metal articles, that is when the heat has restored the malleability. Practice with scrap pieces of metal which have been hardened is desirable. Overheating may approach the melting point of the metal and spoil it.

2. Remove the heat and allow the metal to cool gradually, as sudden cooling may cause it to harden. Do not hammer again until it has become entirely cold.

Cleaning or pickling

Annealed copper and brass will be discolored when they have cooled and the upper layer of metal will have loosened and appear blistered. This scale must be cleaned off or it will be hammered into the metal and make it rough. A black oxide forms on copper which also must be removed.

An efficient method used for years by professional metal workers, requires a solution of ten parts water and one part sulphuric acid, called a pickling solution. This is liable to cause severe burns, so rubber gloves should be worn in mixing the solution and in handling the articles to be immersed.

The container should be of glass, porcelain, or a heavy copper pan of the type made for this pickling and available from suppliers. *The water must always be put in the container first and the acid added very slowly.*

1. Immerse the annealed or soldered article, while warm, in the solution and leave for five to ten minutes. Large articles can be cleaned by rubbing the metal with a swab or cloth tied to a stick. *Never* let any steel or iron tool come in contact with the solution, as it will change the acid. Use copper or wooden tongs to handle the annealed metal. Avoid getting any of the solution on clothing or holes will result.

2. Remove the metal article when the discoloration has disappeared or can be easily rubbed off with the swab. If some of it remains, repeat the immersion process. Some metal workers use the proportions of eight parts water to one (8 to 1) part sulphuric acid to remove copper scales.

3. Wash the article thoroughly in clear water, first using a clean swab, then running water over the metal. Never permit the solution or rinse water to stand in a sink, but rinse out immediately.

Recently a powder called Sparex No. 2 has been developed for pickling annealed metal or for cleaning. According to the manufacturer, "it is a safe dry granular acid powder, which has no corrosive fumes, or offensive odor." The powder is dissolved in water, according to directions, and heated to 179° F., before the article is immersed. A copper pickling pan should be used. Ask your supplier about Sparex No. 2.

Chasing and repoussé methods of metal decoration

Designs may be developed in relief by a process of repoussé or the depressing of the metal from the back with embossing tools. A relief appearance, as in leather tooling, is given metal by stamping down a background and beveling the margins of a design. Simple designs are most effective as developed by either method.

The procedure for embossing or repoussé metal decoration follows:

1. Clean the metal with very fine steel wool and the cleaning solution recommended for the metal to be stamped or embossed.

2. Draw the design with a pencil directly on the metal, or transfer the design with carbon paper. Then scribe the outline with a metal scriber or fine pointed engraving tool, so that it will be distinct at all points.

3. For flat surfaces a firm piece of heavy linoleum or a slab of soft lead is satisfactory for relief embossing. Place the metal face up on the linoleum or lead surface and lightly depress the outline and details of the design with the narrow outline tool, held as shown in Fig. 204, sketch 2.

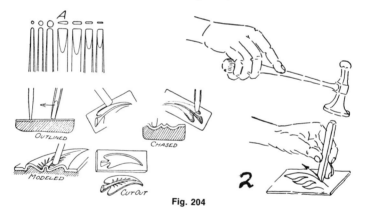

Fig. 204

4. Note that the thumb and forefinger holds the outline tool, while the other fingers rest on the metal to steady it in a slightly slanted position, so that the edge of the tool rides on the metal in the direction of the arrow.

5. Start the outlining of the design at a point or intersection where the line approaches the worker. Move the tool slowly toward you, meanwhile striking it with light, rapidly repeated hammer strokes. Hold the hammer by the end of the handle with the forefinger extended along it, for better control. Keep the wrist relaxed and strive for a rhythm in the movement of the tool and the hammer strokes.

6. In embossed metal work, the outline must be sufficiently deep to reveal the design clearly on the reverse side. Turn the metal and flatten the margins of the design with the smooth embossing tool or, if space permits, the flat end of the smooth chasing hammer to make it appear to stand out slightly on the face side.

7. With a pencil, mark on the reverse side or back of the metal, the areas you wish to appear raised, then with the narrow or broad raising tool, as the space permits, move it toward you along the metal within the marked area, striking it lightly and rapidly as with the outline tool. Inspect the right side frequently and work to produce a modeled effect without visible separate tool impressions.

8. With the metal right side up, redefine the design lines with the outline tool or the pointed graver.

Professional metal workers use a time-tested base for repoussé, called a "Pitch pot", Fig. 205. This is a container, round or square, in which is poured the "Chaser's Pitch," made of 6 pounds of burgundy pitch and 2 pounds of plaster of Paris (Pumice powder may be used instead) melted together. To this is added about ¼ pound of tallow. (Prepared Chaser's Pitch is available from metal craft suppliers.)

In using the pitch bowl, soften the surface with the blow torch so it will harden around the metal and hold it when cold. It provides a firm yet resilient surface to support the metal.

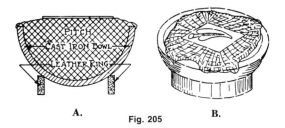

A. Fig. 205 B.

Chased background for repoussé or embossing

Chasing or applying a background texture with various tools provides a contrast in color and texture of the metal surrounding the design element or motif, which has been raised in the embossing process. Types of background processes are:

1. *If the object is to smooth and flatten the background,* apply the narrow of broad raising tool to the area, as described under repoussé. Work from the raised design element to the border or margin of the background area.

2. *Develop a pebbled effect by stippling* the background with the rounded end of a stippling tool or the point of a scriber. With either of these tools, use the ball-peen hammer, flat end, to strike the tool. Move the tool from the design motif to the border of the background in the intervals between hammer strokes, applied lightly with uniform pressure. The making of metal background tools is described on page 240.

3. *Cover the background with the impressions* of the crosshatched tool, hammered in the same way, but with special care to avoid overlapping. Place the tool in an even sequence, fitting the impressions together in close alternating lines. Work *from* the outline of the raised design to the border of the area, as with other types of background.

4. *Carefully redefine the design outline* and the parts which were raised. Use the round pointed graver or metal scriber. Shading of the background for contrast may be done with a burnisher.

5. The illustration of a memorial plaque in Fig. 206 shows a unique design, developed with repousse tools by a master metal craftsman, W. E. Glander of Colorado Springs, Colorado. The decorated disc of copper, with the figures of prospectors in an early day scene of the "Cripple Creek Gold Rush" is mounted in a regular prospector's "gold pan." It commemorates the period and occasion of the famous discovery of the Independence mine by Winfield Scott Stratton.

Fig. 206

Metal stamping tools

The making of stamping tools for metal decoration requires painstaking skill and effort, but is not especially difficult otherwise. The stamping tools illustrated in the sketch, Fig. 207, and the impressions stamped on copper, Fig. 208, show the variety of sizes and designs which can be made.

These tools, singly and in combination, can be used effectively on copper, nickel silver, and brass, but were designed primarily for silver stamping of the Indian symbol type as will be illustrated and described on pages 280 to 304.

Tool steel which is available in round, square, and hexagonal rods, in diameters ¼ inch to ½ inch, but into 3 or 3¼ inch lengths is used in the following process.

1. A special annealed steel in the above sizes is available from suppliers, otherwise the heat treatment described for annealing on page 233 must be the first step.

2. File the face of the selected sized piece of tool steel and rub on emery cloth until it is perfectly smooth and at right angles to the rod length. Next, mark the outline of the tool face with a metal scriber.

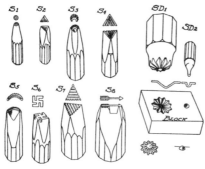

Fig. 207

Fig. 208

3. From a point about an inch down on the steel rod, taper it to the margin of the tool face outline. This can be done by filing, but is shaped more quickly and evenly by rotating it against the revolving surface of a grinding wheel. Keep the surface wet so that the tool will not heat and harden.

S1 *is a small circle about 1/16 inch in diameter,* made by driving a rounded center punch into the center of the tool face as it is held in a vice. File the metal margin of the face of the tool in a perfect circle around the depression, sloping it downward to the rounded part of the rod as shown in Fig. 207. Smooth with fine emery cloth.

S2 *is a triangular shaped tool* about 3/32 inch wide at the base and 1/16 inch high. For this tool use ¼ inch or 5/16 inch annealed tool rod. File five V cuts with a three square jeweler's file, at first lightly, then deeper until a clean cut impression can be made on a piece of leather. *Do not try on metal before the steel is tempered.* Finish the margins and taper the end of the tool by filing and smooth on emery cloth.

S3, *the horseshoe shaped tool* is about ⅛ inch in diameter for which 5/16 inch steel rod is used. File a half-round groove on the face, at the base, about 1/16 inch across and 1/32 inch deep. File eight V cuts with a three square jeweler's file from the groove to the outside margin as indicated in sketch of tool S3. File margins and smooth as before.

S4 is a triangle ⅛ inch on each side and made from ⅜ inch tool steel. File four V cuts with the three square file, bringing the two side cuts to a lower point of intersection as they appear in sketch S4.

S5, the curved border stamp, is about 7/32 inch wide by 3/32 inch high and made from ⅜ inch tool steel, by the method used for S1. Drive an arc-shaped chasing tool into the smooth face of the rod (held in a vise), deep enough to make a clean cut impression. Then, with flat and half round files, shape the tip of the tool until it conforms to the outline shown in sketch S5. File a series of equally spaced V notches along the upper edge of the stamp with the three square file.

S6 is the Navajo Indian symbol for the Four Winds, meaning "Good Fortune." It is made by forming the square area and the four cuts with a thin "equaling" file (a fine oblong file, about 1/16 inch x 3/16 inch which cuts on both sides), or a square end file the width of the cut.

S7, the Tepee, is a triangle with a 5/32 inch base and ⅛ inch high, made from ⅜ inch tool steel. File five V cuts parallel to the base of the triangle as indicated in sketch S7.

S8, the arrow is made from ⅜ inch or ½ inch tool steel, tapered to the width of the arrow, a space of about 1/16 inch as indicated in sketch S8. File the design cuts like the feathers on an arrow.

Matrix and die block SD1 and SD2

1. Shape the metal for the matrix block, a piece of tool steel, ¾ inch x ½ inch x 1½ inch and heat it with the blow torch to a cherry red color. Place the steel block on a sheet of asbestos or firebrick and turn with tongs to insure an even distribution of the heat. The die is described below in Step 3.

2. While the steel is still red hot, place it on the anvil and immediately drive the shaped and tempered die or plunger into it to depress and form the rosette or sunburst matrix. Temper the die block matrix as soon as the red color fades to a straw color by immersing it in cold water. Leave in the water a few minutes until it is cool. The crosssection and appearance of the design is shown in sketch SD1.

3. Shape the die from a piece of ½ inch round or hexagonal steel rod in a lathe or on a grinding wheel to the desired taper with a surface face of ⅜ inch or more. File three V cuts in each quadrant of the circle, which must be exact. In all, make twelve V cuts evenly spaced and of even depth, as shown in sketch SD1. Temper the die or plunger in the same way as the matrix.

4. Form the rain drop (Indian name), in the same way, using the rounded and tempered die to depress the opening which it will fit in raising the design "drop" which is like a small dome.

To use the Matrix and Die Block: Locate the center line on both sides of the bracelet or concha blank and mark the center point, for the sunburst or rain drop, on the back of the metal. With a blunt center punch, depress a small dome at the center point on the metal which is held against a piece of lead, ¼ inch thick.

Place the metal over the matrix, face down, and set the die point into the dome. Hold the metal in place with the pressure of the left hand on the die and strike with evenly repeated blows of the hammer until it is forced into all the grooves of the matrix cavity.

Chasing tools

Chasing and embossing tools are used to flatten design margins to produce a relief effect, also to define the outlines of raised or repousse designs. In sets available from suppliers, several sizes of the essential tools are offered. These are shown in Fig. 210 and consist of:

Narrow and broad outline tools, smooth finished with rounded edges, sketch A.

Rounded raising or embossing tools, sketch B, smooth finished.

Background tools, sketch C, which are used for chasing the background of a relief or repoussé design in a crosshatch, pebbled, or roughened effect.

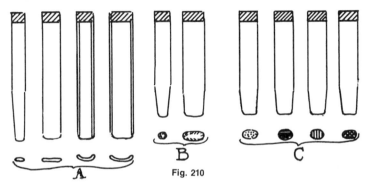

Fig. 210

An adaptation of the standard metal engraving scriber, Fig. 211, and the narrow flat tipped chasing tool is called a "Wiggle Engraver," since it is used with a slight wiggling pressure movement to remove a shallow continuous segment of the metal along the design outline, or to scribe the lines.

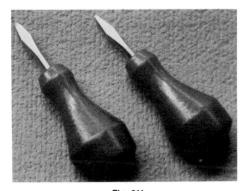

Fig. 211

The tools in Fig. 210 may be made from round or square tool steel, the ¼ inch size which is preannealed but not tempered. Chasing tools may also be made from nail sets (the tool a carpenter used to countersink a nail), but these must first be "drawn out" or have the hardness removed, the reverse of tempering. The tips are heated with a blow torch or on an electric plate to a slight red color, allowed to cool slowly (not in water), and then filed down to the required size.

1. For the outline tools, file the face end to a length of about 5/32 inch and slope this back 1½ inches. Make the narrow outline tool 1/16 inch wide and level the face with a fine file. Smooth on emery cloth and round the edges evenly.

Make the broad outline tool ⅛ inch wide and the same 5/32 inch long as the narrow tool. File and smooth the face and round the edges.

2. Shape and smooth finish the face of the raising tools in the same way, these may be 5/32 inch square with rounded corners, or an oval 5/32 inch by ⅛ inch.

3. After shaping the background tools, place them in a vise and file the lines; close fine diagonal lines which cross to form a fine crosshatch, or closely filed straight parallel lines on a round or triangular face.

File all rough edges and remove metal burrs. Smooth the face carefully so as not to blur surface lines.

Tempering metal working tools

The chasing and stamping tools which are handmade according to the procedure just described, must be tempered before using them on metal. A recommended process follows:

1. Heat the tools, singly or together, in a crucible of molten lead, which surrounds the tools to a depth of two-thirds of the length. The melting point of lead, 621 degrees F. will be retained in the crucible long enough to raise the temperature of the tools to the necessary point, unless several cold tools are added and reduce it too quickly.

2. Place the crucible of lead on a piece of asbestos, surrounded and supported closely with firebricks. Play the torch flame around the crucible until the lead is liquid.

3. Remove the tools, one at a time, from the lead with tongs and dip the tip into cold water to a depth of ½ inch. Lift immediately out of the water and inspect for surface color. Shades of blue, purple, brown, and yellow will appear as the residual heat in the upper part of the tool descends.

4. The colors register the temperatures, decreasing from that of the lead, 621 degrees to 570 degrees, 500, 440, and finally the straw color of 430 degrees F. which is the point at which the tool must be dropped into cold water to quench the heat and temper or harden it. When the tools are cool, remove from the water and wipe dry. An application of light household oil will prevent rusting.

Etching

The background of a relief or repoussé decoration and other forms of metal design development may be etched for contrast. This type of background should be part of the over all design plan, and is best completed before the design elements are applied. The procedure is basically the same for all metals but the mordants or etching solutions differ according to the kind of metal to be etched.

Research and experimentation by producers of craft metals have enabled them to improve and simplify the etching process. They are developing new products which will replace dangerous substances, such as the acid content of etching solutions. A nonacid etching medium for aluminum is now on the market. The directions for its use are provided by the producer.

The choice of a design for an etched decoration is limited by the difficulty of protecting fine lines or other details. In planning a design in which either the design motif or the background will be etched, choose one in which the contrasts will be clearly defined, without intricate detail. Usually the design is protected by asphaltum or a prepared resist, and the background or surrounding surface etched to leave the design in relief.

A beeswax resist is sometimes used to protect the design background. Warm the metal and coat it evenly all over with the wax mixed with powdered chalk. Trace the lines of the design with a metal scriber or slightly blunted tracing tool, to leave a distinct margin of the design motif as well as the finer details. Carefully remove, with a modeling tool, all the wax from other areas or parts of the design to be etched. This wax resist method necessitates an ability of the worker to develop his design directly on the wax or through it to the metal surface, which must clearly expose it for etching. After this is done, remove the wax by warming the metal sufficiently for it to melt.

1. *Note:* The metal must be perfectly clean and free from any finger marks. Wear gloves or use a piece of cloth for holding the metal before etching. Alcohol will clean new metal, otherwise it should be dipped in the pickling solution, rinsed well and thoroughly dried.

2. Prepare the design and draw it directly on the metal or transfer with metal carbon paper. Another method requires the coating of all of the article with a kind of whitewash, called "Chinese white." This comes in a cake and is applied with a watercolor paint brush moistened in water. When dry, it provides a surface for the transfer or the direct drawing of a design with a metal scriber or etching needle.

3. Black asphaltum varnish is a standard resist or protective coating for the parts of the metal which are to remain plain. Apply evenly to these areas and also to the back of the article. Keep the design margins clear and distinct. Remove, with a little turpentine on a fine brush, any asphaltum which has blurred a design margin or spread across a line. Leave to dry completely, preferably overnight.

4. Other commercial resists for use on silver, copper, or brass may be secured from suppliers. A recommended resist is a special formula prepared and supplied direct or through suppliers by Wm. Dixon, Inc. (see suppliers

list). It is easily applied, adheres well, and dries in less than an hour.

5. The etching fluid or mordant for copper and brass is nitric acid in a solution of one part nitric acid to two parts water, mixed in an earthenware or glass container large enough to submerge the metal article to be etched. *Always measure the water and pour into the container first, then add half as much acid very slowly,* while stirring with a glass rod or spoon.

6. Mentioned on page 241 was the nonacid etching medium for aluminum. Inquire as to its availability from your supplier. William Dixon, producer and dealer of tools and supplies for Art Metal Crafts, offers a special mordant for etching silver and another for etching copper, brass, aluminum, and other metals. These are guaranteed.

7. *Pewter* usually does not need or have any surface enrichment, since its soft luster is so attractive on well shaped and perfectly finished articles, such as the example of a tea set, Fig. 5, page 6. The Dixon mordant previously mentioned can be used for etching pewter. The designs should be simple and chosen mainly for contrast, Fig. 234, page 265, of a bookend, small candy or nut dishes and a tray are all from the Penland School of Handicraft and illustrate the principle of simple designs with etched background, Fig. 212, page 246.

There are important precautions in handling etching fluids:

1. Never pour water into the acid or other etching substance which is to be mixed with water. Always pour the acid into the water to avoid violent reactions which will cause the mixture to splash over.

2. Store or mix the acid only in glass or porcelain containers.

3. Wear heavy gloves and an apron. Be careful not to inhale the fumes. Work near an open door or window.

4. Be careful in disposing of residue. If possible, pour out on the ground away from foliage. Otherwise empty in a floor drain with water running in it at the same time.

Steps in the process of etching:

1. If the design is on the bottom of a bowl or tray, pour the etching solution into the area. Dip other articles into it, and immerse them for a specific period.

2. After a few minutes, tiny bubbles will appear and light fumes will be thrown off. Large active bubbles and heavy fumes indicate that the mordant is too strong. In this case, add a little water slowly and mix into the solution carefully. Use a glass stirring rod or spoon.

3. Inspect the metal after about 30 minutes, lifting the article with wooden tongs or a stick. If the etching is not sufficiently deep, return the article to the solution for a longer period.

4. If, after this period, the etching has not started, the solution is too weak (acids vary in strength), so add a small quantity, about ½ cup, half and half water and acid, mixed as before, *acid added to the water,* to the solution. Mix thoroughly and immerse the article for another period. The bubbling action indicates the etching process has started.

5. When the etching process is satisfactorily finished, rinse the metal several times in cold water, then remove the resist with turpentine. Clean the

raised or clear parts of the metal with fine steel wool, polish with fine emery cloth or paper. Protect the finish with lacquer or with the wax treatment described on page 245.

Soldering

Metal edges may be joined, either overlapping or at butt joints with a metal alloy called solder melted along the edges. Solders are supplied as soft and hard solders, the difference depending on the melting temperatures of the combined alloys. For any soldering operation it is essential that the parts are perfectly fitted together.

There are two kinds of solders usually supplied: One is an alloy with a small amount of pure silver and the other a cheaper solder composed of half lead and half tin. These melt at very low temperatures, ranging from 490 degrees F. to 558 degrees F. Because of their low melting points, *soft solders* do not fuse with the metal parts but hold them together when melted across and in the joint, uniting the parts on the outside edges.

Soft solders are limited for use on metals having low melting points. It is less difficult to apply than hard solders, so is usually suggested for a beginner in metal work.

The soft soldering process requires a soldering iron of the type heated in a flame or one with an electric element. The copper tip must be cleaned for each use and filed, if necessary to remove oxidation. The surfaces to be united must also be cleaned, either by filing, scraping, or the action of the acid pickling bath. When clean, do not touch with the fingers which may leave an oily film.

Steps in soft soldering:

1. Heat the tip of the iron in a flame until it just begins to glow, then hold it against a cake of sal ammoniac (supplied with the solder wire), while applying the end of the wire to the tip point and about one half inch of the surface of the iron on all sides. This operation is called "tinning the tip."

2. With a small brush, apply the flux to all the surfaces to be united. This is a substance with an acid reaction, mixed with water to a paste. Powdered borax, fluorspar, or a prepared paste such as "Nocorode" may be used. The flux controls the flow of the melted solder, as it will flow only on the fluxed part.

3. Dip the tip of the hot soldering iron in the flux paste and rub it along the edge of each piece of metal to transfer the heat to it. Apply the solder wire at the point of the tip, held on an edge, and spread a thin coating over one edge at a time, allowing one to cool slightly while the other is being coated and also allowed to cool before the edges are brought together.

4. Apply a little more flux to the edges and reheat the soldering iron, cleaning it in the flux paste as before. Hold it on top of the metal surface if the edges overlap or over the butt joint. This should melt the solder previously applied so it will run along the edges. Remove the iron and hold the edges firmly together with pliers or other support until the solder is cool. File away any excess and smooth the surfaces with emery cloth or paper.

An acid core solder (self contained flux) is recommended for an inexperienced worker. Various types are available from suppliers.

Detailed sketches for soldering silver jewelry items may be found in that section on pages 282 to 290.

Hard soldering

Hard solders are preferable for use wherever the melting temperature permits, as it may be hammered into a joint and made almost imperceptible. They are silver alloys, combinations of silver with copper, zinc, and sometimes tin, and are supplied in three grades: No. 1 with a melting point of 1425 degrees F.; medium with a melting point of 1390 degrees F.; and Easy with a melting point of 1325 degrees F. This range of melting points makes possible successive soldering operations on an article of higher melting point.

As in soft soldering the surfaces to be joined must be perfectly clean and the clear metal exposed. The borax slate, holding tools, and the charcoal or asbestos block must also be clean. The steps in hard soldering follow:

1. Use a metal worker's blow torch, equipped with a special burner for gas, alcohol, or gasoline, depending on the fuel available. Gas is the most efficient fuel, either bottled gas under pressure or natural gas with a compressed air supply or a foot bellows. For soldering small spaces, a blow pipe with air supplied by mouth is sufficient.

2. Apply the flux to the edges to be overlapped or butt joined, either a prepared flux paste which has a borax base, or finely powdered borax in water. Avoid getting any of the flux beyond the edges as the melted solder will follow the flux.

3. Have small pieces of wire or sheet silver solder in the borax slate paste. Pick up the pieces with tweezers or the damp (not wet) borax brush and place closely along the edges to be soldered. Apply heat with the torch gradually until the borax dries. If the rapid evaporation of the water dislodges the pieces of solder and causes one to "snap off," replace with one from the borax paste.

4. When the solder liquefies, it will flow in a line along the fluxed surfaces or edges. For a butt joint it should be visible from the reverse side. A technique termed "drawing around" is the method of drawing the molten solder to a portion of the joint or overlapping edges by applying heat to that part.

Heat the edges and the larger parts to be united first. Apply just enough solder to fill the joint or overlapping edge.

5. If more than one step in soldering is required, the solder of the higher melting point should be used first and that with a lower melting point for the second or third step, so that the first application may not soften and come apart.

6. Remove dried flux and any discoloration with emery cloth and polish with fine pumice powder. There should be no excess solder to remove if only the necessary amount of wire or strip "snippets" are applied.

Note: The tendency of copper to oxidize may cause difficulty. This may be avoided by immersing the pieces, wired together for soldering, in a solution of boric acid, which is then brought to a boil. After they dry, a thin glazed coating will remain. Then apply the flux and the solder and melt the solder with the flame as quickly as possible. Protect from drafts with a baffle of asbestos sheets, firebrick, or other heat retaining material.

For Hoyt's pewter, recommended for the pewter projects which will be described, a special solder, 1/16 inch wire on spools, is available with a special flux, offered by the Hagstoz Company. Dixon supplies a bismuth solder for pewter. This flows at 550 degrees F. Hoyt's special solder for pewter flows at 370 degrees F.

For aluminum a stick solder is available which does not require a flux. The manufacturer's recommended process is to heat the aluminum to 500 degrees F., then rub the stick solder on the parts to be joined.

A brass solder for hard soldering, melting point 1530 degrees F., is inexpensive and satisfactory for copper and brass. It is good for copper jewelry.

Solderall is a trade name for a paste solder that requires no acid nor paste flux. It is claimed by the manufacturer "to be effective for most metals." As with aluminum solder, the metal is heated and the Solderall applied to the joint.

Finishing and polishing

The use of household wax, applied to the heated metal, has been suggested for copper and brass. If renewed occasionally this protective coating will last indefinitely unless the article requires washing in soap or detergent solutions. It can be wiped with a damp cloth. A lacquer finish is applied by manufacturers of metal articles. A special metal lacquer is applied with a soft camel's hair brush to the warmed surface of the metal. Spread a thin even coating with brush strokes that do not overlap and brush in one direction only.

Before any protective finish is applied, the article must be cleaned of any oil, dirt, or oxidation and carefully polished. Various effective household cleaners for most metals are now available with directions for use. All metals can be cleaned and polished with very fine steel wool or emery cloth. Buffing powders and jeweler's rouge applied with a chamois skin will produce a high polish similar to that developed by power machines with felt or cloth buffing wheels and polishing materials.

Metal Craftwork Projects

Fig. 212

We are indebted to Miss Lucy Morgan, the founder and former director of the Penland School of Crafts, Penland, North Carolina for the pictures of the pewter articles shown above, also the tea set on page 6. Other pewter items, made in Penland, are described as project examples in this section.

Miss Morgan started the Penland Program of Crafts, to perpetuate or retrieve the skills of the mountain weavers and potters, as well as the workers in other crafts of the Southern Highlands. She recruited professional instructors to help them improve their products and enable them to benefit from the Penland sales. Today, Penland, one of the largest Craft Schools in the United States," is dedicated to a serious creative craft program for all ages and backgrounds" with instruction from National and International Craftsmen during the summer school of seven sessions.

Napkin clips with pierced decoration

An easy and attractive project in which a beginner in metal work can learn the processes of hammering, piercing, and bending is that of the napkin clips shown in Fig. 199, page 227.

The clips are made as follows:

1. Cut a strip of 16 gauge aluminum, pewter, or nickel silver 5½ inches long and 1½ inches wide and tapered to ⅞ inch at one end. Remove the rough edges with a fine file and flatten any surface irregularities, with the metal on a smooth hard wood surface, with a wooden mallet, as indicated in Fig. 199, page 227.

2. Transfer the selected design to the metal by tracing over carbon paper. A thin wash of flat watercolor or "Chinese white" paint on the surface will provide contrast for the design. (It will wash off with soap and water after the design is pierced.) Trace the design with a hard lead pencil or a metal scriber.

3. Saw cut the designated open areas as directed for pierced work on page 226. Incise lightly the design outline with a metal graver or incising tool.

The flower centers can be raised from the back with a round pointed center punch or nail set.

4. Remove the white surface coating and clean with fine steel wool. Texture the surface and edges with the small end of the ball-peen hammer, while holding the metal against a hard wood block. A smooth surface with a textured edge can be finished with a burnishing tool. Tool marks on the surface can be removed with fine dry pumice powder or emery cloth moistened in oil.

5. Mark a line across the metal for bending and fold it to a right angle against the edge of a smooth wooden block. The fold may be started with the fingers and pressure then applied with a wood or leather tipped mallet to bring it to the desired angle. Shape the metal into a clip according to the directions and sketch 198 on page 227.

Fig. 213

Aluminum or pewter plate with flattened rim

A similar mold formed plate of either pewter or soft aluminum can be strengthened with a rim reinforcement as indicated in the sketches of Figs. 214 and 215. A disc of 16 gauge metal may be obtained from suppliers or cut with metal shears from sheet metal of the same gauge. Fig. 214A is the wooden mold carved from a block. The flat base is used as in Fig. 215.

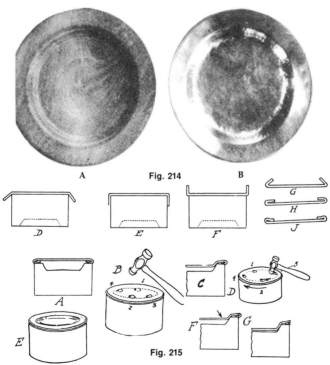

Fig. 214

Fig. 215

1. Place the disc on the flat bottom side of the contour block, braced in a fixed position on the worktable with the bottom uppermost. A purchased block or one lathe turned or gouged out by hand may be used. The bottom surface should be smoothed and perfectly level and the circular edge exactly round and vertical at all points.

2. Position the disc on the contour block so that the edge projects equally at all points, indicated as 1, 2, 3, and 4, Fig. 218. Bend the edge downward at these points with light blows of a hard wood mallet or ball-peen hammer. The wood mallet is preferred. The sketch D shows the correct position at this point with the disc centered on the block. Continue the bending process until all of the edge is in contact with the block as shown in sketch E.

3. Remove the disc from the block and reverse its position as shown in sketch F. Continue bending the upturned edge inward as indicated in sketch G. Then lap it back to the position of sketch H, and finally hammer the edge down until it makes contact with the rim. Sketch J.

4. Follow the procedure given for mold formed metal, in shaping the shallow plate depression, shown in Fig. 215, sketches A to G. Clean and polish as directed for finishing on page 245.

Pewter and Aluminum Projects

Pewter plate and matching bowl

A molded plate embodies the basic principles of molding metal forms. Aluminum and pewter, as now made, do not contain any objectionable substance which can affect food, so they are especially suitable for serving dishes. Neither pewter nor aluminum require annealing, as they do not harden while being worked and so are less difficult to shape by hammering in a mold than other metals. Hoyt's sheet or disc pewter and the "soft roll" aluminum are the best types for craft projects of this kind.

Fig. 216 shows a pewter plate and deep bowl with leaf handles, made at the Penland School of Crafts.

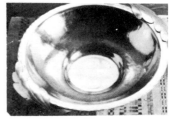

Fig. 216

1. Procure or make a hard wood contour block of the required size for a plate. A wood mallet and wood planishing hammer will be needed, besides a metal disc or circle cut from sheet or rolled metal, 16 gauge for pewter and 18 gauge for aluminum. For a large plate, a heavier gauge of 16 for both should be used.

2. With pencil or compass dividers, mark the position of the plate well or the section to be depressed. Center the disc on the block, with the well corresponding to the contour form and begin the molding. Strike light blows (mallet) just inside the penciled well circle and continue around the margin, rotating the disc and slanting the blows slightly toward the edges of the well. Do not overlap the impressions and keep them evenly placed without visible tipping toward either side. Refer to Fig. 219, on page 251.

3. Continue to hammer around the well margin until the metal is pressed into the mold. Wrinkles may have developed in the rim section, so the next step is to gently press these down smooth with the wood mallet and at the same time bend the rim down toward the surface of the block. Leave the center until later.

4. Press the rim partially down in 4 or 6 equally spaced places at opposite points, then in between. Continue hammering with the wood mallet, applying light strokes, slanting them evenly from the top of the plate well toward the edge of the rim to smooth out any remaining wrinkles. If an irregular edge has developed, use a fine half round file to restore the pattern circle. Smooth with a burnisher.

5. To flatten the bottom of the plate well, if it has become bulged, place it over a reverse mold or stake of the same contour. Gently planish the center area until it is level or has a slight concavity.

6. Texture the rim with a chasing tool or with the small tip of the chasing hammer, with the plate form blocked in the mold so it cannot move. Encircle the rim with light impressions. A design pattern for the leaf will follow.

Deep bowl with ornamental handles

A design pattern for the ornamental handles on the plate and deep bowl, as sketched in Fig. 217, can be modified for the chosen dimensions of either article.

Fig. 217

Cut a similar pattern from stiff cardboard and trace the outline on a piece of metal of the same gauge and cut out the leaf with metal shears. Deepen the leaf indentations and even the outline with a fine half round file. Smoothly burnish the edges.

Use a chasing tool to develop the leaf design. When the plate or bowl is ready, solder the pair of leaf handles in place with the special solder for aluminum or pewter.

Two wooden molds are required to form the deep bowl in Fig. 251. For this project a heavier 14 gauge of pewter or the 16 gauge for aluminum should be used. The molds are the same diameter, 10 or 12 inches according to the chosen size. The first is shaped for the shallow upper part of the bowl and the other for the entire depth but with the same upper contour. The steps follow:

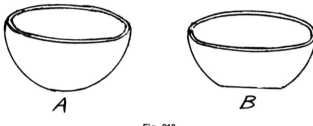

Fig. 218

1. Cut a circle from a sheet of metal or purchase a disc. The size of the circle for the deep bowl should be the diameter plus the depth. Clean it with very fine steel wool and wipe with a clean cloth.

2. Place the disc over the shallow mold and shape the sides around the top. Make sure a full ½ inch is left above for the rim. Keep the metal evenly centered while rotating it for the shaping with a wooden or leather tipped mallet.

3. Move the partially shaped form to the deep mold, which has a small flat base as shown in Fig. 218B. Continue the formation of the bowl with successive light mallet strikes in the same direction, downward in a circular path. Leave the base for flattening later.

4   At this point, bend the rim over the flat rim of the mold within the ½ inch margin but do not flatten until the bowl is formed.

5. Reverse the direction of the hammering to smooth and obliterate all possible mallet impressions from the margin of the base to the top of the bowl. Then with the lightest possible strikes of the wooden mallet or a softer fiber mallet, shape the bowl form into the rounded curve above the margin of the base. Place the bowl over a flat hard wood stake to planish the base and form a slight concavity.

6. Flatten the rim to the required position by rotating on a flat surface. Texture the edge as directed for the plate. Wash in a hot detergent solution, dry thoroughly, and while it is still hot apply a coat of paste wax. When cool, polish with a clean dry cloth. Repeat the wax treatment occasionally to preserve finish.

A rimless bowl with a flat or curved base may be made in the same molds, if the base is rounded or flattened later over a stake of the required contour. The top edge may be textured or fluted as desired.

Fig. 219

Candlesticks and small flower bowl

The attractive but plain pair of candlesticks and small bowl, Fig. 219, were made of pewter, but would also be attractive in brass or copper. They can be made as follows:

1. The tools required for the candlesticks are: ball-peen hammer and burnisher, a wooden contour block, with a half circle depression, a fine half round file, strip of fine emery cloth, soldering flux (special pewter flux for pewter), and wire solder with two melting points, one for joining the candleholder ends and the other, with a lower melting point, to attach the holder tube to the base. Two discs of 18 gauge metal and strips 2¾ by 1¼ inches of the same gauge will be needed. (See Fig. 220, sketches A and B, with contour block sketch E.)

2. Shape the discs in the contour block and slightly bevel the edge with the small end of the ball-peen hammer, holding it flat on the rim of the block. File and smooth with the burnisher any edge roughness or irregularities.

3. Form the candleholders by bending the strips into cylinders, sketch D, using a half circle contour block and the wood dowel pin. Shape into the candleholders and secure with binding wire. Apply flux and solder the joint.

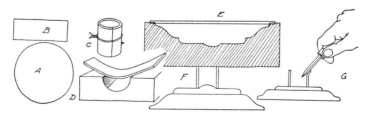

Fig. 220

Place on a mandrel and texture the surface with the hammer. Solder to the base with the lower temperature solder. Smooth with fine 000 pumice powder and remove any scratches.

4. Flare the top with the burnishing tool, sketch G. Polish with tripoli and metal polish. Protect the surface with a spray of lacquer.

5. Make the flower bowl according to the instructions for mold formed metal on page 228. A folded or textured rim may be developed as a finish. Solder the bowl to a base matching those of the candlesticks.

Mold formed plate and bowl

The small copper plate, Fig. 221A, with an elaborate repoussé decoration around the rim was made by a Mexican craftsman. For an ornament or as a small card holder, it is both beautiful and useful. To duplicate the design illustrated, or to apply a less elaborate original design requires a pitch pot as described on page 235, a slab of lead or a thick piece of linoleum. Chasing and embossing tools for raising the relief elements of the design are also required.

The outlines for the four repeat design units were first lightly dented on the face of the disc, so that the design lines are evident on the reverse side, after being traced or scribed accurately on the face. The outline stamping for

A   Fig. 221   B

the margin of the shallow bowl of the plate and the chased background for the floral relief element were both done before the raising or embossing on the back of the disc, according to the process described on page 234. The forming of the bowl in a plate mold was done last.

This little plate retains its soft luster with occasional applications of a household copper cleaner, followed by a very hot water rinse and well dried with a soft cloth before receiving the protective coating of paste wax as described on page 245.

The nut or candy bowl, Fig. 221B, with the hammered and textured rim can be mold formed in the process described on page 228.

1. Procure or cut a pewter or aluminum disc, 6 or 8 inches in diameter. Center the metal on a contour block of corresponding diameter with a ¾ inch rim, and a shallow depression, rounding down to a small base of 2½ to 3 inches.

2. Shape the metal into the sloping contour of the mold or block. Use a leather tipped mallet and press the metal gradually into the mold, without making perceptible hammer marks.

3. Flatten the rim, if it has become uneven, and keep it the same width all around the circumference. Texture the rim with a small ball-peen hammer, both to stiffen and to decorate the surface. If the metal is pewter, hammer with light strokes and avoid making any deep dents.

The spoon with the pierced design is shaped into the rounded oval in a hard wood mold of the spoon contour. This can be carved out with a gouge, then sanded smooth. Pierce and saw out the background areas to leave the open spoon design of the dogwood blossom, before the shaping is done.

Texture the edge of the spoon bowl and handle as the illustration shows. The process is described on page 231.

Shaped serving dish

Pewter or aluminum in 16 gauge are practical and attractive for this type of dish with the three compartments. The original which is illustrated in Fig. 222, was made of pewter at the Penland School of Handicrafts.

Fig. 222

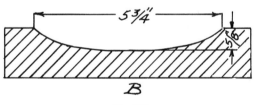

B

Fig. 223

The process for making this dish follows:

1. In planning the pattern, draw a circle, 8 to 10 inches in diameter and divide it into thirds. Make a pattern for the V shaped divisions which will indent the edges about 1¼ inch and round to a slight point at the half circle division of each compartment, exactly opposite the center of the design for the aluminum or pewter dish.

2. Mark the shaped and divided outline on a 10 inch disc of 16 gauge pewter or aluminum. Cut the outline with the metal shears, leaving the V shaped segments between the compartments, also the area of the points to be sawed out later, after the shaping of the metal is done, Fig. 224.

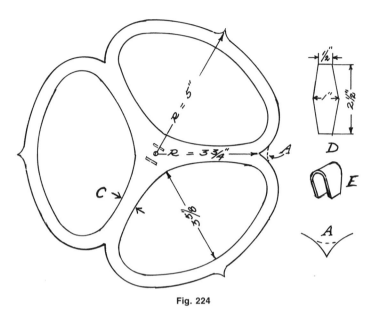

Fig. 224

3. Shape the three sections one at a time in the oval wood contour block, Fig. 223, sketch B. Depress the metal gradually into the block with successive regular strokes of a wood or fiber hammer around the top of the outline, sloping the metal into the curve of the block contour. Avoid overlapping the planishing strokes and keep them level, with no more force in the strokes than the weight of the hammer, as it is dropped about 3 or 4 inches in the swinging rhythm described on page 228, step 3.

4. When about 2 inches of space remains toward the bottom, reverse the direction of the strokes and start from the center, shaping it into the block, then hammer upward in the circular path, without visible impressions as far as possible, until the outer edge is reached, and about ¼ inch margin remains. If necessary, trim any unevenness.

5. Turn the bowl face down over a hard wood stake with the same contour and gently flatten the hammer impressions that are visible, leaving a smooth surface. Complete the shaping of the dish by flattening the dividing space, as shown in sketch C between the compartments and around the rims, about ¼ inch on the rim edges, merging into ½ inch at the V corners for the dividing space.

6. Remove the segments of metal from the corners and at the edge points with a fine jeweler's saw, following the directions for sawing corners, step 9 on page 225.

7. Cut a piece of metal 2½ by 1 inch for the handle, taper the ends to ½ inch, Fig. 223, sketch D and E, and fold together over a dowel pin. Attach to the center of the dish with aluminum or pewter solder. Finish and polish as directed on page 245.

Aluminum trays

A practical size and type of tray is illustrated in Fig. 225. This was made of 16 gauge aluminum, cut 15 by 10 inches and finished 14 by 9 inches with a rim ⅜ inch deep. The rim finish and decoration with textured edge and narrow fluting as formed over a wood stake of the same curvature and the fluting indented with a rounded chisel at measured intervals of 5 on each end and 9 on the sides.

A simple type of stamped or chased border decoration would be suitable for a tray of this size, also a center panel design corresponding in proportions to the outline of the tray. The illustrated decoration of the chased lily and leaf design is more difficult and should not be attempted without practice on a small article with a single small leaf. The steps follow:

1. *Prepare an exact design* drawing on tracing paper, with all outlines clearly defined and the chased leaf design lines and scalloped edges indicated by a wider line for the chasing tool impressions. Have the design ready to transfer to the metal after the surface hammering is done.

2. *Clean the surface of the metal* with a little oil and fine 000 steel wool. Wash with detergent solution, rinse, and wipe entirely dry.

3. *Place the metal on a thick piece of linoleum* (smooth like "deck" linoleum) tacked to the top of a level piece of planed wood on the worktable. (It has been found for the worker to have this at waist height, for the chasing process as well as the hammering.) *Use the flat surface of a wooden hammer for aluminum.*

4. For a form with corners, like the rectangular tray, *start the hammering* about ½ inch from the left, and carefully work toward the next corner, placing the strokes without overlapping. Plan the spacing to avoid hammering in the corner. On the next row of hammer impressions, which should be complete, but with a very slight indentation, place the strokes so that they come just below the point of contact of the two impressions above.

5. Continue the hammering with the same sequence developing the semblance of a diagonal pattern of hammer stroke, until an over-all hammered surface is complete.

6. *Mark the points for the rim fluting,* 5 at each end and 9 on the sides, spaced so that they do not come at any corner. With a planishing hammer or mallet, planish the ⅜ inch rim over a round edge wood or metal stake, to an even ⅜ inch depth. Then use a fluting hammer or a round edge chisel, with the metal held over a shallow grooved hard wood fluting stake, Fig. 200 on page 229, to make the fluting as marked on the rim.

7. *Clean the metal with an aluminum cleaner* to remove any marks from the handling, then position it on a smooth surface, between wedging blocks. Transfer the prepared design with metal carbon paper, over a wash of white watercolor paint. Redefine the straight stem lines and any other outlines that may not be clear with a soft pencil.

8. A metal scriber and three chasing tools will be needed. The scriber to incise the straight stem lines, a smooth rounded tool for the modeled lily blossom, a curved and a straight chasing tool, both with a fine pebbled surface and 1/16 inch wide.

9. *Incise all the straight and curved stem lines,* using a "French curve" drawing guide, then apply the straight background chasing tool to indent the straight leaf lines and the curved tool for the leaf edges. The impressions in Fig. 225 C and D show this detail for the leaf and flower.

Clean and polish with a fine grade steel wool with a little oil. Finish with buffing powder and a chamois.

Aluminum Tray and Rim Enlargement

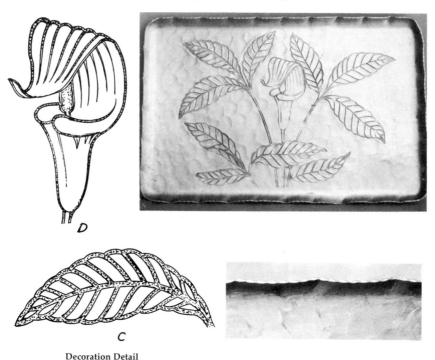

D

C

Decoration Detail
Incised and Chased.

Fig. 225

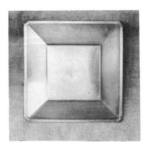

Fig. 226

Copper tray with tile inset

The ceramic tile inset (process is described on page 81), which decorates this copper tray, Fig. 226 with construction detail sketched in Fig. 227, was made according to the following process. Other types of insets would be equally suitable, such as an enameled piece of copper, etched brass or chased aluminum. Polished alabaster or a slab of petrified or agatized wood might also be used.

The pattern dimensions and outline are shown in Fig. 227 for a four inch tile with copper sides 1½ inch deep. One piece of 20 gauge copper 7½ inches square is required for the tray, with corner strips ¼ inch wide and 2½ inches long.

1. Make a woodblock 4⅛ inches square and ½ inch thick. Sand it smooth with the sides and edges exactly square and vertical to the top and bottom surfaces.

2. Scribe the outline of the pattern on the copper and cut out the entire form with the corner sections removed and angles cut to miter together as shown in Fig. 227. Cut the four corner strips which are to cover the corner joints ¼ inch wide and ½ inch long. Bend the ends about ¼ inch at right angles, one to fold over the top of the corner, and the other to extend into the base depression for the tile.

3. Carefully file rough edges on the copper shape and the strips, without changing the straight margins, burnish smooth. Bend back the edges of the tray form ¼ inch to strengthen and finish the top rim, indicated as a reverse edge in the sketch. Flatten this as directed in Fig. 215 G, H, and J, page 247.

4. Mark the square base for the tile or other inset and shape over the woodblock with the wood planishing hammer or smooth mallet.

5. Shape the sides of the tray over a block beveled to a slope which will form an angle of about 35 degrees or until the mitered corners will meet together. Wrap the shaped tray with soft binding wire to hold the joints in place.

COPPER BASE FOR MOUNTING CERAMIC TILE

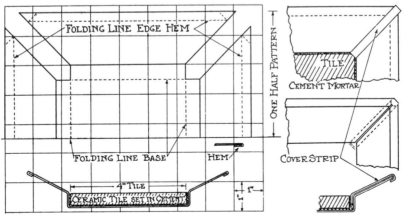

Fig. 227

Copper planter and TV lamp

Planters and planter-based lamps are a modern decorative necessity. The illustrated planter, Fig. 228, shows side A and base B, with the attached TV lamp is unusual in construction and practical as a container for plants as well. A glass insert is a convenience in cleaning the metal, but is not a necessity.

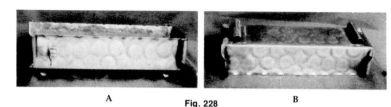

A   Fig. 228   B

The copper pieces required for the planter may be cut from regular 20 gauge metal or from the Dixon soft (cold) rolled copper, which is easier to form.

These are: 1 piece 8 by 16 inches, 2 pieces 2½ by 2½ inches for box and feet, and 1 piece 1 by 2½ inches for the electric fixture bracket.

In addition to the shop metal working equipment, a woodblock, 2¾ by 2½ by 11 inches is required to shape the piece for the box. This must have edges and corners exactly square and be sanded smooth.

The steps in constructing the planter follows:

1. Remove any wire edges from the box piece, 8 by 16 inches, also from the edges of the 2½ by 2½ inch pieces which make the rolled feet, with a fine file.

Coat the surface with Chinese white and trace the construction guide lines from the pattern with metal carbon paper underneath, to transfer the lines to the metal, indicating the area for the base, the triangle corners and lines of fold.

2. Remove the four triangular corners with the metal snips, then place the metal on a piece of linoleum or a lead block, and stamp the impressions with the filed and smooth rounded end of a 1 inch pipe, 4 inches long, in even rows. This will stiffen and harden the metal, so it may require annealing before the stamping is completed.

Immerse after annealing in the pickling or cleaning solution. Clean again after the final stamping.

3. Flute the top of the end and side margins by any of the methods described in Fig. 203, page 232. Small flutes to develop a slightly scalloped edge may be made with the round nosed pliers.

4. Bend the metal along the base outline between blocks of smooth wood held in the bench vise, then finish the shaping over the block of wood, to make the base corners and edges exact right angles.

5. Roll the triangular shaped corner parts of the ends into a coil with the half round nose pliers, overlapping the sides which butt against the ends, and concealing the corners as indicated in Fig. 229.

6. Solder the corner joints from the inside, using Solderall or stick solder with a self-contained flux. Apply heat with a small torch flame.

7. Make the two coiled metal feet by clamping one end of the 2½ by 2½

inch pieces in the bench vise and rolling them into the coil with pliers in both hands gripping the sides at the ends. If necessary, have a helper facilitate the operation with a wooden mallet.

Copper Planter

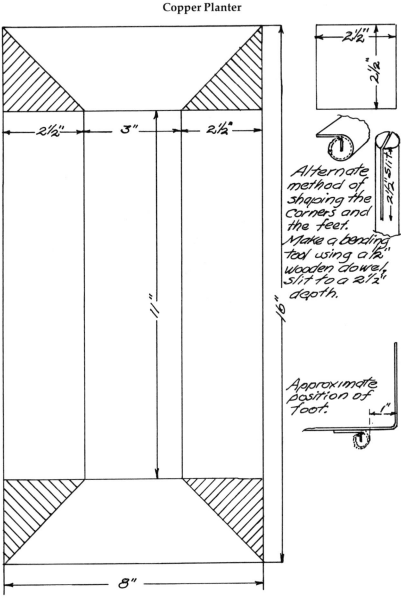

Fig. 229

8. Release the end from the vise and when both pieces are rolled to the same size, solder the flat ¾ inch (approximately) to the base of the planter, about 3 inches from the ends.

Turn the edges of the bracket strip and flatten down, making it ⅝ inch wide and a rigid support for the lamp receptacle which is placed with the stem through a ⅜ inch hole drilled ½ inch from one end. Turn the other end of the strip to form a right angle to solder to the side of the planter, 1½ inches from the right hand end as shown in the photograph.

Clean in the pickling solution, page 233, wash as for other projects, and apply paste wax to the heated surface. Polish when cold.

Hanging Planter

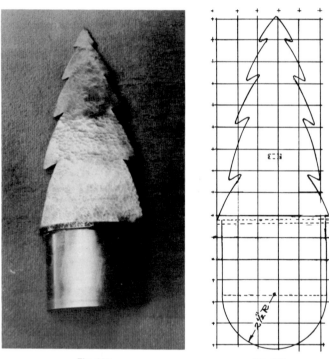

Fig. 230   Fig. 231

Copper hanging planter

The usefulness and popularity of planters of many kinds includes the unusual type shown in Fig. 230, with the pattern and construction detail sketched in Fig. 231.

Required for this planter are the following pieces of copper:

1 piece of 18 gauge copper sheet 5 inches by 16 inches.

1 piece of 18 gauge copper sheet 3 inches by 8 inches.

For the suspension loop soldered on the back for hanging, a strip of 18 gauge copper ⅜ inch by 1½ inches.

For the planter cup rim, a strip of ¼ inch square copper wire 7½ inches long.

1. Carefully mark the outline of the back piece of copper from a stiff paper pattern of the dimensions given on page 260, on a piece of 18 gauge copper. Mark the outline of the planter cup which should exactly fit around the turned out section to form the base, with ¼ inch margin on the sides.

2. Hammer the upper arrow shaped surface with the small end of the ball-pein hammer to develop the decoration indicated, Fig. 231. Hammer the rim strip on the side and top in the same way.

3. Shape the planter cup and solder to the edge of the base and to the margins of the back with the ends bent closely around the back. After these edges are joined together with hard silver solder and have cooled, it is desirable to add a line of solder over the joined edges to insure closing any gaps and prevent water seepage. See soldering directions on page 243.

4. Bend the strip of square copper wire and solder to the top of the cup to strengthen and hold the cup in position. Note that the top and front of the strip are hammered to match the upper part of the planter.

5. Clean with fine steel wool and an approved copper cleaner. Wash in very hot water and after wiping thoroughly, apply a coat of paste wax. When the wax has cooled, rub off all excess and polish with a soft cloth.

A lacquer coating may be applied in place of the wax if desired.

Covered copper, aluminum, or brass server

This practical and attractive server can easily be made after successful experience in applying the metal work processes to the beginning projects.

If made of copper or brass, the server should have a glass or ceramic container for food in the box. This insert is not necessary in aluminum.

Fig. 232

Since the methods of working aluminum have been given in connection with other projects, the steps which follow will detail the methods of decoration and assembly for a server of copper or brass. Aluminum, however, is equally satisfactory for this project. The soft rolled metal, available in 12 inch widths, and lengths as ordered, is preferable, as the quality is less hard and easier to work in any of the processes than the regular sheet metal. The soft rolled metals are produced by William Dixon Inc., Newark, N. J., and may be obtained through suppliers.

1. *The server project requires* the following pieces of metal in the gauges specified:

1 piece 7¾ inches by 9¾ inches, 20 gauge for box.
1 piece 5½ inches by 7⅜ inches, 18 gauge for lid of box.
1 piece 1¼ inches by 9 inches, 16 gauge for the handle.
1 piece ⅞ inch by 1½ inches, 16 gauge for the thumb rest.
1 piece ⅛ inch tubing for the hinge.

2. *Box Formation*

1. Measure a distance of 1⅜ inches in from each edge of the box piece and draw a pencil line. The area within the line should measure 5 x 7 inches, the size of the completed box. The corners formed by the intersecting lines are to be removed to leave the ends and sides.

2. Cut out the corner sections with the metal cutting shears, taking care not to cut past either intersecting line. The ends should be 5 inches long by 1⅜ inches wide and the sides 7 x 5 inches, with the additional ⅜ inch edge to overlap the ends when the metal is folded to form the box.

Bend the ends and sides over a wooden block as described on page 227. Server, with handle, Fig. 232.

3. Note that the outline of the diamond design is marked before the rim line is marked or the surface textured, but is not contour formed until the other decoration is finished.

4. With the small end of the ball-pein hammer, texture the surface of the lid, between the diamond and the border line of the lid, as is evident in the photograph. Anneal copper or brass, if it has become hard, clean as directed on page 233.

5. Crimp the edges with the round nose pliers to develop a slight scallop effect at regular intervals, forming 7 units on the sides and 5 on the ends.

6. Place the metal face down over a contour block with a diamond shaped cavity carved by gouging out the wood, then finish smoothly with a chisel as described in the woodworking section. Mark guide lines on the block for the centering of the design area.

7. Shape the metal into the diamond design contour block, depressing it gently, with the small end of a wood or fiber mallet, so that the impressions are not evident. Reverse the diamond, face side up over a planishing stake, and smoothly planish the surface with the flat end of a planishing hammer. Smooth all the edges with a fine file and the burnisher.

Assembly of the box

1. If ⅛ inch tubing for hinges is not available in the metal used, it can be made according to the directions to be given later. Each hinge requires two pieces ½ inch long and one piece 1 inch long. Make the hinges by passing a wire through the three pieces of tubing, long enough to permit spreading the ends to hold them in the tubing, the long piece in the center and a short piece on either side. The diameter of the wire should be sufficiently less than the tubing to permit free movement without excessive play.

2. Solder the overlapping ends of the box to the sides and solder the end sections of the hinges on the edge of one side, 1½ inches from each corner. Shape the handle by bending one end at right angles, then curving the strip over a rounded mandrel into a handle form that will fit the side of the box at the center between the hinges. Solder the right angled end in a butt joint just above the bottom of the side. Solder the other end, bent under to fit against the side, about ⅜ inch below the top. Before soldering, be sure the strip is formed in the angle and curve that will fit the width of the side. Use special aluminum solder for aluminum and Dixon's Solderall for copper or brass. (See directions for soldering on page 243.)

3. Solder the center section of the hinges and the thumb rest to the lid. Finish with fine steel wool or pumice powder in oil. Wash in hot detergent solution and dry completely with a soft cloth. Apply paste wax to the warm surface and polish until all trace of the wax has disappeared. Occasional coats applied to the heated surface will preserve the finish. A sprayed lacquer forms a more durable protective film.

Making or drawing tubing for hinges or other purposes, from the sheet metal, requires a draw plate and draw tongs, materials for annealing and soldering. It is not a difficult process. (Tubing for silver and some other metals is now available from suppliers.)

1. Shear a piece of the sheet metal into strips, making the width approximately three times the diameter of the tube to be formed.

2. Anneal the strips by heating to a dull red color, and clean or pickle as directed on page 233. Partially form the strip by pressing it into a groove in a wooden or metal block with a round edge chisel or chasing tool. Hammer with a wood mallet, if necessary, to shape the strip into a U form. Remove from the groove and file any rough edges.

3. Close the edges of the U shaped strips into the round O shape by hammering with the mallet over a metal wire. Anneal the strip if it has become hard. Clean as before.

4. Taper one end of a rounded strip and pass through one of the holes in the draw plate, selecting a gauge larger than the size the finished tubing is to be. Draw the tube through the next smaller gauge and repeat until the desired size is obtained.

5. Solder the joint and cut to the sizes required for the hinges.

Bookends, copper, aluminum, nickel silver, and pewter

Two attractive and practical types of bookends are illustrated in Fig. 233.

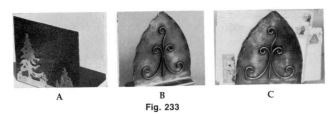

A   B   C
Fig. 233

The first is decorated with an appliqué of pewter on copper and the second is also copper with a scroll design of copper wire. Brass wire is effective on copper, and an ornament of brass appliqué on the hammered copper bookend, Fig. 233A, is equally effective and suitable. The process for the pewter appliqué follows:

1. Plan the bookend design both for shape and for decoration and make a pattern of heavy stiff paper for both. Trace the outline for the pair of bookends on a piece of 18 gauge copper and for the appliqué motif on pewter or brass of the same gauge. Outline the position of the decorative motif on the copper with the bottom coming just to the bending line.

2. With a jeweler's saw cut out the appliqué metal as instructed on page 226. Cut the copper bookend pieces with metal cutting shears, rub with fine emery cloth or a fine file to remove any burrs from the edges. Smooth with a burnisher.

Texture the portion of the copper, which will not be covered with the appliqué, with the small end of the ball-pein hammer.

3. File or trim to the original contour any edges which may have been pressed out of line by the hammering. Mark a line ¼ inch from the edges, also a line to define the panel for the design appliqué. Incise them slightly with the outline chasing tool. With the round-nose pliers, form regular short flutes and develop a slight scalloped edge between them.

4. Drill holes in both the copper and the appliqué metal at points which have been indicated in the pattern and marked when the design was traced. Rivet them together with rivets made of copper wire, cut 1/16 inch longer than the combined thicknesses of the copper and the appliqué metal. Flatten the rivets smoothly on both sides with the ball-pein hammer.

5. Bend the copper on the bottom line of the applique, to form the book support and the base for the upright section. Finish the surface with fine pumice powder applied on a damp cloth. Polish with jeweler's rouge and spray with lacquer or apply a coat of paste wax to the washed and heated surface and polish when cold with a soft cloth or chamois.

For *bookend B and letter holder C*

1. Plan the design for the ornamental scroll, shaped from No. 14 wire, according to the selected proportions of the boodend pattern. Mark the pattern outline on 16 gauge copper and cut with metal cutting shears to the exact outline. Smooth the edge with emery cloth or a fine file to remove any cutting burrs. Apply a chased design about 3/16 inch from the margin and flute the edge slightly as indicated in the print.

2. Trace the line for the position of the scroll, then incise it lightly with a chasing tool. Drill holes at the points marked for the insertion of the wire, bend it at right angles about ¼ inch back from the end, and insert so that just enough protrudes on the back to be bent closely against the metal and spread into a rivet with the ball-pein hammer. A piece of sheet lead placed beneath will prevent the flattening of the scroll.

For the *letter holder,* rivet a pair of the scroll design bookends together with base ends overlapping to provide the desired space between.

The pewter bookends in Fig. 234 are from the Penland, North Carolina School of Handicrafts and are made of 16 gauge metal with an attractive etched decoration, according to the process described on page 242. The edge is finished with a textured design applied with a chasing tool to the edge of the metal, held in a vise with the surface protected with cloth or a piece of leather.

Fig. 234

Note: the bookends and letter holder are all strengthened and stabilized with the reverse fold at the bottom as indicated in Fig. 234. The bending process is described on page 227.

Spring type bookends may be constructed from sheet aluminum, copper, or brass. Nickel silver is also suitable. The metal base is covered with felt.

1. Make a dimension drawing to indicate the size and the curvature desired for the scroll ends. This should be full size to provide a checking guide in bending the scrolls. The example shown in Fig. 235 is one of a pair, which required 2 pieces of 14 gauge metal, 4 inches by 10¾ inches.

2. Before shaping, the metal should be given a satin finish with 000 steel wool and waxed. Hammer one of each blank over a ¼ inch diameter steel rod with a wood or rawhide hammer, to start the form of the outer scroll. Insert the remainder of the blank in a holding jig, made by clamping in a vise two steel rods, held vertically about ¼ inch apart.

3. Bend the scroll gradually by hand or by striking with the rawhide mallet. As the bending progresses, check the scroll frequently with the pattern layout. The two pieces are made in the same manner and must be identical.

4. After completing the scrolls according to the pattern, mark lines on each piece for the bending of the base sections. Clamp the end in the vise between smooth sloping blocks of wood with the bend at the top and the scrolled section projecting upward. With the rawhide mallet hammer the upper section

over the edge of the block in the reverse direction from the scroll, as indicated in the sketch.

5. After a 90 degree bend is formed, remove the metal from the vise and continue to bend it over the edge of a hard wood block or steel form which has an angle of 30 degrees. This should bring the bend to an angle of about 150 degrees, from which it should be hammered into the complete reverse or 180 degree bend. If not completely flat at this point, place the fold in a vise, protected by a fold of cloth and tighten the jaws of the vise over it.

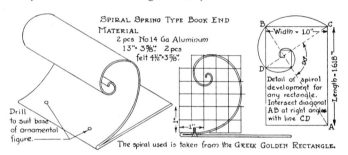

Fig. 235

Metal house numbers or names

Numbers or letters may be cut from sheet aluminum, copper, brass, or nickel silver, 14 gauge or heavier. Either aluminum or nickel will best retain its finish.

1. Design the figures and cut them from stiff paper. Arrange them on a piece of metal, with supporting bars or width of metal connecting the figures or letters at the top and bottom as shown in Fig. 236.

2. Attach these with leather cement which will hold them in place while the outline is clearly scribed on incised with a scratch awl or metal scriber. Go over the lines until the margins of the letters or figures are distinctly marked.

3. Rough cut the figures or letters from the metal sheet with a jeweler's saw, keeping just outside the lines to allow for removal of burrs and accurate finishing with a file. Small sections may be removed with the jeweler's saw, inserted in a drilled hole, if necessary.

4. Drill holes for the attachment of the supporting bars to wood or other wall surfaces. Screws are used directly in the wood. Stone or brick will require an expansion bolt. Smooth with fine steel and apply aluminum polish or a spray of lacquer for a protective finish.

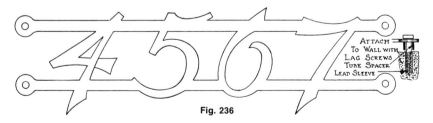

Fig. 236

Fig. 237

Tooled designs on metal foil

Metals in thin sheets, called foils, available in a 36 gauge weight or a thickness of .005 or 5/1,000, are supplied in 12 inch rolls of copper, brass, and aluminum. Copper and brass are especially effective because of their rich color and the contrasting highlights and shadows that can be developed by stamping or stippling the background and polishing the raised design areas.

Tooled metal foils can be applied to a wood base to make bookends, box lids, panels for wood projects, and mountings or overlay designs on other metals. Nickel silver makes a very good background and contrast for copper or brass tooled design units.

Leather working tools of hardwood, shown in Fig. 240, sketch A, also wood manicure sticks, are satisfactory for tooling metal foils. A woodblock, faced with heavy, smooth linoleum or a piece of firm felt, makes a satisfactory base for repoussé or raised elements in design. As in leather tooling, the background work requires a hard surface, glass or marble.

Fig. 238

The procedure for tooling metal foil follows:

1. Prepare a drawing of the chosen design and transfer it to the metal foil. One method is indicated in Fig. 240 sketch B, in which the reverse of the drawing is against the metal foil. A penciled retracing of the outlines is then transferred to clean foil without carbon paper. If this is not sufficiently clear on the face of the foil, a coating of "Chinese white" or watercolor white will show every detail of the design.

2. Remove the drawing and carbon and retrace the design outline with the tip of a leather working tracer. Place the metal on a plate glass or marble surface. Outline the areas which are to appear raised with sufficient pressure to develop clear lines on the underside, Fig. 239.

3. Place the foil face down on a piece of felt or other yielding surface with a double faced cardboard piece underneath. A pad of folded newspapers will serve the same purpose, permitting the depression of the areas in the design for the raised appearance. Use the ball and spoon ends of the modeling tools and work slowly with care not to cut or distort the foil. Develop the border lines if necessary. Refer to the repousse process of tooling leather on page 000.

4. Complete the tooling on the right side of the foil, defining the raised areas with the edge of the tracer or deerfoot tool. To protect and retain the form of the raised areas, fill the back with plastic wood or a caulking material. As in leather tooling a slight relief appearance may be developed on the face of the design by slightly pressing down the foil margin along the outlines as in flat modeling of leather. Use the deerfoot tool to bevel the design lines.

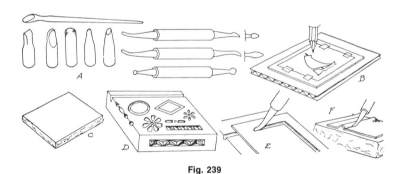

Fig. 239

Contrast backgrounds

1. Fig. 241, sketch C indicates the marginal beveling of a design outline. In some designs it may be desirable to smooth the entire background between design elements.

2. A stippled background is developed on the aquatic scenes in the panels of Fig. 239. With the metal over the felt and firm cardboard surface, tap it with a slightly rounded tool point. A blunted nail set tool can be applied with light hammer strokes to barely dent, not pierce the metal. Fig. 241, sketch A indicates the process. All spaces between borders and design are covered in this way.

Carefully avoid denting the border or design lines.

3. A hammered background, resembling that on heavier metals, is best done with a hardwood dowel. Hammer lightly with a wooden mallet or a small flat hammer as in Fig. 26, sketch B. Keep the impressions uniform and in an alternating path to cover the background area.

4. A simulated wood grain background, as in Fig. 242, sketch E is effective and easy to do. Place the foil on a soft surface and rub with the wood creaser. Experiment with the amount of pressure and length of markings, imitating the grain of wood as nearly as possible. Sketch F shows possible variations.

5. Another type of background can be produced with the cross bars of a metal screen or the pebbled surface of a coarse piece of sandpaper. Place the foil over the screen or sandpaper, with a firm surface underneath, and rub with a blunt metal or wood tool. The round ball modeler can be used.

Fig. 242, sketches F and H suggest tooling design elements.

6. Christmas cards with simulated metal designs offer suggestions for design tooling. The illustrated nativity scene, Fig. 238, is an example. This seems to be both a repousse process for the figures and a tooled or special stamped process for the wing feathers and textured coat of the lamb.

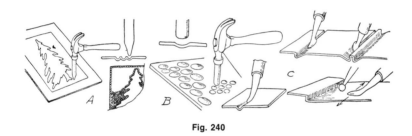

Fig. 240

Fig. 241

Methods of mounting tooled metal foil

1. Attach the finished foil to a wood base with escutcheon pins or small upholstery nails. Pierce the metal, as placed on the wood, with a small drive punch and drive the nails halfway with a hammer. Finish with a nail set, to avoid marring the metal. The tooled panels in Fig. 238 were mounted in this way. A picture frame type of mounting is attractive.

Enameled metal — copper and silver

There is no question but that a piece of perfectly enameled metal, usually copper or silver, has an intrinsic beauty and value surpassing other crafts. It requires a perfection of line, tone, and color in both the plan of design and its execution, demanding a skill superior in all respects.

The decoration of copper, gold, and silver with colored enamels, or, as once known, "glass, colored with different metallic oxides," has been practiced almost as long as these metals were known. The origin of enameling has been attributed to the ancient Egyptians, and it is known that the Greeks and Romans practiced the craft many years before Christ.

Fig. 243

Fig. 244

The Byzantines, who occupied the whole Eastern Empire and the capital, Constantinople, after the fall of the Western Roman Empire in 476 A.D. were noted for their fine closed or cell enameling, named "Cloisonne" years later by the French.

A treasured piece of Cloisonne, now in an English museum, known as the "Jewel" made at the order of King Alfred was found in the ruins of the monastery he founded at Athleney, England. Alfred was king of England from 871 to 899 A.D.

It was centuries later, in 1400 A.D., when the knowledge of enameling was acquired by the Chinese from Arab traders, according to the *History of Art in China*, during the Ch'ing Dynasty, which ended in 1795. The box illustrated in Fig. 244 is decorated with an Arabian design. The little salt and pepper containers, more typical of Chinese enameling, were identified as "Cantonese" when they were obtained by missionaries in 1911, Fig. 244.

The Japanese are presumed to have "borrowed" the techniques of cloisonne from the Chinese and to have perfected them to such an extent that cloisonne enameling has become known as Japanese. They produced large quantities even during the war years.

Definitions

Enamels and glazes are similar. A definition for enamel, quoted from AMACO (American Art Clay Company) states: "Enameling is the art of applying a permanent glassy surface to metal. Enamels are fritted ceramic chemicals, and colorants, which fuse to metals. 'Fritted' means a fused or partially fused material, used as a basis for enamels or glazes."

The finest and most valuable enamel work of the Orient has been done on silver or gold mainly the "old cloisonne" of the 16th century by the Chinese. Transparent enamels over "fine silver" and fine or 24 caret gold do not require an undercoat of flux and do not oxidize. However, both are very soft and usually have an alloy added to harden and stiffen the metal. 75 parts copper is added to 925 parts silver, per 1,000 for "sterling."

Equipment and tools for enameling

*Worktable with smooth wood block and clamps, or other holding device.
Containers for enamel with tight fitting tops, preferably the screw on type.
Deep bowls or pitchers for washing enamels.
Jar with tight cover for saving water from washing.
Copper screen, 80 and 100 mesh, or sieves.
Mortar of agate or porcelain with hard wood or agate pestle and
   cloth cover.
Tile pieces for mixing enamel with surfacing agent or for
   blending colors.
Sifter for applying dry enamels, atomizer.
Enamels as required.
Grooved palette and palette knife.
Gum tragacanth, pumice powder, carborundum stone.
Pieces of clean cloth.
Tracing paper, carbon paper.
Section of metal or stone as base for hot fired enameled work.
Piece of asbestos.
Sulphuric acid or commercial copper cleaner for pickling agent: Sparex
   No. 2 is recommended, also AMACO low acid metal cleaner.
Tongs of wood, copper, or brass.
Running water.
 Metal rests (nonoxidizing) for supports in kiln.
Grills (nonoxidizing) for a kiln support.
Monel wire, binding wire.
Overglaze, brushes of sable hair.

Essential precautions in enamel work

1. In all enamel work avoid inhaling dust or fumes in firing. Enamel has a high lead content (to lower the melting point), which is dangerous.

2. Keep enamels in sealed, marked jars, never in the paper containers in which they may be received. After using moist enamels, be sure and dry any that are left over before returning to jars.

3. Save all water from the washing process and let the residue settle, as it can be used. Do not empty any enamel powder or fragments into the drain; salvage this residue by grinding (with water) in the mortar and sifting or screening. When fine enough to remain in suspension in water solution, it may be used for atomizer spraying or painting.

4. As stated before, the metal must be cleaned thoroughly.

5. Don't ever use a solution for silver that has been used for copper cleaning.

6. Don't use a lead pencil to trace a design on copper for enameling, as the mark will show through the enamel. A faint carbon line, made from tracing a design with carbon paper, will burn off. Use a round point tool for tracing.

7. Use hard silver solder for attachments to copper. Solder with selfcontained flux, such as SWIF or Presto. For the attachment of fittings, when strain is minimum, Elmer's Glue-All adhesive is satisfactory.

Principles and precautions for firing enameled copper

1. Be familiar with the requirements of the enamels and the qualities of the metals, also their reactions with each type of process when fired.

2. Select a kiln best suited for the kind of enameling to be done. Be informed on adaptations and new developments to simplify firing. Consult with the area supplier or agency for standard kilns and compare: initial price, equipment, electrical connections and controls, guarantees, and replacement provisions.

3. Study the details and procedures for operation of the kiln. Be sure all safeguards are included with the equipment. See list of kiln manufactures.

4. Know the causes for defects in fired enamel and avoid them.

5. Ceramic kilns should not be used for firing enamel work. Special enamel kilns are available.

6. A rest or support for the enameled piece is essential, stainless steel or monel metal is best. Stilts and trivets are used for small items. A piece of asbestos or mica under the enameled piece on the support, is recommended.

7. Do not permit the metal enameled piece to come into contact with the side of an electric kiln, and avoid shock or damage to the piece.

8. Allow the enameled piece to cool gradually. Sudden exposure to cold air may crack the enamel.

Choice and preparation of metal

A pure quality of copper is the least expensive metal, and in the 18 gauge, the one most easily shaped and enameled. Thinner copper is less likely to retain its shape and the heavier more difficult to model or shape for enameling.

Suppliers now offer a wide range of copper shapes for jewelry; bracelets, pins, clasps, and other personal ornaments. Bowls of various sizes and flat pieces of all kinds, including ovals and rectangles, are available from metal suppliers or may be cut from sheets.

Preparation of metals — Cleaning

For new copper which is free from oxidation, soil, or grease, use a simple cleaning solution of vinegar and salt (a saturated solution) applied with a soft cloth; fine steel wool, or a brush, will be sufficient if an enameling oil or adhesive such as gum tragacanth is to be used. Wash under running water to remove any particles of the metal or the steel wool. The metal is clean if a film of water will remain over the surface without forming beads.

Precut or items of metal which have been handled are usually cleaned by the process of heating or annealing to a red color, then the process of pickling or immersion in a solution or mixture of one part sulphuric acid, *added to* eight (8) parts water in a glass or porcelain container. Wash under running water, using tongs of wood, copper, or brass. Wear rubber gloves and do not touch with the bare fingers. To remove any remaining blemishes or scratches, rub gently with fine pumice powder, before a final washing. At this point, the metal may be held with a clean cloth or paper towel.

Sparex No. 2 will remove surface oxidation, scale or incrustations from all nonferrous metals and is recommended as being highly effective without being hazardous. A similar compound is Low Acid AMACO Metal Cleaner.

If the enameling is not to be done immediately after cleaning, reoxidation or other discoloration can be delayed by rubbing the metal with a clean cloth dipped in liquid detergent or a gum solution. It can remain in clear water for a short time.

Enamels: kinds and preparation

The two kinds of enamels and uses which will be described are *transparent and opaque*. Another, *translucent*, is an in-between opaque, made in only a few colors and not widely used. White and black enamels are available only in opaque enamel, and many other colors, particularly the pastel shades, are opaque. They have the appearance of jewel stones, and do not require a base flux.

Transparent enamels include the brilliant darker shades in fewer colors that beautify the natural color of the metal without concealing it. A base coat of clear, colorless enamel or flux (sometimes called "fondant") must be fused over the metal before the transparent enamel is applied. Flux not only protects the enamel from being affected by the metal, but gives the colors greater depth.

Both *transparent* and *opaque* enamels are now supplied in an 80 mesh powder. A standard product of the American Art Clay Company, it is carried by most suppliers. Exact firing information is provided for each kind.

In addition to the 80 mesh powdered enamels semimoist decorating colors are available for glassware and for the painting of designs on fired enameled articles. Liquid gold and platinum overglazes are also available for application over fired enamel. All semimoist enamels are to be softened enough with water (well mixed), to make them sufficiently liquid for application with brush or pen. They are made permanent by firing in a preheated kiln (1400 degrees F.) for 1 to 2 minutes.

A specially prepared type of enamel in liquid form is available for developing the crackle finish. It is applied over a base coat of transparent or opaque enamel, by brushing, spraying or dipping.

Formerly enamels were only available in lump or cake forms, and some suppliers now handle enamels only in lump form, except as ground on special order. Some enamelists prefer to grind and wash the enamels they use.

Grinding and washing enamel

1. Wrap the lump or block of enamel in folded cloth or in heavy paper and break over a hard surface or an anvil with a hammer. *Caution!* Do not permit either surface to come in contact with any of the enamel, as the metal will cause chemical changes. The enamel should be broken into pea-sized or granular pieces.

2. Place the small pieces with a little water in an agate or porcelain mortar and pulverize with a stone or agate pestle. Cover as much of the mortar as possible, both to keep the enamel particles from flying out and to avoid inhaling any of the powder which has a lead content of possible danger.

The pieces should be ground to a powder which will sift through an 80 mesh screen. Do not pound with the pestle, but rotate it on the enamel pieces until they disintegrate. The process is easier with the mortar on a bench, so that pressure can be exerted on the pestle.

3. Do not pour off the water which will have become milky. Add about twice as much more and stir well. Then leave the mixture until all the fine enamel settles and only a cloudiness remains in the water. Pour this off and save it in a glass container. Repeat the washing process, stirring well each time, until the water appears clear. Save all the water in a glass container as it is poured off, after the enamel particles settle. If it is not to be used, immediately spread the washed enamel on a paper towel and dry completely. Store in a tightly capped bottle.

4. Washing of the commercially ground, 80 mesh powdered enamels is recommended to remove finer particles which slip through the screen and may cloud the fired enamel. Opaque enamels need but one washing. The transparent enamels are clearer for several washings.

Special techniques for enameling

1. Swirling is a process using lumps of enamels of assorted sizes in a mixture of colored, transparent, opaque, or variegated enamels, which are supplied for this process. The usual method is to apply and fire a first coat of enamel, then a second coat which is heated briefly or until molten enough to

permit swirling or stirring the lumps with a spatula on the molten enamel. If swirled quickly the lumps melt, a trail or scroll of color appears. Glass threads in color or liquid gold are sometimes placed with the lumps before they are swirled. This process requires a type of kiln which can be opened for the insertion of the swirling device. Glass covers permit visual firing and stirring.

2. *The sgraffito technique,* developed for ceramics, can be used effectively on a second coat of enamel which contrasts with the first. The design is "scratched" through the second coat with a sgraffito tool to reveal the background color in the form of the design, just as a similar tool outlines a design through slip or engobe on a ceramics piece.

3. Another technique, similar to ceramic decoration, is the *painting of designs* over the fired coat or coats of enamel. Semimoist and overglaze colors are used. When entirely dry, the overglaze design and colors are made permanent by firing in a preheated kiln (1400 degrees F.) for 1 to 2 minutes.

4. *Counter enameling* or the application of a base coat or flux to the back, before the front is enameled, is an important consideration. It helps to equalize the tension and to prevent warping, cracking, or chipping of the front surface coat of enamel. Mixtures of leftover enamels or the residue from washing may be applied to the back of the metal. If not previously enameled, the front should have a protective coat of transparent flux.

Slightly curved shapes are preferable for enameling because there is less strain or tension on the surface. Counter enameling need not be done, when the face or surface of the concave side of a curved design is to be enameled.

The surface of the exposed side will then require cleaning and polishing.

Flat pieces and those enameled on the convex side require counter enameling. For large shapes it is essential.

When the front and back sides or surfaces are to be enameled separately, the firing should be no longer than to barely fuse the enamel, so that the oxidation scale on the exposed side is kept to a minimum, and more easily cleaned off before the other side is enameled. A protective material called Amacote can be applied to a bare surface to prevent the formation of oxidation scale. It must be removed before the enamel is applied to that side.

Both sides can be enameled at the same time, which eliminates the need for cleaning of oxidation. A first application of enamel on one side moistened with gum tragacanth adhesive solution is allowed to become partially dry to prevent its running off. Then the piece is turned over and supported on a trivet or block stilts, while the coat of enamel is applied to the other side. When the second coat of enamel has been dusted on (as will be described) an overspray of the gum solution is applied to hold the enamel particles in place on the first side while the other is enameled.

Methods of applying enamels

The traditional spatula method of applying enamels on a plain surface, such as the inner surface of a small bowl, requires that either a little gum tragacanth be added to the enamel or an oil based adhesive applied evenly over the surface first. The steps follow:

1. *Prepare a spatula of hardwood* with a flat and pointed tip. (A manicure stick can be shaped for this purpose.) Metal spatulas are included in sets of enameling tools. Warm the bowl in a low oven or on top of the kiln. *Do not overheat.*

2. Begin at the rim of the bowl and tap a very little enamel on to the metal. Spread it as thin as possible over the metal by separating the drop of enamel with the spatula. Spread the added portions as thin as possible, but cover the metal surface. Absorb any water which may run down the surface with a blotter or little roll of paper towels.

3. *Apply the enamel in rows* from the rim downward, merging them by cutting and spreading each application of a tiny mass on the spatula. A needle end tool, to which the enamel is inclined to cling, or a small No. 00 sable brush will help.

4. Continue covering the surface around and up to the rim, then add the enamel with the spatula in the same way to cover successive areas as it is merged together around the entire inner surface, including the bottom. If the enamel becomes too dry to spread, spray it with a very little water from an atomizer. Try to spread and level the enamel in a uniform thin layer over the metal. Permit the bowl to dry slowly in a uniform temperature away from drafts, until all moisture is evaporated.

5. The only difference in applying enamel to a flat surface is to begin at the center and spread the separate little masses together outward. Tap the surface occasionally on one side to cause any air bubbles to rise to the surface and break. A piece of blotting paper or a pad of a few paper towels laid lightly on the enamel will soak up excess moisture. Dry completely before firing.

1. *The dipping of the prepared bowl* or flat shape in a mixture of the finer ground enamel, saved from the washing of the 80 mesh screened enamels, is another method of covering the metal on both sides.

Mix the fine ground enamel with water to a syrup consistency. Immerse the warmed article in the enamel, holding the edge with tweezers or tongs. Remove quickly and rotate to make the enamel flow over the piece evenly with any excess dripping back into the mixture.

2. The metal piece may also be coated with the enamel mixture by pouring enough inside to flow over the curves as the bowl is turned over and rotated, with the excess dripping back into the mixture. Then rest the piece on stick supports and pour the enamel over the back, rotating as before. Place upside down with the rim on a trivet or triangle support, and do not disturb until entirely dry.

3. A third use for the fine ground enamel mixture is to apply a design of contrasting color over a stencil, moistened with a removable adhesive to cover the original enameled and fired color.

Cut the design and moisten the stencil in water before placing on the fired enamel surface. Spray the exposed surface with a gum solution. Sift over it enough of the fine dried powder to cover the surface not protected with the stencil. Carefully remove the stencil and do not move the piece until the enamel no longer runs.

Application of 80 mesh dry enamel

The enameling of bowls or other curved metal items is now most frequently done by the dusting method in which a uniform coat of dry enamel is dusted or sifted over a diluted gum solution which keeps the powder in place. The steps are:

1. Place the metal piece on a clean dry piece of smooth paper. Spray or brush a thin coat of an adhesive or gum tragacanth over the surface to be enameled. Use an 80 mesh strainer or a jar with a perforated top and holes that will prevent grains of any larger than 80 mesh size from sifting through. (This will not be necessary with previously screened and washed 80 mesh enamels.) If some of the surface dries before it is dusted, respray with adhesive.

2. Begin at the edge and work around the area in successive circles until the surface is entirely covered. When using an opaque enamel, one thin layer of enamel at a time is sufficient. Fire the piece, let it cool, then sift on a second layer, and fire again. Repeat until the color and texture of the enamel is satisfactory. A single thick layer will not result in a smooth texture.

3. Two or three layers of a transparent enamel can be applied before firing. It is essential that all areas receive a uniformly sifted cover or unsightly variations in color will detract from the appearance of the article after firing. Spray the piece after the applications of enamel to hold the grains in place while drying.

4. It is possible to blend or shade the transparent enamel colors, like the process with water colors, to produce an intermingling of different tones in a beautiful effect for a design pattern or an "all over" shadowed effect.

5. Mixed opaque colors will result in an entirely different way, producing a pepper and salt effect which is not attractive. It can be used on the back or other surface which is not visible, but only when opaque colors are used on the front.

6. When the metal enameled piece is entirely dry, lift it into the kiln with a wide spatula and place on supports for firing, which is described on page 272.

The process of cloisonné enamel

This type of closed or cell enameling is said to be of the greatest antiquity, although named "cloisonné" in more recent times by the French, as mentioned. In China, the name for the cell type of enameling was "trellis work" at the time of its introduction by Arab traders.

The perfection of cloisonné enameling, as at present in Japan, is evidence of the infinite skill and patience of Orientals to master and improve the ancient intricate techniques of this work. With equal patience and much determination, the skill required for cloisonné enameling can be acquired by anyone.

A typical example of fine cloisonné is illustrated in Fig. 245. This ash receiver with detachable top, formed with metal knobs which rest in grooves in the base or receiver part, has the interior enameled in turquoise. The silver wire seems to be embedded in black enamel, but the cloisonné process required that the square wire be soldered to the metal base and then the enamel filled in all the background by the spatula method. The steps follow:

Fig. 245

1. Preparation of the metal base for cloisonné enamel requires first and always that the surface of the metal be perfectly clean. Rub the surface with fine steel wool and remove all particles of the wool with a damp cloth. Dip in a cleaning solution after heating in the kiln or an oven to remove any film of grease. AMACO low acid cleaner is safer to use than the acid pickling solution, as is Sparex No. 2, also a low acid cleaner. Rinse well in clear water after cleaning, and wipe dry with a soft clean cloth. Avoid fingerprints on the parts to be enameled.

2. Form the design outline in units with fine flat silver wire, rolled from 18 gauge round wire to the dimension of 16 by 22 gauge, with the 16 gauge forming the depth of the silver outline. The fine silver, which has a higher melting point than sterling, is used for the finest cloisonné, and can be soldered to the copper without softening it. (Copper wire can be used in a method which does not require soldering. This will be described later.)

3. For a beginning, do not try an intricate design but rather one with simple lines. Some of the designs for filigree silver can be adapted for cloisonné enameling. See detail of forming wire on page 302. Selected designs for pierced metal or plastics are also suitable.

4. Solder the unit wire enclosures to the clean metal base, using a hard silver solder such as Hagstoz No. 10. File the connecting points so that they fit perfectly and be sure both metal base and solder are clean. Paint the joints of the solder and metal, also the joints of the wire with flux, then place small pieces of solder evenly along the joints. Solder the joints or connecting points of the wire outline of the design first, then position the design unit on the metal and solder together.

5. Solder all the units in place, as indicated in Fig. 275 and 276, page 303. Then cleanse in the pickling solution or in a solution of Sparex No. 2. Rinse in clear water and wipe dry.

6. Moisten each of the colors of enamel to be used with a gum or other adhesive, and have the approximate quantity required on a paint palette or piece of glass. Place tiny portions of the enamel in the wire forms, using the spatula method or a brush, as suggested for simple enameling of a bowl. Be sure and work the enamel into the corners and over all unit surfaces in a thin even coat.

7. Absorb any excess moisture with a piece of linen or blotting paper and leave the enameled piece in a warm place undisturbed until all the moisture has evaporated and the enamel is perfectly dry (at least 24 hours). Be careful in moving the piece not to disturb the enamel particles.

8. When ready to fire the piece, protect all previously soldered joints with damp clay which also should become entirely dry. Do not fire above 1420 F. to prevent melting of the solder. Follow instructions for firing on page 272.

9. Repeat the applications of enamel and the firing two or three times or until the enamel is even with the top of the silver wire or rounded slightly above. Always avoid overfiring which can ruin the enamel. Time the firing periods exactly with the instructions for the kind and color of enamel used. For small items, the firing can be done with a blow torch or bunsen burner.

10. Apply the heat, no higher than 1420 F., from the underside and closely watch the enamel until it settles and liquefies to form a glaze. Withdraw the heat immediately after this point is reached, and do not jar or move the piece until entirely cold.

11. Leave the enamel as a slightly rounded form or "stone" it down level with the wire, so that the flat surface reveals the gleaming margin of the silver edge. This is done with pieces of carborundum, first a slightly rough piece, then finer, followed with a piece of "scotch-stone" which is a very fine abrasive. Melt the surface of the enamel in the kiln or with a torch to restore the luster.

Cloisonné enameling without solder or without wire

Shape square or rectangular copper wire, 20 gauge or less, according to the design which has been transferred with metal carbon paper to the surface to be decorated. The wire should be soft or annealed so that it can be formed around the outlines of the design on the metal, covered with a transparent flux or base coat and fired.

1. Apply a coat of adhesive or gum, which does not conceal the traced design. Arrange the wire on the design outline, then place the moistened enamel between the wires to hold them in place and fire just long enough to melt the enamel. *Watch closely.* After a second application of enamel with the spatula, and firing the same interval, let the piece cool and smooth the surface of the enamel and wire with the carborundum stones and polishing scotch stone as before.

2. A second method is without wire, the separate enamel colors (opaque) being mixed with a small amount of gum tragacanth. Draw or trace the design on the metal, so that contrasting colors will be adjacent. Apply the enamel in one area and permit it to dry completely before applying another color to the adjoining area. Add the enamel to the rest of the design, with the same intervals between applications for drying. When all is dry, fire until barely melted, so that the colors will not fuse together.

Champlevé enameling (without wire)

1. In this method, larger areas of the metal are left bare of decoration and the design units are mostly separate with the enamel applied to an area which

has been etched or cut out with an engraving tool. Opaque enamel in two or more applications, as required to fill the area level with the metal surface, is smoothed in and fired. Leave the enameled units slightly rounded and higher than the metal, or stone the surface level as desired. Polish the metal for contrast, and if stoned, fire the article to restore the glaze finish.

Careful experimentation with original designs and different techniques will enable the craftsman to determine a preference and evolve an individual style.

Silver Metal Craftwork

The method of handling and working silver is much the same as for copper, except for the necessity of annealing silver more often because of its tendency to harden and lose its malleability in the hammering and planishing processes is greater than copper.

Several silver rings are shown in Fig. 246. For a first project and for practice in procedure, a bracelet or ring with a stamped or chased decoration may be selected. An oval or triangular brooch, as will be described later, is also a good beginning project, although it requires the additional step of soldering the pin and catch, as described on page 288.

Types of small brooches with stamped designs are shown in Fig. 246.

Ring Construction and Mounting of Stones

The formation and detail of construction for a shaped ring with oval center for the mounting of a stone is shown in Fig. 249. The bezel base may be round, oval, or diamond shaped, with a bezel band of the same contour for a stone of similar shape or for a stamped ornament, like the rings in Fig. 246, Turquoise mounting with silver balls; B, Freeform mountings; C, Stamped designs; D, Examples of small brooches.

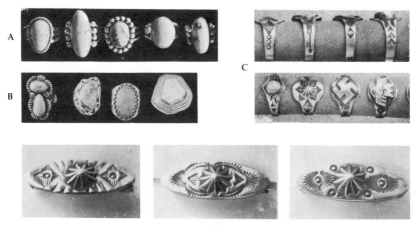

D

Fig. 246

Equipment and material for silver projects

Equipment

Wire

Acid in glass stoppered bottles

    10% nitric acid for nickel
      silver

    10% sulphuric acid for
      sterling silver

Antiquing fluid and brush

Anvil block — grooved for
      stamping triangular
      bracelets. Base drilled for
      ring mandrel. Mortised
      for v-notch sawing
      block and vise

Lead sheet

Pitch bowl

Ring Mandrel

Mounted lead sheet

    ⅜ x 2 x 4 inches

Solder — hard, No. 1-2-3

Soldering tool — probe made from
    bicycle spoke

Stamping tools — matrix and die
    blocks, for sunburst and
    rain drops

Materials

Findings — catches, hinges, jump
    rings, pins, chain

Shapes — rings, bracelets,
    brooches, conchas

Sheet metal — nickel silver,
    sterling silver

Stones — for mounting

Wire

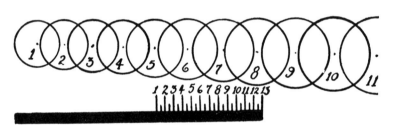

Fig. 247

Ring sizes

The diagram of ring sizes will be found useful in ring making. The numbered circles correspond to standard ring sizes. To use the diagram place a finger ring on the circle it will cover. The number in the circle is the ring size. The scale below the diagram shows the length of metal required to make a ring.

Soldering bezel and balls to a ring

1. Place pieces of solder and silver balls (made as described on page 289) in the borax flux. Dip the bottom of the bezel in the flux and wire in position on the bezel plate, previously soldered to the ring prongs.

2. Apply the borax flux around the bottom of the bezel with a small brush and place the balls in the flux. It will be noted that the balls have a flattened area, where they come in contact with the charcoal in the process of forming from the squares of silver. This surface forms a base for attachment to the metal.

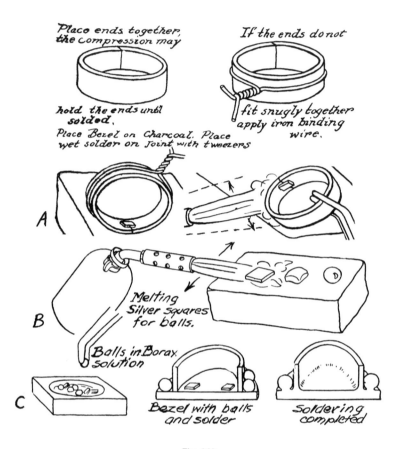

Place ends together,
the compression may
hold the ends until
solded.

If the ends do not
fit snugly together
apply iron binding
wire.

Place Bezel on Charcoal. Place
wet solder on Joint with tweezers

A

B   Melting
Silver Squares
for balls.

Balls in Borax
Solution

C

Bezel with balls
and solder

Soldering
completed

Fig. 248

3. Place small pieces of solder in the center of the bezel and apply heat slowly to dry the flux which cements the bezel and balls in place Fig. 248C. After the flux is dry, apply more heat directly on the edge of the bezel and balls until the solder melts and flows to all parts coated with the flux. In this way, all six balls with the bezel are soldered at the same time.

The heating must be done slowly to prevent the solder and balls snapping off when the flux dries. A sweeping motion of the flame is desirable to produce uniform heating. The charcoal block should also be heated before the ring is placed on it.

4. When the solder flows smoothly around the junction of the bezel band the plate as well as the balls, remove the torch flame and the binding wire. Clean in the solution of sulphuric acid and water as before.

Setting a turquoise in the bezel band

The steps in setting or mounting the stone are shown in the sketches of Fig. 249.

1. The bezel band may be left smooth or notched with a file. Do not attempt to set the stone until the ring and bezel are cleaned by dipping in the acid solution as before.

2. To insert the turquoise, flare the top of the bezel slightly with the burnishing tool. Carefully press the stone securely in place and then press the bezel closely around it as shown in Fig. 249. *Remember that a turquoise is fragile* and avoid breaking it.

3. A device that provides an easy means of placing a stone in the bezel, or to hold it is a small dowel or "dopp stick," to which the stone is attached with sealing wax. This also makes possible the removal of a stone from a bezel without the risk of breaking it.

Making and Soldering a Bezel

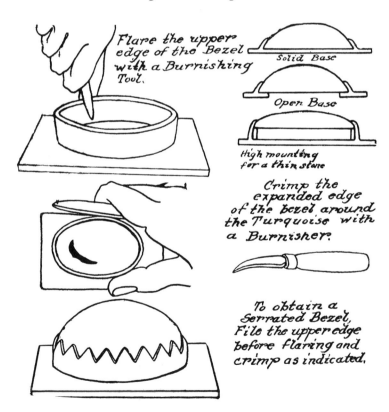

Fig. 249

Prong Type Ring Construction

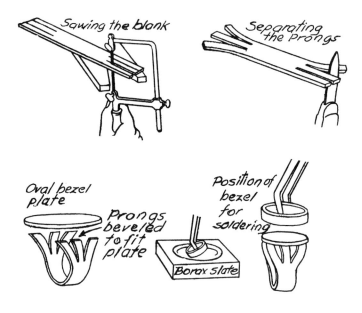

Fig. 250

The prong type ring is a little more difficult to make, but permits added decoration of twisted wire or small silver balls around the bezel, which is soldered to a bezel plate as shown in Fig. 250.

It is essential for both types of rings that the ring blank, bezel plate, and bezel be smoothed and slightly rounded with a fine file. The surfaces to be soldered should also be slightly filed to make a close contact. The ring blank bezel plate and bezel should then be cleaned with fine steel wool and dipped in the pickling solution of 1 part sulphuric acid to 10 parts water, then in clear water. Refer to process of pickling on page 233. For the cleaning or pickling process after soldering, which is necessary, use the same acid solution.

Note: If the liquid flux which is self pickling is used instead of a borax solution, (the "Handy" flux prepared by T. B. Hagstoz and Sons) no further pickling is necessary. The silver solders of the Hagstoz Company are also recommended.

Bracelets

Several of the bracelets illustrated in Fig. 251, A, B were decorated with the Indian type raised rosettes or "sunbursts" impressed with the matrix and die described with the stamping tools, Fig. 207 and 208, page 237. Sterling silver makes the most attractive stamped bracelet, but nickel silver and copper are also used.

For many years the Indians acquired through trade enough Mexican Pesos for their silver work. These were cut in strips and melted down for ingots which were rolled for bracelet blanks or cast for other ornaments.

The use of the Indian "Four Winds," a good luck or fortune symbol, will be compared with the swastika. The Indian symbol is thought to rotate clockwise in the manner of the winds, while the swastika direction is counter-clockwise. The bracelet designs in Fig. 253 were made with a group of Indian design stamps.

When a mounting of turquoise is used on a bracelet, either hammered or with stamped designs, the bezel must be shaped to fit the contour of the shaped bracelet and soldered in place after the bracelet is rounded on the mandrel or the end of an anvil. Blanks sheared from 18 gauge metal sheets may be used or similar blanks obtained from suppliers.

A   B

C

Fig. 251

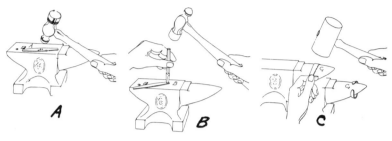

Fig. 252

A hammered or textured bracelet

1. Round the ends of the bracelet blank and also the edges with a fine file, and smooth with emery cloth. Be careful not to change the contour.

If an all over textured or hammered surface is desired, place the blank on a steel block wedged or clamped to the workbench, or on a flat anvil. Either base must be clean and smooth, as the metal will pick up any particles underneath when hammered or acquire the imprint of a rough or marred surface.

2. Hold the ball-pein hammer, Fig. 252, sketches A, B, and C, toward the end of the handle and with free wrist movement strike the surface lightly, working along the center line, then out to the edges to uniformly texture the surface. This surface finish may be used with a mounted stone and no further decoration.

3. Shape the textured blank on a mandrel or the end of the anvil, and solder the fitted bezel in place as indicated in Fig. 250. Twisted silver wire or balls may be added. Clean in the acid solution and polish with fine emery cloth and jeweler's rouge.

4. Setting the stone into the bezel is the last step. On no account should a gem be put into the acid solution. This step is shown in Fig. 249.

Stamped bracelets

As background for a stamped decoration, the blank is usually left with the original smooth surface. If the metal has become scratched or roughened, it should have the surface restored with fine pumice powder or scratch remover and water followed by an application of jeweler's rouge on a soft cloth.

1. In stamping the bracelet blank, the position of the designs can be marked on the metal. With practice, it is possible to place the tool impressions with reference to a line marked down the center of the blank. Hold the blank flat on the anvil or steel plate with the third and fourth fingers and the stamping tool with the thumb and first finger.

2. Hold the tool at right angles to the metal blank and strike a sharp direct blow with the hammer. A glancing blow will make the stamp slip and spoil the impression. A clear impression with one blow is the aim. It is recommended that practice on a scrap piece of metal, until the right results are obtained, precede any attempt to stamp a piece of silver.

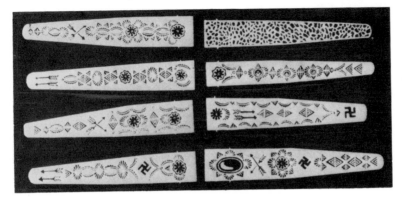

Fig. 253

3. Place the stamped bracelet in a rounded groove in a wooden block to develop a slightly rounded upper surface. Shape the bracelet on the anvil point or on a wooden mandrel, using a wood or rawhide mallet. Clean the bracelet in the acid pickling bath, rinse and polish with fine pumice powder, then rouge on a clean cloth.

4. If a bezel for mounting a stone is to be attached, shape it to the contour of the bracelet and wire it in position for soldering. Follow the procedure for soldering and for the mounting of the stone, page 283.

5. The metal stamping plate, held in a fixed block of hard wood, Fig. 254A, is necessary for stamping beveled or triangular shaped bracelet blanks. The V grooves hold the blanks in the plate in the position for stamping. Designs for this type of bracelet are illustrated in Fig. 251 B and 254 B, and the enlargement shows the relation of the stamped designs on either side of a center line of a triangular bracelet. The stamping plate has a hole drilled in the side for a mandrel or a bench pin.

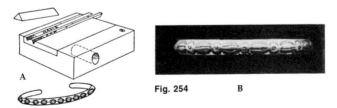

A Fig. 254 B

The brooch designs shown on the small pins in Fig. 246 D are similar to those used on the rings and bracelets. All are of the Indian type, and the symbols all have a meaning which also is expressed in Indian sign language.

1. Other brooch designs are used on round, oval, and triangular shaped blanks, with or without a mounted turquoise in the center. A "thunderbird" shape is popular for a brooch. Two are shown in Fig. 255 which also illustrates other Indian made brooches of unusual shape and design.

Fig. 255

2. The soldering operation for a brooch catch and hinge joint is shown in Fig. 257. Scrape the metal on the back of the plate with a knife blade or scraping tool, until it is bright. Scrape the base of the hinge and joint of the pin, then dip in the cleaning solution and rinse in clear water. Moisten the points to be soldered with a commercial or borax flux and place a little piece of solder on each. Hold the catch or hinge in contact with the solder, using tweezers, and direct the flame of the torch on the solder until it melts and flows around the joint. Protect or baffle the charcoal block to prevent drafts on the work.

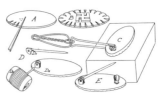

The tool shown above with the brooch fittings was made from a bicycle spoke and tapered at one end which is bent at a right angle. The other was flattened and split into prongs.

Fig. 256

Fig. 257

Buckles for concha belts, strap belts and wrist watch bands

The shapes and designs of the buckle in Fig. 258, A, B, will suggest other types to match or contrast with the varied shapes and stamped designs of the conchas.

The elaborate buckle, Fig. 258 A matches the raised dome and stamped border of the oblong conchas, while the connecting butterfly shapes are similar. They are made as follows:

1. Prepare this or another design and cut a paper pattern to attach to the piece of 16 gauge silver, or the same gauge of nickel silver or copper.

2. Saw cut the outline of the buckle and conchas through the paper, then remove it. Dome centers are formed in a contour block as described on page 262, step 6. Stamp the borders with the S5 metal stamping tool, and file the scallops to correspond. *Note:* This decoration should be applied to the metal before the formation of the domes. Concave the buckle and conchas slightly from the back.

3. In place of the domes, turquoise mountings may be soldered at the centers.

4. Solder loops from copper or nickel silver, ¼ inch by 1½ inches, or to fit the belt strap width with silver solder on the back of the conchas. Make a tongue and tongue bar from flattened silver wire or metals from which the buckle was made, copper or nickel silver.

5. Smaller conchas, with or without the rim scallop, Fig. 258 C, and stamped design, may be made into buttons by attaching (with solder), a button ring on the back.

Make the single belt strap buckles from 18 gauge silver, copper, or nickel silver. Cut the metal to a pattern shape, like the illustration. Apply an all-over decoration by hammering with the edge of the ball-pein hammer or a chasing tool, used with a hard wood mallet, then form in a hard wood contour block.

Smooth file, and burnish the edges, then round the tapered ends.

Solder the buckle bar with the ends attached to the buckle, and attach the belt strap with the three hole fastening. See Fig. 258 D.

Two types of wrist watch straps are shown. Fig. 258 D has a small buckle similar to the belt buckles, but with a stamped design, applied likewise to the keeper bar for the end of the band. In E, the end of the band attaches with a hook soldered to the back of the concha.

Both straps, usually made of strong pigskin or "cordovan" horsehide, are attached to the watch loops with an arrowhead of silver, perforated for the attachment to the band with a goatskin three hole fastening.

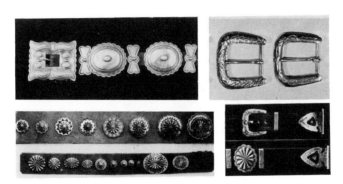

Fig. 258

Silver jewelry from domes, balls, and wire

Very attractive jewelry can be made from silver wire of different sizes, and the combination with cabochon mountings or with half domes and balls offers innumerable design possibilities. Instructions for wire drawing are given on page 293.

The silver balls, Fig. 248 B, are made by a fascinating process which is actually very simple, as described on page 281 and shown in Fig. 248.

1. Dip small cuttings of sterling silver or pieces of wire in borax flux or a commercial flux, place on a charcoal block, and melt with the flame of the blow torch. When each piece becomes red hot, it will begin to curl into a spherical mass under the strain of the surface tension. If the pieces do not melt readily, dip them into the flux again and apply the flame. See Fig. 248B, page 282.

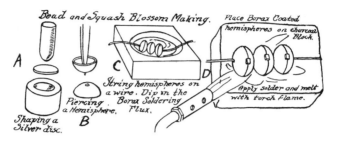

Fig. 259

2. Graduated balls can be made from graduated sizes of silver pieces and evenly matched balls from chain links or pieces of wire of uniform size. Small punched discs are used for the commercial production of balls by this method.

3. Hollow domes of semispherical shape are formed in a "dapping die block," which is a cube of steel into which the metal, 24 gauge, is pressed with a punch or die to form the hollow half ball. Soldered together in pairs or used in the half form, these balls may be strung on wire for necklaces, soldered together or to a base for other articles.

4. The steel block with different sizes of depressions and punch dies to correspond are available from suppliers. The small ¼ inch size can be made by the same process as that described for the "rain-drop" die SD2, page 238.

For the larger sizes, it is recommended that the domes be partly shaped in a hard wood contour block which can be made with wood carving tools. Drill a cube of end grain hard maple about 3 inches square at the center point to establish the center and depth of the depression, then shape the matrix and smooth to the desired diameter with the U gouge, until it conforms to the steel die.

To make the half domes, the following procedure is used:

For a ⅜ inch dome take a ½ inch square of 24 gauge silver and determine the center point. Place it on a similar square marked to center on the depression in the block, and dent the metal at the center with the ball-pein hammer to give the punch an accurate start.

Holding the punch vertically over the square, strike it lightly with the flat end of the chasing hammer. Flatten out the puckered edges of the square piece of silver, and again depress the metal into the matrix with the punch. Repeat these steps, flattening the edges as they wrinkle and turning the silver with each blow to prevent creasing the wood mold.

When the sphere is partially formed, place it in the steel die with the punch against it. Strike the punch once or twice to perfect the shape and then flatten the edge to produce a level clean cut parting line on which the margin may be severed with a file or scissors.

The 26 gauge silver is not too thin for the small domes used for rings or earrings. Large domes for bracelets or brooches should be a heavier gauge and 24 is usually used.

Beads may be made from half domes soldered together and pierced as shown in Fig. 259B. A indicates a single matrix dapping die and a block with a small disc of silver ready to be formed into a dome. D is an oval type matrix in which the oblong bead halves are formed. The silver bead necklace in Fig. 260 was made in similar dies. The process follows:

1. Drill holes in balls or a pair of domes with a reamer, which can be made from a triangular file by filing the narrow end to a sharp point but with the three cutting edges preserved. Mark the exact center of the ball or dome on the inner side as it rests in the depression, made by the dapping die, in a slab or bar of lead. The hole should be just large enough for the bead wire.

2. Solder the domes with hard silver solder on a wire which is large enough to keep the halves from turning on the charcoal block, Fig. 259D. Apply flux with a brush in a line around the joint to which a little snippet of silver solder has been placed with tweezers. Apply the torch flame to warm the charcoal and distribute the heat around the domes as indicated in the sketch. As soon as the solder melts it will follow the line of flux around the joint. The solder should fill the joint with little evidence on the surface.

3. Remove the flame as soon as the solder meets underneath and drop the balls from the wire in a jar of the acid pickling solution. An exact union of the domes closes the joint so perfectly that it is not visible, but any excess solder may be filed down and the ball polished on a cloth buffing wheel or by hand with fine pumice powder followed with jeweler's rouge. To handle the beads, string them again on the wire.

4. Solder the oblong bead halves singly. Hold them in contact with binding wire, twisted at the ends to support the halves on a charcoal block, with the joint in position for soldering. Apply flux to the joint and solder. File a hole for an oblong bead at each end in a tiny half round opening, before the halves are put together and soldered. Be careful not to get any solder in the hole, but if this happens it must be filed or reamed out.

Fig. 260

Fig. 261

5. A necklace of round and oblong beads is shown in Fig. 260, also two types of "Nezzah" pendants. This is the term for the pendant used by the Indian who designed it, indicating it as an amulet which brings good fortune.

6. In addition to the beads which form the necklace chain, and the suspended Nezzah, the attachment of silver balls and a turquoise stone make the necklace a more elaborate ornament, worn in former days by maidens to indicate their eligibility for marriage. The complete necklace is shown in Fig. 261.

7. The second Nezzah, designed by a different silversmith, does not display the Squash Blossom ornamentation, but on the outer strand of the three strand necklace, the attachment of small Nezzahs with a center of mounted turquoise make a colorful and striking addition. Note that these are similar to the large center Nezzah's outer ring which is soldered to the inner ring at the open ends with a single silver ball.

1. The construction detail for the Squash Blossoms which are added to the round beads, on which the Nezzah is suspended, is shown in Fig. 262A. Two cone shaped pieces of silver, slit in three sections and spread in a flare, are soldered to one half dome, and this in turn to another. A pierced segment of flat silver, with one end shaped to the ball curvature and the other rounded, is soldered to the top, the whole being wired together and soldered at one time.

2. The Nezzah pendant for the necklace was cast in a stone mold, Navajo method. The sketch, Fig. 262B, shows the pendant form C, carved or grooved in the surface of a flat stone with an engraving tool.

The gate through which the molten silver was poured and the air vents appear at the top and sides of the bottom mold. B is the mold with cover plate, a smooth flat piece of stone which was held in position with wire while the casting was being poured. Silver scraps and filings for the casting may be melted in a crucible with blow torch or in a charcoal fire with air supplied by bellows. This method was demonstrated to the author by a Navajo silversmith.

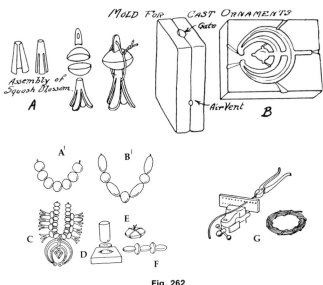

Fig. 262

Wire drawing and chain making

As silver is highly ductile, or malleable, it may be drawn into wire of a specified size by means of a draw plate, a pair of flat nosed pliers, or draw tongs and annealing equipment. A piece of sheet silver, the approximate thickness of the needed wire, is cut into strips, which in cross section are square, and tapered to a point. The tapered point of the silver strip is inserted into the draw-plate opening and grasped by the draw tongs or pliers.

This method is also used to reduce the size of larger wire.

Pull the strip or the wire through the draw plate, Fig. 262G. In this way, the volume of the original metal mass is elongated and reduced in cross section. The process hardens the metal and it must be annealed before a smaller diameter can be drawn, or the wire can be handled for design forms.

The wire may be coiled to insure uniform heating in the annealing process. Place the coil on a charcoal block and play the torch flame around and over it until it heats to a cherry red color.

The procedure is repeated for drawing the wire to a smaller diameter. Each time it must be softened by annealing before drawn again through the draw plate. A little beeswax rubbed on the wire will reduce the friction of wire against the edges of the opening.

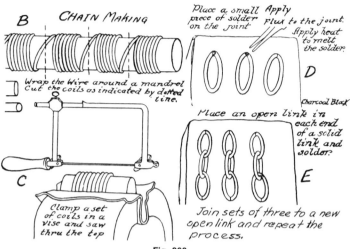

Fig. 263

Chain making

Wire of specified cross section and size may be fashioned into the desired form selected for a link chain. The shape is controlled by wrapping the soft silver wire around a wooden or metal mandrel, Fig. 263, sketch B.

1. Place a few turns of wire on the mandrel coiled closely together. Separate the next set of turns by a space as indicated in sketch B. Continue filling mandrel space as required.

2. Place the wire wrapped mandrel in a vise, protected by a piece of leather to preclude marring the metal surface. Saw the loop apart with a jeweler's saw.

3. Assemble a chain by soldering the first set of links together as indicated in sketch D. Pass the open links into the solid links and solder these in turn. The assembly is a progressive operation as indicated by sketch E.

Round wire rings and bracelets

Two pieces of round wire soldered together at the center and spread at the ends form the shank of the two rings illustrated. The angle is determined by the size of the plate and point of attachment of the wire which must be beveled to join the plate for soldering.

Round Wire Rings

The soldering of a two section wire ring is illustrated in Fig. 264 A, B, C, D and Fig. 265A. The process follows:

1. Shape the soldered shank over a ring mandrel with a rawhide mallet and the fingers. File the wires to fit against the plate for a ring mounting of a gem or a group of balls and solder as shown in Fig. 265C.

2. Place the plate with the bezel and twisted wire soldered in place for a

turquoise mounting face down on the charcoal block. Set the wires in place as directed for a split prong ring in Fig. 265A and solder as shown. After the plate is attached, clean the ring in the pickling solution and wash.

3. Inset the gem mounting as directed on page 283. Additional ornamentation such as leaf or flower forms, or a silver ball, may be placed at the V of the prongs on either side. Such additions should be soldered in place before the shank is soldered to the plate.

4. In making the third ring, Fig. 265C, only the oval shaped plate is soldered to the wire prong ends, and this is the base for the five hollow domes and the solid balls which make the ring decoration.

Twisting silver wire of any size for bezel ornaments, or for forming into rings and bracelets, is a simple process.

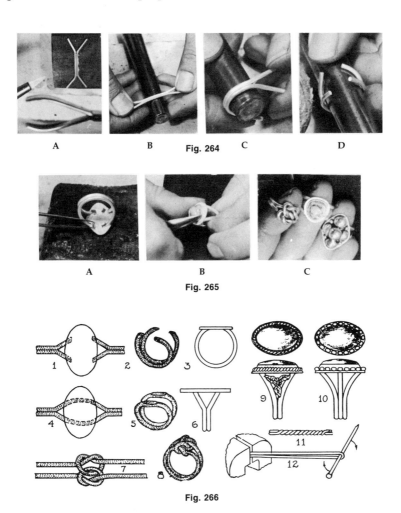

A   B   **Fig. 264**   C   D

A   B   C

Fig. 265

Fig. 266

Wire formed rings and bracelets

1. First *anneal the wire* and clean in the pickling bath. As soon as it is cool form a hair pin loop at the center point of the wire and place the two ends in a vise. Insert a metal rod, dowel pin, or nail through the loop and turn it clockwise, keeping tension on the wires to insure the desired uniformity of the twist, Fig. 266, sketch 12.

2. *Do not relax tension until the twist is complete.* It is a good practice to make one turn with the right hand, then hold the rod in position with tension in the left hand, while reversing the right hand to grasp the rod and continue the twisting.

3. The wire hardens in the process, and the twisted form becomes fixed and molded together so that it can be removed from the vise and rod and be handled without untwisting. Before working, it must be softened by annealing and cleaned in the pickling bath.

4. The wire ring, Fig. 265C, is formed of two strands of round wire with interlaced knots, Fig. 266, sketches 7 and 8. The length of the wire which ties into the knot adds an inch to the ring size. Anneal the wire to soften and tie a single knot loosely in the middle of one length.

5. Run the second wire through the loop of this knot and tie at the same point. Anneal again and with pliers tighten the knot. Shape the wires over a mandrel to the ring form and cut to desired size so that they meet together, sketch 8.

6. *Clean in acid bath* and place on the charcoal block, with binding wire tying the wires together for soldering. Apply flux at the joints and between the wires, place bits of solder on the joint, and apply the torch to melt the solder which will run along the fluxed joints and fuse them together.

Another two-wire construction for a ring shank is made with the center between the equal length wires spread to form an oval opening into which the bezel and plate mounting are soldered. Solid balls, twisted or scroll forms of fine wire, or other decoration may be soldered into the V formed by the spreading wires, sketches 4, 5, 6 and 9.

The twisted wire bracelet with open ends made of heavy wire, 14 or 16 gauge, illustrated in Fig. 251C, page 285, fits the wrist in the same way the band bracelet does. Four wires, about an inch longer than the finished bracelet, are twisted together in pairs. One length may first be twisted by the method shown in Fig. 266, sketch 12, then cut in equal pieces. The ends are inserted into a channel of sheet metal and the joint soldered.

Costume jewelry

The items in Fig. 267 are from a collection of handmade items, designed and made by the late William Bunning of Colorado Springs, a skilled craftsman whose specialty was the fabrication of unique personal items in silver jewelry. Chain necklace pendants, a bracelet with simulated leaf links centered with turquoise settings, hair clips (one plain polish silver with a large turquoise and the others with stamped designs) (picture accidentally taken of the back), and a twisted flat wire. Lapel pins and a tie clip with chain suspended name bar complete the collection.

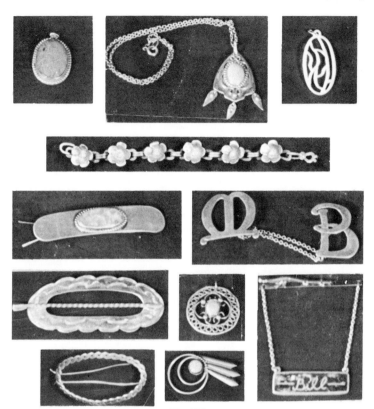

Fig. 267

Fig. 268

Fig. 268 shows items from Taxco, Mexico, the work of a native silver worker of remarkable skill. A brooch of mounted silver domes and a part of a matching bracelet are shown, also the front and back sections of a bracelet indicating the construction.

The grape cluster pin consists of a back or base of 24 gauge silver on which is mounted a cluster of hollow domes, made by the same process as that described on page 290. Two layers of ⅜ inch domes are used for the large pin. Eight are first soldered to the base, which is cut from a triangular piece of silver large enough to include a base for the stem and leaf forms at the corners and center of the top.

The leaf and stem forms are made of heavier silver, 22 gauge, cut as shown and shaped in a small pitch block or stick shellac. The narrow tipped embossing or chasing tool are used to define the markings and a broader tool to raise the centers, then the forms are soldered to the base with the matching outline.

Four more domes above the eight are soldered in place, giving the pin the elevation required. A pin and catch are soldered to the base. The *matching bracelet sections* are made of the same gauge metal, the small domes formed with a "dapping die" and the stem and leaves the same way as for the brooch. The little grape units are linked with circles of silver wire inserted through tiny holes drilled in the sides of the base and concealed by the first group of domes. The loop and link device for connecting the bracelet is shown.

The second bracelet, with the front and back shown, is made entirely of shallow domes ⅜ inch in diameter and ⅛ inch deep, soldered in pairs with holes for the link connections drilled in one edge of each dome. Rings through the holes are soldered underneath the next pair of domes. Fifteen pair thus linked together make the bracelet. A loop of wire on one end pair and a bent strip on the other for a hook provides the connection for the bracelet.

Silver spoons

Hand forged silver spoons from the American colonial period became treasured heirlooms. Some were brought from England or other countries in Europe, and others were hammered from bars or ingots made by the melting down of silver coins or jewelry by silversmiths who came with the Colonists or were trained as apprentices by them. One of these became famous — Paul Revere, the son of an immigrant from France, Apollos Rivoire.

A method of forging silver spoons, similar to that used by colonial silversmiths, can be used by modern craftsmen with comparable results, if the same time and painstaking efforts are devoted to the project. The steps follow:

1. Cast the bar or ingot of silver in a plaster of Paris mold or by the traditional method of pouring the molten metal into a rectangular depression carved in soapstone. Melt the silver in a clay crucible, supported by a charcoal block on a piece of asbestos. Protect the crucible with firebrick on all sides, and melt the silver with the flame of a blow torch. Scrap sheet silver, trimmings, and filings may be melted.

2. For an average size teaspoon, Fig. 269, sketch 1, a bar 4 x ½ x ¼ inches is

required. A cube shaped forging may be rolled to these dimensions. When ready to form the spoon, anneal the bar with the flame of the blow torch, bringing it gradually to a dull red color as it rests on the charcoal block within the enclosure of asbestos sheet or firebrick. This protection helps retain the heat and uniformly raises the temperature of the bar. As soon as the bar is uniformly red, remove the heat.

3. As soon as the color fades to a light pink, the bar is ready for the first step in forming a spoon. Hold the bar on the anvil and strike it with the oval flat end of the ball-pein hammer as shown in Fig. 269, sketch 2. At one end of the bar, flatten it about half for the bowl section. This should be about 1/3 of the total length as indicated in sketch 3. Flatten the handle end slightly.

4. Reheat for annealing as soon as the metal loses its pliability and becomes resistant to shaping. Bring the bar to the dull red point and continue shaping or forging the spoon bowl. At the same time begin to shape and narrow the handle shank by directing the hammer blows to shape and lengthen the metal each way. In the same way spread the bowl at the center and outward into an oval form. Turn the shape on edge, sketches 5 and 6, to hammer the corners into the mass and retain the oval contour.

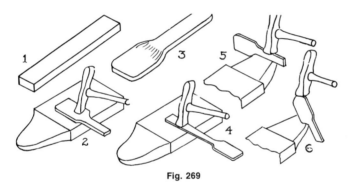

Fig. 269

5. Anneal as often as required. Lengthen and round the shank, reversing the bar at intervals while rotating it over the anvil. "Neck in" or narrow the lower end of the spoon shank as indicated in sketch 5.

6. When the shank is formed according to the pattern, with the rounded taper toward the handle tip and the bowl, hold the neck point over a wooden mandrel, gripped in the vise, and strike it gently with a wooden or rawhide mallet, to develop a slight reverse curve. Flatten the handle tip according to the pattern.

7. The bowl at this point should be a flat oval about 1⅜ inches wide at the widest point, with the thickness diminishing from about 1/16 inch at the center and toward the handle to the thinner bowl edges of about 1/32 inch. Form the contour of the bowl by hammering over a spoon stake.

8. The neck of the shank, as in colonial spoons, may be strengthened by hammering the metal toward a center line with the bowl, as it is held over the rounded stake.

File any uneven edges and round the rim of the spoon bowl and handle with fine emery cloth held over a dowel pin. Smooth and polish the bowl with a very little fine pumice powder applied with a thumb. Finish with jeweler's rouge on a soft cloth. An engraved or stamped decoration may be added.

Fig. 270 is a serving spoon forged by this method and stamped with Indian designs. In Fig. 269, the bowl of the coffee spoon was shaped in a wooden mold. The handle section, cut first as a straight length about ⅜ inch wide, was cut in two identical strips which were twisted together as described on page 295. A small disc of silver with a mounted turquoise was soldered at the end of the handle.

The serving set of a forged silver spoon and fork, Fig. 272, was made by a Navajo silver craftsman, De Pah, on the Navajo reservation near the Crown Point, New Mexico Trading Station and Navajo Indian Center. De Pah designed the pattern and the decoration at the suggestion of the trader B. I. Staples, and gave the set to the writer in appreciation for his hospitality on the occasion of a school demonstration of silver work, weaving, and sand painting. The weaving was done by Ye-Nah Bah, the sand painting by Haska Naya, a medicine man who reproduced a healing ceremony done on the reservation.

Fig. 270

Fig. 271

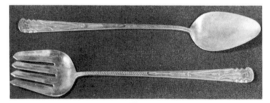

Fig. 272

Filigree silverwork

In ancient times delicate jewel work with twisted and coiled threads of gold and silver was created by the unexcelled craftsmen of the Greeks, Etruscans, and Egyptians for the personal adornment of nobles. Many museum collections of filigree work date back to the sixth century B.C. In medieval times, the skills of the goldsmiths in filigree work were studied and preserved in the monasteries of Europe, and during the Rennaissance many countries revived the craft, including Ireland where a high degree of perfection was reached in the tenth and eleventh centuries. The native craftsmen of India are said to have preserved designs and methods of filigree work from the most remote times until the present day.

Filigree work in silver was practiced by the Moors in Spain during the Middle Ages with great skill, and from Spain it was carried to the colonies of the New World.

In the middle of the last century, many descendants of Spanish colonists of Old Mexico came northward into the Rio Grande Valley of southwestern Colorado. Among them were silversmiths whose skills have been preserved by successive generations and it was one of these fourth generation craftsmen who proudly demonstrated the technique of the filigree work shown in Fig. 273. Changed times and conditions have lessened the demand for this jewelry, but it is to be hoped that the artistry and precise craftsmanship of the filigree silversmith will be appreciated and adapted to other silver craft-work projects.

Fig. 273

Process of Filigree Silver Work

The unit element in filigree work is an area enclosed by a frame made of flattened round wire. The shape of these frames varies with the design employed. The extent to which geometrical shapes in the form of squares, rectangles, ovals, and circles are utilized by the filigree worker is shown in Fig. 274.

The butterfly brooch shows how effective the filigree technique is in portraying insect design motifs. The anatomic body structure, head, antennae, eyes, mouth, thorax, wings, legs, feet, abdomen, and both wing and body markings are all realistically and decoratively portrayed. Equally effective are the pieces based on floral designs. Note in Fig. 274 how each area is enclosed by a frame and the variety of patterns utilized to fill in the framework.

Layout of design

1. Draw to enlarged scale an outline of the project. Sketch in the structural lines needed to provide the required strength and proceed to divide up the space according to the basic elements of the design.

2. Determine position and shape of the twisted wire coils which are to fill each area.

3. Redraw each design element, reduce scale to actual size, and cut paper pattern of each area, marking the quantity of each size wanted.

Make sheet metal forms

4. Cement the paper patterns of each design element to 16 gauge sheet metal, nickel, silver, brass, iron, cut to size and file to shape, Fig. 274.

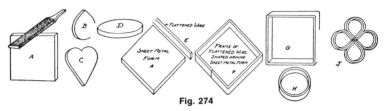

Fig. 274

Shape wire frames over sheet metal forms

The frames used in the filigree jewelry shown in Fig. 275 are made from round sterling silver wire drawn to 22 gauge, and flattened by rolling to a thickness of 30 gauge.

Press the flattened wire against the sheet metal form as shown in Fig. 274, sketches E, F, G, H, and J. Form a butt joint along one side instead of at a corner and solder with hard solder, as described on page 283.

Slip the shaped frames off the forms and solder with torch on charcoal block.

Fill the frame areas with coils of twisted wire according to patterns developed in Fig. 275, sketches F, K, L, M, and J.

1. Use sterling wire, size optional, and draw it to 27 gauge, annealing as required (heat to a dull red in a torch flame, preferably by coiling the strand and placing it on a charcoal block where the flame can be played upon it gently). After each annealing, straighten the coil and prevent kinks by keeping tension on the wire as it is drawn. A 4' to 5' length wire is as long as can be conveniently handled.

2. Double the wire and twist together as indicated in Fig. 275, sketches A to F, until a tight spiral results. The twisting may be done by hand, as indicated in sketch C. Note that the ends of the wire are held in the jaws of a vise, and a small dowel or nail is passed through the loop. Twist the dowel clockwise and at the same time keep sufficient tension on the wire to prevent kinks. When the wire is adequately twisted, the spirals resemble a thin strand of rope.

3. Anneal the twisted strand of wire, taking care not to burn or melt the thin strand.

4. Flatten the twisted strand of 27 gauge wire by passing it through a jeweler's roll as shown in Fig. 275, sketch D, and reduce the combined thickness to 32 gauge. This will require at least two passages through the roll. Anneal after each time through the roll.

5. Coil the flat strand of twisted wire into spirals of the desired shape, size, and number to fill the area enclosed by each frame. See Fig. 275, sketches L and M for method.

6. Fill the frames with the coiled spirals of wire. Place the frame, Fig. 275, sketch M, on a piece of plate glass. Lift the frame L with pliers and insert it in outer frame as shown in sketch M. Sketches K, L, and M show the process of setting the coiled wire forms into the spaces within the frames.

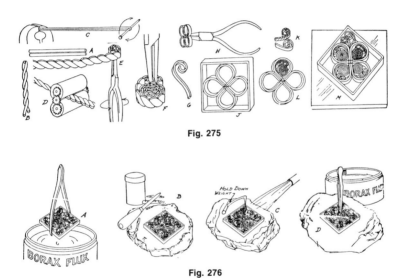

Fig. 275

Fig. 276

Solder the coils and frames in position

1. Lift the assembly from the plate glass with a pair of tweezers (if the coils are properly proportioned and placed together within the frame they will be held by tension), and dip it into the flux, a saturated solution of borax, Fig. 276A. Place on a charcoal block, sketch B.

2. Apply the solder (filings), illustrated in Fig. 276, sketch B, to all points of contact between coils and frame.

3. Apply heat gently to evaporate water in borax by playing the torch on the charcoal block. Gradually raise the temperature of the piece to the melting point of the solder which should flow uniformly over the entire frame, sketch C.

4. Cover the junction of several frames with a ball of sterling soldered in position shown in Fig. 276, sketch D. See detail for making balls or raindrops given on page 282.

Other styles of coils may be used to fill frames as indicated in Fig. 277, sketches A to D. Sketch C shows further enrichment of frame with the addition of a loop band, also a pendant ornament. Sketch D shows a decorative treatment for areas enclosed by concentric circular frames.

Fig. 277

Assemble soldered frames

Place coil filled frames on the plate glass in the position they are to occupy in the assembly. Inspect for unevenness in thickness and contour. File to uniform thickness when necessary, and true up any edge irregularities.

Place adjacent frames in contact, held together by a weight if necessary, Fig. 276, sketch C, on the charcoal block. Apply flux with a brush, sprinkle fine solder on the joint, and bring up the heat gradually until the solder melts.

The enlargements of filigree items of jewelry will suggest many adaptations of the same technique in ornamenting other types of rings and brooches, using heavier wires and less intricate designs. It will be noted that some units of the filigree wire formation, such as indicated in the sketches of Fig. 277 are very similar to those used in combination with balls and domes in more modern costume jewelry items.

CHAPTER 9

Plaiting Methods and Projects

Leather Thongs, Plastic Strips, Fibers, Cord, and Yarn

Types of plaiting were devised or known to the Amerian Indian. Relics from excavations include strands of hair, fur, and fabric. Thongs cut from animal skins were interwoven or plaited. Later as they acquired sheep and learned to make yarn from the wool, they devised ways of plaiting or braiding, before weaving with a warp and woof was learned, or perhaps it was done as a preferred method of making some kinds of costume articles.

It was once believed that the knowledge of some kinds of European braiding came to the Indians by way of Canada, but research determined that the braided or plaited additions to the Canadian soldier's uniform were made and traded by the Indians of that country or the United States. This seems to prove that the skill originated with the Indians of the Northwestern and Southern United States.

Ruth Underhill, in a 1948 publication of the Department of the Interior, Pueblo Crafts, describes the plaiting of the Hopi wedding sash, still made by the Hopi men. She also mentioned the plaiting or braiding of as many as 150 strands of different yarn dyed colors into beautiful costume blankets. This method of braiding, she says, "dates from the very early days, an Indian Art that was not acquired from the European or other white men." An Indian type plaited yarn belt is described and pictured in this book. The men of the Hopi tribe do most of this intricate plaiting.

The frontiersman and the rancher acquired from the Spanish the art of thong plaiting with intricate knots, which was said to have been brought to the Western United States with the horses of the Spanish explorers. From their descendants in New Mexico, Texas, and other areas of the open range and the ranches, the cowboys adopted the plaited bridle reins, lariats, quirts, and other riding equipment of the Spanish horsemen.

For many years, leather was considered the only material satisfactory for plaiting or braided thong articles. Since the introduction of leather substitutes, nearly every former use for leather has been replaced by plastic or other materials which look and wear like leather.

In the equipment of today's horseman, use is made of the recently developed materials. Nylon rope, 7/16" diameter, has replaced the plaited rawhide and leather lariats for both ranch and rodeo use. Weatherproofed hemp and an imported Italian linen is also used for lariats and other equipment.

Materials which are suitable for plaited projects include:

1. *Craftstrip,* a trade name for leather-like thongs, is available in rolls of continuous 50-yard lengths and provides an inexpensive substitute for leather thongs, for plaiting in all the leather thong projects, and for the lacing of frames such as lamp shades. *Note:* Where durability is a first consideration for lacing, goatskin thongs are preferable.

2. *Sisal Fiber,* a product derived from the Maguey plant, widely grown in Asia and cultivated in Mexico and the adjacent states for the manufacturer of hemp rope, can be processed in finer strands, as it is in India and some places in Central and South America. It can be dyed nearly every color and braided for the construction of mats, bags, hats, and other articles. Belts of natural and variegated dyed strands, plaited and sewed together, as well as bags have been imported to this country. A sisal fiber industry in Bombay, India, founded by American missionaries, provides a living for nearly 100 women, who process, dye the fiber, and make many varieties of bags with the plaited strands sewn together.

3. *Swistraw* ribbon is a recently developed *viscose rayon material* imported from Switzerland, which is available in several widths and many colors. Processes for using Swistraw include crocheting, many decorative wrapped foam items, flat plaits for belts, mats, and braids to be sewn together. Information and a catalogue with directions for making projects may be obtained from the importer and creator of the projects, listed at the end of this chapter.

4. *Yarn* entirely of wool or in combination with cotton, rayon, and nylon in almost all desired sizes and colors may be plaited in the round types by the thong or thong plaiting methods or in flat plaits as described on pages 312 and 327. Three and four strand plaits may be sewn together to make mats, hats, bags, and belts. Plaited in four and six strand round patterns, yarn makes excellent bola ties as illustrated in Fig. 293. Fig. 291 and 292 show the use of wood and other kinds of slides and ends, with plaited thongs, cord, and yarn.

5. *Cords* of cotton, rayon, or nylon may be used in many of the ways that leather thongs are used, as they may be plaited and tied in most of the same knots. For square knot and netting projects, firm cotton cord is the recommended material.

Plaited Yarn Belt

The design and making of a yarn belt, similar to the Indian belts, starts, as does the Indian method, with a smooth stick at the center point of the lengths of yarn, measured to make the plaited section waist length and a fringe as long as desired. One end of the yarn strands, 30 as sketched, is attached to a fixed support and reversed for the plaiting of the second half of the belt.

1. Some of the stages in the plaiting of a yarn belt are shown in Fig. 278, A, B, and C. A is the tying of the center strands at the center point on the dowel or pencil with a plain knot; B is the appearance of the center strands which are dark and the lighter strands tied ready to plait.

The first strand is woven to the right as in C. Half of the center design is shown as plaited in D and E. E also shows the turning of the pencil, required to change the direction of the plaiting. F shows the center and one end of the finished belt with the fringe. When the waist length is reached, the 30 strands are divided into 6 units. These are plaited separately by the flat method shown in Fig. 311, page 327. The terminal is a square knot tied with the two center strands of each unit.

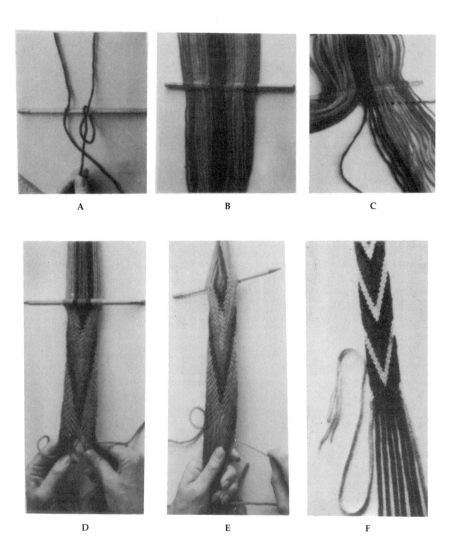

A   B   C

D   E   F

Fig. 278

Detail Yarn Belt

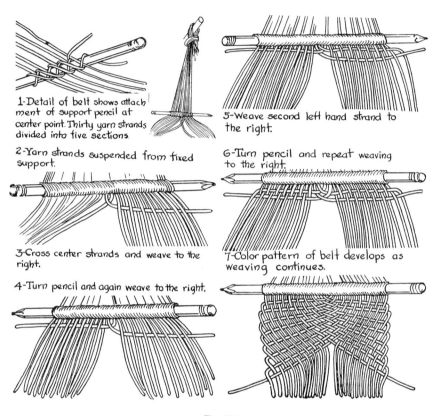

1-Detail of belt shows attachment of support pencil at center point. Thirty yarn strands divided into five sections.

2-Yarn strands suspended from fixed support.

3-Cross center strands and weave to the right.

4-Turn pencil and again weave to the right.

5-Weave second left hand strand to the right.

6-Turn pencil and repeat weaving to the right.

7-Color pattern of belt develops as weaving continues.

Fig. 279

The tie cord in Fig. 278F is a length 30 to 36 inches plaited with the light strands as detailed in Fig. 280. It ends with a square knot tied with two center strands.

Fig. 280

Leather thong cutting methods

Thongs can be cut by hand from discs of leather held on a cutting block with the width controlled by the position of the thumb of the right hand holding the knife as the thong is pulled to the left.

In another method the disc is rotated against a notched piece of wood screwed to the block as the thong is pulled with the right hand from the knife blade, held with the point fixed in the block, by the left hand.

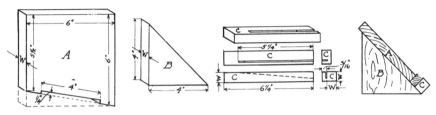

Fig. 281

The construction and use of a wood thong cutter base is illustrated in Fig. 281 and 282. The dimensions of the parts are shown in the sketches A, B, C. To assemble the cutter, screw part C to part A. Mount the A-C portion on the supports B, placing them as indicated. C shows the depth of the saw cut, which controls the width of the thong. All surfaces should be smoothly sanded.

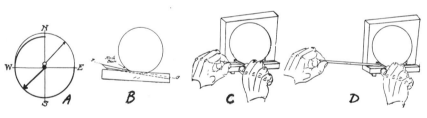

Fig. 282

The discs of leather must be exact circles with the thong W-N started in the desired width. The method of cutting is shown in sketches B, C, and D. The thong is pulled from the fixed knife edge as the disc rotates against the cutter back.

The cutter is held as in sketch C, the leather disc grain surface against the back and the knife blade diagonally across the saw cut at a point exactly the width of the leader thong. Any variation in this position will distort the circle and make the thong irregular. A four inch disc will make a 1/16 inch thong 16-7/10 feet long.

Sharpening the thong knife

The thong knife must be kept razor sharp. The method of sharpening it is shown by the demonstrations, Fig. 283, A, B, C. A thin blade, fixed or extension type, approximately 1/32 inch thick and 5/16 inch wide, can be ground to the necessary shape of a wedge, tapered to the cutting edge, on a fine grit abrasive stone or wheel. It then should be honed or sharpened on an oil stone, followed by strapping on a rouge charged cloth or piece of leather. This step should be done occasionally to straighten turned edges. The polish also reduces the drag which leather exerts on knife blades.

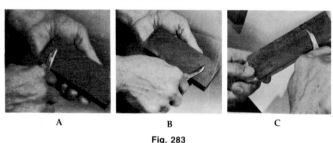

A   B   C

Fig. 283

Methods of plaiting

The start of a strand of four plait round, diamond pattern is shown in Fig. 284A. The first three steps are followed by the positions of the hands and thongs, sketched in Fig. 285. The plaiting steps for the diamond pattern follow:

1. Pass the thongs, preferably of contrasting color, through the ring of a swivel or other fitting, and pull them to the middle point. Place one thong over the other, grain side uppermost, Fig. 284A, sketch 1.

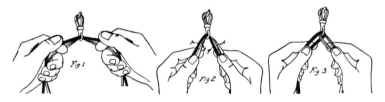

Fig. 284A

2. Carry the uppermost thong to the left, in the position of sketch 2. Count from the left, numbering the thongs 1, 2, 3 and 4. Carry thong 2 over thong 3 and separate the thongs into pairs, 1-3 and 2-4. The color arrangement, with one color on the left and the other on the right is a guide for the plaiting of the diamond design or pattern for any kind of strands.

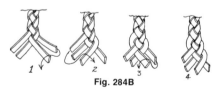

Fig. 284B

The transition of a four plait round strand to a flat plait is shown in Fig. 284B, sketches 1, 2, 3, and 4. At the end of a flat section, round plaiting may be resumed by dividing the thongs again as in sketch 1 in Fig. 284B, following from this position the method for four plait round.

3. Continue plaiting, following the steps shown in the sketches of Fig. 285. Grasp the crossed thongs as in sketch 4. Reach between the light thongs and grasp the upper dark thong as in sketches 4, 5, 6, 7.

4. Remove the left thumb from the position shown in 7 and grasp both dark thongs as shown in sketch 9. The process from here is a repeat, but the manipulation changes from the left to the right hand, as shown in the sketches 10 through 15.

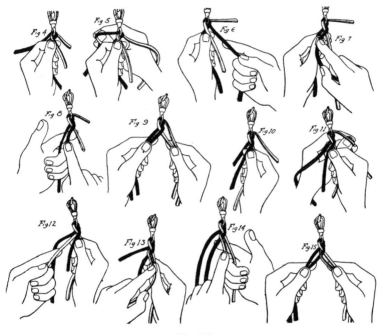

Fig. 285

5. Keep the tension or pull on the thongs as the plaiting progresses. Grasp one thong with three fingers of each hand as in sketches 5 and 6. Continue according to the hand position of sketches 7, 8 and 9, also 12 in which the three fingers of the left hand grasp one light thong. This releases the thumb and forefinger of each hand to manipulate the thongs and hold them in place. Note that these positions keep the tension continuous and steady.

Before the Turk's head ending knot is tied, the plaited strand should be rolled and stretched under a smooth board to smooth out any unevenness and equalize the tension. The rolled strand should equal the width of one of the thongs.

Formation of the terminal Turk's Head knot

The four plait round either diamond or spiral design is ended with the knot detailed in Figs. 286 and 287.

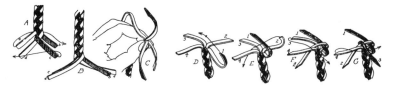

Fig. 286

The continuation of the plaiting is indicated in Fig. 286, sketches A, B.

1. Hold the thongs as in sketch C and follow the arrows through the steps sketched from C to J.

2. From the position of the thongs in sketch J, bring each successive thong up through the center of the square, until all are in the position of sketch Q. Tighten each thong, using the marlin spike or a tracer to open the thongs of the square and pull the ends through the center. This is the terminal knot and the base for the formation of the ornamental crown on crown terminal, detailed in Figs. 289 and 290.

Fig. 287

A spiral design may be developed in the strand of four plait rounds, Fig. 288, sketches E, F, G and H, with the thongs in the position shown, the two light thongs underneath the dark with the left thong crossed over the right. This separates the colors as shown in sketches G and H. The plaiting continues with the thongs numbered as for the diamond design.

Spiral Design

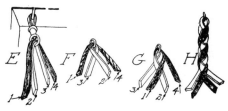

Fig. 288

Formation of the crown on crown terminal

Start with the completed turk's head knot as a base and continue forming the crowns as shown in Fig. 289, sketches A, B, C, and D. D shows the series of crowns formed on the terminal turk's head knot. With the position of the thongs, 1, 2, 3, 4 in sketch D, carry each thong back through the three lower crowns as indicated by the A-B lines. Tighten evenly each of the thongs to form the square terminal and cut off the ends of the protruding ends.

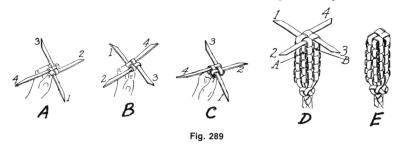

Fig. 289

Spiral reverse

Start in the manner described for the square terminal, build crown on crown rotating each 45 degrees, turning each thong smooth side uppermost. Sketches A to G show the process step by step. Fig. 290, sketch H shows the appearance of the spiral reverse terminal before tucking the thong ends under the next lower crown and trimming off.

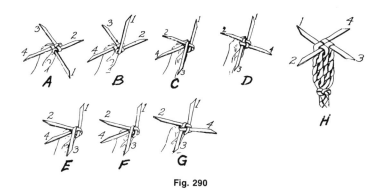

Fig. 290

Plaited strands for bola ties

The slides and the bolas, sketch D, added for weight as well as for holding the plaited strands or leather thongs, latigo leather or lightweight strap, together. (Latigo is oiled horsehide.)

For the plaited strand the sliding knot or other adjustable knots are used. Other slides for plaited strands may be metal, wood, cabochons in silver mountings, or elaborate Indian-made slides with turquoise sets in symbolic designs mounted on silver.

Fig. 292 shows bola ties of plaited strands, leather and yarn, with slides and ends of various materials. Sketches of the detail of the six plait yarn bola tie in A are included in Fig. 291 to show the method of plaiting and ending. Sections of aspen wood are used for the slides and ends. Also for the slides and ends of the plaited strands in D. These and the mounted cabachon slides are adjusted through attached metal channels.

The endings of the plaited strands in B will be recognized as the terminal Turk's Head and the crown on crown described on page 312, also the sliding knot on page 320. The mounting of polished stones or cabachons is described in the silverwork section.

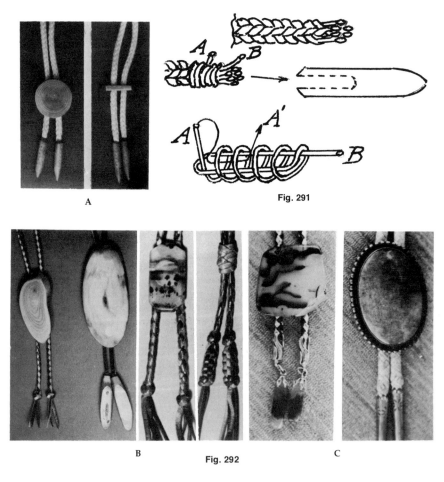

A

Fig. 291

B

Fig. 292

C

The bola tie is an adaptation of a part of the South American Gaucho's (cowboy's) equipment for himself and his horse. The term bola means a weighted strand of plaited leather or a weighted lariat.

Six and eight plait round processes

Possible uses for the six and eight plait round processes are for braiding or plaiting around a core center for quirts and reins and parts of bridles. These are described on pages 324 and 325.

The description of the six and eight plaits without a core, also the twelve and sixteen plait will follow. They are especially suitable for plaiting cord, yarn and Swistraw.

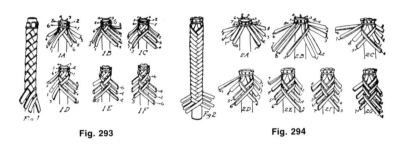

Fig. 293   **Fig. 294**

Fig. 293 and 294 show the pattern and appearance of the six and eight plait strands. In the sketches of the six plait and the eight, the thongs are plaited over a core of rope or rawhide as required for quirts and reins, projects described on page 324. For other uses as mentioned before, with plaited thongs of leather, cord, or yarn, a core is not necessary, and the plaiting is the same. Learning the process may be somewhat easier with a core.

1. Follow the procedure for *Six Plait* in Fig. 293, sketches A through F.
   a. Cross thong 1 over thong 6, sketch A.
   b. Bring thong 4 under thong 5 and over thong 1, sketch B.
   c. Bring thong 3 under thong 2 and over thongs 6 and 4, sketch C.
   d. Bring thong 2 around behind the strand, under thongs 5 and 1 and over thong 3, sketch D. Note that thong 5 is the highest on the left. Bring it behind the strand, under thong 6 and over thongs 4 and 2, sketch E.
   e. Thong 6 is now the highest on the right. Bring it behind the strand, under two thongs and over one as in sketch F. This brings the cycle of plaiting back to C from which it is repeated.

2. The staring process for the *Eight Plait Round* is indicated in positions A and B of Fig. 294.
   a. Divide the thongs as in sketch A and support them over a nail while plaiting. Cross the two inside left hand thongs over the same two right hand thongs, sketch B.
   b. Bring the highest thong on the left around behind the strand, under the two right hand thongs and over two as indicated in sketches C and D.

    c. Change hands and repeat the operation from right to left, as indicated in sketches D and E. Continue plaiting according to the prinple now apparent.

    d. Bring the highest thong around behind the strand, under two and over two. Change hands and repeat, bringing the highest thong on the opposite side of the strand each time.

    3. By changing and combining colors of thongs, the patterns in Fig. 295 sketches J to Q, can be developed. In Q the appearance of four strands sewn together is shown.

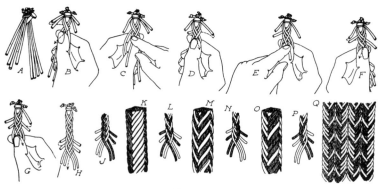

Fig. 295

Twelve and sixteen plait round

    Plaits in multiples of four are plaited in the same way as the eight plait. The sketches in Fig. 295 and 296 follow this principle.

    1. The plaiting is started with the division of the twelve or the sixteen into two groups of three or four thongs crossed from left to right followed,

    2. By the principle of the eight plait in which the highest thong is brought around the strand then under three over three for twelve plait, or under four over four for sixteen plait.

    3. A terminal for two strands of eight, twelve, or sixteen plait, either with or without a tassel is detailed in Fig. 296, sketches A through S.

    4. Wrap the ends of the plaited strands together with a strong thread, as in sketches B and C. If a tassel is to be added, place a section of the fringed material in position D, and tie it tightly in place at the center, sketch E.

    5. Double the upper half of the fringed or unraveled material down over the first thread, wrap and tie thread around to hold it as in G and H. Continue to wrap the terminal with two parallel bands of thread, K, L, and M, caught together in a half-hitch knot.

    6. Conceal the ends of the strands or the tassel with a series of half hitches to unite the parallel bands as shown in sketches N to S. The enlarged detail of the half hitches in T and U show the steps in building the complete covering, shown in S.

Terminals for Twelve and Sixteen Plait Belts

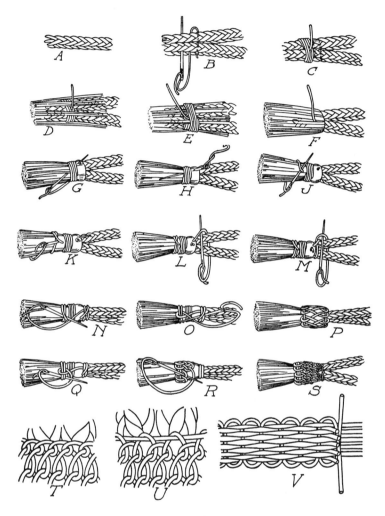

Fig. 296

These methods of plaiting the multiples of four thongs may be successfully used in plaiting colored cord, yarn, craftstrip, or other materials, with the addition of a suitable ending as described above.

Woven fibers are plaited as shown in sketch V. The warp strands are divided equally and the weft strands are passed through the warp strands from opposite sides, then the warp is reversed and the operation repeated. The plaiting (which here resembles weaving) is ended as sketched in Fig. 297, sketch F.

Plaited Strand Belt Assembly

Fig. 297

In Fig. 297, sketches A to H, shows the steps in the assembly of four plaited strands for a belt. A shows an equal number folded back at the center point. B shows an unequal number with the odd strand ending between the folds of the other two.

Place the strands in the position shown and smoothly flatten them in the contour of a belt tongue. Fasten them together with thread of inconspicuous color passed through the strands as indicated in sketch E. Sew the ends to hold the separate strands firmly together, then sew across all the strands to unite them as in sketches E and F. The pattern of this stitching is shown in the enlarged sketches G and H.

The sliding knot

The sliding knot is an essential element in thong work. Its purpose is to unite round plaits and hold them together, also to permit making adjustments for length. Fig. 298, sketches A to J, shows the steps in tying a sliding knot to hold together two strands of four plait round. In the series of single thong knots, this is called the five strand, two bight adjustable knot. (The term bight is of nautical derivation and refers to the contact points of one or more thongs, or ropes, held in position by the friction of their surfaces.)

1. Hold the plaited strands and the end of the knot thong in the left hand, sketch A, and carry the other end over and around the strands to form bight 1. Repeat these steps to form bights 2 and 3 as shown in sketches C and D.

2. Insert a marlin spike under the beginning thong to permit the free end to be passed underneath and around the two strands as indicated in sketches D and E. Insert the spike under bights one and two, sketch E, then carry the free end through and around as shown in sketch F.

3. From this point parallel the single thong, following through the steps of the first operation to complete the knot in sketches G and H. Remove the slack by tightening each bight in turn, just sufficiently to permit the movement or sliding of the knot as required. Trim off any excess length and conceal the end under the previous bight, sketch H. The finished knot appears in sketch J.

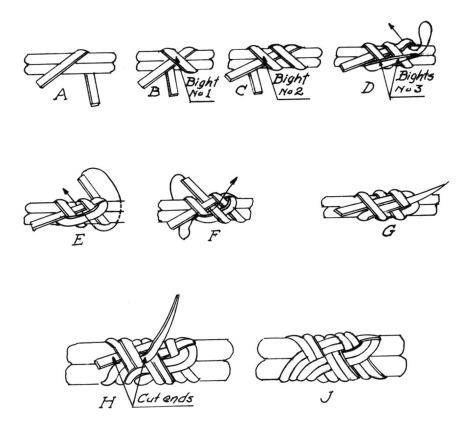

Fig. 298

4. The sliding knot, or five strand two bight knot, may be tied on a single strand or a handle, such as a cane, quirt, or umbrella. The steps and appearance are shown in Fig. 299, sketches A, B, C, D, and E.

Ornamental Knots

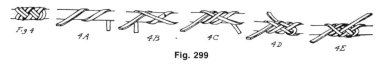

Fig. 299

The three strand two bight knot sketched in Fig. 300 A, B, C, and D is another adjustable knot used to hold two strands, also for concealment of a spliced strand, or just for ornamentation.

Fig. 300

The unit length three bight knot sketched in Fig. 301, sketches A to K, is designed to cover a surface by paralleling the single strand of the knot completed in sketch H with two or three strands for the end of a cane or quirt as in K.

The double length three bight knot is started with two turns of a thong around a core or a quirt handle and continued with steps similar to the unit length knot. This knot may be adjusted to cover the end of a cane, quirt, or other handle by tightening the thong until the last one closes the opening as in Fig. 301, sketch K.

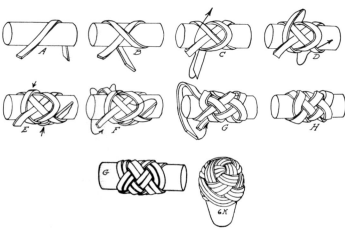

Fig. 301

A four bight knot, made with a single thong, is developed as in Fig. 302, sketches A to H. Sketch H indicates the start of a parallel step which may continue as a triple strand as in sketch 7A if needed to cover a juncture.

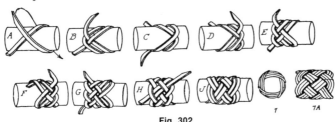

Fig. 302

Five bight knot

1. Place the thong or strand in the left hand, around the fingers, with ends A and B crossed as shown in sketch 1. The knot is tied with the long end B as A remains in the first position and held by the bights 1, 2 and 3 as shown in sketches I and II with thong B wrapped around the fingers, crossing over itself and under thong A. A plaited strand with turks head ending or strap is used.

2. Turn the left hand over as shown in sketch III. Cross thongs A and B as in sketch IV then pass thong B through the openings in the direction of the arrow, pulling the thongs together as shown in sketch V.

3. With the palm of the left hand up, continue to pass thong B along and on the right of thong end A, sketch VI. Parallel the first single thong structure, forming the knot shown in sketch VII. Tighten the thong cut ends and conceal inside the knot as in sketch IX.

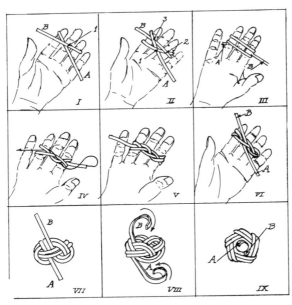

Fig. 303

The gaucho knots

The single and double gaucho knots sketched in Figs. 304 to 306 were developed from plaited work made in South America. These knots are still used by the Gauchos or cowboys of the cattle raising plains or pampas and in the cities by the riding clubs and other horsemen. Cowboys of the South and Western range areas frequently adopt the South American plaited bridles and reins for their horses.

The gaucho knots are useful for terminals, adjustable fastenings, or sliding knots, also for ornamental purposes on bridles, reins, and other cowboy gear. They make attractive neckerchief slides, also bola slides, and for this purpose may be formed over a tubular piece of leather that has been sewn together with waxed thread. This holds the thong or thongs in place during the construction of the knot as indicated in the sketches of the single gaucho in Fig. 304 and 305.

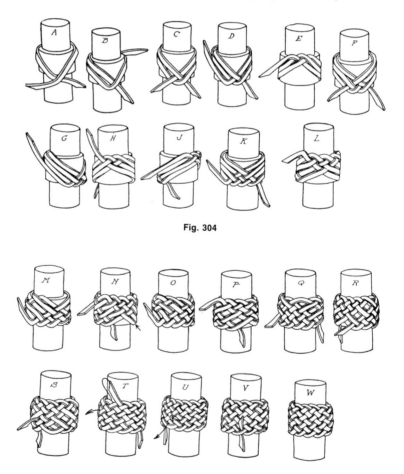

Fig. 304

Fig. 305

The steps for the single gaucho knot, basket weave pattern follow:

1. Make a diagonal loop around the core as indicated in Fig. 304, sketch A. Carry the thong across the end and parallel the loop, following upward on the lower side, as in sketch B.

2. Cross the thong over the first loop and parallel it downward on the upper side, as in sketch C. Repeat the operation, paralleling on the lower side, sketch D, of the thong structure, after the cross over shown in sketch E.

3. Continue paralleling on the upper side, sketch F, downward. The design developed is the basket weave, or over one, under one pattern.

4. Continue the weaving process until the entire core is covered. The appearance of the knot just prior to the completing step is shown in Fig. 305, sketch T. Fill the space between the first and last thong, as indicated in sketches U, V, and W.

5. End the weaving by making the ends of the thong secure with the juncture near the center of the knot, by weaving the thong back under as in V and W.

The double gaucho knot

The steps for the double gaucho knot, herringbone pattern, are shown in Fig. 306, sketches A to T. The principle is similar to that described for the single gaucho knot, except that the pattern of the weave is over two, under two.

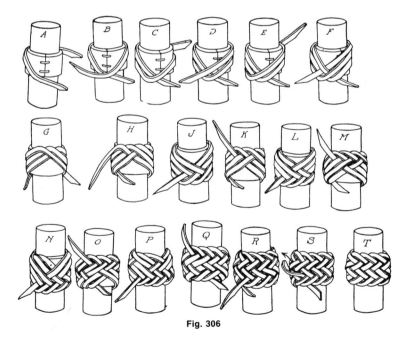

Fig. 306

1. Make a diagonal loop around the core as indicated in sketches A and B. Parallel upward on the lower side as shown in sketch C.

2. Cross over the thong and parallel downward on the upper side as shown in sketch D. Cross over two thongs and parallel upward as shown in sketch E.

3. Cross over two thongs, as shown in sketch F, and parallel downward as indicated in sketch G. Pass the thong under one and over two, sketch H.

4. Parallel upward, pass the thong under one and over two, sketch J. Parallel downward, pass the thong under two over two as in sketch K.

5. Parallel downward, sketch I, then upward, sketch M, passing the thong over one under one, under two, over two. The thong must emerge and cross over two thongs. Hence on the first, third, fifth, and succeeding odd numbers of turns, the thong crosses either under or over a single thong, which is required to make it emerge and cross over two thongs.

6. Pass the thong over one and under two, over two under two, sketches L, M, N, and O. Continue the paralleling and weaving process until the core is covered, sketch P. Fill the space between the first and last thong, sketch Q, and complete the steps shown in sketch R.

7. End the weaving by making the ends secure with the junction near the center of the knot, sketch S. Remove slack and adjust the length of the loops with the marlin spike. Trim off the ends of any protruding thongs, and roll the knot under a board to smooth out any unevenness and make the knot uniform.

Plaited leather quirts and bridle reins

Quirt A, Fig. 308, may be made with a folded strap handle, or with an extension of the plaited section looped back to form a hold for the bridle reins. The required materials for quirt A are:

4 or 6 Latigo thongs, tapered from ⅝ inch to ¼ inch, 40 inches long, 6 ounces weight. The method of cutting is described on page 309.

Strap leather strips for stiffening the core, Hand strap and Lash strap.

Thongs for knots, thong knife, and marlin spike.

Core or body made of a stitched sack of soft leather, tapered from ¾ inch diameter at the top to ⅜ inch at the end. It is filled with buckshot, (lead balls about 1/16 inch in diameter).

1. Prepare the core and sew the ends together. Place the cover strap and the hand strap over the core and secure them with a wrapping of strong twine. Tie the 4 or 6 Latigo thongs to the wrapped core with the flesh side out and the ends extended along the handle.

2. Turn the thongs downward, place the hand strap over a support, and start plaiting as in sketch F. Following the instructions for 4 or 6 plait, Figs. 294 and 295, pages 315 and 316, continue plaiting to the point just beyond the bottom of the core sack.

3. End the plaiting by turning the tapered strand up at the end in the form of a loop. Tie it firmly in place, and cover with a three bight knot.

4. Tie a three bight knot at the top as described in Fig. 301, page 320, and at the bottom, tie the single gaucho knot, detailed in Fig. 306, page 322. Insert the lash strap and tie the sliding knot to hold it in place. This knot is described in Fig. 299, page 320.

In Fig. 308 the reins and attached quirt are around other types of quirts. The hackamore bridle is modeled by the horse in Fig. 309. The enlargement, Fig. 308A, shows the connecting loops of the reins and quirt, also the gaucho knots. The quirt lash is attached under the fringe of the plaited section.

The specifications and method for plaiting the bridle is given on page 326. The reins of latigo or goatskin are plaited over a clothes line core. Snaps are shown for the bridle connection.

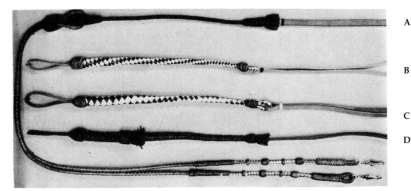

A

B

C

D

Fig. 308

Fig. 309

D1

Fig. 308A

Headstall—Plait two strands of four plait round 28 inches long over a ⅛ inch woven cord. Form a loop on one end and tie a terminal turk's head knot on the other. The loops are for the attachment of the bosal or nose piece as are shown on the bridge in Fig. 309. Fig 310, sketch A indicates the two strands with a sliding knot for adjustment at the top. For the two strands eight ⅛ inch thongs 45 inches long and a ⅛ inch cord core 28 inches long are required.

Throat Latch—Plait a strand of six plait round over a cord, tie a terminal turk's head knot on each end. Sketch F shows the throat latch as connected with a sliding knot after attachment to the headstall.

Browband—Plait two strands of four plait round 12 inches long over two woven cord cores 11 inches long with 3/16 inch wide thongs, 30 inches long. Extend the plaiting 3 inches beyond each end of the core and combine the thongs from the strands at both ends into a flat plaited section as shown in sketch C. Carry this over the headstall and throat latch and secure the ends by working them back into the strands. Cover the juncture with the knot, Fig. 301, page 320, as shown in sketch E. Ornamental conchas may be attached with the three hole fastening.

Bosal or Nose Band—Plait a strand of four plait round 60 inches long over a core of ¼ inch cord and tie turk's head at both ends. Double the strand and tie a unit length knot to form the loop. Fold again forming the band 14 inches long each way and tie a three bight knot over the turk's head terminals to hold them together and enlarge the size. As indicated in sketch J, wrap the strands at points at 1-4 and 3-6 with twine, then cover with a three bight knot extended four times the length of the single knot, Fig. 301. Wrap four complete turns around the two bosal strands before reversing the direction, Fig. 301, sketch B. Sketch H shows the inner surface of the knot covered with a stitched pad.

Bit Loop—Plait a strand of four plait round over a woven cord core ⅛ inch diameter, 13 inches long, Fig. 310, sketch K, to the middle point, then fold the thong ends back and closely bind them with twine to the core. Continue plaiting over these thong ends and core to the opposite end and tie a turk's head knot as shown in sketch L, covering it with a crown knot. M shows a completed bit loop as attached to the loop of the headstall.

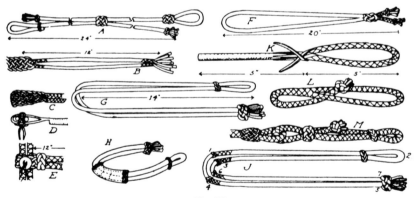

Fig. 310

Variations in Flat Plait Patterns

With some variation in the steps of the patterns, flat plaiting can be done with thongs split from a piece of lightweight strap leather or with cord, yarn, Craftstrip, and synthetic material strands, if firm enough to hold their shape.

In Fig. 311, the series of sketches A, B, C, D, and E, indicate the process in flat plaiting three, four, five, six and seven thongs in the basket weave, or over one, under one design.

A herringbone design can be developed with any even number of thongs. This is an over two, under two method. For an even number of thongs or strands the plaiting may be started over a buckle bar at the middle point. The end is finished with a folded tongue piece of leather or fabric stitched to the ends. If hand sewn, use waxed linen thread and process described on page 211.

Varied patterns in different colored materials may be plaited by the basket weave uneven strand method or the herringbone even strand method. The length and width of flat plaited material is approximately two-thirds of the length and width of the material strands before they are plaited, or one-third more than the actual waist measurement.

Flat Plaits

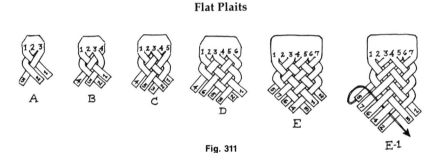

Fig. 311

Variations in Five Plait Patterns

Fig. 312

Buckle and Tongue Detail

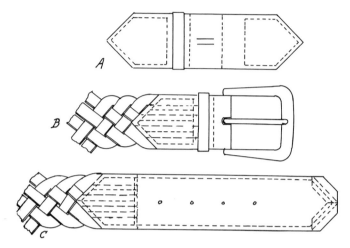

Fig. 313

Three strand basket weave, sketch A
  1. Carry strand 1 over 2.
  2. Carry strand 3 over 1.
  3. Carry strand 2 over 3 and continue this process to complete the braid.

Four strand basket weave, sketch B
  1. Carry strand 1 over 2 and 3 over 4.
  2. Carry strand 4 over 1.
  3. Carry strand 3 *under* 1.
  4. Carry strand 2 over 4 and *under* 3, and continue plaiting bringing the *outside strand* on the *left over one.*
  5. Change to the *right side* of the braid and bring the *outside strand under one and over one.*

Alternately repeat this cycle until the braid is completed.

Five strand basket weave, sketch C
  1. Carry strands 1 over 2 and 3 over 4.
  2. Carry strands 5 over 3 and 4 over 1.
  3. Carry strand 5 *under* 1.
  4. Carry strand 2 over 4 and *under* 5.
  5. Carry strand 3 over 1 and *under* 2. Continue to plait, carrying the *outside strand on the left over one and under one.*
  6. Change to the *right side* of the braid and carry the *outside* strand *over one* and *under one.*

Alternately repeat this cycle until the braid is completed.

Six strand basket weave, sketch D
1. Carry strands 1 over 2, 3 over 4 and 5 over 6.
2. Carry strand 6 over 3.
3. Carry strand 1 under 4.
4. Carry strand 6 under 1.
5. Continue to plait and carry the *outside strand* on the *left* (No. 2 in sketch), *over one, under one, over one.* Change to the right side of the braid and carry outside strand, No. 3 in sketch D, *under one, over one.* Repeat from the left side of the braid, carrying outside strand over and under.

Continue this procedure alternating right and left plaiting until the braid is completed.

Seven strand basket weave, sketch E
1. Carry strand 3 over 2 and under 1.
2. Carry strand 5 over 4, under 2, and over 1.
3. Carry strand 7 over 6, under 4, over 2 and under 1.
4. Carry strand 3 over 5, under 7, over 6 and under 4.
5. Carry strand 6 over 4, under 2, over 1 and under 3.
6. Continue plaiting and carry the *outside strand, on the left, over one* and *under one.*

Alternate and carry the *outside strand on the right over one and under one* continuing this procedure to complete the braid.

Belt straps split for endless braiding
Belt straps may be split for endless braiding by cutting along a traced line, with the rocker knife or by means of the notched gauge, shown in Fig. 314 with plaited and decorated sections.
Buckleless belts
1. After dividing the strap evenly into the number to be cut (2) Crease and bevel the edges, mark off 3 inches for the buckle end and 6 inches for the strap end. (3) Punch size 0 or 00 to terminate the splits. (4) Then follow the steps of the plaiting process, Fig. 316.

Fig. 314

2. For a three section belt strap; pass the lower end of the strap through the slit that separates 2 and 3 in the direction of front to back, as shown in sketch 2. Carry strap 1 over 2 and 3 over 1, then strap 2 over 3 as indicated in sketch 3. This forms bights at points marked A, B, C.

3. Pass the lower end through the mesh below point C, between the straps 2 and 3 as indicated in sketch 3. This removes all twist in the straps, sketch 4. Continue plaiting the straps as shown in sketch 5, forming bights D, E, F. This completes the cycle. Repeat the steps as necessary to fill the space between the straps.

Buckle-less Belt notched tongue inserted in triangular opening.

Fig. 315

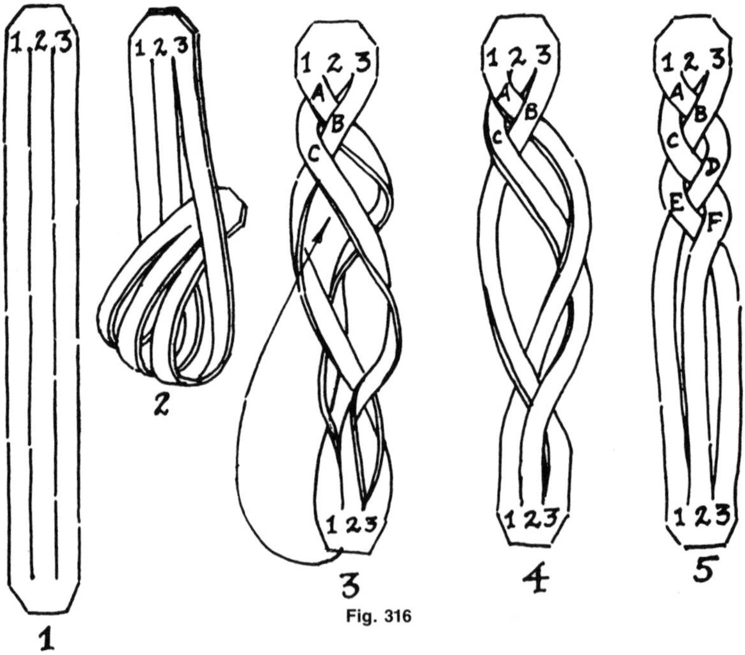

Fig. 316

The steps for a five section belt split for endless plaiting are as follows:

1. Pass the lower end through the slits which separate straps 3 and 4 in the direction of front to back, Fig. 317, sketch 2.

2. Carry strap 1 over straps 2 and 3 as indicated in sketch 3. This forms bight A. Carry strap 5 over straps 1 and 4 as indicated in sketch 4. This forms bight B.

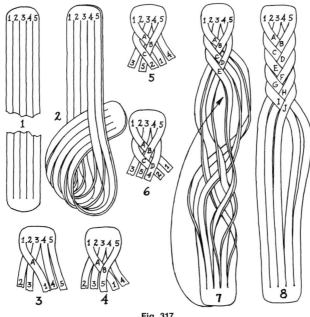

Fig. 317

3. Carry strap 2 over straps 3 and 5, sketch 5, to form bight C.

4. Carry strap 4 over straps 1 and 2, sketch 6, to form bight D.

5. Carry strap 3 over straps 5 and 4, sketch 7, to form bight E.

6. Pass the lower end of the strap through the mesh and below bight E and between straps 4 and 5. Continue to plait until 10 bights are completed, then the straps will be straight as indicated in sketch 8.

From this point, repeat the steps until the space is filled.

Seven section split belts for endless plaiting or braiding can be made by a method similar to the five section (above). The steps are as follows:

1. Pass the lower end of the split strap through the slits that separate straps 4 and 5 in the direction of front to back. Carry straps 1 over 2, 3 over 4 and strap 7 over straps 6, 5, and 1.

2. Form 7 bights by carrying the outside straps over 3 straps alternately. Pass the lower end of the split strap through the mesh below bight 7.

3. Continue plaiting by carrying the outside straps over 3 straps until bight 14 is formed, bringing all the straps straight. Repeat the process for another 14 bights and continue plaiting until all the spaces are filled.

CHAPTER **10**

Plastics Craftwork

Plastics, the twentieth-century marvel of synthetic chemistry, were first developed for industrial uses, and in this field have now replaced many natural materials. In response to the demand from schools, craft suppliers, and individual craftsmen, for types of plastics suitable for hand working, the development of a wide range of materials provides a medium of limitless variation for handcraft projects.

Originally, the Greek and Latin words from which the adjective plastic was derived meant "something capable of being shaped or modeled." The noun form of the word was adopted with the discovery and development of the modern research product, meaning, according to the Monsanto Plastics Research, "materials that, while being processed, can be pushed into almost any desired shape and then retain that shape."

Fig. 323

Classification of Plastics

1. In 1909, one of the first plastics was developed from casein, a natural protein, precipitated by chemical means from milk. After years of research a group of plastics, called the *protein plastics,* were made from soy beans, peanuts, and other agricultural products.

2. *The natural resins,* of which asphalt, rosin, amber, pitch or coal tar, and lac, the basis of shellac, are examples were used as the basis of another classification.

3. *The synthetic resin plastics* are a large group, derived mainly from coal, petroleum, sulphur, urea, and other natural substances in combination with phenol formaldehyde and other chemicals. These are called phenolic plastics. They are hardened by heat and cannot be melted or softened, so are termed thermosets which have many industrial uses, because of their strength, rigidity, and resistance to heat, oil, water, and electricity. Catlin (a trade name) is an example. The projects on page 332 were made of Catlin.

Filaments spun from plastic substances of resin base are woven into different fabrics, which may be made water resistant. Filaments of spiderweb size make nylon hose, one marvel of the plastic industry. Nylon fibers of almost infinite variety are spun for every fabric use, and because of their much greater strength are suitable for many more purposes than fabrics of natural materials.

4. *The acrylic plastics* are crystal clear synthetics which come in brilliant transparent and translucent colors, as well as the water clear form. Plexiglas and Lucite are among the best known trade names. The description of the process of making Lucite gives some idea of the chemical marvel it is: "to make it gases derived basically from coal, air and water are converted into a clear liquid by the tremendous pressure of five tons to the square inch. This clear water thin liquid, called methyl methacrylate monomer, is then caused to polymerize, or change its molecular structure into crystal clear, practically unbreakable solid Lucite.

Fig. 324

A characteristic quality of Lucite is its remarkable optical property of transmitting and reflecting light. Rods and tubing of many sizes are made from Lucite.

Plexiglas is notable for its permanent transparency and resistance to weathering, also its property of conducting light. It is manufactured in many forms and is especially suitable for handmade projects.

The acrylic plastics are all suitable for crafts as they can be readily cut, drilled, carved, engraved, cemented together, and molded. They are all thermoplastic or capable of being softened and formed under low heat (about 150 degrees F.) and hand pressure, then become solid again on cooling. The *phenolic resin plastics,* as mentioned above, are thermosetting, which means that they acquire infusibility under heat and pressure and cannot be melted or remolded. They are available in rods, cylinders, and sheets and can be softened sufficiently to bend under heat.

Other types of plastics include:

Polyester resin which is a liquid form for clear or colored castings, and items embedded for preservation or for decorative appearance. It is thermosetting and when activated with a catalyst, hardens at room temperature. It is manufactured under various names and widely used in industry with fibreglas reinforcement which gives it strength and rigidity. The process is termed laminating and can be adapted for many craft projects.

Poly Paste is a paste form of polyester resin which can be used to cover glasses, ceramic forms, and other materials to hold decorative glass jewels, cabochons, or polyglas, pieces of colored and hardened polyester resin.

Armoplex (trade name) is a granular casting plastic which can be melted in an oven and poured into molds like metal. Other granular and crystal type resin plastics, under different trade names, are handled by suppliers.

Polyethylene is a transparent, thermoplastic resin of natural origin (storax, a tree or bark distillation). It is used in wall tile and kitchen ware.

Vinyl is derived from ethylene and is used in tile floor coverings, lamp shades, raincoats, and similar water resistant articles.

Castolite is a trade name for a crystal clear liquid plastic that can be poured to produce many projects. It sets hard like fine glass, when mixed with a catalyst and heated at 150 degrees F. in an oven, in hot water, or under an electric light bulb. It is a *thermosetting* plastic, which once hardened by heat, cannot be melted or softened. It can be sawed, drilled, or carved like wood and can be colored with special dyes. It has wide usage for preserving biological and other scientific specimens.

Castoglas, produced by the same manufacturer, is a slightly pink transparent laminating or bonding plastic, used for castings to embed flat materials such as leaves, grasses, and flowers which require only a thin layer. When mixed with a hardener, Castoglas requires no heat and hardens in 30 minutes at room temperature. Reinforced with fibreglas, it is used extensively in industry as a structural material, also for many craft projects. Like Castolite it is *thermosetting.*

Castomold is a liquid compound used to produce rubber-like molds, Fig. 331, for castings.

Fibreglas is made from molten glass which is processed into thin filaments. Like steel mesh in concrete, it is used as a reinforcing agent in plastics, also as an insulating material, and for filters.

General Instructions for Plastic Craft Work

Much of the beauty of plastic is in its gleaming clear texture and color. Forms should be designed to reveal these qualities. Surface decoration, except for some types of engraving, should be limited as it detracts from the qualities of the plastic.

A study of metal, glass, and ceramic forms will suggest many ways in which sheet and cylindric plastic may be combined in effective and practical ways. In designing articles of a crystal clear plastic, the reflection and refraction of light from planes, angles, and curves, which are like faceted jewels, must be taken into consideration and this involves some understanding of the physics of light.

Simplicity in all plastic design will insure the most effective and satisfying results.

Plastics: equipment, design and assembly

The equipment for working plastics by hand include:

Engraving tools, hand drill with pivot and twist drills, jeweler's saw with Nos. 0 and 2 blades, bench pin; 6 inch files, round, half-round and triangular, with No. 1 cut, needle files, No. 3 cut; a scraper and bending lamps, also sensitized paper, black and white; sand paper Nos. 3/0 and 7/0, tracing paper, and flexible cement. Supplies of plastic, sheet, rods and blocks, also liquid plastic for casting, with the required prepared cement, hardener, catalyst, and polishing materials.

Transferring the outline design is a process quite similar to that followed for metal. Simple line patterns may be laid out freehand, using a rule or guide which will not scratch the surface of the plastic. Make sure of the position of lines along which the piece is to be cut, then incise them lightly with a metal scriber.

Designs of irregular shape are best cut with the paper pattern outline attached directly to the surface of the plastic with rubber cement. Coat the plastic very lightly with cement, position the paper at one edge first, then roll it into place without wrinkles. Be sure it is smooth and on contact along all design lines.

Dividers are useful in scribing lines equidistant from a square edge. Plastic of cylindrical shape may be marked by rotating it against a scriber fixed at right angles.

The methods of cutting plastic vary with the nature and thickness of the stock. Thin sheets, .080 inch in thickness may be cut with a paper cutter or broken along deeply scribed lines, when held at the edge of a smooth straight block, with another block or a weight on the plastic to hold it firm and square with the design line exactly on the edge of the first block. Break the piece to be removed along the scribed line.

Sheets up to .050 inch may be cut with metal cutting shears. For cutting thicker sheets, use a sharp hack saw with blades 20 to 30 point, for the straight lines, and a jeweler's saw with a No. 1 blade for cutting curved lines. (See metal sawing on page 226). Clamp rods or cylinders, protected with a pad of cloth or leather, in a vise and cut with a hack saw held vertically or horizontally as the direction of the cut requires.

Pierced or cutout decorations are effective on sheet plastic. The desk set and paper knives illustrated in Fig. 326 are examples. The method of piercing or sawing to remove areas of a design in an outline effect is described on page 226. The same process is used for plastic sheets with one important difference. The sawing must be done slowly to prevent heating. If this happens the contact surface will be softened and hinder or stop the sawing. This *caution applies* to all work with metal tools on plastics. Friction induced by rapid scraping, sawing, or drilling will cause heat, and must be avoided.

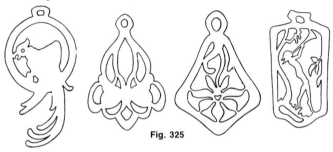

Fig. 325

The above group of curtain or shade pulls of 1/16 inch plastic with cutouts or pierced designs, as well as the desk set, Fig. 326, and series of paper knives, cut from sheet plastic in opaque or translucent plastic are very attractive and fascinating to make. Several of the paper knives and the curtain pulls may be painted with enamel or special plastic paints, in contrasting colors.

Note that these designs were all planned to keep the design segments attached at as many points as necessary to unify and strengthen the article. This must be remembered in using the jeweler's saw to remove the open areas, so as to avoid cutting through an attachment point on any margin.

The desk set and some of the paper knives were cut from an amber colored sheet plastic about 3/32 inch thick with the edges left square, but all roughness smoothed with a piece of emery cloth folded around a dowel stick.

Fig. 326

Plastic Desk Set Units and Paper Knives

Fig. 327

The paper knives vary in thickness from 1/16 to 1/8 inch and all edges are slightly rounded. The letter opener edge must be thinned down to a slightly rounded 1/32 inch or a thinness which will cut paper without tearing.

Fig. 328

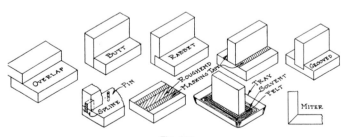

Fig. 329

The assembly of plastic parts may require the recessing of one or more panels into a base, Fig. 329. The steps are as follows:

1. Brace or clamp the piece of plastic, scribe the lines to be grooved with a metal scriber or scratch awl, then saw cut them to the necessary depth with the fine blade hacksaw. If a wide groove is necessary, make a second or third saw cut between the first lines, and exactly the same depth.

2. Remove the saw cut sections with a narrow wood chisel, carefully driving the chisel with a slight shaving movement to lift off the plastic segments, and even the groove down to a uniform depth.

The woodworker's hand routing tool may also be used for this purpose. Smooth the edges of the channel with emery cloth folded around a flat piece of metal or a hard wood stick shaped like a chisel.

3. Start V or U grooves with one saw cut, and finish with a chisel of the proper shape. Use the chisel alone for shallow grooves as in engraving. Cut short length grooves with a file.

4. Square all straight line margins before assembling the pieces. A block plane can be used to level margins of flat pieces. Place them in a vise, with paper or cloth protection, and for a guide in planing off irregularities have level pieces of wood along the sides. Use a piece of fine sandpaper to square the circular pieces of rod or cylinders. If necessary, carefully file curved or rounded surfaces and smooth with fine sandpaper.

Cementing plastic pieces together requires a special plastic cement, which solidifies to unite the surfaces. Unlike wood cement, plastic cement is made of a composition similar to that of the plastic or it may be a solvent which softens the edges sufficiently for them to merge together and thus unite. Suitable cement for each type of plastics is usually supplied by dealers who handle it, together with detailed instructions for use.

1. To prepare plastic surfaces for cementing it is essential that they fit perfectly and are entirely free from dust or moisture. Roughen the contact surfaces slightly with an abrasive to provide a "hold." Various kinds of contacts or surface relationships are shown in Fig. 329. Indicated for a butt joint, or corners where there may be strain is a metal dowel pin inserted in holes drilled in both surfaces. Such pins are put in place after the cement has been applied and the surfaces are ready to be placed together. This is only possible with opaque plastics.

2. Protect the margins above the surfaces to be cemented with masking tape to prevent any spread of the cement or solvent which would mar the surface finish. This use of tape is shown in one of the sketches in Fig. 329 and 330.

Caution: The solvents or accelerators used in plastic cements are powerful and pungent chemicals. Be careful to avoid spilling any on hands or clothing, and work in a well ventilated room.

3. Immerse an edge which is to be attached in a butt or mitered joint in a little cement which has been poured in a shallow glass container. Leave the plastic piece to "soak" for several minutes until a coat or cushion of the cement adheres to the edge and will permeate into the second surface when the two are brought together.

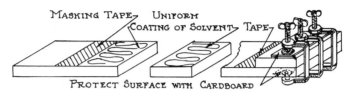

Fig. 330

4. Press the surfaces together but do not use force. If the fit is exact, this will not be required. Tape may be used to maintain contact until the cement sets. Wooden clothes pins of the clamp type may be used on a joint which is not too thick. Quickly remove any cement that presses out before it sets, using a smooth, thin edged piece of wood. Avoid getting any on the fingers.

5. On surfaces which cannot be dipped as described, apply the cement with a small brush, a glass rod, or a stick to the surfaces which have been slightly roughened at the contact points. Hold the pieces a moment before bringing them together. The hardening period varies according to the kind of plastic and the cement. When this is used in conjunction with an accelerator or catalyst, which is usually supplied with the cement, the hardening time is shortened.

6. A laminating cement dye is available which produces a line of color and unites the surfaces at the same time. It may be applied in the form of a design between two surfaces to make a clean line. Clean the pieces well with alcohol and apply the dye with a brush or glass rod.

Cast plastics

The synthetic resin liquid plastics, classified as phenolic, are usually designated for cast projects, as they are thermosetting and once hardened cannot be softened or melted. Some are opaque and others are crystal clear or translucent with color.

Also available from suppliers are the crystalline granular and pellet forms of recently developed plastics which come in many colors as well as the clear, which can be dyed. It can be melted in any mold which will withstand the required oven heat of 350 degrees. and will assume the shape of the mold as it begins to cool. When cold it shrinks from the mold and is easily removed. A flat cast form, while still flexible, can be shaped over a form. This plastic is thermoplastic and can be softened and reshaped when heated.

A feature of the pellet type of plastic resin for casting is the quality which permits it to be melted and cast in aluminum containers or forms. It is available in the clear, also in a number of transparent and opaque colors. Aluminum forms in sizes up to 10 inch diameter, round and 12 inch by 18 inch rectangular are available from suppliers. Highly polished tin molds can be used for the pellets or crystals offered by some suppliers, and as for any kind of plastics, pyrex or other heat resistant glass and porcelain make excellent molds.

This type of plastic is excellent for the embedment of nature items and other small articles. Only the thickness is limited. As with liquid plastics, these types are thermoplastic and the cast forms can be shaped into freeform dishes, trays, ornamental plaques, and similar articles. For the development of such forms, the cast piece is warmed in an oven, about 25 degrees for a few minutes, or until slightly flexible. When shaped and cool again, this plastic will be firm and rigid.

Preparation of molds

The liquid resin plastic can be cast in molds just as plaster of Paris and clay slip is cast. One and two piece plaster of Paris molds, made as described on page 69, can be used and molds of modeling clay are suitable for some projects. Plaster molds are not usable for plastic casting unless glazed. Some kinds of glazed ceramic molds for casting plastic gems, small trays, and desk items, also such molds of heavy plastic, are available from suppliers. Pyrex glass utensils and dishes are satisfactory for similar forms; ash trays, cans and paper cups will also answer for molds, provided the sides are tapered for removal of the form, and a suitable mold release agent is first applied.

Turned hard wood molds, with inner and outer forms which fit together are used for shallow curved and deep bowl forms. With supports to permit pouring the liquid resin between the forms, the desired thickness can be obtained. All surfaces of wood or plaster molds must be sanded smooth and sealed with plastic resin or with lacquer and other wood surfacing materials. The plastic resin, applied with a small brush in three or four coats, is the most satisfactory sealer, except possible types of sealers supplied by manufacturers with specific casting plastics. Fine sanding between each coat is essential. Apply with padded sander.

Hard wood plywood ¼ inch thick, sanded and surfaced with the resin coats, is satisfactory for flat castings. *Each coat must be allowed to cure, one to three hours,* for all forms of wood molds, and given a thorough sanding with 3/0 then 6/0 sandpaper, followed by a fine grit buffing compound to remove all marks from sanding.

A power buffing wheel with an acrylic buffing compound should be used if available.

Caution: The resin must be cleaned from the brush immediately after using, with a resin solvent, acetone, or lacquer thinner. Do not permit to harden or it cannot be removed.

Products for making rubber molds and molds of rubber-like qualities are available from suppliers of plastic materials. Castomold and Castoflex from the Castolite Manufacturers are two of these. There are several special rubber molding preparations on the market.

Pure latex rubber can be applied in several coats, 15 to 20, or sufficient to build up a mold of the desired thickness. This rubber is more flexible than the molding preparations, which are thicker and can be built up in three or four coats, and is more durable than the latex. This is preferable when the figure design requires the flexibility of latex. In either type, it is possible to split the rubber coating in places for easier removal, then seal the joints on the outside for casting.

The original model may be a ceramic article, one of cast metal, carved wood, glass, or cast plaster of Paris. Modeling clay of the kind that dries hard may also be used. The rubber is flexible, and can be pulled from a casting that would require two or more pieces if made in plaster of Paris.

Whatever the model, it must be thoroughly cleaned and dried. Metal must be free from tarnish, polished and washed. Wood models should be smooth finished and lacquered, then sanded again and polished with a fine abrasive. All sanded particles or dust should be removed. Glass models need only to be clean and dry.

Some commercial preparations consist of a thin facing rubber which is sprayed on or brushed on in two or three coats, each of which must dry 20 minutes to an hour before the next is applied. Then a plaster of Paris "backing" (prepared as plaster of Paris for molds) is spread with a spatula to build up a reinforcing coat. Fig. 331 shows such a one-piece plaster shell and rubber mold for a figurine.

A plaster of Paris shell can also be made by the two-piece or split mold technique, that is, half is poured around a clay half of the model in an enclosure and when formed has small round holes drilled or bored at rim points. The clay half is removed and then the second half of the mold poured against the first one. The holes become cone shaped points or "joggles" which later permit the halves to be fitted exactly together in the supporting mold.

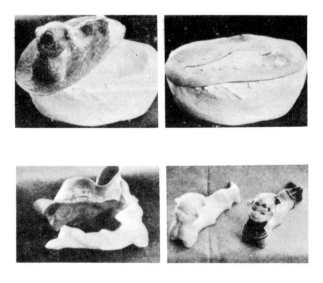

Fig. 331

The first type of brushed on rubber and plaster of Paris mold is necessarily broken open for removal. The second rubber coated type is easily removed intact, so it is reusable.

The process of casting a hollow figurine or a hollow form which may be designed to hold a light or an embedded ornament (in which case clear plastic resin would be used) is called "slush molding." The steps follow:

1. Provide a small opening in the rubber mold and the supporting plaster cast, for the pouring of the liquid plastic. Hold them firmly together with rubber bands. Rinse out the inside of the mold with a mold release prepared for the kind of plastic resin to be used. Thoroughly coat the interior surface and wait for the mold release to dry before pouring the plastic.

2. Carefully pour the estimated quantity of plastic into a paper cup, then add the amount of hardener or catalyst recommended by the manufacturer of the plastic and mix thoroughly with glass stirring rod. Protect clothing and table top. Wear rubber gloves and *DO NOT INHALE* fumes from the catalyst. Adequate ventilation is essential.

3. Pour the mixture into the mold and rotate it slowly to build up a complete coating ⅛ to 3/16 inch thick. Continue rotating until the plastic begins to set, about twenty minutes or longer, depending on the amount of catalyst used and the temperature of the room — at least 70 degrees is desirable. In a few minutes after it begins to set, the plastic will become rigid.

4. When this solidification is complete, remove both the plaster mold and the rubber inner mold. This can be peeled off like a leather glove turned wrong side out. At this point a limited amount of tool finishing or carving can be done.

5. Put the casting in the regulated oven of an electric stove at 140 degrees and leave for two to five hours, unless a type of liquid plastic is being used which will harden more quickly. The manufacturer's directions will specify.

The colorless liquid plastic may be cast clear in other types of molds with almost any desired object embedded in it or tinted with special pigments. Marble effects can be obtained by mixing the desired colors in two separate quantities of plastic, then combining just before pouring.

Plastics and fiber glass

In industry, specially prepared types of sheet and liquid plastic are replacing natural materials for many purposes. When reinforced or laminated with Fiber glass, cast plastic parts have strength and durability and are also resistant to stains and abrasions. An increasing number of household items, including screens, chairs and tables are made with laminated plastics in combination with wood or other materials.

Several manufacturers, such as the Castolite Company, supply prepared plastic and Fiber glass in mats and cloth for numerous hand-built projects, together with detailed instructions. Since this information is adequately presented by them, it is not covered here.

Assembly methods

Perforations in thin plastic sheets may be punched with a leather punch, either the revolving type or a single drive punch used with a mallet on an end grained piece of wood. Hand twist drills will be required for heavier sheets, with the plastic form or sheet against a block of wood.

Carefully mark the position of the hole with a pin or awl and avoid any slipping of the drill point. Drill from the front or face of the plastic piece and operate slowly to prevent heating. Remove the rough margin of the underside with an emery board or fine sandpaper over a round stick. Take care not to make scratches on the surface.

Bore large holes such as are required for the electrical fittings in making a lamp base, with a carpenter's auger and bit. First drill a pilot hole with a smaller hand drill. Such holes can be reamed smooth with a piece of emery cloth wrapped around a dowel pin.

Bending plastic forms

Bookends and desk set articles, Fig. 327, require bending, which can be done as shown in Fig. 332 by immersion in water about 200 degrees F. Some kinds of thermoplastic resins can be bent by hand after heating until flexible. Wear clean canvas gloves wrong side out to protect hands and prevent scratches or finger prints on the plastic.

Wooden forms or jigs, Fig. 332, are made for bending different shapes. A strip of plastic, when warm, can be bent into a curve with hand pressure around a wooden mandrel or a glass jar.

Small trays can be formed with rims by pressing a heated plastic disc into a wooden mold or another tray of similar size. Twisting of rods or flat strips is accomplished by gripping one end in a vise and twisting the other end with pliers.

In *each process the section of plastic article which is to be bent must be softened at intervals in hot water. Caution:* The plastic will crack easily if not sufficiently heated, or if it begins to cool before the bending is done.

1. Bend straight angles, such as the bookends over the square edge of a woodblock or table, protected with a cloth or a piece of thin plastic to prevent scratching the plastic. Press with two smooth woodblocks, one held over the part on the table and the other to press downward against the unsupported portion of the piece. When the desired angle is bent, do not remove pressure until the plastic cools. Bending by the hot water method is not recommended for plastic pieces which are more than 3/16 inches in thickness as sharp angles may break in the process.

2. A specially made strip heater with a coiled electrical element such as are used in irons and other appliances can be constructed for concentrating the heat along the line or portion to be bent. The materials can usually be obtained from an electrical appliance repair shop. The oven of a thermostatic controlled electric range can be used, *with careful watching,* to avoid overheating. Suspend the article to be heated from the oven rack or place on an asbestos sheet. The temperature should be held between 200 to 300 degrees F.

Bending bookends by the hot water process

1. Set the plastic forms in the clamp with the edge against the metal stop

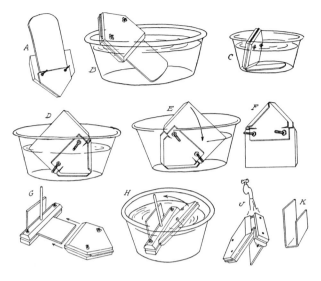

Fig. 332

on the lower part of the clamp, as shown in Fig. 332, sketch A, with the upper half of the clamp removed. Sketch B shows the upper half of the clamp attached and held with set screws.

2. Place the plastic within the clamp in hot (near boiling) water. As soon as the plastic softens, press on the clamp to force the plastic against the bottom of the pan and bend it to the required angle, as in sketch C. Immerse in cold water to chill and set the shape before removing the clamp.

Bending an envelope holder. This process is shown in Fig. 332, sketches G, H, J, and K. Make the first bend as directed above for the bookend. Set the bent piece in the position shown, sketch G for clamp number 2. Attach clamp 1 as indicated and place in the hot water, sketch H. Press clamp 2 firmly against the pan, while moving clamp 1 into a vertical position. Chill the shaped piece in cold water, then remove the clamps. Sketch K shows the finished piece.

Bending blotter corners, sketches D, E and F. Remove the upper part of the clamp, No. 1, and place the plastic piece for a corner beneath the metal plate as in sketch D. Immerse the clamp in hot water and fold the piece of plastic over the edge of the metal by rotating the clamp and pressing the margin against the bottom of the pan.

Sketch F shows one edge of the blotter corner bent over the edge of the metal. Repeat the process for the other edge. Attach the top half of the clamp and press the turned edges in between the upper and lower parts of the clamp. Place the clamped piece again in the hot water until the softened plastic can be bent closely over the metal edge and between the clamps by pressure on the bottom of the pan. Tighten the clamps and set the fold in cold water.

Carving and engraving plastics

The cast resin plastics of the thermosetting type are ideal substances for carving, either by hand or with power lathe tools. Many craftsmen are of the opinion that forms and figures, sculptured from solid blocks or slabs of plastic, may be finished to as near perfection with less effort than is required for any other carving material. Some types of the thermoplastic resins which are suitable for carving and engraving are now available also. Consult a supplier about them.

Many plastics can be carved with very simple tools, but wood carving tools are not recommended. Worn triangular files, ground to a square end or in the shape of a V or U, are the most satisfactory for surface carving. For figures or three dimensional forms, do the preliminary shaping on a lathe and carve the details of the design with the file tools, or with "die sinking" tools such as are used by die makers.

The finishing of carved backgrounds and surfaces in plastic carving is done with a kind of stick abrasive called a "carborundum pencil" also with files and with wood sticks wrapped with emery cloth. If available, an electric hand grinder of the vibro type will expedite this work, unless the individual preference is the completion of the article by hand.

Polish with any of the recommended polishes for plastic.

Tools for the detail carving are mounted in short handles with a broad top like an engraver's tool handle, Fig. 333, sketch G, so that pressure from the base of the thumb rather than the fingers, can be exerted to push the tool. It is guided by the fingers, and the material to be removed is gouged out in shallow cuts. The left hand holds the form in position or rotates it as required. The gouge cuts indicated in Fig. 333 by G 1 and the H and J series of sketches, outline or start the margins or areas to be removed by the square cut file or a shallow U shaped gouge.

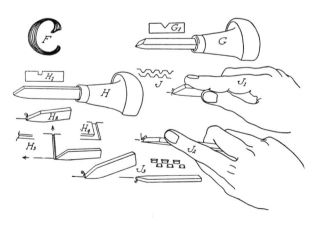

Fig. 333

Fig. 334

Fig. 335

The G and H cuts shown in Fig. 333 are also used in design engraving (see alphabets Fig. 334 and monograms) on flat metal and plastic surfaces. A type of tool called a "wiggle engraver" is an adapted metal engraver developed to cut outlines and design lines 1/16 and 3/32 inch wide. The use of this tool for metal engraving is described in Fig. 211 on page 239.

A form of engraving on plastics is called internal engraving as it is done on the underside of a form or mold of transparent plastic. The optical aspect of the light refraction gives a depth and relief effect which has the appearance of an embedded figure.

Engraved plastic etching plates

Transparent sheet plastic of ⅛ to 3/16 inch thickness will make an etching plate to produce prints closely resembling copperplate etchings. The method of preparing a plastic plate is a much simpler process than drypoint etching or engraving on metal, although the technique is somewhat similar.

An incising tool or graver may be readily made from a crochet needle or from a bicycle spoke, Fig. 336, sketches A, B, C. Anneal or soften the end of the needle or spoke by heating it to a bright red and allowing it to cool slowly. Then bend the tip at right angles, sketch B, and bevel the end to a triangular point on a coarse emery stone or grinder, sketches B and C. Finish the edge on a fine stone. Temper or harden the tool by reheating to a bright red, and cool quickly by plunging it into water.

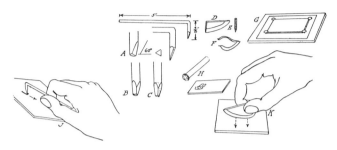

Fig. 336

The scraper may be made from a 1 inch flat file ground to the shape indicated and sharpened on both sides of the blade, Fig. 336, sketches D, E and F.

1. Place the drawing or design tracing upon a piece of blotting paper, cover with the plastic and attach to the drawing board, sketch G. It is desirable to test the tools and practice the cutting operation on a scrap piece of plastic before undertaking the graving of the plate. Control of position and movement, and the required degree of pressure for heavy and fine lines should be determined.

2. Incise the design outline with the graving tool, removing a small shaving of plastic as indicated. Fig. 333, sketch J, shows the correct position of the graving tool and the direction of motion. A clean cut groove should be produced. Sharpen the graver frequently on a fine oil stone or razor hone. Turn the board as required to obtain the proper position for cutting all lines with a pulled or drawn stroke of the incising tools which must be kept vertical at all times. Inspect the grooves for width and depth. This is facilitated by rubbing engraver's chalk (Magnesia) into them so that the exact depth and margins are clearly shown as in the finished print.

3. Develop the background to produce the effect of sky, clouds, foliage, highlights, and shadows with the scraper. Hold the tool as shown in sketch K with the cutting edge at right angles to the surface. A light stroke makes a light tone. Variations in directions and pressure produce the desired contrasts. Test with chalk as the engraving process progresses.

Sandpaper may also be used for producing contrasts. For small areas attach a piece of No. 00 sandpaper to the end of a stick with sealing wax or cement, sketch H. Apply to the plastic with a rotating motion. Large areas may be hand rubbed with pieces of sandpaper.

4. The scraped surface or one roughened with sandpaper can be burnished by rubbing over it a highly polished metal surface, such as a leather modeling tool or metal burnisher. A chamois covered stick rubbed over the etched surface will produce a still softer tone.

5. Remove the sheet plastic from the board and trim it down to the desired size. Wash out the chalk with warm water and a soft brush.

Inking the plate

The application of ink to the etched plate involves not only filling the grooves with ink but the removal of any excess which may adhere to the surface of the plate between the etched lines, Fig. 337, sketch A.

1. Squeeze a small amount of ink from the tube, place a few drops of thinner upon it and work it with a spatula to a uniform consistency on a glass plate. When the softened ink drops from the spatula and forms a mound that flattens out, it is of the proper consistency for use.

2. Make an ink applicator out of cheesecloth or gauze free from lint. Apply the ink to the plate with the pad, starting at one corner. Rub across the plate and back, slightly overlapping each stroke. Continue until the plate has been traversed over both length and breadth. Care must be taken not to wipe ink out of the grooves on the return stroke, sketch B.

3. Remove any ink which has spread across the surface of the plate with a clean cloth. Wipe the plate with a spiral motion beginning at the center without exerting sufficient pressure to remove ink from the grooves. Repeat the process until the cloth appears clean after rubbing the surface.

4. Inspect the inked surface to make sure all grooves are filled with ink. Test the surface afterward with the hand. Unfilled grooves should be refilled with ink rubbed in with the dauber or finger. In some subjects, highlights should be made more prominent by removing ink from the grooves with a soft cloth drawn snugly over the end of the finger or a pencil. Carefully inspect edges of the plate for surplus ink and remove with a cloth dampened in turpentine. Then wipe off all trace of the turpentine with a cloth dipped in gasoline.

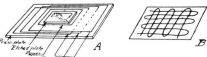

Fig. 337

Preparation of etch printing paper

Papers suitable for printing from etched plates come in varying degrees of smoothness or texture and may also be classified by the hot or cold process of manufacture. Secure the paper from local suppliers.

The paper should be soaked in water for about an hour before it is ready to use. Each sheet is removed from the water bath as needed and placed between two sheets of blotting paper or paper towels and squeezed or pressed with a roller to remove the excess water. The sheet is then ready to print.

Printing from an etched plastic plate

The etched sheet of plastic must be attached to a firm base before it can be printed. There are several methods of applying the pressure required to make clear prints. The screw type letter press is satisfactory since it provides a positive pressure control. Portable commercial presses are available which are ideal for the purpose. A hand roller, Fig. 338B, may also be used successfully.

Fig. 338

1. *Letter Press Method*

1. Apply a piece of bond paper to the sheet metal with household cement and permit it to dry. Mark on the paper the marginal position of both the etched plate and the print paper.

2. Attach the etched plastic plate to the sheet metal in the position indicated for it by the guide lines, using laundry soap as the adhesive. To apply the soap turn the etched plate face downward and rub the bar on the back. Reverse and place it in position on the metal sheet. Cover the etched surface with a piece of blotting paper and apply pressure with the hand to make the metal contact at all points. Wipe off any excess soap exuding from the edge with a damp cloth.

3. Attach two guide strips of plastic to the metal press plate as shown in Fig. 338A. These serve to properly position the paper upon the etched plate.

4. Place on the base plate of the press the following: several thicknesses of newspaper, the plywood board, a piece of blotting paper, the metal sheet with the plastic plate attached, then lay the etching paper over the inked plate. Cover with a few thicknesses of newspaper and apply pressure with the hand screw. Uniform close contact must be made and a few trials will determine the degree of pressure required. Inspect the first print for any inequalities in pressure or insufficient ink. If necessary, level the plate by adding newspaper under the plywood.

5. Remove the print and place between sheets of clean paper (paper towels) to dry. Add sufficient weight to hold the sheet flat but not enough to flatten the ink.

2. *Hand Roller Method*

Excellent results have been obtained in printing from etched plastic plates without a press. The printing paper is forced into contact with the inked plate by the pressure of a hand roller. A rubber covered roller, used in mounting photographs, a drawing board, a piece of sheet metal, galvanized iron about 20 gauge, will be needed.

1. Apply a piece of bond paper to the sheet metal with household cement and permit it to dry. Mark the position of the etched plate on the paper, allowing the same margin as desired on the finished print.

2. Nail the two wood cleats to the drawing board as indicated in Fig. 338C to serve as a stop for both the base plate and the printing paper.

3. Attach the etched plastic plate to the sheet metal using laundry soap as the adhesive. Apply as directed under Letter Press Method.

4. Place the metal plate with the plastic plate attached upon the drawing board and in contact with the cleats. Press three thumbtacks into the board to the position shown to hold the metal sheet in contact with the cleats.

5. Prepare the paper, and ink the plate as described on page 349. Place the etching paper over the metal plate in contact with the cleats and hold it with the hand.

6. Apply the hand roller along the margin of the etched plate with a gentle pressure. Roll each margin toward the cleat in the direction indicated, sketch B, so that the edge of printing paper is held in contact with the cleats. The lower margin of the paper is held firmly against the plate with the left hand during the rolling process.

The moist printing paper is somewhat translucent, and from the top or back of the print a color variation is observed between the inked and blank areas. This is a reliable index of the proper degree of inking and shows where additional pressure should be applied to bring the paper into contact with the ink so that the impression will be uniform. The ink does not come through the paper and when the print is dry this effect disappears.

7. Remove the print and place between sheets of clean paper towels to dry. Add sufficient weight to hold the sheets flat but not enough to flatten the ink.

Care of a plastic etching plate

Each time a print is made the ink is removed from the plate. It must then be re-inked or inked again before another impression is taken. After the last print is made and before the ink is dry, remove all trace by wiping it with a cloth dipped in gasoline. Then wash with soap and warm water and dry with a soft cloth. Remove plate from the metal sheet by inserting a knife blade at one corner to loosen the plastic so that it may be lifted and peeled off. Wash with warm water to remove the soap.

If corrections to an etched plate are necessary, plastic solvent may be applied with a small brush to fill the grooves in the area to be altered.

CHAPTER **11**

Weaving

The weaving of protective coverings by primitive people, who learned to interlace vegetable and animal fibers, is a common heritage in all races. The preserved baskets and fragments of ancient textiles reveal a knowledge of the elements of weaving long before recorded history.

In the beginning, the weaving process was entirely a method of finger weaving, then a support was devised for the strands or threads which dangled freely at one end.

The primitive weaver tried attaching weights to these lengthwise threads and also tied them to his person. In some countries, this practice still exists. Finally, he learned to anchor the threads so that they were held in place, while he interwove the cross threads to make a fabric. When his ingenuity led to the construction of a loom is unknown, as is the distant period when he devised a frame for holding the lengthwise or warp threads taut, as well as the "lease" stick to prevent them entangling, while he interlaced the crosswise or weft threads to form a fabric.

Kinds of Weaving

Hand loom weaving is classified in two ways, pattern weave, in which the design plan is embodied in the lengthwise warp threads, and remains unchanged throughout the length of the warp, and design weave in which, colors, textures, and designs may be varied in the crosswise or weft threads.

The simple plain weave which is the foundation of most patterns and design weaves is sometimes called *"tabby" weave.* It is the oldest and most durable, as well as the most used of all weaves in which the warp and weft threads are equally spaced and interlaced in an even over one, under one pattern.

Fig. 339

352

The warp and weft may be of the same material as in monk's cloth or the linen weaves, also in the wool worsteds. Frequently, however, the warp threads are of a different material, as cotton with wool weft, rayon with linen and other combinations.

Many weaves are derived from the tabby weave by varying the threads or the colors of the weft, also by grouping the threads as they are interlaced. A basket weave of two by two, three by three, or even four by four, as in certain fine wool blankets is used for different kinds and colors of warp and weft. Thread is the common term regardless of the material for both warp and weft.

A tabby weave and its variations may be done on a two-harness loom.

A serge weave is a variation of plain or tabby weave with many patterns. For serge weave a four-harness loom is required. It is developed by grouping the weft and warp threads in an ascending or descending gradation. The weaves, known as twills and chevrons, are in turn variations of the serge weave. A and B in Fig. 339 are two variations of these. C is a design weave; D, border patterns.

The samples shown are: A, twill herringbone; B, hounds tooth; C, cats paw (also known as snails trail); D, borders.

The original interlacing of the warp thread was probably done by lifting each one singly, while the weft thread was being drawn through. Then it apparently became evident to the primitive weaver that a stick could be inserted to hold up every other one of the warp threads to open a space through which the weft thread could be passed. This space is now known as the shed.

Looms or frames for stretching the warp threads have evolved from the simple spacing of stretched threads or strands of limited length across two supports, to the intricate equipment of industrial weaving, yet the basic

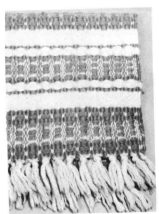

**Rug with Pattern in Weaving of Colored Weft Yarn.
Warp is Light Background.**

Fig. 340

principle of weaving remains unchanged. Looms on which most of the traditional patterns and design weaving can be done may be constructed or obtained from dealers in weaving supplies.

Embroidered Weaving is the term applied to the forming of a design in a plain weave by threading in different colors, usually a different material and texture than the plain weave background.

The design threads are wound on small shuttle sticks or bobbins for this embroidered weaving, and are woven in as the background is woven. Another term for this weft type of design weaving is the *"laid-in"* method. It is more frequently used for borders or corners in linen lunch sets and similar articles in which a contrasting color "laid-in" adds the decorative note as in Fig. 343. The designs in Fig. 343 are typical of Mexican or South American embroidered weaving, used for garments as well as household items.

Brocade weaving is a weave in which the weft threads, of contrasting color and material, are drawn through to form a design on the front, but skip along the back from the area of one design to another. This type of weaving is the method by which the weavers of Mexico and Central America make the beautiful blouses and skirts which typify their sections of the country. This is similar to the decorative weaving of Switzerland and Eastern European countries.

A variation of this brocade weaving is possible by warping the loom with widths of colored threads of a material different from the background or the weft weave. Threads are skipped in a border design shown in Figs. 341 and 342, which shows a single design, front and reverse. The weaving detail for this design element is shown in Fig. 341.

Tapestry types of weaving designs in a fabric are most commonly understood to mean a material in which scenes appear. Laid-in weaves in which the color, carried by bobbins, is woven within a color area to form a design or figure is often called tapestry weaving. The professional weaver uses the term "tapestry" to apply only to a fabric that has the warp completely covered within design areas.

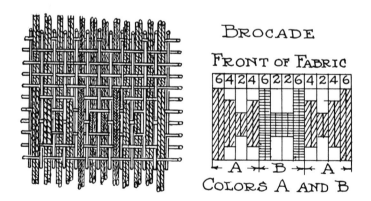

BROCADE

FRONT OF FABRIC

| 6 | 4 | 2 | 4 | 6 | 2 | 2 | 6 | 4 | 2 | 4 | 6 |

← A →|← B →|← A →

COLORS A AND B

Fig. 341

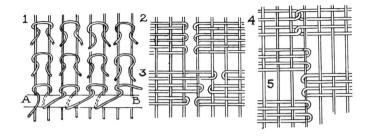

Fig. 342

When variety in weaving was sought, horizontal or vertical stripes of contrasting color were mixed with the warp or weft. Plaids were later woven by interchanging both warp and weft with other colors. A modern development for decorative fabrics is the use in either warp or weft of metallic, plastic, and other synthetic threads.

A distinguishing feature of tapestry is the way in which the meeting of adjacent colors in the vertical parts of the design form slits, which are sometimes left open, and sometimes joined on the back with a buttonhole stitch, after the rest of the tapestry is finished. Another way of connecting the design areas is by interlocking the wefts over and between a warp thread. Sketches 2, 3, 4 and 5 in Fig. 342 show weft detail in tapestry weaving.

Primitive weavers in many areas have developed similar types of weaving design, which is basically a finger weaving technique. The Navajo type, as will be described later, is the best known example in this country. The so-called peasant weaving, as it identifies national costumes in some countries, as well as the famous tapestries woven to decorate the walls of medieval castles, use a similar technique.

Pile types of weaving are those in which loops of the weft threads are brought up to the front in tufts or uncut loops over a bar, as well as those in which the weft is tied in close knots around the warp threads, over a bar or spacer, where the loop is cut. When compressed closely together with the batten, the tufts of the cut loops appear as a pile. This method is used in weaving Oriental rugs.

Embroidered cotton scarf with Guatemalan designs

Different developments of the same design are shown on the ends of the scarf with the same border design above the fringe. Either A or B may be considered the front, as both are finished without visible differences in the embroidery. The center sections, C and D, are embroidered with designs typical of Central America and Mexico. Examples of these are shown in Fig. 343.

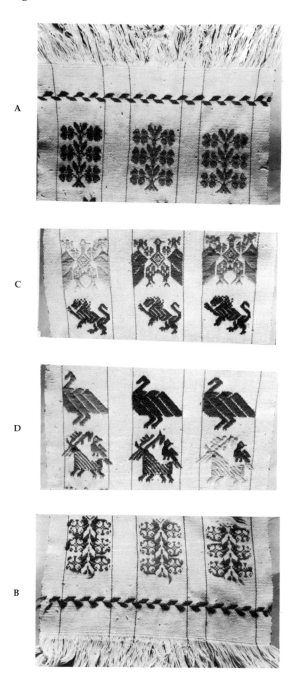

Fig. 343

A portable loom

The loom, Fig. 344 and 345, embodies the essential features of a typical bench or hand power loom. It is designed to fold up into a space within the bed or frame which supports the cloth and warp beams, and will weave fabrics up to 30 inches wide.

Fig. 344 shows the open and closed loom as folded into the body of the frame. This is easily done by first rolling all the fabric on the cloth beam, then loosening the ratchets to relax the tension on the warp sufficiently to permit the reed and heddles to assume a folded position within the loom bed.

Loom C is equipped with folding runners which permit its use by a bed patient. It is "dressed" or threaded and ready for weaving.

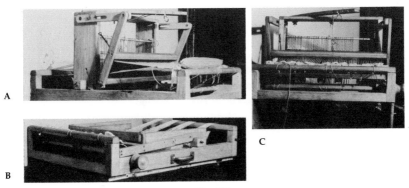

A

B

C

Fig. 344

Portable Loom Specifications

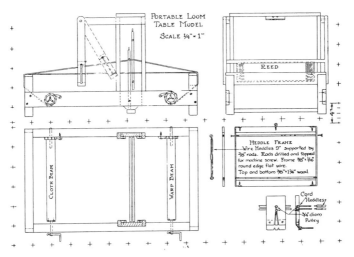

Fig. 345

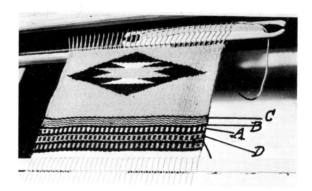

Fig. 346

Weaving plain cloth on the simplified portable loom is accomplished by passing the shuttle stick containing the weft yarn or thread through each warp shed. The blanket in Fig. 346 shows a border pattern in which A indicates a plain stripe in solid color, produced with one shuttle stick. B is a stripe produced by using two weft colors and two shuttle sticks with which each color is passed through alternate sheds. C is a variation of this weave in which the color arrangement is reversed and this will produce a twill effect.

D is a stripe design produced by using two shuttle sticks with different colors. Each weft color is passed through one shed and back through the opposite shed before the second color is passed in the same manner. The double passage of each shuttle stick forms a narrow stripe two weft strands wide.

The threading details for the portable loom are shown in Fig. 347. Sketch 6 shows the cord mechanism used to attach the warp to the cloth beam. Two holes are drilled near the ends of the rod to which the warp is tied and four holes are drilled in the cloth beam. Pass the attachment cord over the center of the rod. Carry each end over the breast beam and through the inside holes in the cloth beam, then along the cloth beam through the outside holes, again over the breast beam and through the holes in each end of the rod. Tie a knot in each end of the cord and adjust the cord through the holes until the rod is parallel to the cloth beam. Place tension on the warp by rotating the cloth beam which is secured by the ratchet and pawl shown in sketch 6. The cord winds up on the cloth beam as indicated in Fig. 347, sketch 6.

Dressing the loom, using a spooled warp

The procedure outlined is for weaving plain cloth.

Place the required number of warp spools on the hexagonal rod, shown in Fig. 347, sketch 1. The arrows showing the direction the warp is wound on each spool should point upward. Allow at least two extra warp threads at each edge selvage for reinforcement.

Break the gummed tape seal on the first spool and unwind one turn of the warp. Attach the band of warp ends to a small block of wood with gummed tape as indicated in Sketch 1. Unwind enough warp to reach over the harness as indicated in sketch 2. About four turns should suffice.

Separate the warp threads from the strand one at a time, taking the right hand thread off the block held in the left hand as indicated in sketch 2. Reach over the harness and hold the thread taut as indicated in sketch 3.

Pass the hook, Fig. 347, sketch 3 through the first heddle wire and draw it through the heddle as indicated by sketches. Repeat this for each spool of warp thread. In case a double thread is used on the selvage two threads will be drawn through the outside heddle wires in each harness. See Fig. 347, sketch 4. This operation is called *threading the heddles.*

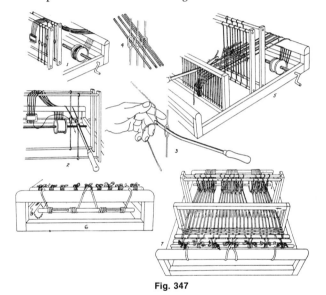

Fig. 347

This hitch may be used with a harness to a treadle. Here a rope is suspended below the harness and the treadle is attached to its center point.

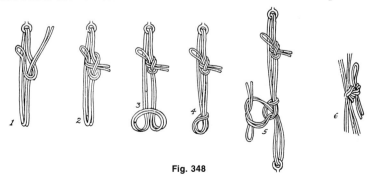

Fig. 348

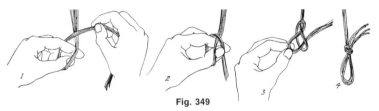

Fig. 349

Place the reed in a vertical position and with the hook passed through each dent, Fig. 347, sketch 5, draw each warp thread in its turn through the proper dent. *This process is called sleying the reed.* After a group of 10 to 15 warp threads have been sleyed, tie a knot in the free ends of the entire group as indicated in Fig. 349, sketches 1 to 4. This slip knot is readily untied and serves temporarily to keep the bundle of warp threads from accidentally passing back through the reed.

Repeat the sleying process until all warp threads and both selvages are carried through the reed.

Untie the knot in the center bundle of warp and divide it into two bundles approximately equal in size, and carry each half bundle of warp around the stick as indicated in sketch 5. A special knot is used which keeps tension on the warp while it is being tied. It may be untied readily and retied in case the tension in any bundle of warp requires adjustment. The method of holding the warp while typing this knot is developed in sketches 6 to 15.

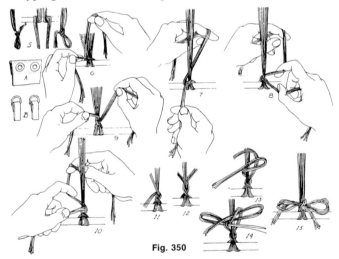

Fig. 350

Attach the warp to the cloth beam. Several devices are used. Sometimes a piece of canvas known as an apron is attached to the warp beam with tacks and the free end is carried to and around the breast beam. In the edge of the canvas, Fig. 350, sketch A, a row of holes or metal eyelets is placed. Each bundle of warp is passed through a hole, and tied to the canvas. Sometimes dees are sewed to a canvas apron instead of using eyelets.

Fig. 347, sketch 7 shows the appearance of the "dressed" loom. The warp has been carried over the spreader beam from the warp spools, through the heddle wires in the harnesses, and through the reed. Just back of the rod to which the warp is attached, two thin wooden slats are shown, one in each shed. Just back of these slats five strands of coarse yarn have been placed in alternate sheds. The purpose of these wooden slats and heavy yarn is to distribute the warp threads and make them equidistant, corresponding to the spacing controlled by the dents in the reed. Also the yarn serves as a pad, cushioning the blow of the reed. To remove the woven fabric from the loom cut the warp in front of the wooden slats. Remove the slats, heavy yarn, and tie an overhand knot in a strand or bundle of four warp threads. Slip the knot up against the weft drawing it taut.

Repairing a warp break

In case a warp thread should break, a method of making the repair is shown in Fig. 351, sketches 8, 9, and 10. Tie a piece of warp thread to the end of the warp which passes through the heddles and reed. Wrap a few turns of this thread around a needle or pin, draw the warp taut between the two adjacent warp threads, and fasten the needle to the fabric as shown in sketch 8. Proceed with the weaving as indicated in sketch 9. Later remove the pin or needle.

Loose ends of weft may be concealed as shown in sketches 11 and 12 by carrying them under a few strands of weft with a needle paralleling a warp thread.

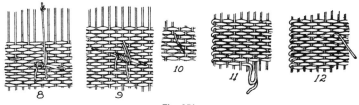

Fig. 351

Warp terminals

A typical warp terminal is made by tying an overhand knot in bunches of warp threads (3 to 5) as shown in Fig. 352, sketch A. A better terminal, which reinforces the edge, also made with an overhand knot, is shown loosely formed in sketch B and drawn down against the fabric in sketch C.

Fig. 352

The two harness loom

Fig. 353 shows the several parts which comprise the simplest form of loom; namely the two harness counter-balanced, two treadle type—designed at first for the weaving of plain and striped cloth, then for the basic plain weave, on which tapestry and brocade weaving designs were added.

Warping and weaving process for two-harness loom

1. Stretch four warp threads, 1-2, 1-2, between supports BB (breast beam) and SB (spreader beam) as indicated in Fig. 353, sketch SL-1. Number these from right to left with respect to the position of the weaver, which would be at the left end of the loom illustrated.

2. The two harnesses used in the loom are indicated by numbers H1 and H2 in the sketch SL-1. These make the "shed" by separating the warp threads to permit the passage of the weft thread, as indicated in sketches SL-2 and SL-3.

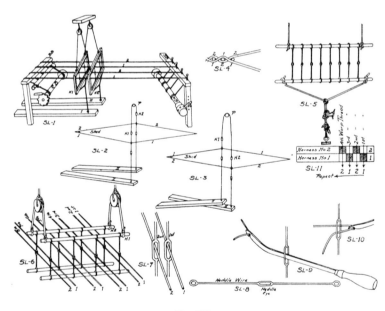

Fig. 353

Attach a dowel rod to the warp beam with strong cord, Fig. 353, sketch SL-1, and attach each bundle of warp to this rod, as described on page 360.

The tie-up of the treadles indicated in Fig. 353, sketch SL-5 has the merit of being adjusted easily and holding fast after it is tied.

3. Press the treadle with the foot to operate the harness, and form one shed as indicated in sketch SL-2, then the opposite shed as indicated in SL-3 in which harness H1 is pulled down as treadle number 1 is pressed down, sketch SL-2. This is controlled by the rope, which is attached to the top of the harness H1 and H2 and passes over pulley P, to lift harness H2 from the balanced position shown in SL-1.

4. Note that each harness, H1 and H2, is made up of a number of heddles (string or wire), which have a loop or eye in the center, sketch SL-8, also a loop for mounting the heddle between the sticks of the harness frame, sketch SL-5. This assembly or harness permits the individual heddles to be moved freely along the end supports.

5. *The warping arrangement* required to produce the two sheds shown in sketches SL-2 and SL-3 is indicated in sketches SL-6 and SL-7 and the steps are as follows:

   a. Pass each warp thread through heddle wires as indicated in sketch SL-7. As in sketch SL-6, pass the first warp thread on the right (no. 1) through the first heddle, mounted in harness H1.

   b. Pass the second warp thread SL-6 through the heddle mounted in harness H2.

   c. Pass the third warp thread through the second heddle in harness H1, and the fourth warp thread through the second heddle in harness H2.

6. The process of passing the warp thread through heddles is known as "threading the heddles," using a threader as shown in sketch SL-9.

   a. Insert the threader through the heddle eye and slip it over the warp thread, then pull it back through the heddle, carrying the warp with it as indicated by sketch SL-10.

7. Usually a pattern known as a threading draft is used to guide the weaver in warping the loom. In sketch SL-11 the method of expressing graphically the threading procedure described above is indicated. The two horizontal bands indicated by numbers 1 and 2 represent harnesses H1 and H2. The black squares in each band represent heddles, their position indicating the heddles in each harness. This form of notation is interpreted as follows:

   a. Pass all four warp threads through both harnesses from back to front of the loom in the direction of the arrow, sketch SL-11:

   The first warp thread through the eye of heddle number 1, harness H1.

   The second warp thread through the eye of heddle number 1, harness H2.

   The third warp thread through the eye of heddle number 2, harness H1.

   The fourth warp thread through the eye of heddle number 2, harness H2.

   b. Repeat this procedure as indicated in the draft, by extending the bands and filling the black squares, progressing to the left.

8. As in sketch SL-1, thread the four warp threads through the heddles in

the harnesses H1 and H2. The arrangement of the ropes which attach the treadles to the lower frame of each harness is shown in sketch SL-5.

9. Step on treadle number 1 as in sketch SL-2 to shift the harnesses H1 and H2 from their original position. So long as weight is applied to the treadle the harnesses will remain in the position shown in sketch SL-2. Note that the number 1 warp thread is down and the number 2 warp thread is up with the passage of the warp thread indicated in the shed, sketch SL-2.

10. Change the shed by pressing down treadle II as indicated by sketch SL-3, to shift the number 2 warp thread down and the number 1 warp thread up. Sketch SL-4 indicates the position of the weft thread through the two sheds. Number the warp threads to show the position with respect to the weft, with the number 1 warp thread below the weft in the first shed and above it in the second shed.

All the warp threads numbered 1 in the draft are controlled by the treadle number I since they are operated as a single thread by means of the harness. Likewise treadle number II controls all number 2 threads.

The process for weaving double width cloth can be reduced to the more tangible form of the draft as in Fig. 354. The loom set-up is essentially the same as the Spanish Colonial type described on page 387. A second set of two treadles, two harnesses (counter-balanced), are added to the two harness loom SD-1, Fig. 353. These harnesses are mounted behind the original set and the additional treadles are placed on the left of the first pair. They number from right to left, and are directly connected to the corresponding harnesses.

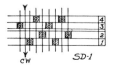

Fig. 354

The draft for double width cloth is as follows:

1. As in sketch SD-1, which indicates the threading draft, pass the first warp thread between the heddles in number 4-3-1 harnesses and then through the heddle in number 2 harness. Pass the second warp thread through the heddle in number 4 harness, also between the heddles of the 3-2-1 harnesses.

2. Pass the third warp thread between the heddles of the 4-3-2 harnesses and the heddle in number 1 harness. Pass the fourth warp thread through the heddle in number 3 harness and between heddles in 4-2-1 harnesses. Repeat this manner of threading for the width of the loom in the order of harnesses 2-4-1-3. Pass an extra warp thread between the heddles of all four harnesses and between the last two warp threads numbers 1 and 3. See extreme left of treadling draft, SD-1. This floating warp thread, although it is in the fold at the left hand edge of the double weave fabric, becomes the center weave in the finished cloth.

3. The treadling draft:
   a. Press down on treadle number 4. This forms a 3-4 shed (all of the number 3 warp threads are down). Pass the shuttle from right to left and carry it over the center warp to the left as indicated in the shuttle diagram, SD-2. This floating or center warp is marked C.W.
   b. Press treadle number 1. This forms a 1-2 shed (all number 1 warp threads are down), that is the number 1 threads are on the bottom of the shed. Pass the shuttle to the left, carry it over the center warp, C.W. as indicated in the shuttle diagram, SD-2.
   c. Press treadle number 2. This forms a shed (all number 2 warp threads are down). Pass the shuttle to the left, carry it over the C.W. as indicated in the shuttle diagram, SD-2.
   d. Press treadle number 3. This forms a 3-4 shed (all of the number 3 warp threads are down). Pass the shuttle to the right. Repeat this treadling process and shuttle passing in the order given, 4-1-2-3, and include the floating warp thread each time it is encountered.

The four harness loom

By the addition of two more harnesses and four more treadles, a two harness loom may be converted into a standard four harness type as indicated in Fig. 355. Sketch 1 shows the detail of the two harness loom with the two heddles counter-balanced and suspended with a rope over a roller. Sketch 2 shows the detail of the converted loom with the four harnesses.

Two rollers are suspended from the top roller and from each of these, two harnesses are balanced against each other and suspended by a rope attached to eyes screwed into the top of the harnesses.

Sketch 3 shows a method of attaching the treadles to the harnesses. An intermediate lever or lam is mounted directly below each harness. These lams are attached to the loom by a loose pin of metal, as detailed in Sketch 2. Six screw eyes are placed on the lower side of each lam, spaced directly over each of the treadles to which they are attached.

Plain cloth, sometimes called "tabby" may be woven with two of the treadles, just as on a two harness loom. The six treadles of the four harness loom are used to produce patterns which are woven according to the design draft. The draft indicates the detailed arrangement of the warp threads, or threading, also the method of attaching the treadles to the lams, which is called the tie-up.

The draft also specifies the order in which the treadles are to be depressed, the process called treadling. The threading process, in which a hook is used to pull the warp thread through the eye of a heddle wire, is shown in Fig. 347, sketch 3, on page 359. For a weaving pattern the draft is developed as indicated in Fig. 356, sketch 3. The harnesses are represented by the four lines 1-2-3-4 in sketch 2.

The number of repetitions required are designated in the draft. A simplification in the draft is shown in sketch 3, where the four harnesses are represented by four spaces on cross ruled paper. The X marks shown in the vertical spaces represent the heddle threading for each warp thread.

A wide variety of pattern drafts are available in weaving references listed at the end of this chapter.

Tying up the treadles for the order, specified in the draft, in which the weft is to pass across the warp establishes the pattern which is followed in the weaving and the treadling. In Fig. 355, sketch 3, a method of mounting the treadles is indicated. The dowel rod which passes through the four lams, Fig. 355, preserves the spacing of the treadles, each of which is attached to any one of the four harnesses according to the draft specifications.

The Four Harness Loom

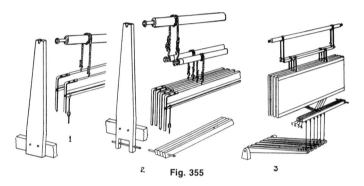

Fig. 355

The threading process, in which a hook is used to pull the warp thread through the eye of a heddle wire, is shown in Fig. 347, sketch 3.

To preserve the alignment in ropes, four points of attachment are indicated on each treadle with screw eyes as shown in Fig. 355, sketch 3. Holes drilled in the treadles are sometimes used instead of screw eyes.

Directly above the treadles and in the lower edge of each of the four lams, the six matching screw eyes are shown. The detail for the adjustable knot used to attach the ropes to the lams is shown in Fig. 348, sketches 1 to 5. The adjustable attachment of the cord to the treadle is also shown in Fig. 348, sketch 5.

Note that each thread from the warp beam passes forward through all four harnesses. It is threaded through the eye of one heddle wire, then drawn through a dent or space in the reed, and finally attached to the cloth beam.

The warp threads (ends as they are called by weavers) go *between* heddle wires in three harnesses and *through* the heddle eye of one harness. The threading of a heddle eye is indicated by an X mark. In the threading draft indicated in Fig. 356, sketch 1, the right hand warp thread, marked end number 1, passes through the eye of the heddle wire mounted in harness number 1. Similarly warp end number 2 goes through a heddle, of harness number 2, end number 3 through a heddle of harness number 3, and the fourth end through a heddle of harness number 4. The first unit of the threading process is completed at this point.

The structure of fabrics depends on the relative position of the warp and weft. In the weaver's terms a weft thread passing in front of a warp is identified as a "read" and when it passes back of a warp it is called an "unread." This terminology seems inadequate, but the significance is definite and in agreement with the draft, which indicates the reads by solid black or blacked out squares and the unreads by white or blank squares.

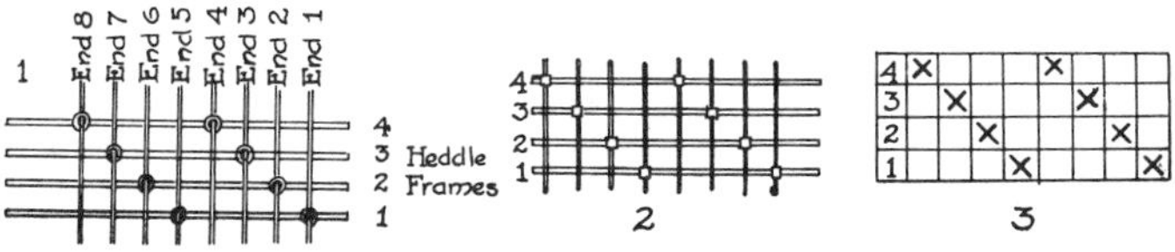
1
End 8
End 7
End 6
End 5
End 4
End 3
End 2
End 1
4
3 Heddle
2 Frames
1
2
3

Fig. 356

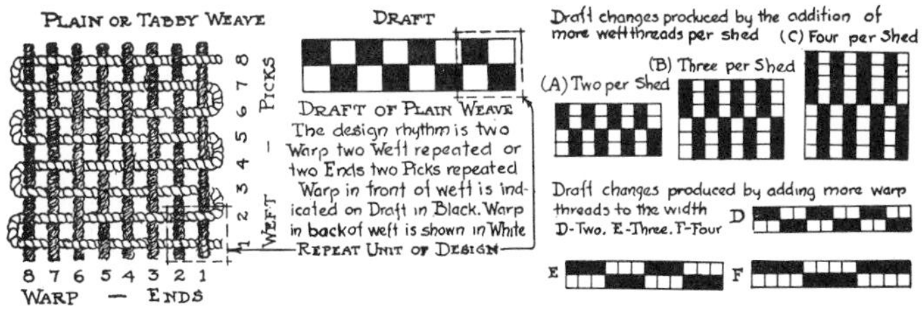
Plain or Tabby Weave
8 7 6 5 4 3 2 1
Warp — Ends
Weft — Picks
Draft
Draft of Plain Weave
The design rhythm is two Warp two Weft repeated or two Ends two Picks repeated
Warp in front of weft is indicated on Draft in Black. Warp in back of weft is shown in White
Repeat Unit of Design
Draft changes produced by the addition of more weft threads per shed
(A) Two per Shed
(B) Three per Shed
(C) Four per Shed
Draft changes produced by adding more warp threads to the width
D-Two. E-Three. F-Four
D
E
F

Fig. 357

Fig. 357 shows a plain woven structure made up of one each warp ends and weft threads or picks. The reads or points where the picks are in front of warp, as at points 2 in the sketch, are indicated by the black squares in the section of the draft and the unreads or points 1 are indicated by the blank squares. Variations of plain weave are shown in drafts A to F.

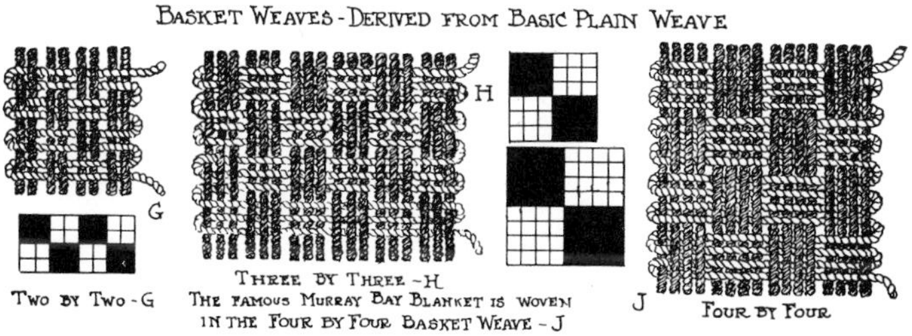
Basket Weaves - Derived from Basic Plain Weave
G
H
J
Two by Two - G
Three by Three - H
The famous Murray Bay Blanket is woven in the Four by Four Basket Weave - J
Four by Four

Fig. 358

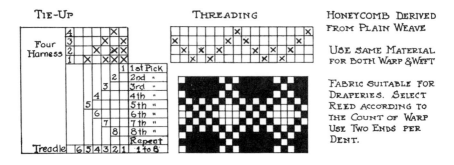

Fig. 359

Example draft of honeycomb weave

Eight warp threads are used in each unit of this pattern which repeats as indicated in Fig. 359. The specified threading is followed according to the draft: In the first step the first three warp threads or ends are drawn through the heddles of three harnesses in corresponding order, numbers 1-2-3-4 of both ends and heddles. In the following steps, ends 4-5 and 6 go through heddles 1-2 and 4 and then ends 7-8-9 and 10 through heddles 1-3-2 and 1 in the order shown in Fig. 359.

The tie-up of the treadles for the honeycomb pattern is also specified as indicated in Fig. 359.

Treadle 1 requires three cords each attached to harnesses 1-2-3.

Treadle 2 requires three cords each attached to harnesses 1-2-4.

Treadle 3 requires two cords each attached to harnesses 1-3.

Treadle 4 requires one cord — attached to harness 2.

Treadle 5 requires one cord — attached to harness 1.

The treadling is also specified in the draft. Treadle 1 is pressed and the shuttle passed through the shed which is controlled according to the tie-up. This operation is called a pick. The shed is changed by pressing treadle 2 and the shuttle passed to form pick number 2. In the same manner treadle number 3 is pressed and pick 3 formed. This operation is continued in the order indicated as 4-5-6-7-8, which produces the basic weave design. The repeat begins again with pick number 1 and continues to number 8 as before.

It is important to consider the principles of proportion and color relationships in planning the weaving pattern. The ratios of widths and the interplay of colors determine the pleasing or unpleasing appearance of the finished material. The weaver, after some experimentation with the possible combinations of colors and of warp and weft materials, will find new interest as well as unlimited suggestion and inspiration in the study of old textile patterns and their modern adaptations in the use of plastic and other synthetic filaments which have provided a new decorative medium.

A New England type coverlet, woven in the Revolutionary period. One half of the design and the enlarged section shows the intricate and meticulous development of the woven coverlet. This type of weaving, in which the colors and design elements are reversed from front to back, is called double weave or double web (weft). The coverlet illustrated is blue with white design on the front and white with blue on the back as in the enlarged section.

An interesting account of the coverlets, made many years ago and still treasured in the homes of the Southern Highlands, was written by Allan Eaton in his book, Handicrafts of the Southern Highlands. This is listed as a library reference, as it is now out of print.

Carding wool

The process of combing and straightening wool fibers preparatory to spinning is known as carding. The tools employed are known as hand cards. To make a medium or coarse yarn, the fleeces are pulled apart with the fingers (teased), and these fluffy masses twisted into yarn without further preliminary preparation. Some yarn is spun in the grease (as it is called before washing or scouring). In fact, yarn spins more readily in the grease than after the natural fat (lanoline) has been removed. It is a commercial practice to restore the necessary oil content to some grades of wool before it is spun. Other grades of wool contain so great an oil content that a portion of it must be removed before it may be readily spun.

Hand cards are available for both materials, cotton and wool. The manufacturer describes the construction of this equipment and makes recommendation for its care. "The wires are flexibly, but firmly set (in leather), uniformly and accurately pitched, and correctly pointed to prevent tearing and breaking of the individual fibers. For longest wear and most satisfactory results, shift cards top for bottom as you use them. Store them face to face away from moisture." A good practice is to keep a bit of oiled fleece between them when not in use. The process of carding follows:

1. Hold the loaded card in the left hand with the elbow on the left knee. The handle points away from the carder as indicated by Fig. 360, sketch 3. Take a small portion of the teased wool (wool fleeces pulled apart with the fingers) and spread it over the left hand card, sketch 1. The appearance of the loaded card is indicated in sketch 2.

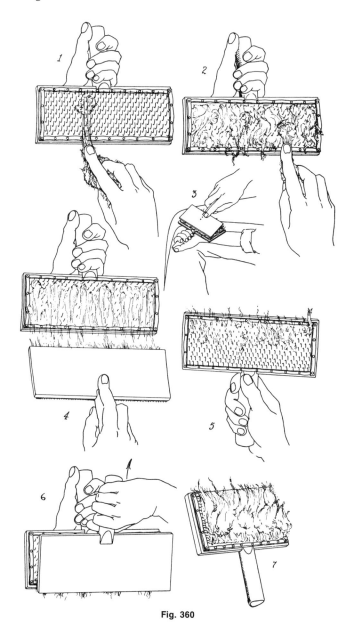

Fig. 360

2. Comb the loaded card by drawing the right hand card lightly over the left hand card as indicated in sketch 4. Repeat this combing several times. A portion of the fleece will then be found transferred to the right hand card as indicated in sketch 5.

3. Reload the left hand card. This is accomplished by drawing the left hand card across the right hand card as indicated in sketch 6. The appearance of the left hand card, after the transfer, is shown in sketch 7. This method is employed by the Indian weavers in the Southwest.

Repeat the combing and reloading twice more. This straightens the strands and the fleece is ready to be taken off.

4. Remove the carded wool and form a batt. The loaded card is held in the left hand, Fig. 361, sketch 8 (handle toward the person carding), and the right hand card is held in the position indicated by sketch 9. The wires in the lower edge of the right hand card are used to lift the wool fibers off the lower card. This is accomplished by merely drawing the upper card across the lower card with a motion indicated in sketch 9. A large, loosely formed batt may be produced by one stroke of the upper card. However, a more compact batt results when the wool is removed in a few short strokes as suggested by the arrows in sketch 9. Fig. 361, sketches 10 and 11 shows finished batt with top and bottom appearance as removed from the card. The next step is to spin the wool fibers as described on page 373.

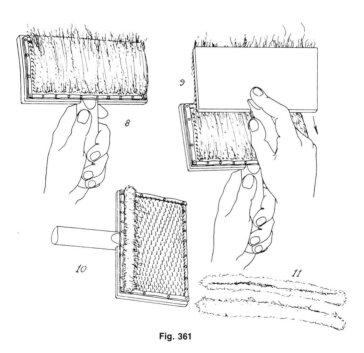

Fig. 361

Carding wool and angora goat hair

Some of the finest blankets are woven with a yarn containing a mixture of wool and Angora goat hair. The long fibers of the goat hair permit making a strong, coarse, loosely twisted yarn. The fabric woven with the large size single strand yarn is quite heavy, very soft, and possesses a lustrous silky texture. The method of carding a mixture preparatory to spinning is similar to the procedure described for wool. The process is shown in Fig. 360.

1. Load the card by placing both wool and goat hair on the card, and combing them together. The portion of the hair and wool mixture adhering to the right hand card is transferred to the left hand card, as indicated in Fig. 362, sketch 6. After the transfer is made, the left hand card has the appearance shown in sketch 7. This combing procedure should be repeated three or more times if necessary to straighten the fibers. Sketch 8 shows the appearance of the straightened fibers.

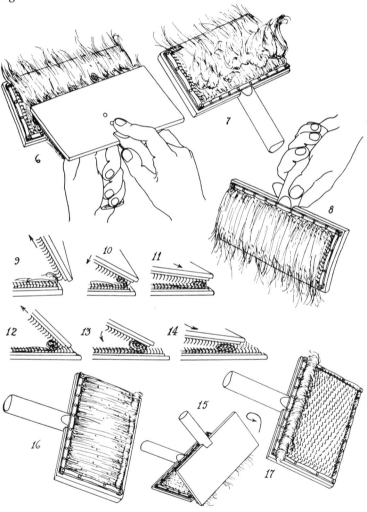

Fig. 362

2. Remove the card mixture as indicated in sketches 9 to 14. The long fibers extending over the edge of the lower card, are folded back upon the card as indicated in sketch 9. Downward pressure applied with the upper card is indicated by the arrow shown in sketch 10. The pressure is carried forward as indicated by the arrow in sketch 11, before removing the upper card. This downward and forward pressure compacts the fibers together preparatory to rolling the bast, the name applied to a roll of long fibered material.

Sketches 12 to 14 is a repetition of the process indicated in sketches 9 to 11. The process follows:

3. Lift the roll at the outer edge, and fold it over the straightened fibers held in the lower card.

4. Compress the roll by a downward and forward pressure applied with the upper card, as indicated by the arrow in sketch 15.

The appearance of the lower (left hand) card with the batt started is indicated by sketch 16, while 17 shows the tightly rolled mixture after the lower card has been cleared and just prior to removing the batt.

Spinning

The art of twisting fibers into threads is very old. Spun threads, remnant fabrics, and the tools used for spinning have been found over widely scattered areas, indicating that spinning and weaving were major activities of prehistoric man. The basic spinning mechanism, a weighted spindle or whorl, devised at that time, has been used for many centuries with only slight modification.

The implement employed in spinning, the weighted spindle or whorl, is selected for the particular kind of fibers to be spun. Fig. 363, sketch 1, represents the general type. Size and weight must be adjusted to suit the size and delicacy of the thread.

Flax and other long fibered batts are spun by drawing out bunched strands from a supply mounted on a support known as a distaff. This is held under the left arm of the spinner. Short fibered material, like wool, is spun from carded batts or rolls. The spinning process follows:

1. Attach a few strands of twisted fibers to the spindle as shown in Fig. 363, sketch 3. Rotate by rolling with the hand against the thigh, also twirling between the thumb and fingers of the right hand.

2. When the weight of the spindle is sustained by the strength of the thread, it is unnecessary to support the lower end. If support is required, the lower end of the spindle may rest in a concavity in the ground, Indian fashion, or in a fixed support.

3. Draw the fibers out into a strand of uniform diameter, using both hands to maintain the necessary tension. Twist the stretched fibers, until the desired strength and size are obtained.

4. Wind the twisted strand upon the spindle. Usually an arm's length of the twisted strand is sufficient. (A skillful spinner can make yarn of uniform size, strength, or fineness comparable to the best produced by modern machinery.)

5. When sufficient twist has entered the fibers drawn from the batt,

sketch 3, slip the right hand upward to the top of the newly made yarn. Give an outward twirl to the spindle to keep it whirling in mid-air. Pull more wool or other fibers, out of the batt, and by separating the hands, permit the twist to enter the strands as described above.

6. Repeat this step, causing the spindle, which will descend, to touch the ground. Then place the newly made length of yarn on the spindle above the whorl. The process follows:

   a. Remove the half hitch from the notch in the spindle and place it where it will remain stationary. Wrap the yarn around the thumb and the little finger of the left hand as indicated by Fig. 363, sketch 4.

   b. Grasp the spindle with the right hand and transfer the yarn (under tension) from the left hand to the cone of yarn on the spindle. The figure eight wrapping forms a satisfactory cone for accumulating the newly spun yarn. Repeat this process until the space on the spindle is filled. The appearance of the loaded spindle is shown in sketch 5.

   c. Unload the spindle by slipping the cone off. Place it on a stationary spindle as shown in sketch 6. In case the yarn cone does not come off the spindle readily, it may be removed by mounting the spindle with the yarn in supports, sketch 7. Wind the yarn directly on a spool, sketch 8.

The yarn produced on the spindle rotated clockwise as described will be a left hand twisted strand. It may be used for knitting or weaving fabrics as it comes from the spindle.

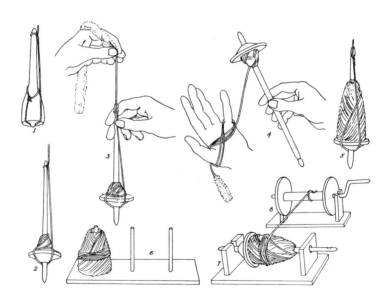

Fig. 363

CHAPTER 12

Woodwork

With your first wood carving underway, you will be more impressed than ever with this wonder of nature, the tree in which your block was formed. As you remember the years of its growth, you cannot but resolve to preserve, without waste, the piece of wood which your hands can transform.

Fig. 383

The art of wood carving has been one of man's first acquired skills, perfected so early in history that few records have been preserved. Relics, such as a recently excavated set of wood carver's tools, prove that even before metal for tools was used, wood was cut and decorated with tools of shell, bone and flint.

The Bible descriptions of the tabernacle of Moses and the temple of Solomon reveal the skill of the wood carvers of that time. Research in the records of the Holy Land at the time of the carpenter's apprentice, who was Jesus, "the man of Nazareth," indicate that he was a "carver of wood," a material so scarce in that land that it probably was not used for any other purpose.

A few existing examples in museums show that wood carving was a highly developed skill in the ancient Egyptian empire, two thousand and more years B.C. In some countries of Asia the intricate carving and inlaid wood has been preserved in temples and shrines for centuries, and the skills were perpetuated from father to son until recent war conditions and lack of materials interrupted this great tradition.

In this country in recent years, the development of other materials has seemed to supplant wood, both for construction, interior finishing and furniture, as well as for decoration by carving, and so the interest in acquiring and teaching the skills of wood carving waned. It is encouraging to the skilled wood carver and individuals who want to learn this creative and satisfying craft, that now with renewed recognition and appreciation, hand carved wood has been restored to favor.

Carving detail of separate
top of cuckoo clock attached
with long wires hooked to frame.

Fig. 384

The cuckoo clock, Fig. 384, came from the Black Forest of Germany, and is typical of the carving skill of the wood and clock craftsmen of that region. They make many more elaborate clock mountings with forms of persons and animals, as well as elements of trees, foliage, and flowers, as if each carver worked to elaborate his clock structure in competition with others. Such clocks are rarely duplicated, but the clock in the illustration is one of the most common models.

For all clocks the same mechanism with wooden gears and other parts are made by hand from applewood, and are so perfectly adjusted that they run without interruption (if regularly wound) for generations, and are rarely replaced with one having metal parts.

Clock building and carving are skills passed on from one generation to another in the Black Forest and in the village of Oberammergau in Bavaria, where the carvers are unsurpassed masters of wood carving for clocks, religious figures, scenes, and many other articles.

At Oberammergau, wood carving is the principal occupation during the periods between the presentations of the Passion Plays every ten years. Each generation in over 1,000 families is taught in the state operated carving schools by the master carvers of this world famous village. The participants in the Passion Play are mostly wood carvers.

Fig. 385 shows some of the ceiling motifs carved in vermillion wood for a Hindu temple, reconstructed with elaborately carved walls in the Nelson Gallery of Arts in Kansas City, Missouri.

Fig. 386 is a massive carved pine door from the Spanish governor's palace in San Antonio, Texas. Many elements in these examples of 16th century wood carving, executed by craftsmen of different races oceans apart, are similar. The parts, upper and lower, of the door were decorated with carved Spanish designs by a Mexican craftsman, taught by a Spanish Friar (a priest with the conquerors). Note the mythological and actual faces, also the pegged construction and heavy hand wrought lock.

Fig. 385

Fig. 386

The carved and painted dower chests, cabinets, and other furniture made in the early period of the Pennsylvania Dutch colonists for their households are now museum treasures. The Metropolitan Museum of Art in New York City shows a large collection of European carved work of the sixteenth and seventeenth centuries, also examples of some of the early American wood carvers and furniture builders, which are an inspiration and an example. To see or to read about them will challenge and enthuse the would-be wood carver.

An excellent historical chapter is included in a highly recommended book — *Whittling and Woodcarving* by E. J. Tangerman.

This chapter has been planned for the beginner in the carving and the construction of wood articles, and will cover descriptions of the preferable kinds of wood recommended for carving, the use and care of tools, as well as the elements of wood carving and construction.

Woods for carving and cabinet making

Complete tables of native and imported woods are obtainable from the United States Forests Products Laboratory, Department of Agriculture, Washington, D.C. These tables will give information on the hardness, durability, shrinkage, elasticity, ease of cutting, and other qualities by which wood is classified. A few of those listed for carving and inlay work are grouped as hard or soft as distinguished commercially, but there is no defined separation between the two. In the hard class, starting with hickory at the top, but not in order of hardness, appear oak, walnut, ash, elm, sycamore, maple, pear, cherry, holly, and many others not so common.

Classified as soft are: Pine, basswood, juniper, cypress, redwood, yew, cedar, poplar, birch and aspen. Among the imported woods, used mainly for veneers and inlay are sandalwood, satinwood, camphor wood, ebony, teak, mahogany, and lemon wood.

The woods offered for carving by the major suppliers usually include cherry, white maple, white oak, walnut, Honduras mahogany, also northern white or sugar pine, basswood.

A sampler of wood for carving and cabinet work (also current lists of available woods and sizes) may be obtained from Albert Constantine and Son, 2050 Eastchester Road, Bronx, New York 10461, a firm which has supplied craftsmen with fine wood from all over the world for four generations. Schools and individual craftsmen may obtain the Constantine catalogue-manual on request. A recently published book, *Know Your Woods* by Albert Constantine, Jr., will be helpful and informative for the woodworker and everyone interested in natural resources and their conservation. (Available only from Constantines at present.)

In the selection of wood for carving, the choice depends partially on the skill of the carver, but mainly on the suitability or durability of the article to be carved, whether it is to be decorative or for household use. In general the quality of the wood should conform to these requirements:

For carving either the hard or the softer wood should be straight grained, with a fine or close texture, kiln dried, and well seasoned, also free from knots, resin, and any tendency to split. Sanded wood should not be selected, because particles of silica from sanding remains embedded and it is ruinous to the edges of carving tools. *Pieces for carving should be planed on all sides.*

Wood carving tools and equipment

The wood carver's chisels and gouges are his instruments, and although dozens of shapes are made, the essential ones are few in number and may be used for many difficult operations. The tool shapes will vary somewhat with individual preference and also with the kind of wood and the nature of the carving. The skew chisel, together with straight and curved shapes, three or four gouges, and fine veiners are the basic tools with which all kinds of carving may be done. Some expert carvers and whittlers consider a good pocket knife or sloyd knife to be a necessity.

The indispensable tool for chip carving is the skew chisel with an angle of approximately 30 degrees. It is beveled equally on both sides and the taper may vary with the kind of wood. About 20 degrees or less for soft wood makes a clean cutting edge. The harder woods require a stronger edge on which the taper may be 25 degrees or more.

A kit of the eight tools, shown in Fig. 387A with the addition of the small 3/32 inch V and U veiners, will be adequate for most work. These are:

3/8 inch skew chisel	5/16 inch veiner	chip carving knife
1/2 inch straight chisel	1/8 inch veiner	sloyd knife
3/8 inch long radius gouge	1/4 inch V parting tool	
3/8 inch short radius gouge	3/32 inch U veiner	
5/16 inch short radius gouge	3/32 inch V veiner	

These tools should be of the best quality, as inferior tools will not hold the essential cutting edge. For sharpening, slip stones, a white slightly abrasive stone known as Arkansas slip stone (mined in Arkansas), Fig. 387A, are shaped to fit the inner curves of the veiners and gouges.

Other required sharpening equipment includes: a carborundum or grit stone with coarse and fine surfaces, two heavy leather strops, one to use with jeweler's polishing rouge and the other treated with saddle soap, with which to complete the polishing edge of the sharpened tool.

Wood Carving Tools

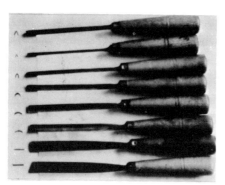 

Fig. 387

The workbench should be equipped with a motor driven grinder for the reshaping of tools. The grinding wheel should be a fine grit aluminum oxide type, which is preferable to an emery wheel because it generates less heat, with less possibility of damaging the tool. The process of sharpening is described on page 405.

The carver's workbench should be the best working height for the individual, then it must be attached to the floor or wall, so as to be immovable during the carving processes. The following items, in addition to those listed above, are required or will expedite work. They can be stored in drawers or cabinets above the workbench:

Bracing blocks and clamps

Cutting block, hand plane

Hand drill and set of drills

Hand saw — coping saw, jeweler's saw

Electric router, wooden mallet, vise

Scraper, burnisher

Small brush, pieces of clean soft cloth, paper towels

Set of fine files, round, triangular, half round

Flat file and wood rasp, riffle files

Background stamping tools, dot series, rosettes, crosshatch. See page 170

Wood paste filler, shellac, lacquer, wax

Three grades of fine sandpaper

Pumice and emery cloth

Pieces of wood for practice and for sampler

Sharpening of woodworking tools

There are three steps in sharpening tools: grinding to shape, beveling the blade to a taper, and polishing the cutting edge. New tools usually require grinding although some types may be purchased ready to use. Tools broken or with edges chipped from use must be ground to restore the cutting edge. Continued use, especially on hard woods, gradually makes the edges blunt. Repeated whetting on the stone alone may shorten the taper and make the edge too thick for satisfactory cutting.

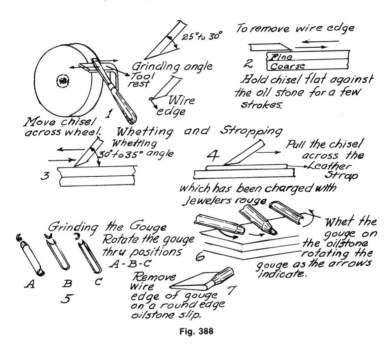

Fig. 388

1. Rotate the grinding wheel toward the cutting edge of the tool, held on the face of the stone at an angle of about 30 degrees, Fig. 388, sketch 1. The friction of the tool against the wheel generates heat. Contact, prolonged beyond a point that is comfortable to touch, changes the temper of the tool and may render it useless. Dip the tool in water at frequent intervals. Do not grind the tool edge longer than is necessary to reshape the bevel and the line of the edge. When a fine burr develops, the tool is ready for the whetting operation. Longer grinding will produce a coarse burr which is difficult to remove. Move the tool back and forth across the wheel to avoid wearing grooves.

2. When an edge is broken, the bevel must be re-established and the edge ground back. For this operation, hold the tool at a right angle until the line of the tool edge is restored. Then bevel it and reshape the edge.

To sharpen a straight end chisel, square it on the grinder and shape to restore correct bevel.

3. After grinding remove the wire edge or burr by whetting on the oil stone as indicated in Fig. 388, sketch 2. Then whet and strop the edge as shown in sketches 3 and 4.

4. Grind and bevel gouges of short radius with the bevel slightly longer on the bottom than on the top. Vary the angle of the bevel between 8 and 10 degrees, depending on the wood and the preference of the carver. Slightly round the corners of flat or long radius gouges. The grinding of a gouge is shown in sketch 5, as it is rotated on the wheel through positions A, B, and C and then whetted on the oil stone as in sketch 6.

The wire edge or burr which develops on the inner edge of the gouge must be removed with an oiled Arkansas slip stone as shown in sketch 7.

5. Veiners and V shaped tools are beveled with the point or tip extending slightly beyond the top edges of the V, Fig. 389, sketch 3.

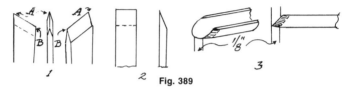

Fig. 389

The whetting operation, Fig. 388, sketch 3, is done on a combination stone made with two grades of carborundum, coarse with 60 to 80 grit on one side and fine, 120 to 160 grit on the other. After whetting a tool, remove burr particles, which may adhere to the surface with household oil or water. Use the coarse stone first and finish whetting the tool on the fine surface, Fig. 388, sketch 2. Hold the tool at a low angle at first, then lift until the level of the edge is even with the stone.

The direction of the stroke is forward against the stone, which is held in the hand or fixed in a recess in a block. The fixed position is preferable as it permits the use of both hands for the whetting. Hold the tool with the right hand and control the pressure with the left fingers. Lift the tool between strokes in a vertical rotary movement and keep it moving from side to side on the stone to prevent wearing grooves on the surface.

Honing always follows the whetting with the same direction of the strokes to produce a smooth edge and bevel. This is done on the natural fine grit stone quarried in Arkansas and known as Arkansas slip stone. The set shown in Fig. 387 includes wedge shaped and tapered slips for removing burrs from the inner edges of gouges, veiners, and V tools. Flat and beveled chisels are honed on the flat surface of a slip stone. A little oil should be applied for each operation.

Stropping, Fig. 388, sketch 4, polishes the beveled surface back of the edge and prevents "drag" by friction on the wood fibers. Glue the first strap, flesh side uppermost to a piece of wood and coat the surface with jeweler's rouge. Treat the surface of the second strap with saddle soap occasionally to keep it soft and pliable. For curved tools and small gouges, fold the piece of leather over a finger or dowel pin. The direction of the strokes are the reverse of movements in whetting and must be *from the bevel to the edge*.

Wood finishes

Varieties of wood differ in the kind of finish that will penetrate and preserve the surface and not change the color, especially when carved.

Nineteenth century so-called Victorian furniture with its ornate carving was generally of oak, darkened and heavily varnished, a durable finish as the long life of this furniture proves. This is not popular in modern times.

Expert woodworkers and carvers maintain that penetrating oils, applied warm, which replace the natural oils, preserve the appearance and the wearing qualities of the wood. Repeated light coats of linseed, thinned with turpentine and well rubbed between coats is standard for many furniture items. Applications of paste wax on the warm surface of the wood, repeated three or four times with a thorough rubbing between coats is also a common practice.

Shellac, with two or three coats lightly sanded with a final application of paste wax will produce a satiny finish, but this will not withstand water, oily food particles or alcohol. For table tops, trays and similar articles a sprayed lacquer in several light coats is recommended.

For some projects of the carved colonial type, a light coat of flat white paint and partially rubbed stains of brown, blue and grey are suggested. Another type of antique finish is that obtained with the application of varying amounts of burnt umber well mixed with gasoline, approximately a teaspoonful with a pint, wiped before the color becomes streaked or too dark. When dry this finish is rubbed with paste wax and polished.

Modern wood finishes and paints that are resin or plastic based are now numerous. A liquid oil and resin mixture, a Danish product, recently imported by some suppliers is said to be nontoxic and entirely resistant to water and food stains.

The non-grain raising stains now available greatly simplify wood finishing. Kleartone, a Valspar product is an example. No sanding between coats is necessary and it can be followed when dry with a clear lacquer or wax applications.

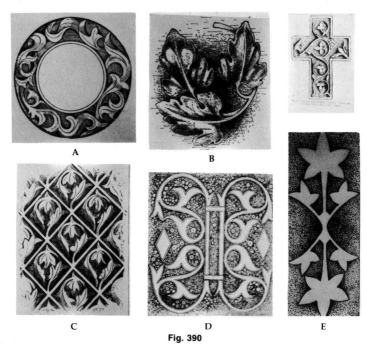

Fig. 390

The relief carved and outlined designs with stamped backgrounds were taken from an excellent book, now out of print, "Wood Carving" by Charles E. Leland, an English educator and craftsman. A revised edition was published in 1931 by Isaac Putnam and Sons, Ltd. of London and New York. It is now a library reference.

The tray or frame A in Fig. 390 has a leaf design, also the cross B and the motif C. All were carved with the background leveled to leave the design in relief. The panel design in D has similar leaf designs within identical diamond shaped spaces. The English term for this type of carving was "diaper carving."

Units D and E were outlined and the backgrounds depressed with rosette and star stamps or stippled with the rounded point of a tracing tool.

The wood carver's sampler

To practice and to experiment are as necessary for the person who undertakes wood carving, as love of the material and inspiration for design. A sampler of individual steps and completed motifs is not only the proof of developing skill but is a reference in design.

From time to time, the beginning carver can add new and more difficult elements, making the sampler something of a permanent record of his progress and work.

Cutting shallow lines or grooves with the ¼ inch U veiner is a first lesson.

1. Mark across the grain of a piece of smooth white pine wood, several light pencil lines about ½ inch apart. Clamp the wood securely to a clean smooth board attached to the workbench or table.

2. Hold the tool as indicated in Fig. 391, the handle firmly in the right hand, with the forearm resting on the table and the first two fingers of the left hand pressed on the face of the blade, about an inch from the cutting edge.

"Keep your mind on your work—a careless movement may cause a slip of the tool and ruin the work—or you" is an admonition of the master carver.

3. Remove a thin shaving the entire length of one line, then deepen until a clean cut groove about 3/32 inch results. Continue cutting the parallel grooves along the marked lines. Study your motions and see where you can accomplish the same result with less effort and fewer motions. *Learn to relax the muscles which are not in use.* This process corresponds to the carving technique of line or grooved carving and will be used in many designs which are simply outlined with a flat background.

4. If you are not satisfied with the first set of parallel lines, study them to know what to avoid, then make a second set. The widths of the grooves and the spaces between the lines should be exact.

5. When you have mastered the cutting of straight grooves, mark lines at right angles and proceed to cut the cross barred grooves. *Note the angle at which the lines intersect* as indicated in Figs. 391A and B. As these are straight grain lines, even more careful use of the veiner is necessary to avoid cutting a splinter. The angles of intersection must be uniform and exactly the same depth as the first set of lines. This detail is most important, as the way it is done in a design could perfect or ruin an entire project.

6. Practice cutting curved and circular intersecting lines in an original design. Learn how to carve overlapping lines to produce an interwoven effect. These four types of line carving are indicated in Fig. 391A. When this procedure is mastered, relief carving and inscriptions or lettering can both be successfully done.

7. The next step is the carving of leaf and flower elements. The procedure in carving a simple leaf is illustrated in Fig. 391C and E. Other leaf designs are shown in Fig. 391E. These are examples of low relief carving or modeling in which the background is slightly carved down with a flat gouge, after the outline is cut or incised with the veiner.

Many flower elements are similar and it will be found from the study of traditional and historical carving, that innumerable combinations are possible, with variations in the depth of the modeling and the treatment of the background.

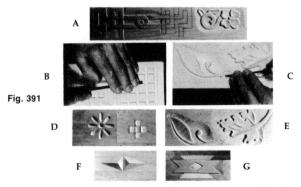

Fig. 391

The units A, B, C and E of the carving sampler show the geometric and floral elements previously described. Units D, F and G are symbols of the Southwestern Indians; Sunburst, Morning Star, Medicine Man's Eye and Butterfly.

Elements and types of carving

The steps on the carving units just described may be recognized as types of wood carving techniques, which in general are grouped as 1. *outline*, 2. *modeling a line design in low relief*, 3. *design modeled, with beveled background* for elevated relief effect. Other types of carving as in lettering, as well as design background, requires the lowering of the background to a level from an average of 3/32 to 3/16 inch.

Figure carving or carving in the round is considered the most difficult, but as a practice experiment, can be done with a pocket knife and the whittling technique. Birds, small animals, or a cartoon figure can serve as models. It is desirable to prepare a scale drawing from which to plan the measurements of the figure. (See Fig. 419, page 437.)

Bas-relief figure carving is very similar to modeled relief carving, usually with lower backgrounds.

The pierced or cutout carving of the Gothic motif is illustrated in Fig. 392. The high relief appearance of this historic type of openwork carving is developed by the contrasting levels of the panel border, the enclosure of the motif, and the lowered background. For this example, a ¾ inch thick pine board was carved as follows:

1. Outline the design enclosure and the marginal border. Make a continuous incision or even depth cut approximately 3/16 inch deep, so that it can be deepened to a full ¼ inch as the background is lowered. Do not cut on the pencil line, but leave a slight margin, about 1/16 inch for a protection in the background carving. Remove this margin when the background is finished. Use a skew chisel or a straight chisel for the straight outlines, then a chisel with a corresponding curvature for the outlining of the motif or cutout. Avoid under cutting. On pine and other soft woods, sufficient pressure can be exerted with the palm of the right hand, while the left holds and guides the tool. It may be necessary to use a mallet in carving hard wood.

2. Remove the background to a ½ inch level with the slightly curved gouge, making shallow cuts in the same vertical (according to the shape of the motif) direction to remove thin layers over the background surface in succession until the desired background is level. Finish it smoothly with the chisel. Avoid using any sandpaper if possible, as any embedded particles of the abrasive will spoil the edge of the chisel or other tool.

3. Make sure the detail of the design is clear, and in exact proportions for the diamond shaped points and the horizontal curves.

a. Carefully saw cut the outline with an 8 inch coping saw to remove this section, first making a vertical and a horizontal saw cut to within ½ inch of the line margin.

b. Use a small gouge to carve down the diamond shaped corners to a level of the background, then carve down the margins of the opening to a thickness of ¼ inch sloping them evenly from the surface edge or rim. Depending on the varying curvature, use a short radius or a long radius gouge. Finish the surface as smoothly as possible with the carving tools. Do not use sandpaper except on outside edges.

A   B

Fig. 392

Chip carving

The type of wood carving developed from simple geometric elements with a single tool, the skew chisel, is associated in this country with the carving and painting of household furniture by the Pennsylvania Dutch. They brought this type of decorative carving from Germany. It is typical of much of the wood decoration known as Scandinavian, but historically it is said to have been devised originally by the South Sea Islanders and to be common now in other primitive parts of the world. The early missionaries from Germany to the South Pacific Islands admired and learned the skill which they brought back with them, according to one explanation of the development of chip carving in Europe.

Fig. 397 shows examples of a few chip carving motifs and others will be illustrated with the description of techniques to follow.

The geometric elements of chip carving seem simple in comparison with other types of carving, but the designs must be drawn and carved with mathematical exactness not required in other carving, when variations and adaptations of the original design may emphasize the carver's interpretation.

The master carver uses only a skew chisel, as sketched in No. 1, Fig. 389, although a veiner may simplify the cutting of some lines of depth carving. The designs and steps which are demonstrated as panels of the same repeated units, with varied rosettes, illustrate the main use of chip carving in borders or centers.

The variety and charm possible in combinations of the carved rosette appear in the adaptation in squares for the decoration of a small chest, illustrated in Fig. 392. The carving detail in Fig. 396 shows a variation with sections cut out or pierced for grill work. These areas can be left plain or have a carved unit as indicated in the sketch.

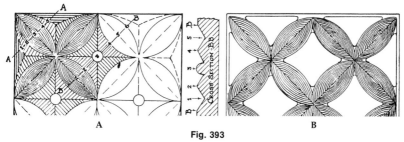

A   B

Fig. 393

Guide line pattern for chip carving

1. Determine the size and position of the design motif, which will be carved in one or more units and draw a geometric layout as indicated in Fig. 394. Draw the lines as in the unit 1, Fig. 394 and note the equal triangular forms and proportions.

2. Bisect each angle of the triangle as indicated at point D and draw the lines to intersect at points H, J, and K. When carved, the sloping depth of this point has the appearance of a shallow inverted pyramid.

3. Fig. 393, sketch A, shows the layout for a rosette design, carved as illustrated in Fig. 392B.

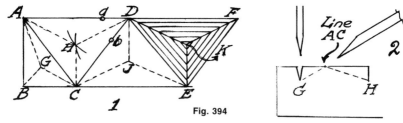

Fig. 394

Chip carving procedure

In Fig. 395A, the penciled design for a frame border, with the first cut of the corner triangle, is shown. B shows the position of the chisel for this cut. C shows the corner cut completed and the starting of the second. D shows the completion of this second cut. Note the position of the right hand, with pressure from the left sufficient to cut a thin shaving or "chip" from the first curve of the edge decoration.

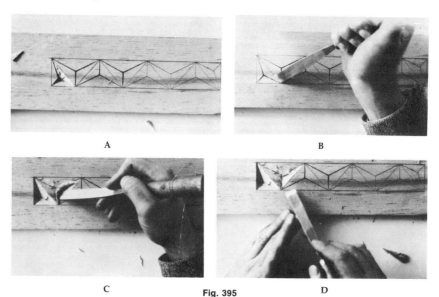

A

B

C

Fig. 395

D

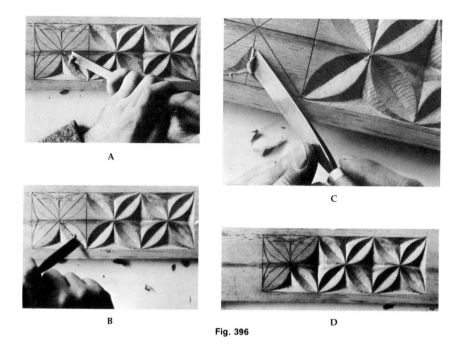

Fig. 396

When following the process of the wood carver in Fig. 396A, B, and C, the completed design element is D.

1. Mark the design on the wood to be carved. (Be sure the piece is smoothly planed and without marks or stains.) Practice the right and left positions or cuts of the chisel, as shown in A and B of Fig. 396.

2. Lightly stab a cut on a guide line, with the chisel held perpendicular, then place the heel of the chisel at a point of intersection of the guide lines and cut along one to the next point of intersection in the design.

The chisel is sharpened so that the bevel of the cutting edge is the same on both sides, making it sharp in the center to cut from one side and then from another, to avoid splitting the grain.

3. A of Fig. 396 shows a carved triangular element, with the removal of a pyramid shaped piece of wood completed, and the start of the next element. In B and C, the carving of this element is shown. D shows both elements smoothly carved to the same depth as the other two rosettes of the panel. An enlargement of an illustration of the carving of the pyramid or triangular element is shown in 396C, as demonstrated by the carver, who is removing thin shavings, "chip by chip" until the desired depth of the inverted pyramid is cut.

Note that the slope of the chisel corresponds to the curve of the sloping design element, as it is rocked along to cut a shaving of the wood.

4. A of Fig. 397 shows the upper and lower or right and left inverted pyramids, carved in reverse or alternating for a narrow border or frame design

and D, a wider border made up of three or any number of rosettes. B and C are rosette variations, C having curved lines which result in a rotating effect. A study of the oblong design or rosette E will reveal similar elements as in D carved with an elongated effect.

5. Before starting a panel of the curved edge rosettes, practice a sweeping circular movement with the chisel, to make a sloping curved depth cut on a separate piece of wood, with the rocking kind of pressure used on the straight cuts of the border design. Both hands are required, the left to guide the chisel and the right to exert pressure as shown in Fig. 398A and B.

6. In drawing the design or layout for the squared rosettes, make sure the connecting points or apex of each triangle come exactly together in a horizontal line, so that the combined curved sided triangles come together to form another unit of the design. This is detailed in Fig. 393, sketches A and B. In 393A, the addition of a round cap in the center emphasizes the effect of this unit.

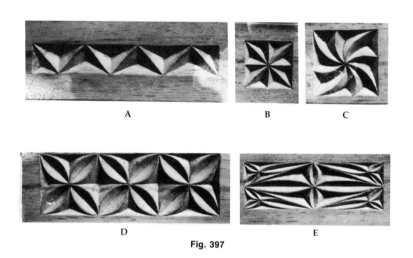

Fig. 397

Carved decoration for edges

The adaptation of chip carving methods to an edge of a table, a frame, or similar articles is illustrated in Fig. 398. The profile of the carving appears on both faces or surfaces as it is carved on both, with each half of the design at right angles to the other half.

The first step is to inscribe penciled guide lines parallel to the edge on both horizontal surfaces, inside and outside. A template cut from a folded paper pattern can be used as a guide for marking the opposite lines accurately.

Make the cuts on the lines with the straight edge chisel held as indicated in Fig. 398. The combined curves of equal depths form an oval unit on the edge.

In the same way, carve the triangles from opposite sides, of equal depth and height so that together the carved unit appears as a diamond shaped form.

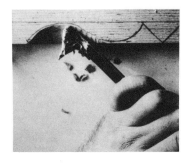

A   **Fig. 398**   B

Projects with chip carved decorations

Two practical projects, bookends and a waste paper basket, are sketched in Fig. 399 and Fig. 400. They also show the geometric type of chip carving. The assembly process is given.

1. For the bookends, cut two pieces of clear, smooth planed pine wood, 4½ by 4 inches and ½ inch thick. Obtain from a sheet metal shop two pieces of 18 gauge, rust proof metal, 4 inches square. 16 gauge copper will make an effective contrast to the wood. Trim and round the edges to the approximate outline of sketch A design.

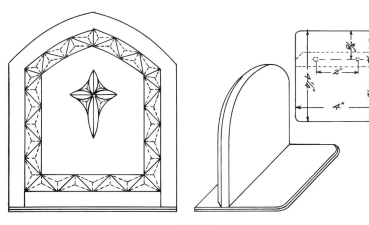

Fig. 399

2. Draw the outline of the triangular rosette in the center of the ends and the border outline and design guide lines about ⅜ inch from the margins. These conform in reduced size to the chip carving elements shown in Fig. 397, page 414.

3. Clamp the pieces in turn to the worktable, and carve the design with the skew chisel. The detail is sketched to show an enlarged design element in Fig. 395B. Keep the angles and depth cuts with the chisel exact as any irregularity will detract from the appearance of the carving.

4. When the carving is finished on both ends, lightly sand the surface with No. 0 sandpaper, rubbing only with the grain of the wood. Wipe off all dust particles with a clean cloth. Use a small brush to clean the cavities of the design.

5. Stain (if desired) with a prepared oil stain, or use a light application of a solution of one tablespoon of burnt umber in oil mixed with one pint of gasoline. Apply to the carved elements with a fine brush and wipe out at once with a cloth wrapped around a small stick, to avoid the darkening of the cross grain cuts. Apply to the surface with a cloth swab dipped in the stain or umber solution. Wipe with a cloth to unify the color and remove any excess.

6. When the wood is completely dry, sand again rubbing only with the grain, with No. 000 sandpaper, then finish with shellac or well rubbed paste wax. Avoid leaving any wax particles in the design.

Attach the metal base with countersunk wood screws. Drill holes in the metal, an inch from the corners of the wood ends, for the screws. Place the metal so that a supporting margin of one inch extends toward the outside from the bottom of the wood. Cement a piece of felt over the metal.

Waste basket with chip carving

This project requires six panel pieces 6 inches wide and a hexagonal base cut from a 10 inch by 10 inch square of wood. All parts are ½ inch thick, and two of the panel pieces are 20 inches long to allow for the hand holes. The other four are 18 inches long or high.

1. Bevel the inside edges of the side pieces with a plane as indicated. Drill the holes in each panel as marked for the assembly lacing.

2. Cut the hand holes in pieces 2 and 4 and shape the top and bottom ends of the other side pieces. Shape feet on panels 2, 4, and 6, Fig. 400.

3. Mark lines to show the exact position of both sides of the bottom inside the panels. Saw 3/16 inch cuts along these lines which should be the same width as the thickness of the bottom. Saw a center cut the same depth. Remove the wood with a chisel to the even 3/16 inch depth.

4. Clamp the side panels to the worktable and carve the designs. Note that the center diamond shaped rosettes are carved only on the panels with the hand holes, with the corner units on the others.

5. Finish the panels by lightly sanding, then apply stain and sand again as for the bookends. Wax in the same way or shellac.

6. Loosely lace the side panels together with two rawhide thongs, 5 feet long by ¼ inch wide, which have been softened in water for about thirty minutes. Pass the thongs through the holes so that the edges of the panels are covered. Secure the ends with a tack inside a panel.*

7. Apply a light uniform coat of household cement to the grooves in the panels, press the bottom into them, then tighten the rawhide thong to hold the panels firmly together, so that they also hold the bottom in place with the edges cemented into the panels.

*Source—rawhide thongs, see page 454.

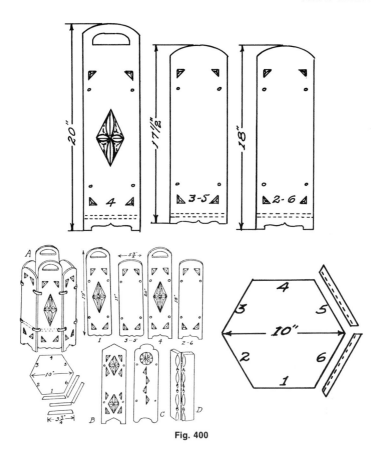

Fig. 400

The front and back of a safe and effective knife for chip carving is shown in Fig. 401A and B. The replaceable razor blade is encased in a metal holder. Straight geometric elements can be carved singly or in combination with this tool in the softer woods, birch, pine and basswood. Curved elements, as in the rosette of the demonstration carving, require a chisel type blade. C and E are holders for other types of encased replaceable razor blade knives. D has a special blade which is adjustable.

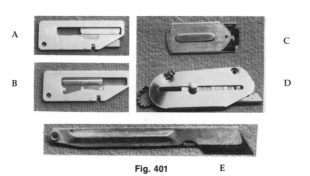

Fig. 401   E

Frames for mirrors and pictures

The mirror frame, Fig. 402, with elaborate carving combines nearly every type: high relief and modeled elements, cutout or pierced with the borders and medallions of chip carving. It was designed for a family wishing to display the ancestral crest in this way. The details are shown in the enlarged sketches of the floral elements, medallions, and left finials. These may be used as decorative motifs on various articles as well as frames.

Fig. 402

The picture frame in Fig. 402B shows a simple gouged decoration which relieves the plain surface of the sides and ends. It can be reproduced with a short radius gouge and a chisel. Note the slanting form of the characteristic gouge cuts which resemble thumb prints. As evident in the illustration, the gouge cuts can be painted with colors which harmonize with the picture.

The chip carved edge decoration consists of the same geometric elements as those described and illustrated in Fig. 396. In place of the side and end motifs used on the frame illustrated in Fig. 392, a design like that shown in Fig. 397A will effectively match the edge decoration. Other suggested borders or panels for frames are shown in Fig. 397D and E.

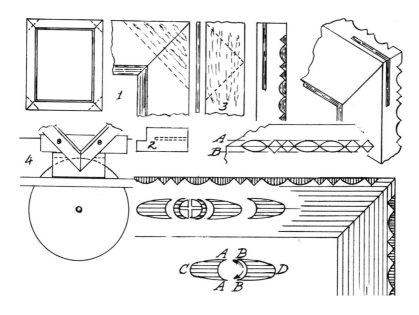

Fig. 403

1. For the carved frame, select from a local supplier a length of clear, planed pinewood, without knots, ½ inch thick and 1⅛ inch wide, sufficient to cut the two 10 inch side pieces and the two 8 inch ends, allowing for the mitering of the corners. Rabbet the groove or recess along the inner edge of the back of the four pieces, 3/16 inch deep and ¼ wide.

2. Lay out and carve the design selected for the ends and sides of the frame, also the edge decoration. Lightly stain the surface with a wood stain or the mixture of burnt umber and turpentine or mineral spirits. Wear rubber gloves and avoid inhaling fumes. Apply two or three coats of wood paste wax and rub each coat thoroughly.

3. Place the glass (if used) in the frame, then the picture and backing. Secure with glazer's points and cover with a durable paper glued to the frame and even with the lower edge. Trim if necessary.

The second picture frame in Fig. 402D is finished with a simple but effective hand hewn effect, accomplished with a short radius gouge, about ¼ inch. The grooves, parallel but not all vertical, are gouged to variable depths and lengths, giving the surface both highlights and shadowed effects. An application of flat white paint, tinted with a little ultramarine blue in oil, rubbed to remove excess and reveal the highlights, harmonizes perfectly with the sky colors in the picture.

The frame has no glass and both frame and picture are protected with a fixative applied with a sprayer.

The assembly process for both frames follows:

1. For the hand gouged frame, Fig. 403, sketch 1, obtain a length of pine wood 1⅛ inches wide and ½ inch thick without knots, long enough to cut 12 inch side pieces and 10 inch ends, allowing for miter cuts at the corners. Rabbet the groove or recess along the inner edge of the back of each piece, sketch 2, about 3/16 inch wide and ¼ inch deep. Set the saw guide at 45 degrees, test with a try square for accuracy, and cut the corners for mitering.

2. Clamp each side and end to the table top with the mitered ends fitting closely together and the corner in position for sawing the cut (known as a kerf) to receive a spline. A more exact method is to screw a piece of lath or batten to the back of a side and end as indicated in Fig. 403, sketch 4, in which a power table saw is to be used.

3. Cut the spline, sketch 3, to fit the saw cut from a firm piece of wood, making the thickness vary slightly less than the saw cut or kerf. It will be snug when the glue, applied to both sides of the kerf and the spline, has set. Apply cold glue, Weldwood, Elmer's or the equivalent, and press the spline gently into place. After the glue has set, remove the protruding ends of the spline with a small plane. Smooth joints and ends of splints with a sharp knife.

4. Follow the same process for all four corners, then proceed with the carving of the gouged surface on the assembled frame. Finish as suggested above with tinted paint which harmonizes with a selected color in the picture.

5. With the frame face down on a smooth surface (after the paint has dried), lightly sand the recess, if necessary, then place the print, photograph, or painting in the recess, cover with a close fitting piece of stiff cardboard, two if needed to fill the space above the picture to the level of the back of the frame. Insert two glazer's points in the frame on the sides and ends, to secure the picture and backing. Cover all with a durable paper glued to the frame and trimmed evenly to the edge of the back.

The pair of round tile, framed in soft brown colored wood with Spanish style carving, is very decorative on any wall. They show the skill of Mexico's tile artists and wood carvers. The costumed Senorita, fiesta bound with her flower tray and water jar, and the horseman bedecked as "El Gaucho" for a riding contest, are rarely seen in modern Mexico except at fiesta times.

Tools and materials for frame

Carving tools, including the ⅜ inch gouge, ⅜ inch chisel, ⅛ inch veiner, and a knife, all very sharp are required for the circular frame carving. A hand plane, drill, compass with pencil and a hand saw will also be needed.

The materials are: A circular tile, bas-relief carving or a silhouette, all suitable for the inset: A square of wood large enough to make a frame and allow corner space for the carving motif. The example, a piece of knot free, planed wood 12 by ¾ inch with ¼ inch plywood the same size for the back. All edges must be smoothly finished.

The process of carving and assembly

1. With the compass and pencil carefully mark out the center opening of slightly less diameter than the face of the tile or other inset, about 1/64 inch. Draw the corner motifs on tracing paper for transfer to the wood or preferably mark them directly in identical spaces at the corners. Lay out the edge design so that the corners can be rounded. Leave a margin of ¾ inch on the three sides. The detail is revealed in the enlarged section of the illustration.

Scribe the circle of the lower edge of the opening on the back of the frame, making it the circumference of the bottom of the tile. This is usually slightly larger than the top. If not, build it up with a little tile grout or patching plaster in a slope upward of about 1/64 inch and permit to harden when it can be smoothed with a piece of abrasive cloth to make the tile circumference perfectly even.

2. Carve the edge decoration, then the corner motifs, finishing all grooves with the tools as *sanding on the carving elements must not be done.*

3. Cut out the center opening with the coping saw, first drilling a sloping hole to correspond with the upper and lower edges of the circle to permit the insertion of the saw blade. Carefully saw out the opening with the slope that will make the lower edge large enough to hold the base of the tile or inset when it is put in from the back. Finish the inner edge with a piece of emery cloth wrapped around a piece of wood with the same slope as the opening.

4. Mark the opening on the plywood in the same position. Apply a coat of tile cement to the lower surface of the tile and also the plywood and leave for the time required for it to slightly harden, then apply weldwood glue to the for a few minutes, then leave under a weight several hours, overnight is best. Carefully smooth the edges and apply a clear or tinted finish as directed on page 407.

Carved pine wood box

The pine wood box in Fig. 404, with inscription in Spanish and the typical Spanish type "sunburst" or "rayo de sol" rosette decorations, was built of ¾ inch selected, planed boards, matched for grain and glued together, making a box 24 inches high and 38 inches wide, with the exception of the rope carved corner posts. The end panels are 24 by 24 inches and the 1⅛ inch thick lid, 40 by 30 inches, projecting over the panels to the extent of the carved edges, about 2½ inches.

The carved inscriptions on the lid and the three panels in Spanish are: Cajon Para La Leña (Box for Wood), Piñon Y Pinovete, Para del Fuego (Piñon and Pitch Pine for the Fire), Almagordo (Cottonwood), and Amigos Viejos (for Old Friends). The rounded relief modeled letters, with the flat gouged background, are simplified Gothic style, not difficult to carve if carefully spaced.

The carved letters were designed and spaced on tracing paper to fit the background areas on the top and panels, then redrawn over the impression on the reverse side with a soft pencil so that this could be transferred to the wood when the original was retraced. Any blurred or incomplete outlines were corrected.

Fig. 404

The steps in carving the wood box follow:

1. Mark the ¾ inch wide channels in the posts for the recess and attachment of the panels, the back as well as the front and ends. There should be two in the center of each post at exact right angles to each other and 1 inch deep.

Make three saw cuts for each channel, on the marked lines and in the center between them. Remove the wood with the chisel and level the bottom of the cuts.

Mark off and carve the chosen oblong element at the top of the posts, using the guide line method of the chip carving units, described on page 413.

2. Round all vertical edges of the posts, then draw on them the spirals for the ropelike identations, which rotate in opposite directions on the front and end panels, as they appear in the photographs. The carved motifs at the tops of the posts, and a part of them, extends to within an inch of the edge of the lid. This area is the size of the square post, 2¾ inches after the 3 inch rough finished square piece was planed. In appearance and slope, the spiral is around the posts.

3. With a mallet and sharp chisel, incise the lines on the posts to a depth of ½ inch for 2 or 3 inches at a time, rounding and completing the groove of the spiral, before continuing the incising. Keep the spaces in between as even as possible, likewise the margins of the groove. Note that the spiral terminates at the lower edge of the panels with a horizontal groove of about the same depth. Cut with the grain from left or right, never against it if possible to avoid, as otherwise splinters may develop. Be careful to end the spiral smoothly at the saw cuts.

4. Glue the boards together with contact cement, clamp and leave until the glue hardens, approximately 30 minutes.

5. Lay out the circles for the sunburst design on front and ends, centering them in the approximate proportions shown in the photographs. Mark the quarter circle divisions and divide them, on the circumference, into 5 segments each. Mark a 3 inch diameter center and extend the segment border lines to the center circle, each perpendicular to it. This requires a narrowing of the segments to fit exactly together as they end on the center circle.

6. Go over all the marked lines to be sure there are no variations and the tapers from approximately 3/16 inch on the divided outer circle to ⅛ inch or less on the center circle are maintained evenly.

7. Incise along the lines, defining the sunburst segments or "rays," about 3/16 inch deep. With a rounded long radius gouge carve out the segments, smoothly and to a depth, slightly rounding down from the dividing lines. The sunbursts are the same diameter on the three panels.

8. Make a pattern for the inscriptions and the background areas on the lid and the three panels in the proportions indicated in the photographs. Make sure that the spacing and heights of the letters leave room for carving the background. Transfer the pattern to the wood by tracing the reverse outline as previously mentioned.

9. Evenly incise the outline of the letters and the background panels ⅛ inch. (The latter may be done along a straight edge.) Round the edges of the

letters with a chisel, keeping the design width and height exact, and the depth margins clean of any roughness or tiny splinters. Remove the background to a depth of ⅛ inch with the gouge. Then stamp over it with stippling tool.

10. Adze the front and end panels to appear hand hewn, also the lid which will be attached with hinges. Apply a wood adhesive to the sides and bottoms of the post channels, also along 1 inch of the side edges of the sides and ends. Press all four panels into the channels in an upright position. Secure with padded clamps until the adhesive has fully hardened.

11. Finish with a light brown stain and three successive coats of wood paste wax, well rubbed after each application. Avoid leaving any particles around the letters or in the post grooves.

The copper hinge strips on the lid are not connected with the box hinges, but are decorative only and in appearance like the Spanish hand hammered metal hinges on such chests.

Tea Wagon

A practical item of studio furniture, Fig. 405, is the adaptation of the tea wagon to the Spanish type of "mesita trastero" or little table cupboard. It occupies only 20 by 30 inches of floor space, yet holds a complete tea and coffee service for eight persons, including electric appliances. The doors on the four sides and sliding shelves make all the equipment readily accessible. The interior has a light reddish brown stain under a coat of shellac, and the exterior has a smoothly planed surface and a natural finish with one coat of shellac and two of well rubbed wax.

The doors, with the Spanish type pierced panels, are latched with hasps of hammered copper, similar in design to the wrought iron hasps of Old Mexico.

Fig. 405

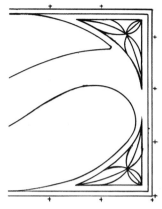

Fig. 406

Drop Leaf Desk

The eighteenth century style drop leaf desk of carved wood, Fig. 407, is an example of the fine cabinet work and skilled designer-carvers of that period. It was made of oak with the characteristic grain preserved by a natural clear varnish finish.

The carved low relief designs on the panels of the front (with leaf closed) and the ends were probably done by a German trained carver. Note that the balanced scroll and leaf design for the irregular end panel is a complete unit, with extensions of the central motif filling the space. The detail of the modeled design outline was possibly carved after the background was depressed with a fine crossbarred metal stamping tool. The impressions are not evident in the illustrations.

The similar stamped background on the front was unfortunately darkened, seemingly for greater contrast with the raised effect of the scroll and leaf design units. These in effect are like individual plants, related as a whole by the enclosing scrolls. Both of these designs are suitable for the ornamentation of oak or walnut furniture of many kinds.

The unique over-all carving on the drawer front resembles a Greek design for panels of frames, called the "Parthenon."

Fig. 407

Pine Chests with Carved Decoration

Fig. 408

The dimensions of the carved chest are:

Height of corner posts from floor to top of lid	29″
Finished posts, rounded from 3 inch square pieces	2¾″
Width of front between posts	40″
Width of front with ends mortised into posts	42″
Width of sides, including mortised ends	17″
Width of sides between posts	15″
Depth of completed box (space to floor 5½ inches)	22½″
Dimension of lid, with corners cut to fit posts	22″ by 44″

Exact parallel lines were cut with a veiner ¾ inch from the edges on two sides for the right and left posts at either end, leaving space for the carving of the rope type decoration 1¼ inches wide, as it appears in the photograph, and ¾ inch at the top of the rounded posts. These extend beyond the cutout corners of the lid and hold it in place.

Spaced 1½ inches apart the spiral slanted grooves, carved to a depth of 3/16 inch and slightly rounded at the margins, rotate in opposite directions, leaving the spaces between evenly rounded in a relief effect.

Panels in the ends are carved with a sunburst modified to fit the panel rectangle. Each quarter was divided into 4 segments, spaced to bring the center diagonal groove to the corner points with all the grooves perpendicular to the circumference of the center circle.

The intricate high relief carving on the front and the lid combines many elements, in a unified and balanced design, of religious significance to the carver, a man of Spanish ancestry.

All the decorations were accentuated by the finish of antique ivory, highlighted by rubbing. This finish, particularly adaptable to pine wood, consists of white oil based paint. A thin priming coat was applied first, followed by a covering coat. When this second application was almost dry (slightly "tacky" to the touch), powdered burnt umber was dusted over all surfaces, lightly in the design grooves. Later when the paint was fully dry, all surfaces were well rubbed with a linen cloth to produce the shaded ivory finish. Two applications of paste wax, followed by more rubbing, made a durable soft matt surface with shadowed copper brown shades in the depths of the carving.

Spanish Chest with Relief Carving

Fig. 409

The beautifully executed carving in low relief, with flat smooth chiseled background, resembles eighteenth century European decorations. The perfect symmetry of the design, proportioned exactly for the chest space, and the carving were done by Eva Clark Keller, the artist who illustrated many of the processes, and mastered all the techniques of design and procedure in this and previous editions of *Handicraft*.

Features of the chest are: The dovetailed corner construction; the type of base supports extending beyond the chest; and the peg attached lid with side pieces dovetailed into the top, in the same way as the corners of the chest. All of these construction details are typical of the Spanish type found in Old Mexico.

Walnut Bench

Another furniture item, useful and attractive in any setting, is the small bench and book rack, illustrated in Fig. 406. It was made of solid walnut with lathe turned legs and a smooth planed top with book supports beneath. The unusual feature of the top is the pierced and carved hand hold with carved corner decorations, shown in the illustration and in the sketch, drawn to scale.

The lathe turned section of the legs, between the upper and lower scalloped rails, is 13½ inches long with square sections, adjacent to the rails, mortised to receive the tenons (projections), on the rails. Glue or an adhesive like Weldwood hold them securely together. The legs are spread or splayed from a width of 8 inches at the top rail to 10 inches at the floor level and the front spreads from 4 inches to 15¾ inches. Overall the legs are 19 inches long and 2 inches by 2 inches square.

The pierced top, one inch thick is 14 inches by 20 inches with a slightly rounded margin, sloping from panel 11½ inches by 17¼ inches to an edge ⅜ inches thick and ¼ inches wide, defined by an incised line.

The Spanish Colonial type furniture in the home of Mr. and Mrs. H. Merril Taylor in Farmington, New Mexico is decorated with intricate carvings of adapted Spanish designs, all done by Mr. and Mrs. Taylor who are both skilled craftsmen. Mr. Taylor is shown as he carves the background of a large design unit for a chest. All of the carving on the bedroom set was done after the parts were assembled. Knot free pine wood was used and the finish given an antique grey tint with light blue in the recesses. Note position of Mr. Taylor's right and left hands.

Carved Single Piece Projects

The hot plate trivet, Fig. 410, was carved with a dogwood blossom design from a piece of smoothly planed applewood finished in a square ¾ inch by 6½ inch by 6½ inch. To produce this unusual trivet, these tools are needed:

Hand saw, coping saw, pencil compass, ½ inch flat chisel, ½ inch skew chisel, ⅛ inch and ⅜ inch gouges, a veiner and mallet, also a riffler type fine rasp.

Carved Applewood Trivet

Fig. 410

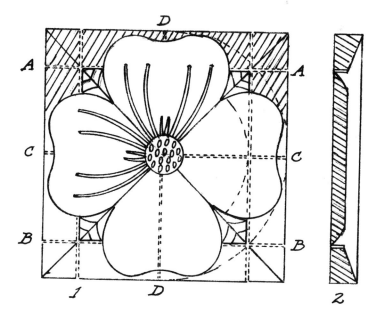

Fig. 411

The steps are:

1. Draw the design and trace it on the block, placing the little leaf ends, which are the tops of the feet, on the cross lines from opposite corners of the square and on the circumference of a circle which touches the four sides, at the ends of the petals, as indicated in Fig. 411.

Be sure the design is placed so that the pairs of little feet are aligned with the direction of the wood grain.

2. Attach the wood square to the workbench by framing it with pieces of ¾ inch by 1 inch by 8 inch wood, using a ⅜ inch thick wood spacer to raise the block ⅜ inch above the frame, which is nailed or screwed to the bench.

3. Carve the design of the dogwood blossom, using a veiner for the outline of the petals and the leaf ends, then the ⅛ inch gouge for the development of the petal design, the center of the blossom, and the lines on the leaf ends.

4. Reverse the wood block, wedging it firmly within the frames. Scribe a circle at diameter D, which forms the bottom of the trivet between the feet. Locate the feet in the same position on the bottom as on the top, and mark the outline of the petals with the two points of each petal and the end of the feet on the circumference of the outer circle, as indicated in sketch 1.

5. Mark the guide lines across the block from A to B and from C to D, at the points between the feet and petals, also at points centering in the curve of petals at opposite edges of the design, E and F.

6. With the hand saw, make cuts across the block on the three lines, not more than ⅜ inch deep. Turn the block, and saw cut cross lines from the inner V of the feet and the center of the curved petal, ⅜ inch deep across the block.

7. With the ½ inch skew chisel and gouge, remove the wood from the area within the circle to a depth of ⅜ inch or the bottom of the saw cuts. The cross section, sketch 2, indicates this level. Shape the feet between the outer saw cuts with a chisel or knife, and bevel smoothly as shown in Fig. 410.

8. Use the coping saw to cut away the corners of the block and around the outer circle, following the inward curve of the dogwood petals. Carefully trim down the bottoms of the petals with the ½ inch chisel sloping them from the inner circle D to an edge of about 3/16 inch. Round the curves to the V at the edges of the feet.

9. Remove the wood from the frame and then round the edges toward the bottom with a knife or file keeping exactly to the outline of the petals and feet. Redefine the petal outline and design lines with the small veiner and the center markings with the ⅛ inch gouge.

Lightly rub the sloping bottom area and undersides of the feet in the direction of the grain with a fine abrasive treated cloth. Wipe off dust or carving particles with a clean cloth, then apply three light coats of paste wax and polish well in between. If necessary, lightly rub the top with 0000 sandpaper, taking care not to blur any of the design lines or change the contour. Apply wax and rub well.

The leaf sandwich tray, Fig. 412, was made of cherry wood. Other suitable woods are maple, ash and applewood, as these are less likely to affect the taste of food. A ¾ inch thick piece 10 inches long and 7 inches wide, smoothly planed on both sides and the edges, is required for the making of this useful tray. The simple steps are:

Outline the contour of the leaf, Fig. 413, and the enlarged stem or handle for the tray, then mark the center line continuing the main leaf vein from the stem to the tip point. Also mark the lines which radiate from the stem and the center vein across the leaf vertically to end at the edges, in a variation of leaf vein lines.

1. Block the piece of wood on the worktable with 8 inch strips of wood about 2 inches by 3 inches on all edges, so that it is immovable.

2. Shape the center stem with even chisel cuts along the defining lines, then round it at the top, making it like a divider for the tray 3/16 inch by ⅜ inch. Evenly level the surfaces from the center vein for 2½ inches toward the edges on either side and along the stem. Slope the other inch of space upward to the same height at the margin as the dividing vein, or midrib of the leaf.

3. Smooth the surface of the leaf form with fine abrasive cloth and wipe with a clean cloth and a little wax to remove all particles of wood and abrasive.

4. Carve the vertical marked lines or veins of the leaf with the ⅛ inch U gouge keeping them exactly even and lightly cut as indicated in the sketch and photograph.

5. Turn the piece of wood over, block it firmly again in position to cut the outline with the coping saw, marked exactly as it was on the surface of the leaf form. In sawing, carefully follow the line to keep the contour curve even, also the size and position of the stem handle.

6. Leave the center section flat for a space about 4½ inches wide from the end of the stem and following the contour of the leaf to within 1½ inches from the tip, and 1½ inches from the margins, as indicated in Fig. 413, sketch B. With the ½ inch flat gouge, remove the wood from this base to the margins of the leaf and a thickness of 3/16 inch, like the level base of a plate or platter, with sloping rim.

7. Remove from the frame and round the edges of the leaf and the stem. Rub lightly with the grain, using an abrasive cloth and fine 000 sandpaper. Apply three coats of wax and rub well after each application.

Fig. 412

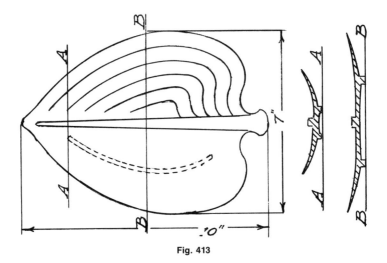

Fig. 413

The octagonal trinket box illustrated in Fig. 414 was made and carved in Latvia. The material is applewood and the size 5 inches in diameter at the points of the octagon with a depth of 1 inch finished, without the lid which is 3/16 inch. The over-all outside size is 5⅜ inches by 1 3/16 inches.

The box and the lid may each be cut in one piece and the inside areas removed with an electric router on a circle tangent to the octagonal sides, and the angles cut out with a chisel and V tool, with the inside dimension of the lid 1/16 inch wider at all points to fit down over the box.

A square or circular piece of wood 5⅛ inch in width or diameter and 1¼ inch thick is needed for cutting the sides of the box and a piece ⅜ inch by 5¼ inch for the lid. If made entirely by hand, the bottom piece can be separate, 5⅛ inches by 3/16 inch.

An easy way to make a pattern, Fig. 415, for each of the circles, inside and outside, is to scribe similar circles on paper, fold in the center for half, then in quarters, and last in eighths, without any variation. By connecting the points of the folds on the circumference, the resulting octagon should be perfectly proportioned for the similar division of the circles on the piece of wood.

Fig. 414

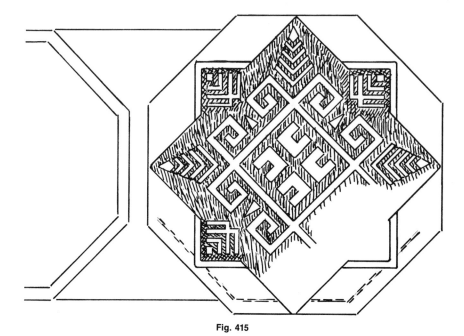

Fig. 415

1. With the piece of wood supported by a frame or clamped to the workbench, make the octagonal sides of the box first, starting with a circle tangent to the outside edges of the square, or just within the margin of the circular piece. Mark the equally divided segments for the 8 sides of the octagonal box and then cut them at exactly the same angle top and bottom, with a fine blade in a hand saw.

2. Draw and incise the inner circle to make a thickness of 3/16 inch for the octagonal sides and cut out the area within the circle with a coping saw. (To insert the detachable blade, drill a hole large enough to put it through the wood.) Finish removing the wood in the angles of the 8 sides with a chisel and ⅛ inch gouge, leaving them slightly rounded. Use a fine grit abrasive cloth to smooth the inner margins.

3. Mark a circle on the bottom piece exactly the same as the outside circumference of the sides, divide the circle into segments for the octagon which must match the lower edge of the 8 sides. Slightly round off the edge of the base, with a piece of fine sandpaper and smooth the surface of the bottom in the direction of the grain. Keep the upper edge of the bottom and the lower edge of the sides flat and level so that they will glue together without a crevice.

4. Apply a colorless wood adhesive to both the lower edge of the sides and the same width space on the bottom. Clamp them together to set, unless the adhesive will adhere sufficiently while held by hand.

5. The lid should be made in one piece, cut from a square or circular piece of wood ⅜ inch by 5⅜ inches. Mark two circles, slightly larger than the outside

and inside circles, at the top of the sides and 3/16 inch apart. Measure off the segments on the circles corresponding to the octagonal sides. If a router is available, use this to remove the area of wood within the inner circle to an even depth of 3/16 inch, then cut the corner angles between the 8 sides and the circle, leaving them 1/16 inch wider in circumference than the sides, so that the lid will fit down over them. If done by hand, use the ⅜ inch gouge to remove most of the wood finish with the skew chisel and the ⅛ inch gouge in the corners. Make the top of the lid no less than 3/16 inch.

6. Round down the margins of the top of the lid octagons from the square design area, Fig. 415. Smooth the surfaces and edges with a fine abrasive cloth, followed with 000 sandpaper. Do not rub against the grain in any part. Wipe with a clean cloth to remove the particles of wood and abrasive.

7. Carve the design on the top of the lid with the smallest veiner. If desired, emphasize the design with a colored stain applied with a small paint brush, or give it a jeweled effect with an inlay of enamel.

8. Three successive coats of paste, well rubbed after each application, will develop a soft, lustrous and durable finish.

The beautifully carved stamp box, Fig. 416, also from Latvia, requires the use of a wood turning lathe with a face plate. This part of the work can be done by a woodworking or cabinet shop.

1. The piece for the lid, Fig. 417A, of walnut should be 5 inches by 5 inches by ¾ inch to allow a margin for attachment to the face plate of the lathe with wood screws. When turned, the finished disc will be 4⅜ inches in diameter and ⅝ inch thick. The knob for the top of the lid is turned out of a piece of walnut, ¾ inches by ¾ inches by 2½ inches. When finished the knob will be ⅝ inch in diameter and 1¼ inches long.

2. To attach the knob, after it is carved, drill a ¼ inch hole 3/16 inch deep in the lid for insertion of the extended ¼ inch diameter post, which is also 3/16 inch long. After the top and knob are carved, apply wood glue to both the hole and the post, press the post into the hole, holding them firmly together for a few minutes, until the glue sets. The cross section sketch, Fig. 417, indicates the position, also the contour of the lid and its relation to the bowl or bottom part of the box.

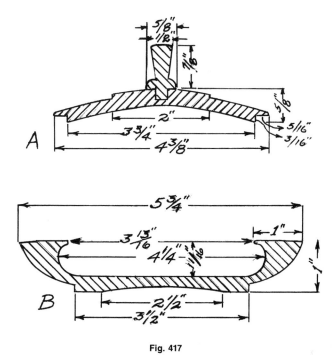

Fig. 417

3. The overall diameter of the circular box when finished is 5¾ inches and 1 inch thick, with the inside space 11/16 inches deep and 4¼ inches in diameter, narrowing to the top to 3-3/16 inches in diameter. The piece required for the lathe turning of the box is 7½ inches by 7½ inches by 1 inch, as indicated in the cross section sketch, Fig. 417B. This also shows the contour, and diameter of the finished box of maple which is used for this part. Lightly smooth all surfaces with an abrasive cloth, follow with 0000 sandpaper, and wipe with a clean cloth to remove all particles.

4. The design of the carving of the lid and the rim of the box is clearly shown in the illustration from which a tracing, with the dimensions indicated on the cross section sketch, can be made for transfer to the wood. Note that the four carved elements on the rim of the lid join four of the eight triangular points which in turn match every other one of the sixteen grooves in the rim of the box, which taper inward from a width of about 3/16 inch on the edge of the rim to meet the points on the lid.

5. Stain the outside and rim of the lower maple part of the box with a brown shade matching the natural walnut color of the lid. Leave the inside of the bowl part of the box the natural maple color. Apply to all surfaces the kind of one-coat finish which dries to a polished appearance without rubbing. This is available from sources listed on page 457.

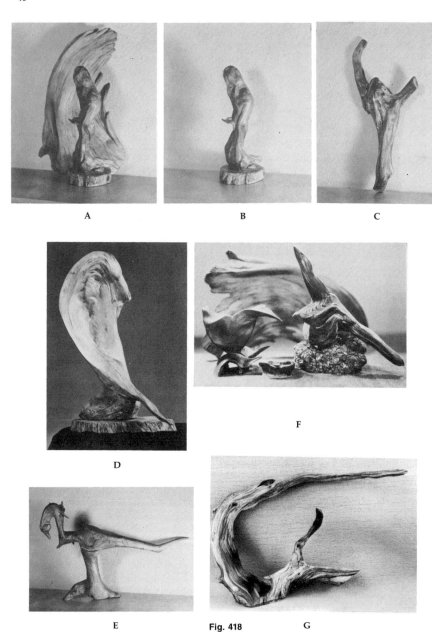

Fig. 418

The six figures, A, B, C, D, E and F were made from pieces of driftwood or weathered roots from fallen trees by the late Mrs. Aubrey Kempner of Boulder, Colorado. With imagination and great skill she revealed the forms here reproduced. A and B are the same angel and A has a sheltering wing. C is the figure of a prophet, D a nuclear cloud and E a bird survivor. F was called a symbol of spring. G is a root from a pine tree blown down at timberline and polished by wind and sand.

Finishing natural wood forms

Who has not observed a strangely fascinating piece of driftwood carved by nature with water, wind, and sand into fantastic shapes with beautiful gray-brown colors, and longed to seek and disclose its elemental form? The search and discovery of such shapes is a rewarding experience in the mountains or along nearly any waterfront.

The careful removal of decayed layers and pockets can be accomplished with a flat gouge or knife (not too sharp) and a fine wood rasp. Particles of bark and decayed wood can be removed with a stiff brush, revealing the weathered pattern of the wood grain and the natural shape which has resisted all the decaying forces. When completely clean, the smooth areas will show a gleaming surface with a little wax and lots of rubbing by hand. Occasional rubbing by hand with a very little furniture oil will maintain the polish and keep the form clean.

Whittling and figure carving

Many boys of all ages and times have found a diversion and a satisfying activity in whittling, and some famous figure carvers began with a pocket knife, a piece of wood, and the idea of depicting his dog or favorite pet. To a certain extent the skill or knack of whittling seems to come naturally, but the whittler has to learn a few essential and finger preserving points, namely:

Fig. 419

1. Get a knife of good steel, which is easy to keep sharp.
2. Follow the grain of the wood away from the figure outline.
3. Never cut toward yourself. Keep fingers out of the way of the blade. Remove thin layers of wood at a time.

4. If the figure outline, cut with a chisel blade, comes against the grain, make slanting or diagonal cuts to clear the outline until a straight cut with the grain is again possible.

The pictured figure of a farmer with his scythe, pipe, and scythe sharpener, Fig. 419, the only parts made separately, and then placed in the usual positions, was carved from a single piece of wood, the base of which seems to be carved like a rock pedestal.

The farmer's garments, green stained waistcoat, brown pantaloons, white socks, and shirt give him a very realistic appearance. They also make the work of carving him more simple than with a different outfit, such as western or southern farmers would wear. He represents a European farmer, and was carved in Switzerland.

The figure carver usually works from a profile outline of a picture or a model, from the front and side, adhering to physical measurements of body, arms, and face, unless he is making a caricature. A study of the famous carved figures from Oberammergau, and practice with them as examples, will enable almost any student carver to develop skill sufficient to carve any figure he may want to undertake. Pictures of the Oberammergau carvers and their work can be obtained from the German Tourist Bureau in New York City.

Fig. 420A is a practical adaptation for a lamp base of part of an old Colorado cedar root, finished by Mrs. Lillian Hemmie, the rock shop artist of Rock Creek, near Colorado Springs.

The arrow head lamp, Fig. 420B, was made from a section of an old cedar fallen log. Hand whittled, the reflecting copper colored surfaces give the light an effective background. The electric wire service was brought in from the back and the socket concealed by a circular section of cedar, which has been hollowed out. This slips down over the socket before the lamp is screwed in place. The holes through which counter sunk screws attach the arrowhead to the wall are concealed by dowel pin plugs. A sconce type shade can be attached if desired.

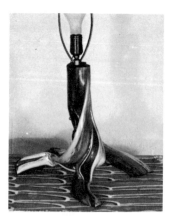

A   **Fig. 420**   B

Fig. 421

Woodwork, Mexican lathe turned method

Fig. 421 illustrates an exhibit of Mexican turned wood from the village of Paracho, where the chief occupation of the native worker or "paisano" is the forming and decoration of hollow ware from the madrona wood. This is seasoned by months of immersion in water, then completely dried, a process the workers claim which eliminates any tendency to warp, shrink, or split.

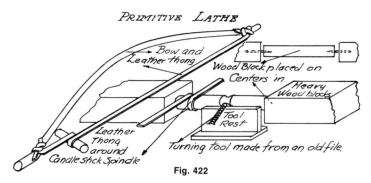

Fig. 422

The Paracho woodworkers have devised a primitive hand powered lathe as sketched in Fig. 422 for the aid of any ingenious craftsman, who prefers to dispense with powered devices, or is without electricity. The sketch shows how the spindle which holds the tool, made from the end of an old file, is turned by a thong, attached to the end of a bow, rotating the spindle and tool against the wood candlestick. It is held by the right hand, while the left moves the bow forward and pulls it back, winding and unwinding the leather thong to operate the spindle and tool to accomplish the turning of the wood.

The landscape on the lower part of the vase or lamp base, of the madrona wood, depicts the famous volcano, Paracutin, which erupted in a cornfield in 1947, and is said to be still active. This was painted with a brown stain on the natural light colored madrona wood, then the vases polished and rubbed to glasslike smoothness by burnishing against a piece of the wood.

The dark color on the candlestick was produced by friction induced heat, as a piece of soft wood was held against the rotating candlestick form, until sufficient heat was developed to char and blacken the area. The design was then produced on the dark areas with an engraving tool.

The little boxes were decorated with an incised design, contrasting with the dark stained surface. The knobs and inlay are of bone.

Inlay and Marquetry

Veneering or the covering of the surface of cheaper woods with thin layers of rare or more costly wood veneers was a practice of skilled woodworkers of the earliest civilizations. Furniture items found in the tombs of ancient Egypt's kings were veneered, and other civilizations of about the same time (3500 B.C.) left records of the work in items revealed in excavations. As wood was then scarce in the countries of Asia Minor, it may have been an early conservation practice as well as one of decoration, since the word veneer applied to the overlay of ivory, tortoise, or precious stones, as well as rare wood.

Veneer of contrasting dark, light, and figured grain wood is of interest to the craftsmen for work with inlay and marquetry or the assembly of wood pictures, a variation of woodworking. It has a great deal of appeal because of the originality possible for design combinations and the skills involved in construction.

Types of veneers and the steps in modern methods of producing them are fully described in *Veneering Made Easy* by Herman Hjorth and revised by Albert Constantine, Jr. It is now published by Albert Constantine and Son, Inc., New York importers and suppliers of wood and tools for craftsmen. Inquire of your area supplier for sources of veneer wood.

Veneer adhesives

Formerly an animal glue, or one made from the hoofs and horns, applied hot with the wood parts clamped together for at least 24 hours, was an essential process in veneering. Since resin plastic adhesives and catalysts, rubber based compounds and other synthetic materials became available, the use of glue which had to be applied hot and the practice of clamping will soon be a process of the past.

In veneering, as used in furniture making, as well as with veneer woods for inlay and marquetry craft work, modern adhesives have greatly simplified the procedures, to the great benefit of all who have undertaken this fascinating kind of craft work.

Elmer's Glue-all is a ready mixed adhesive which sets in 20 to 30 minutes at a 70 degree temperature. Pressure for the setting or curing period must be applied before the glue dries. It is transparent and does not stain, but must not come into contact with metal because of an acid content. It is one of the group of poly-vinyl resin products. Elmer's waterproof glue will withstand all kinds of weather conditions when applied and cured at temperatures of 70 degrees and above. The curing time varies according to the room temperature. Pressure for 4 to 6 hours is applied after 10 to 15 minutes of drying the separate parts before the glue covered surfaces are put together. It is a liquid to which a powder catalyst is added just before applying.

Cascamite and Weldwood are resin glues widely used in veneered furniture production as they are light in color and do not stain. They are water resistant and cure rapidly, 4 to 6 hours at 70 degrees with pressure. The time may be shortened to as many minutes with heat at 200 degrees F, obtainable with heated rubber blankets and other methods. Both are supplied in powder form with a catalyst and are mixed in water just before using. Sustained even pressure during the curing period is required.

Adhesives which unite pieces of wood or other materials to wood on contact are the latest significant improvement, which is a great advantage in all kinds of veneer work, and especially the inlay and marquetry craft projects which are described in this chapter. A temperature of no less than average room (70 degrees) is necessary. Surfaces to be united must have been fitted perfectly and leveled exactly alike, as no fitting or testing is possible after the glue is applied. The bond which is made on contact cannot be changed. Some contact adhesives are Weldwood Contact Cement and Constantine's Veneer Glue, both called "pressure-sensitive synthetic rubber and resin glue."

The above information is condensed from *Veneering Made Easy* by Herman Hjorth with the supplement, *Veneering Without Clamps* by Albert Constantine, Jr., published by Albert Constantine and Son, Inc., 2050 Eastchester Road, Bronx, New York 16461.

The minimum equipment for inlay and marketry projects:

Materials	Tools	Finishing Supplies
2 pieces ⅛ inch plywood of pine or gum 5 inches by 8 inches.	Jeweler's saw with blade No. 2/0 or 3/0.	Abrasives, Nos. 0 and 000 Garnet paper No. 280A wet or dry.
Sheets of veneer and veneer backing.	Hand drill and 1/32 inch bit, hammer, wire brads. Razor blade and holder or veneer saw.	Wood filler, shellac sticks to match veneer.
Veneer cement and brush. Inlaid bands and veneer for frame of picture.	Heavy straight edge, ⅜ inch by 1¼ inch by 18 inch. Design sheet carbon paper, pencil, veneer tape, square.	Alcohol lamp and alcohol. Knife, sanding sealer. Rubbing compound, wax. Spray gun and lacquer or varnish.

(Several other contact adhesives have recently been developed. Ask your supplier for his recommendation.)

Inlay

As the name indicates, inlay refers to a contrasting piece of material set into a cavity of the same size, shape, and depth in another material. The process embodies some of the elements of wood carving, and is an effective way to relieve a plain surface.

Carving for an inlay is like that of intaglio, in that it is the reverse of carving for relief or removing a background. A mold or impression from an intaglio produces a relief, the same principle as that used in making plaster molds.

1. A monogram or silhouette makes a good beginning project. Trace the design with a pencil as for a relief carving, then proceed to cut out the design, leaving the background intact. Be very careful, as the accidental removal of a chip beyond the design line margin may spoil it.

2. Use the incising knife and small 1/32 inch veiner for the lines and note that none should be too narrow to permit the inset of the decorating material or the inlay. Decide on the depth of the base according to that of the inlay, and level it smoothly with the curved gouge and a riffler file.

3. A helpful step is to form a pattern for the inlay with modeling clay, in separate sections for the kinds of wood veneers which will build the design. Trace the parts of the design on the selected veneer pieces. The standard 1/28 inch thickness of commercial veneers are suitable and more easily handled than other kinds of wood which must be planed or surfaced to the required thinness.

4. Drill a small hole for the insertion of the jeweler's saw blade and (as described for the technique of piercing wood, page 225, carefully cut out the sections of inlay as indicated in the design. Compare with the model and file a slight bevel downward on the lower edges to match the upward slope of the cavity.

5. Test the inlay sections and if any parts do not press readily into the cavity parts, file the edge very slightly. Coat the surface of the cavity and also the base of the inlay very lightly with a veneer glue and press them into place. *Follow directions for using any of the several types of modern veneer glues,* described on page 440.

If several sections have been required, plan the order for placing them in advance.

6. Apply the veneer glue to each section just before placing it, following the planned order for placing the larger and more difficult pieces first.

The trinket box in Fig. 414 was made of South American woods, native to the countries making up the continent, in corresponding inlays. These include prima vera or white mahogany for the top piece, rosewood, tulipwood, dark reddish brown mahogany, and other tropical woods from Brazil. The inlay technique was used in making the lid of the box and the construction detail, indicated in the illustration of the open box, is detailed for the marquetry box on page 444.

7. The inlaid tray with the nautical motif, Fig. 423C, is a simple and attractive project. A lathe-turned walnut tray, obtainable from wood craft suppliers, was routed out to a depth of ⅛ inch for the inlay of the center circle of redwood, in which the ship and wheel of white holly were previously inlaid.

Marquetry projects

The processes for projects in marquetry are similar to that described for inlay, except for the number of areas of the design which forms a unit and constitutes the entire surface for a picture, a panel, the lid of a box, or a decorative motif to be inlaid in a table top, chest, book cover, or other previously built article.

Marquetry is a French term and the technique was developed from the ancient practice of inlaid wood decoration by Jean Mace who was the first French marqueteur. In the 16th and 17th Centuries as furniture decoration it became popular in England and Europe. Another Frenchman, Andre Charles Boulle, who became the King's marqueteur, invented the method of making parts for four marquetries by cutting out two sets of interchangeable parts of a design.

The lids of the boxes with marquetry designs, illustrated in Fig. 423, were constructed as indicated in sketches 2, 3, 4 and 6. The material requirements follow:

Select hard wood for the box frame which is light or dark, and a contrasting shade for the bottom of the box and the base of the top, or lid part, on which the marquetry assembly will be placed. The sizes of the parts of the box are:

2 pieces of wood 5½ inches by 1⅜ inches by 5/16 inch for the sides.

2 pieces of wood 3½ inches by 1⅜ inches by 5/16 inch for the ends.

1 piece contrasting hard wood 3½ inches by 5½ inches by ⅛ inch for the bottom.

A   B

C   D

Fig. 423

Marquetry Box

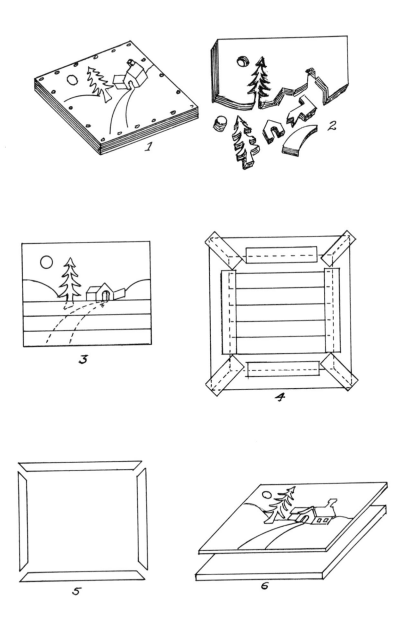

Fig. 424

1 piece contrasting hard wood 3½ inches by 5½ inches by ⅛ inch for the
top.

For the marquetry, 2 pieces of each color or grain of wood in the design or
picture plan. (Do not try to cut more than four pieces at one time.) Also required
are 2 pieces of veneer backing for a supporting cover and base for the veneer
picture parts while they are cut or sawed.

1. Assemble the box frame, sides and ends, with the corners mitered as
shown in Fig. 424, sketch 5. Glue them together with Elmer's Glue-all or the
equivalent. (It is essential that the workroom temperature be maintained between 60 and 70 degrees.) Follow directions carefully for the gluing process,
then wrap a length of Scotch wrapping tape or a heavy strip of rubber around
the frame and leave it to set or "cure" for 6 to 8 hours.

2. When the sides and ends are firmly united and the glue set, attach the
top and bottom pieces to the frame with the same cement. Wrap the box with
rubber bands and place it under the clamps as before. After 6 to 8 hours for the
glue to set, attach the marquetry assembly to the top.

3. Plan the marquetry design for the box lid, and for the first experiment
choose one without intricate detail. Simple landscapes for which two or three
color effects and variations in distances or elevations can be depicted with
different wood grains are satisfactory. Ships or boats with simulated water are
less difficult to reproduce with veneer wood than more detailed scenes.

4. Place the selected pieces of veneer wood together between the pieces
of veneer backing for support, with the grain of each piece in the direction
required by the design. Hold the pieces all together with Scotch tape as indicated
in Fig. 424, sketch 3.

5. Trace the design on the top wood backing piece with carbon paper,
unless it is possible to draw it freehand. The top piece of veneer backing may
have a coating of Chinese White paint if there is difficulty in getting a clear
design outline (see page 241).

6. Drill an opening for the insertion of the jeweler's saw blade and proceed to cut out the parts in sequence, placing them so that they can easily be
reassembled. Follow instructions for pierced work on page 225. *Caution.* It is
essential that the margins remain intact so that the design parts can be fitted
together interchangeably with no spaces between.

7. Test the parts, as they will be fitted together on the top piece of hard
wood, so that any variation in height may be corrected by sanding.

Assembly process

8. *Assemble each picture* on a piece of glass or any smooth level surface,
holding them together with tape as indicated in Fig. 424, sketch 3. Add pieces
and tape until the marquetry is complete. Compare with the hard wood top
piece, which will be the base for the marquetry picture, and carefully trim
any irregularity with a razor blade, Fig. 425, sketch 14, in a holder or a veneer
saw, Fig. 427B. Place on a piece of masonite or cardboard.

1. With the marquetry base on the hard level surface, apply an even coat
of veneer contact glue. Coat the base of the assembled marquetry, held face

down with the tape, and leave both, without any contact between for at least 30 minutes, but no longer than an hour. A test for the right degree of dryness is to press a piece of paper to a corner surface. If the glue does not adhere, it is sufficiently dry for the pieces to be put together.

2. The placement of these parts in exact alignment is the most particular step, as the bonding begins immediately and there can be no shifting after the surfaces touch each other. Spread a little rubber cement along opposite edges of the bottom of the hard wood base to keep it from moving on the glass when the marquetry is placed in contact.

3. Holding the marquetry in the right hand, place the glued surface of the *lower left hand corner* on the same corner of the base and press lightly with the left forefinger to hold it in position while carefully uniting the margins in alignment along the left end. Keep the marquetry assembly from touching the glue coated base until the end margins are evenly together, then smooth both parts together.

4. Press them with a roller, Fig. 427A, from one side across to the other, then reverse the direction and press back. Do the same with the ends. A rolling pin may be used, or if neither is available, it is possible to press all of the surfaces together with a rubber mallet. It is essential that no spots be missed in using the mallet.

5. Finally this top is ready to be glued to the box frame, Fig. 426, sketches H and J. Apply the contact cement to the edges and after 30 minutes or more delay, press them together with the rubber mallet or roller. Leave the tape in place on the face of the marquetry and then cut the box apart to make the lid ⅝ inch deep. A table saw, Fig. 426L with a guide, is necessary for this process, which may be done at a cabinet wood shop, if none is available otherwise. Carefully remove the tape from the marquetry face.

6. Finish the box according to the finishing process given on page 416. Then attach the hinges to complete the project.

Detail Marketry Box Top

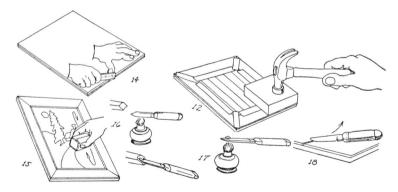

Fig. 425

Detail Marquetry Box Top

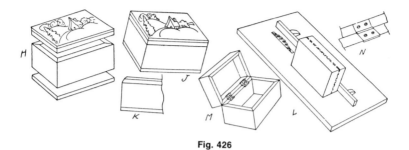

Fig. 426

Veneering Tools

A B

Fig. 427

A marquetry panel picture

1. Saw cut and assemble the wood picture, Fig. 428, in the same way the marquetry top for the little box was prepared. Square the corners and trim any irregularities as for the box project. Use the razor blade in the holder, or the special veneer saw, which is available from suppliers.

2. Place border strips of inlaid bands around the trimmed picture, Fig. 425, sketch 12. (The bands are available in a variety of patterns from suppliers.) For the frame, cut border strips from contrasting veneer and fit them to the marquetry panel, overlapping the corners. Attach tape on the front to hold the marquetry and the bands together.

3. Measure and mark them exactly alike for the cutting of the miters. This should be done along a straight edge with the razor blade or veneer saw. Place a strip of tape along the mitered corners on the face side to hold them from breaking or separating, until all parts are glued to the base.

4. Prepare a suitable base of ¼ inch plywood, pine or gum. Masonite press board will also make a satisfactory base. Cement the marquetry picture and frame to it using the veneer contact cement and method of applying as given for the box lid, or one of the resin type cements. Trim any edge unevenness and bind the panel with a matching veneer tape.

Marketry Panel

Fig. 428

Table with mosaic top

The photograph, Fig. 429 illustrates an unusually attractive table with an assembly of six separable units in a size useful for individual serving. The sketch of the unit construction detail, Fig. 430, indicates the method of making the wood frame and insets for the top. *The following material items, in addition to the assortment of Venetian tile,* are required for each unit:

For the six 24 inch by 24 inch by 24 inch unit hexagon shaped table shown in the photograph and sketch;

Base—1 piece—¾ inch plywood 24 inch by 24 inch by 24 inch triangle;
Hard wood inset for each unit. One piece ¾ inch walnut or other hard wood, 12 inches by 12 inches by 12 inches;

Legs. Three pieces 1½ inches by 1½ inches by 12 inches. Lathe turned and
tapered to 1 inch square (or commercial type table legs of similar
dimensions). Three #9 wood screws 2½ inches long;
screws, 2½ inches long;

Edge. Three pieces ¼ inch by 1¼ inch by 25 inch walnut.

Fig. 429

Assembly procedure

1. Cut the plywood to size.

2. Lay out the position of the legs and drill with a 1 inch diamond drill
to receive the screws.

3. Counter sink the top to receive the head of the #9 screws.

4. Screw the legs to the plywood top.

5. Glue the triangular piece of walnut to the plywood top.

6. Miter the walnut edge frame pieces, fit closely (sand if necessary)
around the top of the plywood. Glue together with contact cement.

7. Finish the hard wood pieces and polish.

8. Mount the Venetian tile in Mosaic cement on the space in the plywood
top of the base of the triangle of hard wood. (Directions on page 450.)

All six units are identical in size and construction, equilateral triangles
that are assembled together make a perfect hexagon. The tile for the top sections
12 inches by 12 inches by 24 inches should be placed in even or random
patterns according to a planned design of harmonious colors and sizes,
similar to the table shown in the photograph. This was designed and tiled by
Heidi Brandt, artist-craftsman and designer.

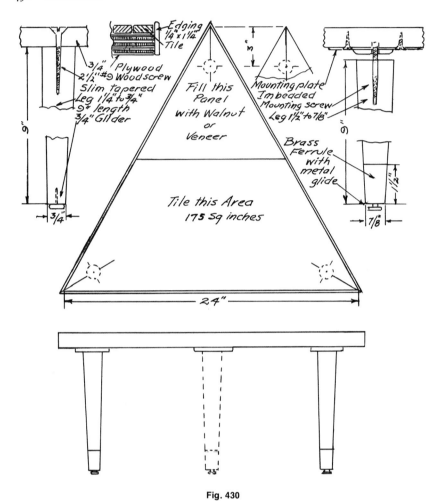

Edging
1/4 x 1 1/4
Tile

3/4" Plywood
2 1/2" #9 Woodscrew
Slim tapered
Leg 1 1/4" to 3/4"
9" length
3/4" Glider

9"

3/4"

Fill this
Panel
with Walnut
or
Veneer

3"

Mounting plate
Imbedded
Mounting screw
Leg 1 1/2" to 7/8"

Tile this Area
175 Sq inches

9"

Brass
Ferrule
with
metal
glide

1/2"

7/8"

24"

23"

Fig. 430

GENERAL CRAFTS SOURCES OF SUPPLY

1. American Handicrafts Corp., Division of Tandy Leather Company and Agencies, 1515 S. University Drive, Fort Worth, Texas, 76107. (Write for location nearest Agent.)
2. Arts and Crafts Material Corp., 321 Park Ave., Baltimore, Maryland, 21201.
3. Craftools Inc., Woodridge, New Jersey, 07175. (Agent for Triarco Arts and Crafts.)
4. William Dixon Inc., 32-42 East Kinney St., Newark, New Jersey, 07101.
5. Griffin Craft Supplies, 669 — 20th Street, Oakland, California, 94604.
6. Handcrafters, Manufacturer and Distributor, Waupun, Wisconsin, 53963.
7. Patterson Brothers, Division of Paxton National Inc., 45 Samworth Road, Clifton, New Jersey, 07012.
   Paxton, Equipment and Supply, Division of Paxton National Inc., 7401 South Pulaski Road, Chicago, Illinois, 60629.
8. Sax Arts and Crafts, Division of Sax Co., 1103 N. Third St., Milwaukee, Wisconsin, 53203.
9. Triarco Handicraft Supplies, available from agents:
   Delco Craft Center, Inc., 30081 Stephenson Highway, Madison Heights, Michigan, 48071.
   Gager's Handicraft, 1624 Nicollet Ave., Minneapolis, Minnesota.
   J. C. Larson Co., Inc., 820 S. Tripp Ave., Chicago, Illinois, 60624.
10. Western Manufacturing Co., Sto-Rex Craft Dept., 149 Ninth Street, San Francisco, California.

Consult your local dealer for location of agency
or write the company for information.

REFERENCES AND SOURCES OF SUPPLY

Basketry

Reference Books:

Christopher, Frederick J., *Basketry,* Dover Publications, Inc., New York, N.Y., 10014, 1952.

Eaton, Allen H., *Handicrafts of the Southern Highlands,* Russell Sage Foundation, New York, N.Y., 10017. (Available in libraries, at present Out of Print.)

James, George Wharton, *Practical Basket Making,* J. L. Hammett Co., Boston, Massachusetts, 02142.

Lee, Martha L., *Basketry and Related Arts,* D. Van Nostrand Co., Inc., Princeton, New Jersey, 08540, 1948.

Wright, Dorothy, *Baskets and Basketry,* C. T. Branford Co., Newton Centre, Massachusetts, 02150, 1959.

Sources of Supply:

American Reedcraft Corp., 417 Lafayette Ave., Hawthorne, New Jersey, 07507.

J. L. Hammett Co., 48 Canal St., Boston, Massachusetts, 02142.

Handcrafters, Waupun, Wisconsin, 53963.

Le Jeune Inc., Sunnyvale, California, 94080.

H. H. Perkins Co., 228 Shelton Ave., New Haven, Connecticut, 06506.

(See also, General Crafts Sources of Supply, page 451. Refer to numbers 1, 2, 5, 6, 8, 9, and 10.)

Bookbinding

Reference Books:

Banister, M., *Pictorial Manual of Bookbinding,* Ronald Press Co., New York, N.Y., 10010, 1958.

Corderoy, John, *Bookbinding for Beginners,* Watson-Guptill Publications, Inc., New York, N.Y., 10036, 1967.

Klinefelter, Lee M., *Bookbinding Made Easy,* Bruce Publishing Co., Milwaukee, Wisconsin, 53201, rev. ed. 1960.

Lewis, Arthur W., *Basic Bookbinding,* Dover Publications, Inc., New York, N.Y., 10014, 1952.

Sources of Supply:

Craftools, Inc., Woodridge, New Jersey, 07075.

Patterson Bros., Division of Frank Paxton, 45 Samworth Road, Clifton, New Jersey, 07012.

Paxton Equipment and Supply, 7401 S. Pulaski Road, Chicago, Illinois, 60629.

(See also, General Crafts Sources of Supply, page 451. Refer to numbers 2, 5, 7, 9.)

Ceramics

Reference Books:

Binns, C. F., *The Potter's Craft,* D. Van Nostrand Co., Inc., Princeton, New Jersey, 08540, 4th ed. 1967.

Drake, Kenneth, *Simple Pottery,* Watson-Guptill Publications, Inc., New York, N.Y., 10036, 1966.

Kenny, John B., *Complete Book of Pottery Making,* Chilton Books, Philadelphia, Pennsylvania, 19106, 1963.

Long, Lois Culver, *Ceramic Decoration,* American Art Clay Co., Indianapolis, Indiana, 46222, 1958.

Nelson, Glen C., *Ceramics: A potter's handbook,* Holt, Rinehart & Winston Inc., New York, N.Y., 10017, 1966.

Magazines:

Ceramics Arts and Crafts, Detroit, Michigan, 48227.

Ceramics Magazine, 4175 N. High St., Columbus, Ohio, 43214.

Sources of Supply:

American Art Clay Co., 4717 W. 16th, Indianapolis, Indiana, 46222.
Bell Ceramics, Inc., Rt. #10, Tabor Road, Morris Plains, New Jersey, 07952.
Carmona Creations, Ceramic Designs, 4351 Hasken, Bay City, Michigan, 48106.
Ceramichrome, Inc., P.O. Box 2086, Gardena, California, 90247.
Cress Co., Inc., (kilns), 323 W. Maple Ave., Monrovia, California, 91016.
Denver Fire Clay Co., (kilns, refractories, clay, insulating brick) 3033 Blake St., Denver, Colorado, 80205.
Newell Studios, 6707 W. Boulevard, Inglewood, California.
Skutt and Sons, Inc., (ceramic kilns, electric potters wheels), 2618 S.E. Steele St., Portland, Oregon, 97202.
Stewart Clay Co., 113 Mulberry St., New York, N.Y.
Van Horne Ceramic Supply, 1185 S. Cherokee St., Denver, Colorado, 80223.
Jack D. Wolfe Co., Inc., (construction materials, electric kilns), 724-734 Meeker Ave., Brooklyn, N.Y., 11222.
(See also, General Crafts Sources of Supply, page 451. Refer to numbers 2, 3, 5, 8, 9.)

Decoration of Fabrics, Paper and Wood

Reference Books:

Adams, Ruth, *Pennsylvania Dutch Art*, World Publishing Co., Cleveland, Ohio, 44102, 1950.
Eisenberg, James and Francis J. Kafka, *Silk Screen Printing*, McKnight and McKnight Publishing Co., Bloomington, Illinois, 61702, 1958.
Hobson, J., *The Hand Decoration of Fabrics*, Craftools Inc., Woodridge, New Jersey, 07175.
Kafka, Francis J., *The Hand Decoration of Fabrics*, McKnight and McKnight Publishing Co., Bloomington, Illinois, 61702, 1959.
Kent, Cyril and Mary Cooper, *Simple Printmaking*, Watson-Guptill Publications, Inc., New York, N.Y. 10036, 1967.
Steffan, Bernard, *Silk Screen*, Pitman Publishing Corp., New York, N.Y., 10017, 1963.
Trevelyan, Julian, *Etching*, Watson-Guptill Publications, Inc., New York, N.Y., 10036, 1964.

Sources of Supply:

Patterson Bros., Division of Frank Paxton, 45 Samworth Road, Clifton, New Jersey, 07012.
Paxton Equipment and Supply, 7401 S. Pulaski Road, Chicago, Illinois, 60629.
(See also General Crafts Sources of Supply, page 451. Refer to numbers 2, 3, 5, 8 and 9.)
(Consult local dealers in artist's materials)

Lapidary

Reference Books:

Baxter, William T., *Jewelry, Gem Cutting and Metalcraft*, McGraw-Hill Book Co., New York, N.Y., 10036, 3rd edition, 1950.
Dake, Henry C., *The Agate Book*, International Gem Corp., New York, N.Y.
Dake, Henry C. and Richard M. Pearl, *The Art of Gem Cutting*, J. D. Simpson, Spokane, Washington, 99206, 7th ed., 1963.
Kraus, Edward H. and Chester B. Slawson, *Gems and Gem Materials*, McGraw-Hill Book Co., New York, N.Y., 10036, 1947.
Pearl, Richard M., *Popular Gemology*, John Wiley & Sons Inc., New York, N.Y., 10016, 1948 — also in paperback, 1965.
Sinkankas, John, *Gem Cutting*, D. Van Nostrand Co., Inc., Princeton, New Jersey, 08540, 1962.
Sinkankas, John, *Gem Stones of North America*, D. Van Nostrand Co., Inc., Princeton, New Jersey, 08540, 1959.
Victor, Arthur E. and Lila May, *Gem Tumbling and Baroque Jewelry Making*, J. D. Simpson, Spokane, Washington, 99206, 1965.

Magazines:

Earth Science Digest, P.O. Box 1357, Downers Grove, Illinois, 60515.

Gems and Gemology, Gemological Institute of America, 11940 San Vicente Blvd., Los Angeles, California, 90049.

Gems and Minerals, P.O. Box 657, Mentone, California, 92359.

The Lapidary Journal, P.O. Box 2309, San Diego, California, 92112.

Rocks and Minerals, P.O. Box 29, Peekskill, New York, 10566.

Sources of Supply:

Behr Manning, Division of Norton Co., (coated abrasives), Troy, New York, 12181.

Covington Engineering Corp., (lapidary equipment), 112 First St., Redlands, California, 92373.

The Gem Exchange, (gems and supplies for lapidary and jewelry), Gem Village, Bayfield, Colorado, 81122.

Griegers, Inc., (gems and supplies for lapidary and jewelry), 1633 E. Walnut St., South Pasadena, California, 91106.

Highland Park Manufacturing Co., (precision lapidary equipment), 1009-1011 Mission St., South Pasadena, California, 91030.

International Gem Corp., (gems, equipment and supplies), 15 Maiden Lane, New York.

Lloyd's Art Shop, (alabaster preform shapes), 1505 N. College St., Fort Collins, Colorado.

3M, Minnesota Mining and Manufacturing Co., (diamond coated abrasive discs), St. Paul, Minnesota, 55119.

(See also, General Crafts Sources of Supply, page 451. Refer to numbers 3 and 4.)

(Consult your local dealer for location of agency or write the company for information.)

Leather Craftwork

Reference Books:

Cherry, Raymond, *General Leathercraft,* McKnight and McKnight Publishing Co., Bloomington, Illinois, 61702, 1958.

Leland, Charles G., *Leather Work,* Isaac Pitman & Sons, London & New York, N.Y., 11017, library reference, 1926.

Willoughby, George A., *General Crafts,* Charles A. Bennett Co., Inc., Peoria, Illinois, 61614, 1959.

Instructional Material:

Stohlman, Al, Leather Projects Instruction charts and booklets, Craftool Publications, Woodridge, New Jersey, 07075.

Sources of Supply:

Robert J. Golka Co., and New England Handicraft Supplies, 400 Warren Ave., Brockton, Massachusetts, 02403.

J. L. Hammett Co., 48 Canal St., Boston, Massachusetts, 02142.

Fred Mueller Inc., 1415 Larimer St., Denver, Colorado, 80202.

Oregon Leather Co., 110 N.W. Second Ave., Portland, Oregon, 97209.

Tandy Leather Co., 1515 S. University Drive, Fort Worth, Texas, 76107.

(See also, General Crafts Sources of Supply, page 451. Refer to numbers 1, 2, 3, 4, 5, 7, 8, 9, and 10.)

(Consult your local dealer for location of agency or write the company for information.)

Metal

Reference Books:

Adair, John, *The Navajo and Pueblo Silversmiths,* University of Oklahoma Press, Faculty Exchange, Norman, Oklahoma, 73069, 1954.

Baxter, William T., *Jewelry, Gem Cutting, and Metal Craft,* McGraw-Hill Book Co., New York, N.Y., 10036, 1950.

Buhler, Kathryn C., *American Silver,* World Publishing Co., Cleveland, Ohio, 44102.

Hagstoz & Son, T. B., Metal Craft Department, *Craft Metals*, Philadelphia, Pennsylvania, 19100.

Manzoni, Peter, *Metalcraft for Amateurs*, The Beacon Press, Boston, Massachusetts, 02108. (library reference) Out of Print.

Mattson, E. B., *Creative Metalworking*, Bruce Publishing Co., Milwaukee, Wisconsin, 53201, 1960.

Pack, Greta, *Jewelry and Enameling*, D. Van Nostrand Co., Inc., Princeton, New Jersey, 08540, 1961.

Rose, Augustus F. and Antonio Cirino, *Jewelry Making and Design*, Dover Publications, New York, N.Y., 10014, revision in paperback, 196?.

Spielman, Patrick E., *Modern Projects In Wood, Metal and Plastics*, Bruce Publishing Co., Milwaukee, Wisconsin, 53201, 1964.

Sources of Supply:

Anchor Tool and Supply Co., Inc., 12-16 John St., New York, N.Y.

Grieger's Inc., (jewelry supplies), 1633 E. Walnut St., Pasadena, California, 94640.

Revere Copper and Brass, (Britannia Metal [pewter], foils), 196 Diamond St., Brooklyn, New York, 11222.

Southwest Smelting and Refining Co., 1703 Jackson St., Dallas, Texas, 75221.

T. B. Hagstoz & Son, (sheet metals and jewelry supplies), 709 Sansom St., Philadelphia, Pennsylvania, 19106.

White Metal Rolling & Stamping Co., (pewter sheets and circles), 80 Moulfire St., Brooklyn, New York, 11222.

Additional Metal Craft Suppliers:

American Art Clay Co., (enameling and mosaic materials), 4717 West 16th St., Indianapolis, Indiana, 46222.

C. R. Hill & Co., (metals, tools, jewelry findings), 35 W. Grand River, Detroit, Michigan, 48226.

Jack D. Wolfe, (materials and equipment for enameling), 724-34 Meeker Ave., Brooklyn, New York, 11222.

Mosaic Arts Co., (American and imported tile, tools and equipment), 3522 Blvd. of the Allies, Pittsburgh, Pennsylvania.

Stewart Clay Co., Inc., (metal enameling supplies, mosaics), 133 Mulberry St., New York, New York.

Thomas C. Thompson Co., (copper shapes and materials for enameling), 1539 Old Deerfield Road, Highland Park, Illinois, 60038.

Additional Book References:

Berry, John, *Making Mosaics*, Watson-Guptill Publications Inc., New York, N.Y., 10036, 1967.

Thomas, Richard, *Metalsmithing*, Chilton Books, Philadelphia, Pennsylvania, 19106, 1960.

Untracht, Oppi, *Enameling on Metal*, Chilton Books, Philadelphia, Pennsylvania, 19106, 1957.

(See also, General Crafts Sources of Supply, page 451. Refer to numbers 1, 2, 3, 4, 5, 7, 8, 9, and 10.)

Plaiting Methods and Materials

Reference Books:

Belash, C. A., *Braiding and Knotting for Amateurs*, Charles T. Branford Co., Newton Centre, Massachusetts, 02159, 1947.

Grant, Bruce, *Leather Braiding*, Cornell Maritime Press, Inc., Cambridge, Maryland, 21613, 1950.

Griffith, Le Jeune, *Swistraw Ribbon Craft Ideas*, Le Jeune, Inc., Sunnyvale, California.

Underhill, Ruth, *Pueblo Crafts (Of the S.W. Indians)*, U.S. Indian Service, 1948. Education Division, (library reference), Out of Print.

Vaughn, Cy, *Uses for Craftstrip*, The Rex Corp., W. Acton, Mass., 1954.

Sources of Supply:

J. L. Hammett, (handcraft supplies including cord, leather & yarn), 48 Canal St., Boston, Massachusetts, 02142.

Le Jeune Inc., (swistraw), Sunnyvale, California.

P. C. Herwig, (cord and square knot materials), 264 Clinton St., Brooklyn, New York, 01201.

Raymond Cornell (rawhide thongs) 7500 Arapaho Street, Boulder, Colorado 80302

(See also, General Crafts Sources of Supply, page 451. Refer to numbers 1, 2, 5, 7, 8, 9, and 10.)

Plastics

Reference Books:

Cherry, Raymond, *General Plastics, Projects and Procedures,* McKnight and McKnight Publishing Co., Bloomington, Illinois, 61702, 1966.

Plastics Industry, *Modern Plastics Encyclopedia,* McGraw-Hill Book Co., New York, N.Y., 10036. (Annual issue for subscribers of "Modern Plastics Magazine".

Spielman, Patrick E., *Modern Projects In Wood, Metal and Plastics,* Bruce Publishing Co., Milwaukee, Wisconsin, 53201, 1964.

Steele, Gerald L., *Fiber Glass Projects and Procedure,* McKnight and McKnight Publishing Co., Bloomington, Illinois, 61702, 1961.

Swanson, Robert S., *Plastics Technology, Basic Materials and Processes,* McGraw-Hill Book Co., New York, N.Y., 10036, 1965.

Sources of Supply:

The Castolite Co., Woodstock, Illinois, 60098.

Immerman and Sons, Inc., 16912 Miles Ave., Cleveland, Ohio.

Plasticraft Inc., 2800 N. Speer Blvd., Denver, Colorado, 80212.

Plastics Products Co., P.O. Box 1415, 2340 S.W. Temple, Salt Lake City, Utah, 84110.

Poly-Dec. Co., Inc., P.O. Box 431, Bergen Point, New Jersey, 07002.

Jack D. Wolfe Co., 724-34 Meeker Ave., Brooklyn, N.Y., 11222.

(See also, General Crafts Sources of Supply, page 451. Refer to numbers 1, 2, 5, 7, 9, and 10.)

Weaving

Reference Books:

Atwater, Mary Meigs, *Design and the Handweaver,* 1961 Craft and Hobby Book Service, P.O. Box 626, Pacific Grove, California 93950.

Atwater, Mary Meigs, *Pattern for Handweaving,* 1957 Craft and Hobby Book Service, P.O. Box 626, Pacific Grove, California 93950.

Atwater, Mary Meigs, *The Shuttlecraft Book of American Handweaving,* 1959 Craft and Hobby Book Service, P.O. Box 626, Pacific Grove, California 93950.

Beutlich, Tadek, *The Technique of Woven Tapestry,* Watson-Guptill Publications Inc., New York, N.Y., 10036, 1967.

Black, Mary E., *New Key to Weaving,* Bruce Publishing Co., Milwaukee, Wisconsin, 53201, 1957.

Davenport, Elsie G., *Your Handspinning,* 1964 Craft and Hobby Book Service, P.O. Box 626, Pacific Grove, California 93950.

Ludgate, H. T., *Popular Netcraft.*

Matthews, Washington, *Navaho Weavers, Vol III,* Bureau of American Ethnology, Smithsonian Institute, Washington, D.C., (library reference).

The Netcraft Co., (materials for nets), 3131 Sylvania Ave., Toledo, Ohio, 94086.

Tidball, Harriet, *Handloom Weaves,* 1957 Craft and Hobby Book Service, P.O. Box 626, Pacific Grove, California 93950.

Tidball, Harriet, *Handweavers' Project Book,* 1960 Craft and Hobby Book Service, P.O. Box 626, Pacific Grove California 93950.

Tidball, Harriet, *The Inkle Weave,* 1952, *Mexican Motifs,* and others, Craft and Hobby Book Service, P.O. Box 626, Pacific Grove, California 93950

Tidball, Harriet, *The Weaver's Book, Fundamentals of Weaving,* Macmillan Co., New York, N.Y., 10022, 1961.

Weaving

Sources of Supply:

J. L. Hammett Handweaving and Handicraft Supplies, 48 Canal St., Boston, Massachusetts, 02142.

The Handcrafters, (supplies for handcraft and occupational therapy), Waupun, Wisconsin, 53963.

The Lily Mills Co., (supplies and weaving accessories), Agent for Leclerc L'Isletville, Quebec, Canada, 44102.

Structo Manufacturing Co., Division of King-Seeley Thermos Co., Freeport, Illinois, 61032.

(See also, General Crafts Sources of Supply, page 451. Refer to numbers 2, 3, 5, 7, and 8.)

Woodwork

Reference Books:

Aller, Doris, *Wood Carving,* a Sunset Book, Lane Magazine & Book Co., Menlo Park, California, 94025, 1966.

Capron, J. Hugh, *Wood Laminating,* McKnight and McKnight Publishing Co., Bloomington, Illinois, 61702, 1962.

Hjorth, Herman, revised by Constantine, Albert Jr., *Veneering Made Easy,* Albert Constantine & Son Inc., Bronx, N.Y., 10461.

Gottshal, Franklin H., *Woodcarving and Whittling Made Easy,* Bruce Publishing Co., Milwaukee, Wisconsin, 53201, 1962.

Graveney, Charles, *Woodcarving for Beginners,* Watson-Guptill Publications Inc., New York, N.Y., 10036, 1967.

Hunt, Ben, *Whittling with Ben Hunt,* Bruce Publishing Co., Milwaukee, Wisconsin, 53201, 1959.

Spielman, Patrick E., *Modern Projects In Wood, Metal and Plastics,* Bruce Publishing Co., Milwaukee, Wisconsin, 53201, 1964.

Stanley Tool Division, Education Department, *How to Work with Tools and Wood,* The Stanley World, New Britain, Connecticut, 06050.

Tangerman, E. J., *Whittling and Woodcarving,* Dover Publications, Inc., New York, N.Y., 10014, 1936.

Sources of Supply:

Albert Constantine and Son, Inc., 2050 E. Chester Road, Bronx, N.Y., 10461.

Craftsman Wood Service Co., 2727 South Mary Street, Chicago, Illinois, 60808.

Lusky, White & Collidge Inc., 214-216 W. Monroe Street, Chicago, Illinois, 60606.

(See also, General Crafts Sources of Supply, page 451. Refer to numbers 3, 4, 5, 6, 7, 8, 9, and 10.)

INDEX

DESIGN IN HANDICRAFT

Design, elements of, 1; examples, 2-5; Ancient Mexican motif, 3

Ornamental design, principles of, 6; examples, 3

Structural design, principles of, 6; examples, 6

BASKETRY

Equipment and materials, 8-9; commercial, 9; natural, 8

Historical notes, 7, 8

Indian techniques: Apache, 17; Cherokee, 37; Hopi, 15, 16; examples and construction, 15; Mexican, 18

Types of baskets and methods of weaving, 11, 13; harness frame, 34; oval basket with handle, 31; pack basket (Adirondack), 34; patterns, 10; pine needle, 18; preparation of materials — spokes, 8; weavers, 8; round mats, plate holders, trays, 12; splint, 25; stitches for coiled baskets, 16; terms, 9; willow, 23

BOOKBINDING

Guild period, 40; hand binding, 41

Preparing a new case (cover), 45

Rebinding a book, 41; restoration of case, 44; reinforcing the back, 43; attaching to case, 45

Small books: construction and binding, 45; albums, 46; notebooks, 46; scrapbooks, 46

Terms: backstrip, 41; boards, 41; case, 41; contents, 41; signatures, 41; tape 41

CERAMICS

Casting clay forms, 70; cast formed jars, 75; molds 70

Classification of clay bodies, 54

Composition, 48; chemical 48, 54; organic, 48

Containers, 69; bats (Plaster of Paris), 69

Decoration, 59; application of coloring, 63; engobe, 60; design painting, 61; ceramic paints, 63; crayons for underglaze painting, 62; incised designs, 60; sgraffito, 61

Drying, 53

Engobe preparation and use (slip), 62

Equipment, 48

Firing: bisque or green ware, 52; glazed, 56; porcelain, 54; stages of temperature, 54

Glazes: kinds available, 55, 56; methods of applying, 55, 56; substitutes, 55

Grog: how prepared, 53; when used, 53, 59

Gum tragacanth, 82

Historical, 47, 48; pre-historic pottery in Denver Art Museum, 4, 5

Handles: press molded, 75

Indian methods: Maria Martinez, 108; designs, 106; sources, 103

Kinds of clay: ball clay, 53; fireclay, 54; kaolin, 48

Kilns: (Electric) materials and plans for portable, 58; stationary, 57; temperature, 56

Making of molds: preparation, 69; pouring of slip, 71; (Plaster of Paris), 70; press mold, 75; reverse mold, 67

Parting compound of sizing, 70

Preparation of clay: drying, 49; grinding, 49; mixing, 49; screening, 49; testing, 48, 49, 85

Projects: cast, 70; coiled, 84, 86; hand built, 65; ash tray, 65; dish, 78; Planter, 66; mold formed bowls, 70; jars, 75; plates, 68; porcelain flowers, demonstration Mrs. Gloss, 102

Mosaics: kinds and sources of tessarae, 80; setting, 97; ceramic, 96; glass, 96

Mosaic projects: tile, 97; table top, 101; wall hangings, 99

Pyrometric cones, 51

Qualities of clay: density, 51; plasticity, 49; porosity, 50; shrinkage, 51; vitrification, 50

Throwing on the wheel, 91; demonstration Fred Wills, 92-95

Tile making, 80; examples from Desert House, 83

Van Briggle Pottery examples, 95

Workshop experiments and projects, (Lewiston, Idaho), 86; bowls, 89, 90; dripping fountain, 91; lamps, 89; teaset, 89

DECORATION, Fabrics, Paper, Wood

Batik 1. Javanese Wax resist method, 124; Batik 2. Dye stopper method, 126

Design painting on wood: projects: plates, 114; covered bowl, 113; Pennsylvania Dutch designs and use, 113

Design printing on fabrics, brush method, 111

Printing from linoleum blocks on paper and fabrics, 117

Silk screen design printing, 120

LAPIDARY

Abrasives, 138

Agates: agatized wood, 130; cabochons, 132; specimens, 132

Alabaster: methods of working, 144; carving, 144; polishing, 145
    Projects: hand built, 144; lathe burned, 145; with cedar, 145

Diamond saw: operation, 131; precautions, 132

Equipment for gem cutting: grinding, 133; polishing, 137; tumbler method of polishing, 139; turquoise, 140

Gem stones: classification 130; scale of harness, 130; synthetic gems, 139; turquoise, 140; spheres, 141

Motor driven arbors: polishing wheels, 138; sanding wheels, 137

Pump drill for bead hole drilling, 142

Stone flaking, 149

Stone sculpture, 143

Tumblers: kinds and operation, 139

Wheels: abrasive, 133; polishing, 138

LEATHER

Assembly processes: edge finish, 161; edge lacing, 168; making of lacing, 163; principles and steps in lacing, 165; splicing, 166; sewing with waxed thread, 211

Classification of Leather, 151; tanning methods, 153; primitive, 153; modern, 153; sources, 454

Cutting: projects, 153; thongs for lacing, 163

Decoration: design selection and transfer, 157
    design background: modeled, 158; stamped, 158; stippled, 159
    design tooling: beveled outline, 157; double bevel outline, 158; repousse, 159

Equipment and essential tools, 144, 155

Fastening devices: snap fasteners, 176; slides, 192; thongs, 163

Gussets for purses, 156; for camera cases, 183; brief cases, 207; process of lacing, 185

Key plates, 176

Perforation of edges for lacing, 162; punching, 162

Projects: For calfskin and steerhide tooling leather:
    Bill folds: construction process, 180; patterns, 180
    Book ends: construction process, 182; patterns, 182
    Brief cases: construction process, 206; patterns, 205; portfolio style, 204; with slide fastener, 205
    Coin purses: double, 178, folding, 186; memo, 179; single 178
    Designs for tooled leather, 160
    Envelope purse: construction process, 195; pattern, 195
    Hand purses: small folded, 188; slide fastener, 192; patterns for hand purses, 191
    Knitting or utility bag: construction detail, 199
    Moccasins: construction detail, 212; pattern making, 213
    Notebooks: attachment of metal binder, 184; cover type of manuals, 181
    Photograph Album, 182
    Projects for cowhide or strap leather: carved, 206; stamped, 206
        Belts: cutting and preparation for carving or stamping, 171
        Brief case: regulation style, 206; construction detail, 207; stamped design, attachment lock, straps, 209
        Camera Case, 183; gusset detail for lacing perforations, 185
        Carved leather box with thong assembly, 202; designs, 203
        Leather box with waxed thread assembly, 201; making wax thread, 211

Stamping tools: process of making, 170

Western Riding bridle: assembly detail, 210; specifications, 210

METAL

Characteristics of craft metals: aluminum, 219; brass, 219; copper, 220; nickel silver, 220; pewter, 221; silver 221

Costume jewelry, 296

Designs: Indian symbols, 285
Equipment: tools, 223; materials, 223
Facilities for metal work, 223
Filagree jewelry: design forming process, 300; examples, 301
Fluting Jig, 232
Forms for bending metal, 227
Matrix block and dies for making conchas, 238
Melting points of craft metals, 222
Memorial plaque, (copper repoussé design) 236
Processes in metal craftwork: Annealing: brass, 283; copper, 233, silver, 233; bending, 226
    Chasing or engraving, 235; tool making, 239
    Cleaning: abrasives, 234; solutions, 233; cutting, 224
    Etching: aluminum, 241; copper, 241; pewter, 241; finishing, 245
    Fluting of rims, 231
    Hammering, 228; to decorate, 228; to shape, 228
    Making hinges, 263; tubing, 263; wire, 293
    Raising or forming a metal bowl, 230
    Repoussé or relief design development, 234
    Sawing, 225
    Soldering, 243
    Stamping, 236; stamping tool making, 237; tempering, 240
    Tooling metal foil, 267; examples, 267
Projects: Aluminum, copper, pewter (Penland examples), 246
    Bookends, 264; bowls, 248; divided server (3 sections), 253
    House numbers, 266
    Planters, 258; hanging type, 260; with T.V. lamp, 258
    Spoons: nut spoon, pewter, 252
    Trays: aluminum, 255; copper with ceramic tile, 257; copper with cover and handle, 261

ENAMELED METAL, copper, silver

Development:
Champleve, 279
Chinese, Egyptian, Japanese, 270
Cloisonne, 277
Enamels: Opaque, 273; transparent, 273
Making of design forms, 278

Methods of applying, 275; of firing, 272; grinding, 274
Precautions in handling, 272

SILVER JEWELRY MAKING

Balls, 289; beads, 291; bezels, 281; domes, 290
Bracelets: design stamping, 286; shaping, 287; gem setting, 283
Brooches: design stamping, 287; soldering pins, 288
Buckles for belts, 288
Cast ornaments, 293
Chain making: drawing wire, 294; soldering links, 294
Conchas: forming with matrix and dies, 289; stamping, 289
Costume Jewelry (Mexican examples), 296; construction detail, 297
Filigree, 301
Necklace of hollow beads, 291
Nezzah necklace, Indian symbolic designs, construction of Nezzah parts, 292
Rings from sheared blanks: mounting turquoise, 283; shaping and soldering split prong rings, 284; twisted wire rings, 294
Serving spoon, silver, 298

PLAITING METHODS

Belt projects: Cord, fiber and yarn, plaited in multiple strands for flat patterns, 306; terminals, 312
Buckle attachment for split leather and strand belts, 328
Cutting leather thongs, 309; cutter specifications, 309
Endless plaiting of split belt straps, 331
Flat plaiting of split leather, 327; 3, 5, 7 sections, 331; finishing of ends, 331
Four plait round patterns: Diamond, 310; Spiral, 313
    Terminals: crown knots, 313; Turk's head, 312
Multiple thongs or strands in 6, 315; 8, 315; 12, 316; 16 plait round, 316
Ornamental knots: Gaucho, 322; sliding, 318; uniting of plaited sections, 318
Plaited leather riding projects: Bridle (hackamore type without bit), 324; Reins, 324; Quirt, 324
Plaited yard sash, multiple cord or yarn (Hopi Indian type), 306

PLASTICS

Classification: Acrylics, 333; casein, 333; resin, 334; thermoplastic, 334; thermosetting, 334
Definition, 332
Designs for projects: book ends, 338, desk set, 337
Equipment, 335
Molds for cast plastic projects; figure casting, 341
Processes: bending, 345; carving, 346; cementing, 339; cutting, 335; engraving, 346; piercing, 336; printing from engraved plates, 347
Solvents, 339

WEAVING AND NETTING

Beams (loom), roller type, 357
Blankets: Chimayo (Spanish), 338; design development, 385; Navajo (Indian), 384
Cloth weaving patterns: basket weave, brocade, 354; herringbone, 353; honeycomb, 368; pile, 355; plain or tabby, 352; serge, 353; tapestry, 354
Coverlet, 369
Design development: embroidery, 354; warp and weft, 367; variations, 355; weaving in contrasting colors or materials, 355
Double width weaving: blankets, 387; cloth, 365
Draft pattern honeycomb weave, 368; for heddle threading, 359; for weft weaving, 367
Dressing a loom with spooled warp, 358
Embroidery on woven cotton (South American), 356
Finger weaving (Navajo), 385
First blanket, Navajo legend, 375
Harnesses: counter-balanced, 353; heddles, 359
Looms: Portable table type, 357; Two harness, 362; Four harness, 365; primitive Navajo, 378; Spanish, 386
Preparation of wool: cleaning and fleece, 376; scouring and washing wool, 376
Preparation of yarn: carding of wool, 369; spinning, 373; spinning Navajo method, 377; skeining, 374
Process of threading, 359
Repairing a warp break, 361
Warp terminals, 361
Weaving process, 382

NETTING

Construction detail for grommet, 393; needle and mesh stick, 392
Cord weaving or netting detail for a fish landing net, 397; hammock, 392; tennis net, 395
Principles of netting, 391

WOOD

Adhesives: veneer, 440
Carving equipment: facilities, 404; tools, 403
Carving elements, 410; example Gothic motif, 411
Carver's sampler: designs, 409; steps in carving, 409
Choice of wood for carving, 402
Chip carving: geometric guide lines, 412; positions for skew chisel, 412
Designs, 408
Figure carving or whittline, 437
Finishing, 407
Gothic motif as example of carving elements, 411
Marquetry, 440
Mexican lathe turned forms, 439; lathe construction, 439
Sharpening carving tools, 405
Projects with chip carved decorations: Book ends, 415; frames, 419; for pictures, 418; for ceramic tile, 421; small chest, 411; waste paper basket, 416
Projects with varied carving elements: Desk, early American oak, with relief carving and stamped background, 425
End table with book trough, walnut, carved top, 427
Four post pine chest; carving detail, 426; construction detail, 426; specifications, 426
Furniture, Spanish colonial, 428
Serving table-cupboard, (Spanish "mesita trostero"), 424
Single piece wood projects: Round carved trivet, 429; round stamp box with lid, 434; shaped tray with carved leaf design, 408; octagonal trinket box with lid, 432
Spanish colonial type carved chest, with separate base supports, 427; construction of; 427
Wood box with carved inscriptions, 422